Architecture and Nature   The word "nature" comes from *natura*, Latin for birth – as do the words nation and native. But nature and nation share more than a common root, they share a common history, where one term has been used to define the other. This has been especially true in the United States, from the idea of the noble savage to the myth of the frontier. Narrated, painted and filmed, the American landscapes have been central to the construction of a national identity. This book explores changing ideas of what nature has meant for the United States and how it has been represented in buildings and landscapes over the past century.

It begins with the close of the frontier and the rise of the conservation movement in the 1890s, and it ends with the opening of the "final" frontier of outer space and the rise of the ecology movement in the 1960s. In this 75-year period, certain American myths about nature have endured while others have been invented, reworked or abandoned. The buildings and landscapes that have resulted from this dynamic process represent the dreams and ambitions of the country for its relationship to nature: the architecture of the national parks, the streamlined dams of the Tennessee Valley Authority, the modernist dream houses of post-war California, and the geodesic domes of the countercultural sixties.

Each of these buildings and landscapes were iconic representations in their era – symbolizing a perfect ideal for life in harmony with nature. Commissioned by either government or business interests, they can be seen as way stations in the development of a national identity. The authors explore the meanings of these seemingly familiar buildings from a new perspective, using them to shed light on the country's complex and often controversial relationship to nature.

Christine Macy is a professor of architecture and architectural history. **Sarah Bonnemaison** has a doctorate in human geography and a professional degree in architecture. They both teach at Dalhousie University in Canada.

Architecture and Nature

creating the American landscape

Christine Macy and Sarah Bonnemaison

LONDON AND NEW YORK

First published 2003 by Routledge
11 New Fetter Lane, London EC4P 4EE

Simultaneously published in the USA and Canada
by Routledge
29 West 35th Street, New York, NY 10001

Routledge is an imprint of the Taylor & Francis Group

© 2003 Christine Macy and Sarah Bonnemaison

Typeset in Sabon by Wearset Ltd, Boldon, Tyne and Wear
Printed and bound in Great Britain by TJ International Ltd, Padstow, Cornwall

All rights reserved. No part of this book may be reprinted or reproduced or utilized in any form or by any electronic, mechanical, or other means, now known or hereafter invented, including photocopying and recording, or in any information storage or retrieval system, without permission in writing from the publishers.

British Library Cataloguing in Publication Data
A catalogue record for this book is available from the British Library

Library of Congress Cataloging in Publication Data
Macy, Christine.
   Architecture and nature : creating the American landscape / Christine Macy and Sarah Bonnemaison.
      p. cm.
Includes bibliographical references and index.
  1. Architecture–United States–20th century. 2. Architecture–Environmental aspects–United States. I. Bonnemaison, Sarah. II. Title.
  NA712 .M3 2003
  720'.47'0973–dc21
                                                             2002009266

ISBN 0-415-28358-2 (hbk)
ISBN 0-415-28359-0 (pbk)

For our parents:

Michel Bonnemaison, Geographer
Colette Dumur, Artist
Alfonso Macy, Architect
Lillian Ruppe Macy, Social Worker

Contents

Illustration credits	ix
Acknowledgments	xi
Introduction	1
1 Exhibiting wilderness at the Columbian Exposition, 1893	13
2 Accommodating the nature tourist in the national parks, 1903	71
3 Putting nature to work with the Tennessee Valley Authority, 1933	137
4 Nature preserved in the nuclear age: the Case Study Houses of Los Angeles, 1945	223
5 Closing the circle: the geodesic domes and a new ecological consciousness, 1967	293
Selected bibliography	347
Index	362

Illustration credits

The authors and the publisher would like to thank the following individuals and institutions for giving permission to reproduce illustrations. We have made every effort to contact copyright holders, but if any errors have been made we would be happy to correct them at a later printing.

A. Quincy Jones Architecture Archive 4.44, 4.45, Plate 18
Allan Wexler 4.40
André Blouin Archive, Collection Centre Canadien d'Architecture/Canadian Centre for Architecture, Montréal 5.4
Archives Nationale du Quebec 5.3
Atlanta Journal-Constitution 3.3
Bibliothèque Mazarine, Paris 1.18
Boeing Business Services Company 4.14, Plate 14
Chesley Bonestell, Space Art International 4.32
Chicago Art Institute 1.4, 1.8, 1.10, 1.13, 1.19, 1.23
Chicago Historical Society 1.2, 1.3, 1.5, 1.7, 1.9, 1.15, 1.20, 1.22, 1.23, Plate 1, Plate 2
Chicago Public Library 1.6, 1.11, 1.21
Clark Richert Plate 24, Plate 25
David Morris and Fred Pflughoft 2.17
David Travers 4.9, 4.10, 4.13, 4.37, 4.38
Doris Ullman, University of Oregon 3.31
Earle S. Draper, Jr. 3.30, 3.35, 3.36, 3.37, 3.38, 3.40, 3.42, 3.43, 3.44, 3.45
Edward E. Ayer Collection, Newberry Library 1.17
Eric Mendelsohn 3.11
ESTO 4.34, 4.36
Garrett Eckbo 4.11
Glacier Natural History Association 2.11
Grace Chan 4.35
Harold Leydenfrost 4.33
Hartley and Marks 5.21
Herbert J. Cowling 2.29
Hildegard von Bingen 5.18
Institute for Lightweight Structures Archives 5.9, 5.10, 5.12
Jack Fulton 5.20, 5.22, 5.23
John de Visser 5.6, Plate 20

Judy-Ann Obersi 2.21, 3.2
Julius Shulman 4.5, 4.7, 4.8, 4.12, 4.15, 4.21, 4.23, 4.28, 4.29, 4.30, Plate 15, Plate 16
Larry Keenan Associates 5.2
Louise Almack 4.26
Marvin Rand 4.27, 4.39
Minnesota Historical Society 2.1
Montana Historical Society 2.5, 2.6, 2.7, 2.12, 2.13, 2.15, 2.16, 2.18, 2.22, Plate 4, Plate 9
National Archives 2.2, 2.3, 2.4, 2.24, 2.25, 2.26, 2.27, 2.30, 2.31, 2.32, 2.34, 2.35, 2.36, 3.4, 3.10, 3.13, 3.24, 3.25, 3.26, 3.27, 3.28, 3.33, 3.52
New Alchemists/Ocean Ark International 5.24
New York State Library, Albany 1.14
Ralph Rapson 4.1, 4.2, 4.3, 4.4
Robert Cameron 4.46, 4.47
Rohm and Haas 4.18
Rosengarten Collection 5.13
Sierra Club Books 5.25, 5.26, 5.27
Tammen Company and Montana Historical Society 2.19
The Eames Office 4.16, 4.19, 4.20, 4.22, 4.24, 4.25
The Estate of R. Buckminster Fuller 5.1, 5.5, 5.7, 5.8, 5.11, 5.14, 5.15, 5.16, 5.17, 5.19, Plate 21, Plate 22, Plate 23
The Fred Harvey Collection, Grand Canyon National Park 2.33
The trustees of the Boston Library 1.1, 1.12, 1.24
Time Life Syndicate 4.17, 4.41, 4.43
TVA 3.1, 3.5, 3.7, 3.8, 3.9, 3.12, 3.14, 3.15, 3.16, 3.17, 3.18, 3.21, 3.22, 3.23, 3.29, 3.32, 3.34, 3.39, 3.41, 3.48, 3.49, 3.50, 3.51
UC Santa Barbara, University Art Museum 4.6
Union Pacific Historical Collection 3.19
University of Nevada at Las Vegas, Special Collections. 3.6
Ville de Montréal – Gestion de documents et archives Plate 19
Washington University Gallery of Art, St. Louis 1.16

Acknowledgments

A book, like a building, is always a collaborative effort that involves the contribution of many people over a long period of time. Yet our first acknowledgment in this collaborative project must be to each other – this book has developed out of countless conversations, shared adventures and sustained work over six years. In the process, we've turned to disciplines we know – architecture and geography – and confronted those we do not – history and the craft of writing. The overall ideas and arguments for *Architecture and Nature*, the research and the chapter outlines were worked out collaboratively, as was the writing of Chapters 1 and 5. Of the remaining chapters, Sarah wrote the Introduction and Chapter 2 and Christine wrote Chapters 3 and 4.

We are very grateful to the many people who welcomed us into their workplaces and homes, gave us tours, opened up their personal photo albums and shared with us their memories, in particular Duane Bailey, Katherine (Kay) Potts Bianculli, Earle S. Draper Jr, Thomas J. Hallin, Elaine Sewell Jones, Clark Richert, Ruth and Leslie Quinn, and Peter Wank. Among the archivists who had the patience to look for the impossible to find, we would especially like to thank Brian Shovers of the Montana Historical Society, Barry Cantor from TW Engineering, Mike Dobrogosz, Bob Cole and Patricia Ezzell of the Tennessee Valley Authority, and Alan Michaelson of University of California at Los Angeles.

Portions of this work were presented at the "Gendered Landscapes" conference at Penn State and at ACSA conferences in Baltimore, Waterloo and Halifax. We are especially grateful for the comments and suggestions we received from reviewers of this work as it developed: Annmarie Adams, Richard Bartlett, Michel Bonnemaison, Robert Bruegmann, Thomas Fisher, Sandra Gillespie, Laura Hartman, Hilde Heynen, Peter Jacobs, Shelagh Mackenzie, Mark Macy and Marian Moffett. We would also like to recognize the work of the anonymous referees who contributed very helpful comments at several stages.

The Canada Council for the Arts and the Graham Foundation for the Advancement of Architecture funded the research for this work. The Faculty of Architecture and Planning at Dalhousie University in Nova Scotia and in particular our Dean Tom Emodi, gave us financial support and never asked when the book would be finished. Anita Regan, curator of the Architectural

Resource Centre at Dalhousie, was a tireless detective in tracking down hundreds of images and securing permissions to reprint. Finally our thanks to Caroline Mallinder, the senior architectural editor at Routledge for trusting us with our first major publication and giving such warm support and encouragement. All attempts have been made to reach the copyright holder of the following images: 3.11, 3.20, 4.11, 4.26, 4.31, 4.40, 4.42 and 5.18. Copyright holders of these images should contact Routledge, 11 New Fetter Lane, London EC4P 4EE.

Introduction

The word "nature" comes from *natura*, Latin for birth – from which the words nation, native and innate are also derived. Not only do nature and nation share a common Latin root, they share a common history where one has constantly been used to define the other. Many countries have defined their national identity through their landscape, one can think of the role of the forest in Sweden or the white desert in Canada. But in the United States, the relationship between nation and nature has been central to its colonial history, from the discovery of a "lost" paradise and the construction of the myth of the "noble savage," to the mythology associated with the frontier and the conservation of islands of wilderness.[1]

While the American colonists declared their independence from England in 1776, it was not until the powerful winds of nationalism swept across western nations in the nineteenth century that the United States began to look for their own national identity. As Roderick Nash argues,

> Almost desperately, Americans sought sustenance for their national ego. They needed something valuable and distinctive that could transform embarrassed provincials into proud and confident citizens. Gradually cultural nationalists began to sense that in one respect their country was different: nature in the New World had no counterpart in the Old. Specifically, it was wilder.[2]

The odd thing of course, is that according to the latest research on precontact America, the first wave of Europeans who settled North America did not experience wilderness at all. The forests of New England, for example, were so well maintained by controlled annual burning that one could drive a carriage under the canopy of trees. One might even say that far from destroying pristine wilderness, European settlers created it. As European diseases devastated human populations in the Americas and Native communities could no longer carry out controlled burning, wilderness quickly took over. "If 'forest primeval' means a woodland unsullied by the human presence," William Denevan says, "there was much more of it in the late eighteenth century than in the early sixteenth."[3] Therefore we might say that wilderness was neither eternal nor God-given when Americans turned to the landscape to construct their national identity.

Popular albums show us how in the early nineteenth century wilderness became a source of pride. "A number of illustrated 'scenery' albums, for instance, made clear the link between nationalism and nature. As early as 1820, plans were made for a volume entitled *Picturesque Views of the American Scene* that would show 'our lofty mountains . . . the unexampled magnitude of our cataracts, the wild grandeur of our western forests unsurpassed by any of the boasted scenery of other countries.'"[4] Early American writers discovered wilderness as a subject, like James Fenimore Cooper who became a national literary hero for his *Pioneers*. Landscape painters were also drawn to the rough beauty of the American wilderness, from Thomas Cole's early paintings of the Catskill Mountains to the later works of Albert Bierstadt, Frederick Church and Thomas Moran. The drama of a raw and wild land was expressed by shattered tree trunks, fallen timber and surging storm clouds. Some of the sites depicted as wild landscapes, like the Hudson River, were in fact inhabited with houses and factories, but artists went to great lengths to portray a land devoid of human presence. The work of photographer William Henry Jackson for the US Geologic Survey proved influential in setting aside land for the national parks and the more recent photographs of Ansel Adams have become synonymous with the pristine California wilds. In the twentieth century, film directors sent their location scouts across western states, searching for the broad horizons and stupendous backdrops appropriate to stories about the frontier. Prairie skies and monumental rock formations silently witnessed epic re-enactments of the battles between farmers and ranchers, settlers and Indians. This is the "western."

Architecture has also expressed ideas about the American landscape yet few historians have looked at it seriously. Yet examples abound. In the twentieth century, one has only to look at the rustic materials of an Arts and Crafts bungalow, the regional architecture of US military installations and other federal works, or the horizontality of Frank Lloyd Wright's "prairie style" houses to see that architects have been fascinated with representing the natural world in their work.[5] Today, we find nature called on in a wide variety of buildings that at first sight would seem to have little in common: the organic architecture of Eugene Tsui, the crystalline geometries of Antoine Predock, or the "sustainable" designs of Sim van der Ryn and William McDonough. These buildings – and their press coverage – have created a discourse about nature in architecture that can be traced. This has not been a fixed discourse of eternal and unchanging truths; rather, it has changed as the nation has changed over the past century.

CHANGING NOTIONS OF NATURE

The book stretches over a short century of American history: from the closing of the western frontier in the 1890s and the beginnings of conservation, to the opening of the "final" frontier with the space program in the 1960s. We have sliced through time at key moments when Americans' relationship to nature was changing and we chose buildings that expressed these changes. At these key moments, the idea of nature resurfaces to be re-interpreted according to specific historical conditions.

In the nineteenth century, for example, as American elites began to argue for the conservation of wilderness, it is generally accepted that their view of nature was shaped by the romantic movement of Europe. While this may be true, it does not explain why conservation began in the United States. At its core, the American conservation movement was a lament by the country's elite for the passing of the frontier. Its strongest advocates were a peculiar American combination of big game hunter, gentlemen explorer and transcendentalist. They saw the wilderness as a place where they could maintain their virility through hunting, camping and exploration. Their sense of themselves – what Michel Foucault calls "subjectification" – occurred through "roughing it" in the wild and recording their experiences for science and posterity.[6] And the federal government, imbued with the conservationists' ideology of purity and isolation, set up legal structures to protect pockets of wilderness: creating national parks, national forests and – in a sign that the myth of the noble savage was still operating – the Indian reservations. Associated with nature and the "wild," American Indians were to be physically isolated from the rest of the country.

Once the national parks were established, wilderness began to be seen as a sellable commodity. The budding tourism industry in the early twentieth century saw in the parks an opportunity to bring people from across the country for short vacations touring national wonders. And at this time of tremendous urbanization and industrialization, idealized nature is commodified for the middle classes. Young urbanites were exhorted to appreciate the "simple life" in craftsy suburban bungalows and to spend their leisure time outdoors. In this context, nature was seen less as a lesson in civic virtue or a romantic reminder of the frontier, but as a modern space of leisure, a space that was entertaining, safe, and increasingly accepting of women's participation. As the number of nature tourists grew, they became more diverse in class and gender. Citizens had to learn to change their conduct with respect to nature, replacing sport hunting with nature photography. And families toured national parks as a collection of regional and representative landscapes which became a way to visualize and conceptualize the whole country.

If the end of the frontier represents our first catalyst for change in a national discourse of nature, the economic crash of 1929 represents the second. In the Depression years, nature reappeared in an entirely different light. On the one hand, there was a discussion of how to heal a landscape damaged by reckless exploitation and on the other, we see the efforts of government to pull the unemployed out of cities and put them back on the land and back to work. Nature was understood to be a valuable resource to satisfy the basic needs of food and shelter at a time when the economy had collapsed. Citizens were not encouraged to consume nature as they had been two decades earlier – and there is little money to spend – but to return to it, healing it and themselves in the process and making both productive again. It is a collective effort, requiring an army of bodies sweating and toiling to construct a new landscape under the benevolent aegis of government. Like in an old-time barn-raising, everyone must push up their sleeves and participate in the project. Working people would be re-integrated into nature in New Deal programs like the Civilian Conservation Corps (which brought inner city youth to the outdoors) and the Resettlement Administration (which brought unemployed city dwellers onto rural homesteads). The beneficent influence of modern technology completed the triangle of a re-engineered landscape in programs like the Tennessee Valley Authority and Rural Electrification Administration. Nature was to be an integral part of a well-administered plan to put the country back into production.

In contrast to the ideology of conservation that argues one must isolate nature in order to protect it, the Depression years reveal a desire to reconcile human inhabitation and a landscape in need of repair. The old frontier of the Tennessee Valley became the setting for a flagship project in which the federal government would heal and modernize the landscape through tree planting, contour farming, fertilizer production, flood control and electricity generation. The nineteenth century lament for the lost frontier was replaced with discourse about nature that included people in the renewed landscape.

After the Second World War, as the economy recovered and American expansionism resumed, there was great pressure to build housing. As the suburbs spread into endless tracts of previously agrarian landscapes, the lawn acquired new meanings. In this patch of nature growing in front and in back of the house, converged a discourse about domesticity, leisure, and nationalism. Before the war, backyards were work areas containing basic utilities like outhouses, wood sheds and cisterns. After the war, the backyards of the burgeoning middle class became spaces of leisure, furnished with barbecues from the campground or the war theater, fitted out with indoor–outdoor furniture and shady trellises. Once again, nature was commercialized. But this time, people were not looking for the pleasures of a simpler life, but rather learning to better themselves on their little plot of land – a relationship to nature that was intensely private and internal, we might even say paranoid. The government supported this suburban expansion with roads, highways and low cost mortgages for first-time homeowners. As the populations moved out from the cities and stretched over the landscape, each house contained its own private bit of nature.

Children who grew up in these suburban environments saw first-hand the effects of urban sprawl as fields, forests and wetlands were ceaselessly replaced with new tracts of starter homes.[7] And with the first images of Earth beamed back from outer space, the interdependency of all natural systems became increasingly self-evident. At the same time, every evening brought television coverage from Vietnam, showing defoliation and devastation that eerily mirrored the warnings about chemical poisoning, carcinogens and pollution at home. Here lies a third shift in the subjectification of Americans' relation to nature. As the idea of protecting nature expanded beyond national boundaries, the discourse of ecology as a planetary project began to take shape. This is the era of back-to-the-land movements and eco-politics. Again, just as the discourse about wilderness took root once there was no more frontier, we see in the 1970s the emergence of a discourse about recycling and waste reduction, about "organic" food, "natural" births and "natural" products, when virtually the entire country is urbanized, food production is mechanized and products all seem to be produced on the assembly line and packaged. Among the ecological activists of the counterculture, this return to nature was formulated as a critique of institutions and large corporations and as a measurement of the moral value of the self: the ecologically-conscious person contributed to a cleaner environment by picking up after themselves, recycling, composting, carpooling and taking a five minute shower.

WHAT BUILDINGS WE LOOK AT AND WHY

These are the slices we have made through this period of American history. They are key moments when nature as an idea was pressed into the national debates and in the process, reinterpreted according to the social, political and economic struggles of the time. In choosing buildings designed at these key periods, we searched for works that spoke eloquently about nature. Now some people believe that buildings cannot express ideas, that they are mute objects in the landscape. And "ideas" in buildings may remain obscure to those who take the built environment for granted and use buildings without reflecting on what they mean. But like painting and sculpture, architecture is part of a discourse that includes both a practice (with its traditions and references) and critical and theoretical commentary. Virtually all aspects of a building communicate bigger ideas: from the way the plan is laid out and the building façade is composed, to the materials used to make the building, how people's movements are orchestrated through space, how rooms are named and distributed, who gets the corner window and so forth. Some buildings communicate a belief in progress through technology, others communicate ideas of democracy, respectability, power, wealth, or impregnability. Here we are interested in buildings that express ideas about nature.

By interpreting buildings in this way, we are using a formulation developed by Michel Foucault. He speaks of *statements* that make up part of a larger *discourse*. The buildings we look at are statements – material objects produced by people that may be "specific and paradoxical objects,"

> one of those objects that men produce, manipulate, use, transform, exchange, combine, decompose and recompose, and possibly destroy.

> Instead of being something said once and for all – and lost in the past like the result of a battle, a geological catastrophe, or the death of a king – the statement, as it emerges in its materiality, appears with a status, enters various networks and various fields of use, is integrated into operations and strategies in which its identity is maintained or effaced.[8]

To conceive of buildings as statements allows us, as Paul Hirst says, "to pose questions not merely about discourses *on* architecture but about discourses *in* architecture.[9] That means not only larger ideas about architecture as a discipline and field of study, but to see architecture as a vehicle for expressing ideas about society, nature, even God.

There are three groups that we see as crucial in developing a discourse about nature in American architecture. One group is the federal government, a second are the capitalists that invest in, transform, build and destroy landscapes. A third group are the architects who give visible form to the statement. The buildings and landscapes we chose to investigate have an intimate relationship to the state since they were built, more or less directly, as the result of governmental initiatives. We singled out the national parks, the regional development project of the Tennessee Valley Authority, the proliferation of suburban housing that resulted from the GI Bill and federal support for interstate highways and lastly, national representation in world expositions abroad. The buildings that resulted from these federal initiatives were used by government to promote ideas important to *them* – ideas such as conservation, rural resettlement, increasing productivity or establishing a home-owning population. Circulating in national media, images of these projects had a far greater influence on popular understandings of the American landscape than a single work of architecture ever could. Although they were not built as monuments, many of the buildings we look at here acquired the status of national icons. The publics that visited these buildings and read about them in the press felt they stood for a bigger idea. Capturing the national imagination, they were prototypes for a way to build and dwell the American landscape.

For their part, entrepreneurs and investors hired architects in the hope of making their enterprise look good and garner public support, increase visitors, sell more product and so forth. The "look" of resort hotels in a national park was used to sell holiday packages, vacation cabins, camping paraphernalia and domestic furniture. The "look" of the California lifestyle in the post-war era was used to sell household appliances, Vogue patterns, and food products. Such businessmen who hired architects often held strong ideas about how nature and landscape should be expressed in architecture. Similarly, on the government end as well, architectural design is often used to "sell" a new project or initiatives to a voting public or to influence diplomatic relations with foreign nations.[10]

In either case, the architect acts as a mediator: between governmental agencies and the voting public or between private enterprise and its market.[11] And architecture becomes a means of communication – with its own concerns and agendas that provide a useful arm's-length discourse for both government and private enterprise to reach their constituencies. Far from being puppets of government or private enterprises, we will see that architects possessed a certain degree of autonomy. They influenced discussions, created priorities, organized space, and ultimately gave form to buildings that we can still see today. Thus the proposal framed by this book raises questions about the relationship of architecture to both capitalism and democracy, but underlines the importance of the agency of individuals in the government, corporations and architectural profession.

OUR HISTORICAL APPROACH

Our decision to investigate how nature is a significant subject of American architecture over the course of a century raises methodological questions that must be addressed from the outset. There are two layers to our reading: a *symbolic* and a *materialist* layer. As symbols, the buildings we explore here have been designed and interpreted in terms of religious myths such as the Garden of Eden or the idea of regeneration, and secular myths like the frontier.[12] But we also work with a materialist reading of architecture, trying not to separate our interpretation of buildings from the social and political forces which led to their design and construction. In this regard, we are indebted to the pioneering work of Diane Ghirardo and Dolores Hayden for their insistence that gender, race and class are crucial to a critical analysis of architecture. Their work stands as a reminder to all of us that architecture affects real people in real places.

Where we differ from a strictly materialist approach is in our view of history. The book is, in a sense, a history of the *idea of nature* in architecture as much as it is a history of specific buildings and why they were built. As national interests changed and certain political agendas evolved in the context of a newly imperial nation, multiple wars, economic crises and so forth, nature was pressed into service time and again as a useful referent – a trope to justify whatever particular battle was at stake. By no means did the idea of nature "evolve" in the United States. Rather, it was employed at certain times by certain groups for certain ends. And it never "talked back."

Methodologically, the analysis of each building draws from notions of "intertextuality." Roland Barthes is perhaps the best-known proponent of this way of working which shows how a text can be interpreted as a series of overlapping, at times contradictory, texts.[13] This was a way for him to counteract what he saw as an undue emphasis on the writer as the sole creative source of a text. Transposing Barthes' notion of intertextuality onto an interpretation of architecture requires us to accept that a building, its plans and its representation in images, can be read and interpreted as a series of texts. If one accepts that notion, intertextuality can be a useful tool for the analysis of architectural works. Such an approach has been used in the interpretation of landscapes, in the work of the cultural geographers James Duncan and David Ley.[14]

Intertextuality is most evident when we begin to see a building not as the creation of one architect but as the result of many people – from masons and carpenters to developers, clients, bankers and even politicians – all of whom make decisions that affect the building for their own reasons. Far from being unified into one coherent work, these "texts" are often contradictory with some holding sway over others. What we see in the built work then, is the outcome of this dynamic process. Our intent is to hold onto the dynamic, and not to reduce our reading of the architecture so that it appears to be evidence of a single intention.[15] Similarly, when we try to understand how a building has contributed to larger ideas, we see that many different people are involved in its inhabitation, interpretation, promotion, and criticism. As we worked in the archives we looked at all kinds of sources for our material: newspaper articles, caricatures, promotional literature, scrapbooks, governmental documents and letters, and during our visits to buildings we spoke with builders, workers, managers and visitors.

Most of the buildings we analyze are not well known in the canon of architectural history. Although architects like Robert Reamer and Roland Wank produced large amounts of work and were recognized as influential designers in their day, they have yet to be the subjects of significant monographs. Work on Buckminster Fuller is just beginning, which is surprising when one considers that he assembled perhaps the most voluminous archive of any twentieth century architect. This does not mean that their buildings were not well known at the time they were built. On the contrary, they were intensely covered by the media and reviewed in architectural journals. And according to Beatriz Colomina, modern architecture is manufactured as much in the media as it is on the building site.[16] While not all of the buildings we study here are "modern" in this sense, their representation in the press forged for them a place in the popular imagination of the American landscape. This "imagination" did not occur spontaneously because the buildings were intrinsically meaningful.[17] These buildings became meaningful because certain groups of people wanted them to be. At times, the private sector used images of these buildings to promote their business ventures, and at other times the government used images to promote ideas. Either way, the circulation of images is highly political and should be treated as such.

Finally, we share Nietzsche's desire to "turn historical ideas to creative purposes."[18] As architects, we believe in taking ideas developed into the past and making them work for us today. If the experiment of the TVA is inspiring, it is because it had a vision of creating entire towns based on cooperative living and using electricity generated by the force of flowing water.

Today, the equivalent would be for the government to subsidize the building of new communities that would run on solar and wind power and have communal greenhouses as treatment plants for sewage and community gardens.

Notes

1. The literature on this subject is extensive. The classic texts in this field are: Henry Nash Smith, *Virgin Land: the American West as Symbol and Myth*, Cambridge, MA: Harvard University Press, 1950; Leo Marx, *The Machine in the Garden: Technology and the Pastoral Ideal in America*, Oxford: Oxford University Press, 1964; Roderick Nash, *Wilderness and the American Mind*, New Haven: Yale University Press, 1967. Subsequent texts which address the myth of nature in the American cultural history include: Annette Kolodny, *The Land Before Her: Fantasy and Experience of the American Frontier, 1630–1860*, Chapel Hill: University of North Carolina Press, 1984; David E. Shi, *The Simple Life: Plain Living and High Thinking in American Culture*, Oxford: Oxford University Press, 1985; John F. Sears, *Sacred Places: American Tourist Attractions in the Nineteenth Century*, Oxford: Oxford University Press, 1989; Richard Slotkin, *Gunfighter Nation: the Myth of the Frontier in Twentieth-Century America*, New York: Atheneum, 1992; and Simon Schama, *Landscape and Memory*, New York: Alfred A. Knopf, 1995.
2. Roderick Nash, "The Cultural Significance of the American Wilderness," in Maxime E. McCloskey and James P. Gilligan (eds), *Wilderness and the Quality of Life*, San Francisco: Sierra Club, 1969, p. 66.
3. William M. Denevan, *The Native Population of the Americas in 1492*, Madison: University of Wisconsin Press, 1976. See also William Cronon, *Changes in the Land: Indians, Colonists, and the Ecology of New England*, New York: Hill and Wang, 1983.
4. Nash, "Cultural Significance of the American Wilderness," p. 67.
5. Passive solar energy design received a significant boost in the United States during the oil crisis of 1973. In California, the State Architect Sim van der Ryn advocated solar energy systems in government buildings, solar and bicycle-friendly subdivisions were realized in the university town of Davis, and the energy-conservation law Title 24 spawned the growth of firms such as Sol-Arc that aided architects in calculating energy loss in buildings. Similar activities were occurring in other solar energy centers of the Southwest, Minnesota and Massachusetts.
6. We use Foucault's notion of "subjectification" as the theoretical construct to relate the changing notions of nature to the buildings we chose to interpret. Subjectification "concerns the 'way a human being turns him or herself into a subject' ... those processes of self-formation in which the person is active." Foucault is primarily interested in isolating those techniques through which the person initiates an active self-formation. These take place through a variety of "operations on [people's] own bodies, on their own souls, on their own thoughts, on their own conduct."
7. For the debt of the ecology movement to suburbanization, see Adam Rome, *The*

	Bulldozer in the Countryside: Suburban Sprawl and the Rise of American Environmentalism, Cambridge: Cambridge University Press, 2001.
8	Michel Foucault, *The Archeology of Knowledge*, London: Routledge, 1972, p. 105.
9	Paul Hirst, "Foucault and Architecture," *AA Files* 26 (1993), pp. 52–60, 52.
10	On these two subjects see Lois Craig, *The Federal Presence, Architecture, Politics and Symbols in United States Government Building*, Cambridge: MIT Press, 1978; and Jane C. Loeffler, *The Architecture of Diplomacy: Building America's Embassies*, New York: Princeton Architectural Press, 1998.
11	In the same vein, but for planners instead of architects, see Richard Foglesong, *Planning the Capitalist City: the Colonial Era to the 1920s*, Princeton: Princeton University Press, 1986.
12	In his study of the mythology surrounding the American skyscraper, Thomas van Leeuwen shows that imagery of natural growth was used to speak about these new constructions. Thomas A.P. van Leeuwen, *Skyward Trend of Thought: the Metaphysics of the American Skyscraper*, Cambridge, MA: MIT Press, 1988.
13	Perhaps the most famous of his textual studies in that vein is Roland Barthes, *S/Z*, translated by Richard Miller, New York: Hill and Wang, 1974. For a more abstract treatment, see his *Image-Music-Text*, translated by Steven Heath, New York: Hill and Wang, 1977.
14	James S. Duncan, *The City as Text: Politics of Landscape Interpretation in the Kandyan Kingdom*, Cambridge: Cambridge University Press, 1990; James S. Duncan and Trevor J. Barnes, *Writing Worlds: Discourse, Text and Metaphor in the Representation of Landscape*, London: Routledge, 1992; and James Duncan and David Ley (eds), *Place/Culture/Representation*, London: Routledge, 1993.
15	For example, the decision to build Yellowstone National Park's Old Faithful Inn out of local materials meant that park trees had to be felled for its construction, yet the park was a site protected from cutting. For an excellent analysis of the multiplicity of forces that affect buildings, see Michael Baxandall, *Patterns of Intention: On the Historical Explanation of Pictures*, New Haven: Yale University Press, 1985.
16	Beatriz Colomina, *Privacy and Publicity: Modern Architecture as Mass Media*, Cambridge: MIT Press, 1994.
17	Here, we take issue with the architectural theorists Geoffrey Broadbent and Charles Jencks who were inspired by structuralist linguistics to propose that architectural language can be broken down into its constituent *morphemes*, much as language was theorized to possess *phonemes*. The difficulty with this approach is that it implies that buildings are read the same way at all times and by all audiences. Hans-Georg Gadamer and Paul Ricoeur offer an important corrective to this view in their approach to interpretation. See Geoffrey Broadbent, Richard Bunt, Charles A. Jencks (eds), *Signs, Symbols, and Architecture*, New York: Wiley, 1980; Hans Georg Gadamer, *Truth and Method*, trans. by Joel Weinsheimer and Donald Marshall, New York: Continuum, 1988 and *The Relevance of the Beautiful and other essays*, trans. by Nicholas Walker, Cambridge: Cambridge University Press, 1986; Paul Ricoeur, *Hermeneutics and the Human Sciences: essays on language, action, and interpretation*,

edited, translated, and introduced by John B. Thompson, Cambridge: Cambridge University Press, 1981 and *From Text to Action*, trans. by Kathleen Blamey and John B. Thompson, Evanston, IL: Northwestern University Press, 1991.

18 Refer to Hayden White, *Metahistory*, Baltimore: John Hopkins University Press, 1973, p. 331.

1.1 "Noble" redwood in the US Government Building.

Chapter 1
Exhibiting wilderness at the Columbian Exposition, 1893

While the slow-moving wheels of the Corliss steam engine were the centerpiece of the American Centennial Exhibition that was held in Philadelphia in 1876, the agrarian fair that surrounded the giant engine showed that even after the Civil War, the United States was still a farming society. If, as Leo Marx has suggested, the Corliss engine represented "the machine in the garden," we find only seventeen years later a reversal of this symbolism in the World's Columbian Exposition in Chicago. How the nation changed in less than a generation! In the rotunda of the US Government Building, in the heart of an exposition dedicated to civilization and progress, we find a giant redwood tree. Now the "garden" was in the "machine" (see Figure 1.1).[1]

The giant tree was the most popular exhibit of the Chicago fair. It was not, of course, a whole sequoia, for how could such a large tree be transported and kept alive? Instead, visitors crowded to see a 23-foot diameter section of a giant redwood (once 300 feet tall) from General Grant Park in California's Tulare County. Those who had never seen the giant trees of California were informed by the exhibition catalog that this was "the largest section of redwood ever moved." Inside the 14-inch thick enclosure of bark, a spiral stair brought visitors up the tree past a series of photographs showing how it had been felled fifteen feet above the ground and carried eastward on ten railroad boxcars.[2] The "big tree" of California functioned as a symbol of the republic. In the usual nationalistic rhetoric of nineteenth century exposition catalogs, it was described as "a fitting natural emblem of the powerful and beneficent republic that has also grown up on American soil."[3] In that respect, the fact that it was named in honor of General John Noble, Secretary of the Interior, was not without significance. Throughout the 1880s, the American Forestry Association and the American Association for the Advancement of Science had been arguing that the vast stands of virgin timber on public lands should not pass into private ownership. In 1891, Noble secured an amendment to the General Land Law Revision Act which granted the President authority to create forest reserves by proclamation.[4] In honoring Noble, the exhibit in the US Government Building reminded the public that the government had acted wisely in preserving forests for future generations. In that sense, the "big tree" expressed the late nineteenth century optimism for progress through management. For if there was no longer a frontier, there were still areas of virgin forest that were being saved from private ownership through governmental authority.

The tree was also a testimonial to the grandeur of American wilderness. As Julie Brown says, "this was perhaps the perfect exhibition artifact: authentic, imposing, and without replication."[5] Rhetorically, it stood in for the wilderness. As visitors climbed the inside of the tree, they were able to touch the real thing, smell the potent perfume of its bark, and be overwhelmed by the sheer size of this arboreal monster. Clearly, the stump did not draw crowds for its intrinsic beauty. Like a relic, its power rested rather in its authenticity, in the fact that it was once three hundred feet tall, eighty feet in circumference, and over two thousand years old.

As visitors reached the top of the staircase, they stepped out onto a panoramic viewing platform under the rotunda. In keeping with the nineteenth century's love for lofty vantage points, the platform allowed the public an overview of the building's interior, which extended like a cross into the four wings of the exhibitions.[6] On the platform, visitors could turn their bodies to the four compass points and view the achievements of civilization in the new world. Brilliantly colored paintings on the second story of the surrounding rotunda depicted the transformation of natural resources into manufactured products. The catalog explained, "the respective leading industries of the north, south, east and west are allegorically represented in the panels, viz. lumber and mining, cotton and shipping, manufactures and agriculture."[7] Thus, the major American industries were completely surrounding this relic of nature. And why is nature in the center of the exposition? At one level, the redwood tree in the US Government Building symbolically represented the beginning of government efforts to conserve natural resources and designate areas of the American west as national preserves. But at another level, the privileged place held by this authentic bit of wilderness represents a shift in the way Americans conceived of nature in general and wilderness in particular. This chapter explores how this shift was carried out, metaphorically and literally, in the landscapes, buildings and statuary of the World's Columbian Exposition in 1893.

By 1893, most people knew that the continent had been settled, that the open plains with roaming buffalo were a thing of the past. The nation had been cautioned by the federal government to inventory its resources. But perhaps the most succinct expression of the significance of this fact was made by Frederick Jackson Turner, in his paper "The Significance of the Frontier in American History" before an audience of two hundred historians assembled for the exposition.[8] The 1890 census had officially declared the end of the frontier – defined as a density of two or more inhabitants to the square mile next to unsettled land. In his paper, Turner linked the frontier experience to American development of democracy and character. "The most important thing about the American frontier is that it lies at the hither edge of free land" he argued, and the advance of each successive frontier was "the outer edge of the wave – the meeting point between savagery and civilization."[9] Pointing to the frontier as the essential formative experience of Americans,

Turner stressed the central importance of the encounter between "man" and "wilderness."[10] That encounter was seen as overwhelming, "at the frontier the environment is at first too strong for the man. He must accept the conditions which it furnishes, or perish."[11] By showing that the encounter with wilderness was a fundamental part of American identity, Turner recuperated the past to construct a national identity for the future.[12]

Thanking him for a copy of the paper sent the following year, Theodore Roosevelt congratulated Turner, "the pamphlet on the Frontier ... struck some first class ideas" he wrote, and "put into definite shape a good deal of thought which has been floating around rather loosely."[13] And as Turner's paper drew more attention, he was offered a prestigious post in the history department at Harvard University. Clearly, Turner's formulation of the significance of the frontier experience to a specifically American identity echoed many ideas shared by the country's elite, which explains its immediate success and the endurance of his "frontier thesis."

Since the mid-nineteenth century, the wilderness cult had been gaining adherents and Turner's focus on the point of contact between "man" and "wilderness" simply added to a general belief among reformers that "without some contact with nature, civilization constricted to the American city would not survive."[14] But with the official declaration of the end of the frontier, people began to confront with a degree of embarrassment the country's disfigured landscapes and inhuman cities, and to recognize that there were no longer large expanses of "free land" or wilderness. Up to the late nineteenth century, the frontier had operated in the collective imagination as a gate of escape. After the civil war, the dramatic escalation of the US Army in eradicating Indian settlement on the Great Plains paved the way for the railroads to move in and take the best land. Farmers then came for what was left.[15] By the 1890s, little arable land remained and renting had increasingly become the only option for those moving west to farm. With the close of the era of continental expansion, the nation was now, in Turner's words, "thrown back upon itself." If, as Turner suggested, the frontier experience had been essential to Americans becoming who they were as a people, without the frontier the future of the nation as a democracy was full of uncertainty.

The year Turner gave his lecture at the exposition, there was plenty to worry about. The economy was in collapse, factories had closed their doors and relations between labor and capital were explosive. M. Christine Boyer explains that by the end of 1893, "a quarter of the capital invested in railroads was in receivership; mills, factories, and mines had been shut down in large numbers, furnaces were slack, and capital timid, new construction was suspended, some five hundred banks and fifteen thousand businesses had failed, and a ruinous wheat crop and limited European demand had cut back agricultural output. Employment, especially in northern cities, began to fall drastically."[16] As a consequence, hundreds of thousands lost their homes and were roaming the streets looking for the means to survive. The struggle for alternatives, however, was stronger than ever. The 1880s witnessed almost ten thousand strikes and lockouts in the country, and 1893 represented the year when, in the view of historians such as Alan Trachtenberg, the frequency and violence of the conflicts between robber barons and workers had effectively culminated in a "class war."[17]

With the end of the frontier, symbolizing for industrialists the end of economic expansion, both industrial and governmental elites felt the need to take control of the nation's resources. Both conservation leaders and corporate elites shared a "mutual revulsion against unrestrained competition and undirected economic development. Both groups placed a premium on large-scale capital organization, technology, and industry-wide cooperation and planning to abolish the uncertainties and waste of competitive resource use."[18] For the governing bodies, there is no doubt that conservation was a convenient way to cut through the conventional political lines of Republican and Democrat. Ultimately, their shared enemy was the working class and conservation became a way to close ranks on a common cause. As the political and technical aspects of conservation began to take shape, a *discourse* about wilderness as an experience of the past also began to develop. Artists such as Frederic Remington depicted the grandeur of the American landscape populated with noble Indians and free-roaming game, and novelists such as Owen Wister created legendary figures such as the genteel Virginian who is drawn to the harsh unrelenting terrain of the west. Landscape architects like Frederick Law Olmsted advocated the preservation of wilderness scenery like Niagara Falls, and architects such as Henry Hobson Richardson developed a style of architecture that drew from geological imagery.

In naming their pioneering building type of the skyscraper, the business elites of Chicago turned to tropes of wilderness and frontier. The best-known example is perhaps the Monadnock Building, Burnham and Root's massive masonry skyscraper of 1891, named after the mountain in Maine (see Figure 1.2). The Katahdin, designed by Holabird and Roche in 1893 directly adjacent to the Monadnock, referred to another mountain in Maine, famous as the site where Thoreau had his seminal vision of the wilderness as an awesome, untamable force. Richardson's "geological" architecture celebrated the rock the country was built on, using massive masonry to express the lofty ambitions of the business classes in the new building type. Indeed, as Robert Bruegmann says, "the skyscrapers were viewed as some kind of immense and uncontrollable force of nature." Examples pairing skyscrapers with wilderness abound: the first skyscraper, the Montauk (1881), as well as the Pontiac (1884–91), Marquette (1891–5) and Lakota (1893) buildings are all named after Indians and frontiersmen. In the Marquette building, sculpted cameos of Indian chiefs and white explorers, executed by the sculptor Edward Kemeys, alternate with mosaics of frontier encounters. Such architectural ornamentation served to glorify the frontier spirit of capitalists, breaking new ground.

In the Columbian Exposition, we find exhibits that speak to this chang-

1.2 The "Monadnock" block, Chicago, 1891. Architects Burnham & Root.

ing view of wilderness which took place at the turn of the century.[19] This emerging discourse is at times conflicted and contradictory, partly because it is still in the process of formation. It includes exhibits like the giant redwood tree and it sheds light on the design of the exposition grounds, in particular the lagoon and wooded islands in the center of the exposition, which represent the value of wilderness as a precinct put aside from everyday life (see Figure 1.3). A small log cabin situated on one of these islands presents a third view. Known as the Hunter's Camp, this cabin and its nearby animal statuary represents an argument for the conservation of big game animals on wilderness preserves. We have isolated these three elements – the redwood tree, the islands in the lagoon and the hunter's camp – from the rich array of exhibits

1.3 Wooded Isle seen from the roof of the Manufacturers Building.

19 | Exhibiting wilderness

at the fair in order to study the emerging discourse on wilderness and conservation at the end of the nineteenth century. Turning to the plan of the fair and exploring the relationships between its constituent parts, we find these three elements in the heart of the exposition grounds. Once again, the "garden" is in the "machine." A closer analysis of the plan reveals to us that they indeed represent wilderness, not nature as we see it in the rest of the fair, transformed by the civilizing and colonizing process (see Figure 1.4).

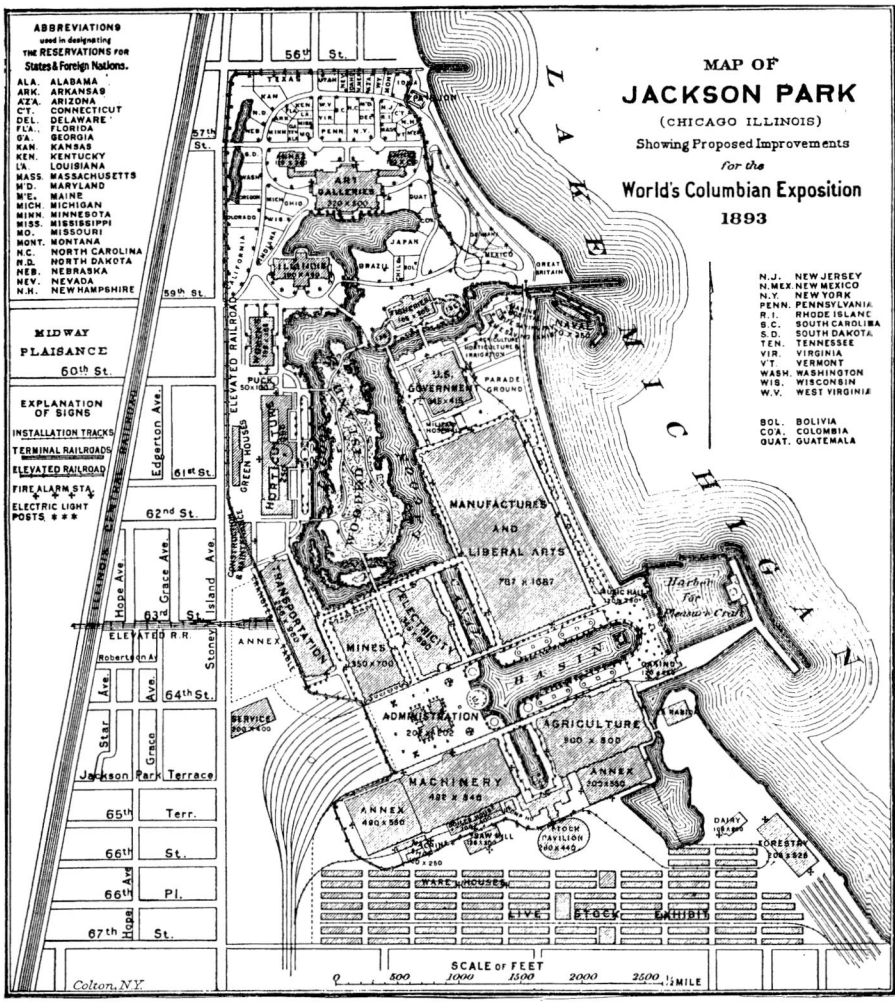

1.4 Plan of the World's Columbian Exposition.

20 | Exhibiting wilderness

Like the famous expositions of London in 1851 and Paris in 1889, the Columbian Exposition celebrated industrialism and expansion through colonization. Planned as the quatercentenary of Columbus's landing in the Americas, it was sponsored by Chicago businessmen. Its location in the westernmost metropolis of an expanding country charged it with the additional task of glorifying the transformation of nature into products. Facing the western prairies, linking the Great Lakes with the Mississippi, at the epicenter of the new rail networks, Chicago was the hub for processing and transporting stock, grain, lumber and minerals from the west to the markets in the east and abroad. The plan of the fair itself recapitulates at a smaller scale the central position of Chicago with respect to incoming raw products.

On the outermost margins of the fair we find exhibits of raw materials and peoples associated with nature, far removed from western civilization. We see living displays of Native Americans brought in for the event and confined to special areas, storage sheds for raw materials, and acres and acres of animal pens, blurring the lines between the fairgrounds proper and the adjacent stockyards and meat processing plants of southern Chicago (see Figure 1.5). These displays are "beyond the Pale" – they depict raw, unprocessed

1.5 Union Stockyards in Chicago.

nature before it is transformed by the civilizing influence of the industrial city. From the Inuit encampment on the northernmost lagoon to the "Indian villages" and miniature replicas of Mesoamerican civilizations on the southernmost lagoon, these displays are linked not by fancy colonnades, but by a rattling elevated railway, the agent of civilization to come (see Figure 1.6). Visitors chancing on these areas of the fair could witness first hand the relation between raw material and manufactured good. They could see civilizing forces at work in the model schools run by the Department of Indian Affairs cheek by jowl with anthropological exhibits of the "typical," pre-conquest "Indian villages."[20]

At the heart of the fair we find the aptly named "White City," an urban ensemble which glorified Anglo-Saxon civilization and American empire. The exhibits on display exalted the machines and manufactured goods of the young nation. Mountains of produce towered over fields of harvesting and threshing machines. Acres of locomotives lined up in rows behind the "Golden Door" of Louis Sullivan's Transportation Building. But it was the visual impression of the White City that best expressed differences between

1.6 View north-west from the intramural powerhouse.

civilized and uncivilized, processed and unprocessed, white and non-white.[21] The neoclassical designs of the massive exposition buildings, finished in a uniform white stucco, created an overall impression of a harmoniously orchestrated modern metropolis (see Figure 1.7). As the fair's designer Daniel Burnham said, "the plan is the thing." Linked by broad avenues and courtyards, hastily planted with trees and decorated with fountains and statuary, stitched together with magnificent peristyles facing expanses of water which reflected the symmetrical façades, the memory of the White City continued to exert an influence in American urban planning for decades, an influence that has been well charted by generations of architectural historians.[22] The image of the White City served well the aspirations of American capitalists for progress and expansion, and it did this in a way that spoke to the ambitions of social reformers and municipal governments for a civic society. Properly speaking, the White City extended from the Illinois State Building in the north, con-

1.7 Court of Honor. Photograph by C.D. Arnold.

tinued along both sides of the lagoon and culminated in the highly orchestrated urban ensemble of the Court of Honor. While most of the fair was devoted to industry, the federal government was given a prominent location between the industrial buildings to the south and the state buildings to the north. Near the towering rotunda of the US Government Building, the army set up a sample field hospital and filled the adjacent plaza with white tents lined up in rows like on a battlefield. When we realize that the exposition was held only thirty years after the national trauma of the Civil War, five years after the incendiary riots of Chicago's Haymarket Square, and three short years after the US Army's assault on the Sioux at Wounded Knee, South Dakota, the presence of the army in the center of the White City is not without significance.[23]

In the heart of the White City, in the midst of this seamlessly unified urbanism of the future, we find a many-fingered lagoon harboring two wooded islands. Why are these representations of wilderness located in the heart of the White City, rather than on its peripheries, with the Indian encampments and raw materials of the frontier? The plan reveals the relationship between nature exploited and nature conserved: "wilderness" hovers like a jewel, well protected by the surrounding White City from a sea of raw products endlessly multiplying in all directions. In other words, wilderness will be protected by those who conceived of and paid for the White City. On these islands, we begin our investigation into the "construction" of wilderness in 1893.

WILDERNESS AS A REFUGE FROM CIVILIZATION

As visitors stepped off the trains and onto the fairgrounds they left the dirty workaday world behind. Like the Bostonian who slept for over a hundred years in Edward Bellamy's turn of the century novel *Looking Backward*, only to wake up in a new, magical city of the future, visitors to the World's Columbian Exposition found themselves in a landscape quite different from the raggedy "brown cities" of the nineteenth century United States. Once they circled past the towering Administration Building, they were faced with an extraordinary prospect – a long, uniformly white courtyard around a central basin, brilliantly illuminated with the new technology of electricity. At the head of the court stood the imposing "Columbian Fountain" by Frederic MacMonnies. On the right, descending into the distance, stretched the massive Agricultural Building by McKim, Mead and White, and on the left the even larger Manufactures and Liberal Arts Building by George B. Post. The far end of the basin was partly closed by a semicircular peristyle revealing Lake Michigan beyond. From this stupendous prospect, smaller courtyards flanking lesser canals led visitors to other regions of the fair. Following these paths less traveled, some visitors chanced upon a peaceful lagoon in the very center of the grounds. In the middle of the lagoon, in a seemingly natural body of water, which was in fact designed by the renowned landscape architect Frederick Law Olmsted, there stood two islands fifteen acres in area, providing a sylvan retreat secluded from the rest of the fair. Olmsted called these the "Wooded Islands."

With few exceptions, the Wooded Islands were the only area of the fair without buildings. Surrounded by a lagoon, they were bordered by aquatic plants and covered with bushes, flowers and numerous trees, giving much needed shade to visitors in the blasting heat of the summer. Olmsted recommended to the board that, "as far as it is possible, the lagoon must be made to look like a natural bayou, secluded, shallow and placid, but not suggestive of stagnancy or any form of foulness, or unhealthfulness. Its low, sterile shores must be given a rich affluent and picturesque aspect, in striking contrast alike with the present ground, the expanse of the Great Lake, the margins of the basin in the central court, and the canals yet to be formed."[24] In this statement, Olmsted is telling the board that although the island is entirely constructed, it will present a picture of wilderness that is more dramatic than the natural landscape currently on the site and that it will work as a counterpoint to the urbanism soon to be constructed. It was not a minor feature in his design. In fact, as Daniel Burnham later acknowledged, the concept of the lagoon and the wooded island was the only original idea in the design of the fair.[25] The question we explore here is why this small area of undeveloped land was important to Olmsted's scheme for the fair, and how it was meant to work on the visitors to this ideal city, a model for American civilization (see Figure 1.8).

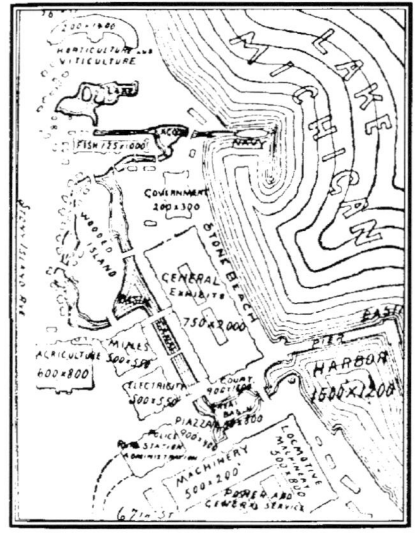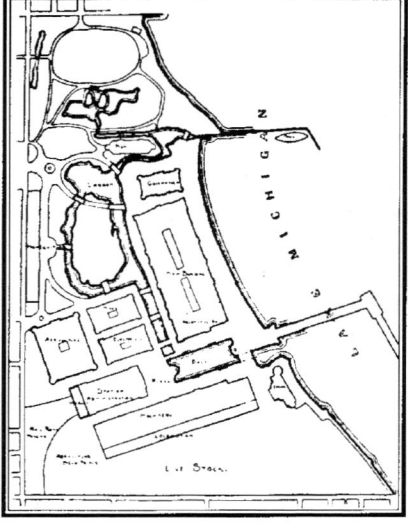

1.8 Schematic plans for the exposition grounds, November and December 1890.

Like all of Olmsted's previous designs, the lagoon and wooded island, once completed, gave the impression of always having been there. But a great deal of labor was required to move rocks, earth and plants to accomplish such a transformation. To begin with, the original grounds were, without question, forbidding. They might have been "natural" but they certainly were not picturesque. "Nowhere else had the opportunity for forming agreeable scenery been so lost," Olmsted remembers.[26] The entire area consisted of three ridges of beach sand, and the swells between them were sporadically occupied by waterlogged and stunted bushes. Today, people might find such windswept dunes attractive, but at the time of the exposition the severe landscape was seen as a "morass," with an "air of nakedness and poverty of vegetation" (see Figure 1.9).[27] The "low sterile shores" were meticulously transformed by dredging, contouring, and planting to create a picturesque landscape.

In his design for the wooded island, Olmsted played with the laws of perspective, creating large masses of greenery and elaborating complex

1.9 Jackson Park before construction. Photograph by Laban Deardorff.

patterns of light and shade through themes and variations in the choice of plants. The laws of perspective allowed him to create certain illusions, "to make an agreeable foreground over which the great buildings of the exposition will rise, gaining in grandeur of effect upon the imagination, because appearing at a greater distance and more lofty than they would but for such a foreground."[28] The techniques of landscaping used different kinds of foliage, textures, colors and light and shadow to create "a mysterious poetic effect." "Anything approaching a gorgeous, garish, or gaudy display of flowers was to be avoided."[29] Scenic wilderness for Olmsted was a landscape that could be read as a painting. Perspective, masses of vegetation and subtle variety in the patterns of light, shade and shadow, were all necessary ingredients for creating a discourse that spoke of the beauty and intrinsic value of wilderness.

Perhaps not surprisingly, photographers quickly grasped that the islands represented wilderness. C.D. Arnold, the official photographer of the fair, worked with the contrast between the natural island and the artificiality of the architecture surrounding it, by creating an opposition between nature as a picturesque wilderness and nature as a human transformation. In a number of views, Arnold "exploited the planned relation between Wooded Isle and its surrounding buildings using the Island as foreground." With these, Peter Hales argues, "Arnold set two conceptions of the relation of nature and man in juxtaposition: nature as teacher, in the Wooded Isle, and nature as material for exploitation and transformation, in the Horticultural Building."[30] In a number of Arnold's photographs, the island edges out the buildings in the frame, asserting the importance of wilderness. Contemporary paintings used similar strategies, as in Charles Caryl Coleman's lyrical "The Afterglow in the Lagoon" (see Plate 1).

The press also picked up the idea of wilderness and explored its picturesque qualities in their articles on the fair. Hamilton Gibson, for example, writing for *Scribner's Magazine*, described the entire fair as if one were on a walk in the countryside. He takes his readers botanizing, starting with the lagoon, then strolling in the wilderness of the wooded islands, visiting the rose garden and finishing with the Fisheries Building, richly decorated with aquatic scenes. The article is written in the genre of nature walks combining botanical and wildlife descriptions with humor. After stepping out of his boat onto the island, he says,

> Follow me through this winding path, embowered with its snowy banks of spiraea. Pry your way here beneath the branches. A few more steps, and the ripples gleam through the branches before us, and we emerge at the water's edge beneath a tangle of willows, while a brood of white ducks, disturbed at our approach, glide out upon the mill-pond – for such indeed is the irresistible association from the surroundings. This hap-hazard chaos of willows and alders disarms all suspicion of artificial planting.[31]

The reader is made aware of the artifice required to construct this miniature wilderness, while encouraged to admire the artistry of the gardeners who created this wild refuge in the center of the fair "embowered with its snowy banks of spiraea."

Contact with nature is a social good

Olmsted, of course, was renowned for his parks, following his mid-century design for New York's Central Park. He was the first person consulted by the fair organizers about the design of the park, and became one of the three key designers for the exposition – joined by the chief architects Burnham and Root and the chief sculptor Augustus Saint-Gaudens. After it was decided the waterlogged and singularly unlovely Jackson "Park" would be the site, the fair organizers recognized that Olmsted was perhaps the only person in the country qualified to manage the difficult water conditions. He was familiar with the site, having drawn up a plan for it some twenty years earlier. Olmsted, however, brought more than expertise in water management to the design of the fair – he brought a philosophy with respect to the natural landscape of the United States. The landscape architecture of the World's Columbian Exposition was the last project of his extraordinarily productive career, which included "scores of city parks, entire communities, ... college campuses, the grounds for state capitols, hospitals and railroad stations, conservation designs for Yosemite and Niagara Falls, and private estates such as Biltmore in North Carolina."[32] The landscape design for the exposition reflects the concerns and skills of a mature designer. We can see the design of the fair as the result of a whole career dedicated to the importance of nature in modern society, in the form of urban parks and preservation of wilderness sites. He had been part of a movement of social reformers who believed that nature, in the form of parks and playgrounds, played a strategic role in the quest for a more stable society. Boyer reminds us,

> The back to nature movement, which spread across the urban mentality of the late nineteenth century, valued woodlands and meadows for their spiritual impact; they were places of simple virtues and pleasures on the edge of urban disquietudes and troubles. Andrew Jackson Downing, F.L. Olmsted and Charles Eliot Norton, Jr., were among those promoters of landscape design and urban parks who believed a civilization of cities would not survive if it was cut off from nature. Nature not only held the power to uplift it also had the power to instill in men the best ideals from America's rural democratic past.[33]

Advocates of parks in the nineteenth century believed that in order for western civilization to persist, people required regular contact with nature for spiritual and physical renewal. For Olmsted then, the scenic beauty of parks such as the Wooded Islands was not only an aesthetic decision to serve as a visual counterpoint to the White City, but served a larger social function.

As tree-lined roads were denuded with each widening or paving, industrial dumpsites served as playgrounds, and the task of keeping water supplies untainted by effluent began to concern city governments, parks began to be seen as a remedy for bodily and moral disease. Many people believed that "foul air prompts to vice, and oxygen to virtue."[34] In that regard it is not surprising to learn that during the Civil War, Olmsted was the first Secretary General of the United States Sanitary Commission, a post that enabled him to advance the connection between natural environments and public health. Using European examples of sanitary plans, philanthropic societies argued for the installation of underground sewers and water pipes. The introduction of patches of greenery in a dense urban fabric, it was thought, would bring fresh air where there was none before and allow light to pierce the "darkest" areas of the city. These parks were designed with recreational opportunities for laboring adults such as areas for ball games, boating and picnicking. The working class child, it was argued, needed vigorous play, which would help children to develop a wholesome moral and ethical life.[35] In fact, the first real playground opened on a vacant lot in Chicago the year of the exhibition, a project managed by Jane Addams' Settlement House. For the government, the establishment of parks was a way to legitimate their position as a democratic institution by financing and maintaining open public spaces, while not interfering with the interests of the business class. For the business community, parks in poor neighborhoods were seen as a minor concession to the reproduction and education of the labor pool; and in wealthy neighborhoods, landowners were quick to realize that a new park increased the price of adjacent properties. As a result, Chicago in particular saw the planning and construction of an entire ring of small parks.[36]

There are two kinds of parks, Olmsted would explain to his clients: parks for roaming about, in which groups of people might spend the day picnicking; and parks for contemplation, smaller in size, which offer temporary relief from the busy streets of the city. His landscape design for the Columbian Exposition considered both of these aims, since the entire fair served to distract, entertain and educate, while the islands in the center of the lagoon were designed as a quiet and wooded retreat from the crowds. While the laboring classes, it was understood, would picnic on the beach or stroll by the sideshows of the Midway Plaisance, the middle and upper classes were expected to bring their families to the more refined restaurants on the grounds, to walk along the promenades facing the Court of Honor and circulate by boat around the lagoon. For both groups though, the Wooded Islands was meant as a place of temporary relief from the noise and crowds of the fair, and as a site for instruction. The "genteel" visitor, assumed to be knowledgeable about wildlife and plants, was informed by the press that the Isle would provide an interesting lesson on plant cohabitation. The laboring class, presumed ignorant of botany, were meant to be simply uplifted by such a display of natural beauty.

Isolating and purifying wilderness

If we look again at the plan of the exposition drafted in Burnham's office, and turn the pages to focus on the islands in the lagoon, we can begin to meditate on their significance. We have already discussed the idea that these areas of wilderness were meant to contrast with the urbanism of the White City. But what arrests our attention now is their configuration on the general plan. We need to pause and reflect on why wilderness is represented as an island. Could not the same argument for wilderness have been made with a park or a peninsula? The essential point here is that wilderness needed to be isolated from settlement to remain pure and unaffected. The process of isolation – literally, "creating islands" of protected areas – is an idea which became fundamental to the ideology of the conservation movement in America.

We already know how wilderness was defined in the nineteenth century – as a place that possesses qualities of a scenic beauty, like a painting. Once wilderness is defined, the second move is to create a boundary which surrounds the wilderness area and sets it apart. In the Wooded Islands, this is a contoured and sinuous line which describes its shore, a line which could hardly be in greater contrast to the rectilinear basins and canals of the White City. One speaks of order and artifice, the other of untamed nature. The water surrounding the island is perhaps the clearest expression of a separation between the two realms. The water is a barrier which protects the wilderness from encroachment and keeps it a place set apart (see Figure 1.10).

Nature preserved is thus encircled and defended. In the exposition, points of entry to the Wooded Islands are clearly established. Two bridges connect to the island from the Horticulture and Transportation Buildings, one from the courtyard between Mining and Electricity (toward the Court of Honor and entrance to the fair), while the last bridge weaves its way from the Fisheries Building. Each bridge, or point of entry, is well guarded by oversized sculptures of elk, wildcats, bison and bears – the "big game" animals of North America (see Plate 2). These bridges and their imposing animal sculptures create a threshold over which visitors must cross to pass from the profane world of the exhibition to the world set apart on the Wooded Islands. As visitors climb the rustic bridges, they are encouraged to pause and discover the scenery and changing views (see Figure 1.11). Small docks demand a similar transition for those taking gondolas or other water craft – they must slowly approach the edge of the island and moor before stepping out onto firm land.

Once inside the borders of "wilderness," the rules governing the composition of the landscape reveal the logic of nature: the island paths are narrow and curvy in contrast to the straight esplanades and canals of the

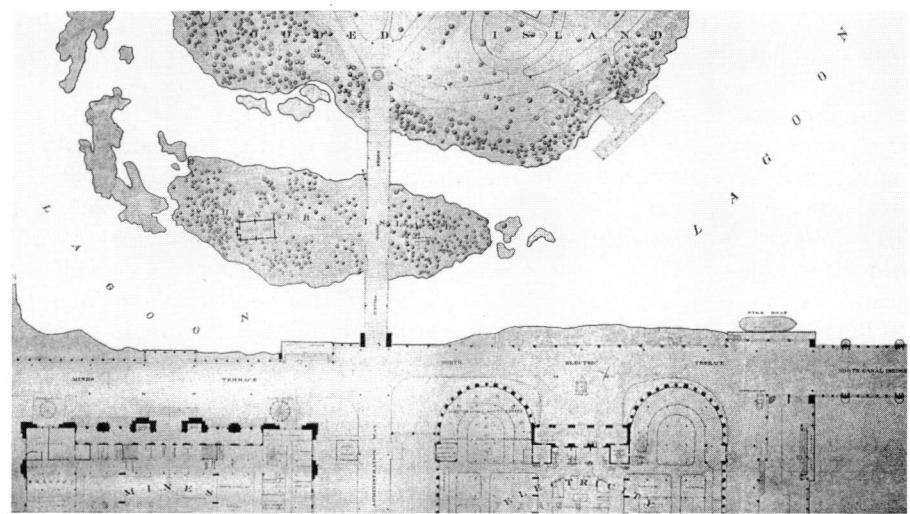

1.10 Detailed plan of Hunter's Island, 1893.

1.11 Undulating bridge to Wooded Isle. Photograph by C.D. Arnold.

White City, its woods are dense and irregular in opposition to the regular plantings bordering the major buildings of the fair, and its grounds are covered with vegetation in contrast to the denuded paving of the promenades. But such an opposition between inside and outside is always susceptible to reversal. In order for the islands to maintain the distinction between nature and civilization, the design of the Wooded Islands had to constantly reinforce binary oppositions such as inside/outside, natural/artificial, sacred/profane, and protected/unprotected. The success of Olmsted and others in asserting these oppositions in the construction of wilderness landscapes can be seen in the fact that they endure until today. It is a dualism, William Cronon says, that "sees the tree in the garden as artificial – completely fallen and unnatural – and the tree in the wilderness as natural – completely pristine and wild."[37]

At the time of the World's Columbian Exposition, the idea of isolation was already being practiced on a large scale in North America with the establishment of the Indian reservations. Indeed, virtually all the Native peoples of North America were, by 1890, living on enclosed areas which entirely restricted both their movements and their traditional ways of life. But wilderness reserves, on the other hand, were in their infancy. In the west, the Yellowstone National Park had been declared a park in 1872 but was not yet managed as one, while Yosemite, General Grant (Kings Canyon), and Sequoia had been established just three years before the fair, in 1890.[38] In the east, there was only the Adirondacks Preserve. Private game reserves were also gaining in popularity across the country – the "Bear Swamp Game Park" of New Jersey, for example, fenced a thousand acres of wooded land and stocked it with deer, and Canadian and Belgian hares.[39] A powerful and growing lobby advocating the creation and good management of national parks included conservationists such as the Audubon Society and the Sierra Club, sportsmen's organizations such as the Boone and Crockett Club and the many rod and gun clubs, Campfire clubs, and the general Federation of Women's Clubs.[40]

Although we see in the nineteenth century both popular and elite conceptions of wilderness inextricably linked "wild" regions with the aboriginal inhabitants, the possibility of allowing Native people to live in wilderness preserves was never considered. As a political and military solution for the pacification of the Native Americans, their isolation on reservations allowed the conquest of the frontier to proceed unchecked. The establishment of wilderness preserves, on the other hand, was viewed as a resource for the exclusive use of the "civilized peoples" of the continent. Black Elk saw this clearly when he said, "the white man has been making islands for us and for the four-legged, and the islands are getting smaller and smaller."[41]

It seems that the idea of isolating the "Indian" on one side and "wilderness" on the other, each confined to its own small territory, was too deep, too fundamental to Western culture to be questioned. As Timothy Mitchell explains in his book on the 1889 Universal Exhibition in Paris, the idea of isolating, which he calls "enframing," was a fundamental practice of the West in the nineteenth century.[42] Enframing an object gives the viewer the impression of being able to study it objectively, without disturbances from the rest. We can see the effort required to maintain this process of enframing by exploring the isolation of Native peoples even at the scale of the exposition. Turning again to the plan of the fair, we see Native Americans isolated as subjects of anthropological investigation: displayed, for example, as relics of a bygone era in dioramas set up in the US Government Building and as "ethnographic villages," again isolated in pockets on the peripheries of the fair. The Penobscot, Inuit and other encampments distributed on the margins of the exposition site were situated next to displays that evoked the march of progress, such as the elevated railway, the replica of La Rabida monastery, from which Columbus departed for the New World, and the Indian School run by the Departments of Corrections and Indian Affairs.

One of the anthropological dioramas in the Government Building showed an "Indian chief and squaw" described in the catalog as "picturesque types of the valiant Sioux nation" (see Figure 1.12).[43] At the first level, this is

1.12 "Red Cloud" diorama in US Government Building.

an ethnological display of a "representative" couple dressed in traditional clothes and adorned with objects associated with everyday life – a bow in the hand of the man and a basket in the hand of the woman. But if one were to read the catalog description, one is faced not with a "typical Indian," but with a historical account of an actual person. The man is identified as Red Cloud, a famous chief of the Sioux nation who coordinated with Sitting Bull the victory over Custer at Little Big Horn. "Under Sitting Bull," the catalog reads, the Sioux "again broke out in war during 1876, the conflict being chiefly memorable for the disaster on the Little Big Horn in which Custer and his command were annihilated."[44] We see here the volatility of the process of enframing. In attempting to set forward representative types, it is undercut by the more vivid and specific history of the recent past. Most revealingly, the story related is cut short in 1876, omitting mention of the final solution to the Sioux problem, carried out by the US Army only three years before the fair: the massacre of the Sioux at Wounded Knee in South Dakota. The enframing of Native Americans, turning them into ethnographic displays, was a political move accomplished with some urgency, because the people being represented were still seen to be a national menace. But it is clear that enframing was far from being conclusive. In a characteristic slippage, the figure of Red Cloud refuses to stay put. He reappears in many forms in the fair: in this ethnographic display, and in a heroic sculpture entitled "Indian Scout," flanking the "Cowboy" in front of the Transportation Building (see Figure 1.13). As a scout, he is even re-cast as an agent of the white man, although Red Cloud was nationally recognized as a Sioux chief, strategist, diplomat and warrior – and a formidable opponent of American settlers and of their government (see Figure 1.14). He surfaces again as a character in Buffalo Bill's Wild West show, near the reconstruction of "Sitting Bull's Cabin" on the Midway, featuring nine Sioux men and women. The multiple representations of Red Cloud show how visitors to the fair had to flip back and forth between ethnography and history, between science and popular culture.

Putting the isolation ideology into practice on a national scale was a violent process. Once a site was deemed worthy of being protected from encroaching exploitation of natural resources, once it was encircled and controlled points of entry were established, the wilderness reserve needed to be "purified" of all human traces. This purification of the national parks and sites of scenic beauty, carried out in the years of the exposition, came at great human cost. In Yosemite Park, the resident tribe was virtually hunted down by the army, captured and expelled. In Yellowstone Park, the Shoshone and Nez Perce were expelled, although they returned time and again to their traditional herding grounds before they were finally incarcerated.[45] In other words, the isolation of wilderness to protect it had disastrous consequences on human lives. It also erased cultural landscapes created by Native peoples and white settlers alike. Clearly, the practice of purification was meant to

1.13 "Indian Scout," A. Phiminster Procter.

remove human traces, to render the land ahistorical, and to re-cast it in an eternal present. The erasure of human traces was also meant to remove traces of work. As Richard White argues, "work is a fall from grace. In the beginning none labored. In the beginning there was harmony and no human mark on the landscape."[46] In the World's Columbian Exposition, work occurs outside the Wooded Islands: in the Mining, Electricity, Manufactures and Horticulture pavilions. There, work is elevated to astonishing quantities of production by the power of machines and human labor. Inside the islands, there is no trace of work. The lagoon represents "the beginning" as a harmonious and picturesque landscape.

Within this sacred precinct, there are two islands, a large and a small one. On the small one, called the Hunter's Island, there is a small building, the only building erected on the islands with Olmsted's approval. If we agree with the religious metaphor put forth by White, this building would have to be a shrine to nature. Introduced in an area entirely dedicated to wilderness, it reveals the human desire for dwelling in perfect wilderness. What kind of building could this be to further Olmsted's argument for the protection of

1.14 Delegation of Sioux to Washington DC, 1875.

wilderness? We may, or may not, interpret it as a shrine, but either way, the question of what it looks like and what it contains is worth exploring, to find out what kind of architecture spoke to conservationists in the 1890s. We now turn to our third and last object in the study, the Hunter's Cabin.

A LESSON IN NATURAL LAW

When asked to recall his favorite memories of the World's Columbian Exposition, the fair's designer Daniel Burnham included on his list "Boone and Crockett Club." By piecing together this clue with other references to the club's building at the fair, we can see that this modest exhibit, known as the Hunter's Camp, made a memorable impression on the most privileged visitors to the exposition. Receiving an invitation from Theodore Roosevelt to attend a club dinner to celebrate the opening of the exhibit on June 15, 1893 ("no dress suits" was written at the bottom), Burnham jumped at the chance for an evening out "with the boys."[47] Leaving the courtyards of the White City behind at the end of the day, he had to cross over a rustic bridge and pass statues of wild elk on either side to reach the island. Ensconced in the dark woodland setting, the club exhibit, a rustic two-room log cabin, was filled with the bulky figures of Victorian gentlemen in informal garb. Warmed by a blazing campfire and hearing the sounds of the fair muted across the water, Burnham joined other men of power and influence for a night of eating, drinking and talking. Always the genial host, Roosevelt had gone so far as to arrange for his friend

Elwood Hofer to send elk meat by train all the way from the wildlife preserve of Yellowstone National Park, so he could host an "authentic" barbecue on this small patch of wilderness in Chicago (see Figure 1.15).[48]

What was the attraction of this evening for the men invited? Was it the camaraderie between men that is possible when women are not present, an experience they were familiar with in the men's clubs so characteristic of the era? Was it the feeling of being away from responsibilities, "let loose," so to speak, where they could taste "the simple life" and share physical companionship? This simple unpretentious cabin was a great deal more significant rhetorically than its modest dimensions might suggest. Targeted to a specific elite group of men, and employing tropes familiar to that group, it was designed to persuade these men of the value of conservation. We are going to analyze this cabin in some detail to understand how it played a role in creating a new way to experience "wilderness," and how this new experience served larger political and social goals important to business and governmental elites in turn of the century America.

The cabin was sponsored by the Boone and Crockett Club of New York, a club of sportsmen and conservationists founded in 1887. In their

1.15 Boone and Crockett Club House, World's Columbian Exposition, 1893. Photograph by C.D. Arnold.

description of the exhibit, they state their intention to represent "so typical and peculiar a phase of American national development as life on the frontier."[49] Club members were delighted with the site suggested by the fair organizers – a small wooded island well protected from the fairgrounds by the lagoon. It is noteworthy that Olmsted did not oppose the building on this site, but rather saw this "temporary camp" as totally in keeping with the spirit and aim of his "wilderness preserve" of the Wooded Islands. The president of the club, Theodore Roosevelt, personally supervised every detail of the exhibit. Looking for architects to design the building, he turned to one of the best firms in Chicago, Holabird and Roche, who he had probably met at the Coleman Lake Club, a hunting resort in Michigan that was designed by Holabird and was popular with Chicago businessmen looking for an escape from city life. Edward Renwick, an employee of Holabird and Roche, recalls the day Roosevelt came to the office to commission the work.

> One day I was sitting in my office trying to concentrate on writing specifications when I was disturbed by a voice in the outer office which had all the musical qualities of a buzz saw. It was a terrible voice, I never heard anything like it. I looked out and there, talking to Roche, was an individual with a red bandanna around his head, dressed in a red flowered smoking jacket with a pattern like an ingrained carpet of the '80s, in red Turkish slippers the toes of which coiled up, and hanging from his mouth a long German pipe with a spark arrester on top. I wondered who this apparition could be, but as his voice was disturbing me I got up quietly and closed my office door. Pretty soon Roche came in and said, "What do you go slamming doors in people's faces for?" I said I hadn't slammed the door but I was trying to get some work done and had to close it to get some quiet. I added, "Who was the crank anyway?" Mr. Roche answered, "A man whom you greatly admire – Theodore Roosevelt." He had walked from the Beau Rivage Hotel which was on Michigan and Adams over to our office, about five blocks, in that get-up. From that day to the end of his career I have seen among his very fine sterling qualities, that same desire not to be unnoticed.[50]

Roosevelt took a great personal interest in this exhibit, as we see from this story of his trip to Chicago to commission its design. The description of the exhibit published by the Boone and Crockett Club in the year of the exposition suggests that each detail of the cabin, inside and out, from the furniture to its rustic ornaments such as the elk antlers or prairie schooner framing the entry door, had been carefully considered and discussed by the members. Roosevelt arranged for Elwood Hofer, an outdoor guide he had befriended during his years in Montana, to be hired by the club to act as an interpreter for the cabin.[51] Although the Hunter's Camp was open to all exposition visitors in the daytime, it came to life at night during events such as the opening night dinner. The sculptor Edward Kemeys recalled fondly that when "Roosevelt visited the World's Fair this cabin was his resting place part of each day and there on this settee before another fireplace, the three old mountaineer friends (Kemeys, Roosevelt and Hofer) sat day after day and recounted pioneer experiences."[52] When we read that Roosevelt thought nothing of bringing a cook, pack boy and 26 horses to accompany him and two guides on a trek through the Yellowstone region, perhaps "pioneer experiences" is a bit overstated.[53]

The point here is that the cabin was an exhibit which worked best when one was invited to participate. Certainly, part of its appeal for those invited was its exclusivity. But we must keep in mind that the contact with nature which it was meant to bring about was not intended for everyone. The Boone and Crockett Club was an unusually exclusive men's society, even by the rarefied standards that governed admission to men's clubs at that time. Restricted by its by-laws to one hundred persons, the membership of the Boone and Crockett Club reads like a roster of *Who's Who* in 1893. The club included influential politicians such as Elihu Root, the ultra-expansionist Senator Henry Cabot Lodge (who co-founded the club with Roosevelt), Senators Redfield Procter and G.G. Vest, Congressmen Thomas Reed and Bellamy Storer. The historian Frances Parkman, much admired by Roosevelt for his romantic and nationalistic history of the west, was listed as an honorary member even after his death in 1892. The army was well represented, from the honorary memberships of generals from the Civil War and the Indian Wars (William Tecumseh Sherman, W.H. Jackson and Phil Sheridan), to officers active in the administration of the young Yellowstone National Park, such as John Pitcher and George Anderson. Other members were scientists who advocated conservation: from the anthropologist George Bird Grinnell and Arnold Hague of the US Geological Survey, to the Harvard botanist Charles Sprague.[54] Artists in the club included the architects Daniel Burnham and Frank Furness, along with the painter of western landscapes Albert Bierstadt and the novelist who would invent the Western genre, Owen Wister.[55] Of course, the main body of the club consisted of that solid stock of east coast privilege who needed only to satisfy the main requirements for entry (other than family connections), which was to kill one animal according to the rules of "fair chase." These included Chanlers, Winthrops, and Roosevelts from New York, Penroses from Philadelphia, Williams from Virginia, and a few persons representative of the new railroad money out west, Crocker, Gould and Van Dyke.

One could hardly imagine a more effective group of men to carry out the conservation agenda: there were men of science to provide scientific rationale and tools, politicians to establish policy, military leaders to act as the enforcing arm, and artists and writers, specialists in rhetoric, to persuade and convince. With a small but active membership widely distributed across the country, the club had eyes and ears everywhere to track the progress and setbacks of the conservation movement. They were not unaware of their reach and influence, as we see from an article celebrating their tenth anniversary, "With a membership which though small, reaches from the Atlantic to the Pacific, covering alike our largest cities and States, which are only just beginning to develop their resources, the club covers a vast territory, and the precept and example of its members come to a great many people."[56] The club was an avant-garde for wilderness advocates, a marching pack for conservationists. Suffused with the sense of their own self-worth, these men turned to an ideology of primitivism to promote their goals of economic and political expansion. They employed a myth set out by the historian Francis Parkman, in which the heroic figure of the natural aristocrat turns time and again to the wilderness and, in the process, gains in natural virtues and moral purity, enabling him ultimately to lead the way to civilized progress.

Naming the club

In that regard, the decision to name the club after Daniel Boone and Davy Crockett is not without significance.[57] They were very popular figures in the nineteenth century, historical persons around whom myths had developed. For the Boone and Crockett Club, the power of these figures rested on the fact that, as frontiersmen, they had chosen a simple life away from civilization, and that choice distinguished them from the merely poor. "No populous city," Boone declared, "with all the varieties of commerce and stately structures, could afford so much pleasure to my mind, as the beauties of nature."[58] The willing primitivism of Boone and Crockett had a hard edge too, which was appropriate to the kind of ideology the club wished to justify. The violence of conquest associated with the frontier, naturalized through hunting, was seen as necessary to the act of "blazing the way for civilization." The paradoxical position of the frontiersman who refuses civilization and at the same time initiates and facilitates development was deeply embodied in the figures of Boone and Crockett. The club saw no ambiguity in this formulation.[59] In contrast to antimodernists of the late nineteenth century, who criticized technology and modern civilization, club members did not see the virtues of frontier life as a rebuke to the values of commercial society, but as an embryonic form of those values.[60] Identifying with these frontiersmen, they saw themselves as "natural" leaders, the cutting edge of civilization, the "carriers of the big stick," the avant-garde of ever further expansion into new frontiers (see Figure 1.16).

To spend time in the cabin, to hunt or tell stories about the hunt, was a way to come closer to the simple life and martial virtues associated with the frontiersmen who, mythically speaking, formed the country. A renewed emphasis on primitivism would ensure the survival and future greatness of American civilization. Spartans of the Gilded Age, the well-heeled members of the Boone and Crockett Club exalted simple needs, simple wants, and

1.16 George Caleb Bingham, "Daniel Boone Escorting Settlers through the Cumberland Gap," 1851–2. Oil on canvas, $36\frac{1}{2}"\times 50\frac{1}{4}"$.

contact with nature as a way to build moral fiber and civic virtue in themselves and others. In architectural terms, this meant a return to first principles – a clearing, a rude shelter, walls, a hearth and a roof.

The primitive hut
The little cabin designed by Holabird and Roche is full of meaning, although this meaning is not communicated through the classical techniques of decoration and symbolism omnipresent in the buildings of the White City. Rather, the Hunter's Cabin is striking for its ability to say so much with so little. As an exhibit, the architecture of the cabin, as much as the objects on display, functions rhetorically to convince the public of the value of conservation. Its siting on the island is significant as well. If we imagine instead that the cabin were located between two large Beaux Arts buildings of the White City, it would still be a cabin but it would not work as a hunter's retreat, perhaps the most important aspect of the exhibit for the Boone and Crockett Club. For the cabin to be seen as a Hunter's Camp it needs the forest of the Wooded Island surrounding it, hiding it even, from the rest of the fair. If the trees are an important visual and sensual element to speak about a cabin in the wilderness, the sculptures of wild animals framing the bridges to the small island reinforce the idea that it is a wilderness populated by American big game

animals. Landscape architecture, sculpture and architecture all come together to speak about conservation, and to convince its public of the urgency to protect wilderness and its animals as a living memory of life on the frontier.

We can interpret this cabin by Holabird and Roche in terms of certain ideas about national architecture that were hotly debated in architectural theory at the time the cabin was built. The question of the "national character" of architecture had led a number of theorists in the nineteenth century, like John Ruskin or Viollet le Duc, to turn to what we call now vernacular buildings in their search for deeper principles which underlay the architecture of any particular "nation." They did this in reaction to the academic styles so well exemplified by the architecture of the White City. There, the references to Greek mythology and the forms of Roman antiquity were assumed to be international, which actually meant the Western world. A national character to architecture, on the other hand, was meant to present the essence of a nation in a building type. The year of the Chicago exposition, Ruskin published "The Poetry of Architecture" with the significant subtitle, "The Architecture of the Nations of Europe Considered in its Association with Natural Scenery and National Character."[61] Joseph Rykwert suggests that in this essay, Ruskin uses the English cottage and the Swiss chalet, the country house in Britain and in Italy, "as instancing national character, as expressing a faith."[62] By turning to the cottages of farmers in his search for "authentic" expressions of national culture, Ruskin was following a wider fashion current in literature, music and painting of the nineteenth century, in which the peasant cultures in daily contact with the soil epitomized national virtues and traits.[63] National identity, in this formulation, stemmed from the very soil a nation was built on; it was not to be found in the cities that represented rather a nation's highest achievements. We find very much this kind of reading in a meditation by the philosopher Martin Heidegger about a painting by Van Gogh of a pair of worn out shoes. He sees a peasant woman's shoes; covered in grime and worn out from toil, they symbolize for him the essential relationship between the earthly elements of soil and blood and the soul of a people, or a nation.[64] In the same manner, Ruskin interprets the Swiss chalet as the architectural expression of the simple daily life of a family taking care of the cows in the green landscapes of the Swiss Alps. Likewise, the English peasant cottage was "a part of nature, because the peasant could immediately mirror this national character in forms he derived from nature: that nature which Ruskin continuously scrutinized for the way in which surface revealed structure, and the structure the process of making."[65]

In the charged context of "national" readings of simple cottages, the cabin of Holabird and Roche can be seen as representing the essential American "national" character – if one could speak of a "Swiss" chalet and an "English" cottage, then certainly one could do the same of an "American" log cabin. Why a log cabin, we might ask, rather than a Cape Cod saltbox or a south-western adobe? The adobe, unfortunately, carries with it a most inconvenient Spanish and Indian heritage, for the resolutely Eurocentric and Protestant myth makers of the nineteenth century United States. Conversely, the saltbox, relying on milled lumber, is too redolent of industrialization. An "essential" American architecture, like the English cottage of Ruskin, had to reveal its surface through its structure. Every mark of the ax, every knot in the log, revealed the experience of frontier life in the wilderness. It is, of course, a temporary dwelling, but then these are a people on the move, pulling up roots and moving onward with every expansion of the frontier. As long as the hunting and farming is good, the cabin endures; once it is time to move on, the roof will collapse, the logs will fall to the ground and rot away, and the architecture will return to nature.

Not only does the log cabin carry national characteristics, it also speaks of *origin*. As we have seen, the Hunter's Cabin was meant to represent the memory of the frontier. It was predicated on an originary moment when wilderness began to be transformed into civilization. The log cabin thus had to carry the seed from which civilization will grow. It is an archetype that expresses the "American" character – individualism, courage, and self-reliance. The materials for the cabin can be obtained by one person (so the story goes), it is set deep in wilderness and requires no special technology to erect it. In that respect it is shown as the original American building (see Figure 1.17).

To explore how the log cabin might speak of origins, we turn to the famous engraving of the primitive hut, published by Abbé Laugier in his *Essais* of 1753 (see Figure 1.18). That image depicts a hut made of four tree trunks and a roof made of branches. In the foreground, a female figure (standing for architecture) calls on the viewer to interpret this rustic hut as an allegory. Laugier believed that architecture was the art of mimesis, of copying nature. He tells us that man "leaves the cave determined to compensate by his industry for the omissions and neglect of nature. Some branches broken off in the forest are materials for this purpose. He chooses four of the strongest, and raises them ..."[66] and so on. From this simple hut, Laugier derives all the essential elements of architecture, the rules which govern them, and the combinations which may arise from them, "the upright pieces of wood suggest the idea of columns, the horizontal pieces resting on them, entablatures. Finally, the inclined members which contribute the roof provided the idea of pediment."[67] Laugier's hut is an artificial construct, an abstraction reducing architecture to its essential principles. In that regard, his essay is a philosophical meditation on the origins of architecture. "Laugier's little hut ... built on Rousseau's river bank" developed a following through the eighteenth century, when to construct a *fabrique* (a thatched roof hut) in the "English garden" became quite the fashion throughout Europe.[68] Turning again to Olmsted's landscape design for the fair, which was influenced by the picturesque English garden, we can now see the American log cabin as a *fabrique*. We know that for Olmsted, the cabin struck no discordant note in his

1.17 "An American log-house." From Georges Henri Victor Collot, *Voyage dans l'Amerique septentrionale . . .*, Paris, 1826.

carefully guarded nature preserve. Even the Europeans could see the connection – in the words of the German theorist Gottfried Semper, "today Europe's overcivilized sons, when they wander in the primeval forests of America, build themselves log cabins."[69] While we recognize that the cabin designed by Holabird and Roche does not speak of strictly architectural elements in the way Laugier's does, what is important for us here is the idea that the origin (in their case, of a national character) is embodied in a small, simple building that looks natural. Laugier's hut set up the argument for the original shelter as one that draws from nature and that is what we recognize here.[70]

Built at the end of the nineteenth century, and not in the middle of the eighteenth, there is no doubt that the cabin fits squarely into a Darwinian world view. Created without technology, but drawing from the natural environment, the log cabin rises from the ground. It is the bottom rung of the evolutionary ladder that will lead to the modern architecture of Chicago skyscrapers. Whether we read Turner's frontier thesis, or turn to Roosevelt's, we find the same sequence of frontiersmen, trappers, farmers, and city-dwellers, each one replacing the previous. In that respect, the log cabin plays right into the myth "from cabin to presidency" in which someone from the humblest

1.18 "The primitive hut," drawing by Charles Eisen. From Abbé Laugier, *Essais sur l'Architecture*, Paris, 1755.

beginnings might end up, one day, as head of the country. In the cabin, the evolution of an entire society – from frontier to modernity – is recapitulated in the lifetime of one man. Be he Abraham Lincoln (and we find such a cabin labeled as Lincoln's birthplace on the Midway of the fair) or the willing primitive Theodore Roosevelt, the American myth holds out the possibility of such a trajectory.

Yet unlike the European examples of national architecture, such as the English cottage and the Swiss chalet, the American log cabin, as it is represented in the Hunter's Camp, is not a home for a family. Any reference to family life – the women and children who, for example, followed Daniel Boone through the Cumberland Gap – were nowhere to be seen as visitors entered the Hunter's Camp. When we compare it to another log cabin at the exposition, the New England Kitchen on the Midway Plaisance, this omission becomes all the more striking (see Figure 1.19). The interior of the Boone and Crockett Club is resolutely a masculine place (see Figure 1.20). We see pegs and deer antlers driven into the wall to support chaps, buckskin shirts, broad hats, stock-saddles, and the like, but no signs of baby cradle, spinning wheel or other objects depicting family life on the frontier. If the cabin were meant

1.19 The "New England Kitchen" at the World's Columbian Exposition.

1.20 Interior of Boone and Crockett Club House, 1893. Photograph by C.D. Arnold.

to depict frontier life as set out by Turner, it would have been a house for a family because, for Turner, the farmer occupies center stage. According to Turner, it is precisely the work involved in transforming wilderness into productive farmland that formed a unique American character[71]. But for Roosevelt, and for the Boone and Crockett Club, the farmer and his family are secondary figures. The hero of the frontier is a man alone in the wilderness. In this sense, the Hunter's Camp mirrors the European *fabrique*, a hut in which a single man meditates on nature and women are present only as allegories for a larger idea – be it "Architecture," as in the case of Laugier, or "Columbia," as we see in the Chicago fair.[72]

If we were to pause for a moment and reflect here what might have been if farming instead of hunting took a central role in the conservation movement of the Boone and Crockett Club, we uncover several points for meditation. First, the type of landscape to be protected would be entirely different. Small fields would have surrounded a rustic house with the forest beyond; such a landscape would speak of human effort and cooperation, perhaps tinged with regret for a time now past. We can well imagine that protection of the early frontier landscape instead of the wilderness would have gained popular support in a country where frontier life and early farming were still in living memory. Certainly more recently, contemporary commentators on the American landscape such as William Cronon, J.B. Jackson and Richard White have argued convincingly of the importance of protecting cultural landscapes that speak of work rather than leisure. By focusing on the hunter rather than the farmer, the Boone and Crockett Club's conservation ideology accommodated rather the mythic history begun by Boone, developed by Cooper and culminating in the nationalistic and heroic vision of the past we see in the writings of Francis Parkman. The frontier, in this vision, is not "a collective process in which nearly everyone participates," but the domain of an exceptional person – a hero, if you will.[73] Daniel Boone is his allegorical double, replacing in the Hunter's Camp Laugier's allegory of Architecture in the primitive hut.

A club of naturalists

If we look further at the photograph taken by C.D. Arnold of the Hunter's Cabin we are first struck by the rough appearance of the interior. The point is clear: this is not a home to stay in long; it is a shelter used for a few months of the year, no more. The photograph is taken from the door leading to the second room, looking toward the fireplace and the back door. Rough-cut log walls, snugly chinked, are interrupted by windows and doors made of split boards with leather curtains. The simple furniture consists only of a square table, a rustic settee and a wooden trunk for a bench. The settee, of mountain pine from Yellowstone Park, is put together with wooden pegs and covered with a red bull's hide, while the clay floor is strewn with skins and furs. A generous hearth is flanked with rustic cookware and cluttered with animal skulls and bone fragments, a pair of crossed snowshoes on the mantel and crowned with a large set of antlers.

Unlike other exhibits at the fair that were simply didactic, this exhibit functioned at two levels. On the first level, it showed how a "frontiersman" lived, among his hunting gear and rude furnishings fitted to a simple life in the wilderness. But on another level, it could be read as a book. For those "in the know," each object in the cabin referred to a story recently published by a member of the club in the popular journals of the day, such as *Scribner's* or *Outing* magazine. Most members of the Boone and Crockett Club wrote for publication, some professionally, like Owen Wister who became famous for his western novel *The Virginian*, or George Bird Grinnell who was the editor of *Forest and Stream*, the most influential outdoors magazine at the turn of the century.[74] The president of the club, Theodore Roosevelt, was a hugely productive author who had developed a significant reputation by the 1890s as a historian of the west and a chronicler of big-game hunting.[75] The fireplace in the Hunter's Cabin then, represents a place where stories about wilderness are told, commented on, and elaborated before finding their way onto paper. Storytelling was one of the most important activities of the club; through this exchange, information about wilderness was passed from one member to another, and passion for nature was shared among like-minded men.

The buffalo skull on the mantel, for example, evokes Grinnell's lyrical essay "The Last of the Buffalo," published in *Scribner's Magazine* in 1892 and reprinted for the first *Book of the Boone and Crockett Club*, which appeared the year of the fair. Grinnell starts his meditation by gazing at bleached bones near the fireplace, and his reverie takes him to a time now past when hordes of buffalo roamed the great plains.

> On the floor, on either side of my fireplace, lie two buffalo skulls. They are white and weathered, the horns cracked and bleached by the snows and frosts and the rains and heats of many winters and summers. Often, late at night, when the house is quiet, I sit before the fire, and muse and dream of the old days; and as I gaze at these relics of the past, they take life before my eyes. The matted brown hair again clothes the dry bone, and in the empty orbits the wild eyes gleam. Above me curves the blue arch; away on every hand stretches the yellow prairie, and scattered near and far are the dark forms of buffalo. They dot the rolling hills, quietly feeding like tame cattle, or lie at ease on the slopes, chewing the cud and half asleep.[76]

In the same spirit, the bear skin on the ground might well refer to "Nights with the Grizzlies" by W.D. Pickett, and the elk horns above the fireplace to "A Day with the Elk" by Winthrop Chanler, both of which also appeared in the first book of the club. Members of the club saw their stories about big game hunting in wild regions as a way to contribute to the increase of knowledge about wild animals and their habitats. "However agreeable it may be for a number of hunters to dine together and to exchange experiences and swap hunting stories," we read in an editorial of *Forest and Stream* celebrating the tenth annual meeting of the club, "the Boone and Crockett Club aims at something higher than being a mere social organization, ... among the objects named in the constitution of the club are the promotion of travel and exploration in wild and unknown portions of the country, the working for the preservation of large game in this country, by furthering legislation for that purpose ... and inquiry into and recording observations of the habits and natural history of various wild animals."[77] In other words, they were a social hunting club with higher aims.

Partly because of the privileged background of club members, but also by choice, the club had many close ties to national institutions of science. The club helped national institutions to obtain specimens of wildlife, both dead and alive. The stuffed trophies prized by club members as souvenirs of a memorable shoot led to their support for taxidermy, many of which still populate natural history museums in major American cities.[78] The club also assisted in capturing live animals for the many budding zoological societies around the country. Elwood Hofer, the Yellowstone guide hired by the club to manage the Hunter's Cabin during the Exposition, carried the title "Smithsonian Hunter," for his job in capturing wildlife in Yellowstone National Park for the National Zoological Park in Washington.[79] By the 1900s, urban zoos took it for granted that the national parks were a resource to supply them with animals. The military administration of Yellowstone was besieged with requests to capture pelicans, grizzlies, mountain lions and, of course, elks.[80] The animals in greatest demand were those which represented the American wilderness. Revealing the influence of the Boone and Crockett Club, the newly-formed New York Zoological Society stated in 1897, "it will naturally be the first object of the Society to bring together a series of North American types, and of these the great game animals will be the first chosen ... buffalo, moose, elk, mountain sheep, caribou, antelope, deer." Almost as an afterthought, the Society mentions those animals less suited to the hunt, "bears, wolves, foxes and other mammals which will find their place here."[81]

Club members who were politicians were well placed to arrange for members with scientific backgrounds to be appointed advisors to government on questions of land use and resource management. Arnold Hague, for example, was on a panel of experts nominated by the National Academy of Sciences to advise the Department of the Interior on the establishment of forest preserves. As a result of the recommendations of this panel, 21.4 million acres of forest reserves were proclaimed by President Cleveland in 1897.[82] Gifford Pinchot, a long-term friend of the club and a future member, was the "father" of scientific forestry in the United States.

As naturalists, the Boone and Crockett Club wished to explore and study the big game animals in their wilderness habitats. And in keeping with their sense of class entitlement, they saw themselves as the nation's experts on wilderness matters. The binoculars on the table of the Hunter's Cabin, the ink bottle nearby, and the little phials of chemicals sitting on the mantelpiece all speak to that commitment. These objects of observation and recording reinforce that the stories these men relate about wilderness are drawn from observation, not hearsay, while at the same time they set this group apart as upper-class men. The impression we may have at first glance of the cabin – a rough and rustic place – slowly transforms as we realize who was meant to inhabit this rustic structure. No signs here of physical labor, no piles of furs gathered by a trapper, no farming implements, no heaps of logs like those next to that other log cabin at the Chicago Exposition, the Michigan loggers' camp. We see, rather, a newspaper on the settee. The Hunter's Cabin, for all its rustic atmosphere, is a place where gentlemen study and hold forth about wilderness. "Conservation above all, was a scientific movement," Samuel Hays tells us, whose "leaders brought the ideals and practices of their craft into federal resource policy. Loyalty to these professional ideals, not close association with grass-root public, set the tone of the Theodore Roosevelt conservation movement."[83] And if conservation is to move forward, members of the club believed, it would be because of well-reasoned arguments set forth by wilderness experts such as themselves. Denuded forests could be replanted, zoos would serve to breed American species and restock wildlife preserves, waters dammed in arid areas – in short, any problem relating to the perpetuation of American wilderness could be solved by the informed advice of experts. Such beliefs reveal to us the "deep sense of hope which pervaded all those at the turn of the century for whom science and technology were revealing visions of an abundant future."[84] Such faith in expert management was carried to its fullest expression in Roosevelt's progressive conservation movement. The Hunter's Cabin then, clearly shows us that the conservation crusade should be led by those who have the education to promote it and the leisure time to enjoy it.

The animalist sculptor
In the description of the exhibit published the year of the fair, the club draws the attention of big-game hunters to the "colossal figures of moose, elk, bison, bear and cougar which guard the various bridges [to the island]; some are by Procter, and some by Kemeys" (see Figure 1.21).[85] We know that the sculptor Edward Kemeys (1843–1907) had crossed paths with members of

1.21 Kemeys and his wife at work.

the Boone and Crockett Club prior to the fair – he met Roosevelt as early as 1886, when a series of thirteen articles he wrote for *Outing* magazine about his western trips followed on the heels of a similar set of serialized stories by Roosevelt.[86] Roosevelt began to acquire some of Kemeys' smaller bronzes and eventually became a significant patron of the wilderness artist, to the point where it was said of Kemeys' sculptures that they "came to attract all the money Theodore Roosevelt could spare for art."[87]

We have seen that the club supported scientific research into wilderness regions, but we have not yet looked into their support for artistic representations of wilderness and wildlife. But patrons of the arts they were, both by privilege of their class, and because of their passion for raising public support for wilderness conservation. Albert Bierstadt, for example, was a club member who enjoyed a national stature for his heroic landscapes of wilderness scenery. But Kemeys' work attracts our interest here not only because his animals inhabit the spaces of the Wooded Island surrounding Hunter's Cabin, but because his sculptures were admired by club members for their power to depict, with great realism, a moment in the life of an animal in the wild. Clearly, such knowledge came from long and disciplined observation.

The intensity of Kemeys' observation often had him described as a mystic. In an interview he explains, "I always had, in some way, an intuitive conception of what animals would do under certain circumstances. I could see them – see them in groups. I knew nothing about conventional composition, but I could see my subjects, every gesture, intuitively. I could sit down before an animal and drink him dry."[88] In spite of his love for animals, Kemeys – raised in New York City – had little exposure to wild animals other than those inhabiting Central Park, where he worked on the grounds, or those kept inside cages in the zoos. With his first public sculpture commission in 1871, he earned enough money to go west and draw animals in their natural habitat. He plunged into western life as only an easterner filled with romantic fantasy could, reveling in encounters with Indians, trappers and hunters. Thereafter, he returned only sporadically to the West, but his fifteen-month trip had made a big impression on him, providing source material for the stories he would later serialize in *Outing* magazine. He draped the floors of his New York studio with furs and hung hunting trophies on its walls. He affected Indian dress and photographs of him reveal his fierce, one might even say intentionally savage countenance. These attributes contributed to his public persona as the first American animal sculptor, a self-taught artist and a self-made man. In the words of his friend Emerson Hough, the editor of *Field and Stream* magazine, "If ever there was an artist who became such independently, without study, without imitation and wholly upon his own initiative, then surely it was Mr. Kemeys."[89] This self-made quality was doubtless appealing to the members of the Boone and Crockett Club. But the fundamental point of rapport between Kemeys and the club was that Kemeys saw hunting as an essential precondition for creating his sculptures of wild animals. Hunting was at the core of the club's philosophy and to be a good hunter was in itself a recommendation to Theodore Roosevelt. And in every interview about his art, Kemeys brought the discussion back to the hunt. This, he explained, was the source of his anatomical precision in depicting wild animals and the secret behind his ability to communicate every nuance of their movement. Reviewers of Kemeys' work ate this up, as we see in an 1894 article from *The Graphic*,

> ... what gives Mr. Kemeys even greater insight into animal nature is his love of the chase. He is an ardent sportsman, yet his eagerness is not so much for the game as that he may study the animal, pose it while body is warm, or later skin and dissect it.[90]

Kemeys elaborates,

> Every night I had all the animals I could use for dissection and posing. ... I wanted to go to the very heart of the wilderness, and then came to the mountains! I went all through them. I met the mountain animals, I killed them, grizzlies, sheep, wolves. ... I went to the heart's core of our American wilderness, and it yielded up its most carefully guarded secrets to me.[91]

Kemeys' intention in his work was two-fold: to create sculptures of American animals to show their beauty (a beauty based on certain ideals), and to document a wilderness, which he believed would soon vanish from existence. Thanks to this type of sculpture, American animals and their behavior in the wilderness would be kept on record for ever.

His dual emphasis on artistry and scientific verisimilitude distinguishes his work from the more traditional animal sculptures at the fair. The monumental animal groupings by Edward Clark Potter (of shorthorned bulls or draft horses) or Theodore Baur functioned as allegories, representing abstract ideas like "work" or "progress." Kemeys' wild animals, by contrast, radiate vitality and power, as if they could jump out of their casts and run away at any moment. The allegorical animals carry the weight of their European heritage – they are tame, garlanded with flowers or harnessed to the plow (see Figure 1.22). By contrast, the sculptures of the wild American animals appear (even today) free of such references – they are rough, they are wild, and they are revealed to the viewer in all their natural idealism (see Figure 1.23). They are to sculpture what the Hunter's Cabin is to architecture – an expression of the frontier experience and the wilderness ideal. The frontier was doubly represented in Edward Kemeys' work: in its content of wild animals, and in its new, untutored but truthful style, a kind of American animalism. As the first sculptor to focus entirely on American wildlife, his obituary compared him to that other pioneer, "He will stand always as uniquely pioneer in the

1.22 Sculptural group for Agricultural Building. Photograph by C.D. Arnold.

depicting of this part of American life, as Daniel Boone stands as the Pathfinder."[92]

The incipient nationalism of the sculptures was picked up and reinforced by the press, "we of America have awakened to the beauty of our own land, its superior possibilities for the artist in whatever field, and to our obligation to present to posterity in enduring form the native life of mountain and plain."[93] And in the years following the fair, public support grew for sculptures of wilderness animals in public parks and plazas.[94] Writing about Kemeys' work in *Field and Stream*, Hough suggests to his readers that such sculptures of wilderness animals not only provide a permanent record of a vanishing fauna, but also hold a deeper lesson for the public:

> The government at Washington has at its hand the very man who could put into parks and avenues of the Nation's capitol what ought to be there – a series of colossal sculptures of American wild animals. These would be a better influence, one is disposed to think, than ... statues of

1.23 "At bay: A female panther ready to defend her lair against attack," Edward Kemeys.

> American statesmen and martial heroes. ... American wild animals and the country that bore them will presently have become things gone forever.[95]

Kemeys' animals, then, can be seen as the sculptural equivalent to the literary efforts of the Boone and Crockett Club, a rhetorical tool which glorifies wilderness, presents it as a lesson in national virtue, and brings conservation home.

The strenuous life of the hunt

By now, we have seen that the Boone and Crockett Club played a central role in wilderness conservation at the turn of the century. What is not yet clear is how they reconciled their seemingly contradictory goals of big game hunting with their advocacy of wildlife protection and glorification of "American wild animals." In this contradiction lie some of the darkest aspects of conservation – aspects that continue to haunt it to the present day. The wilderness preserves advocated by the club were to be isolated and protected from uncontrolled development, expunged of "squatters" and "poachers" as they had been of Native peoples, and full of big game running freely. But the signs of disappearing wilderness were omnipresent. As we look through issues of *Forest and Stream, Field and Stream, Outing* and other magazines of that period, the pages are dotted with alarming titles such as "Vanishing Wild Flowers," "The Future of the Wyoming Elk," "Game Extinction," and "Extermination of the Buffalo." To preserve their vision of a hunter's paradise, the club recognized that big game hunting should be restricted to certain periods of the year and that entire areas should be set aside as "nurseries and breeding grounds of game . . . which are elsewhere inevitably exterminated by the march of settlement."[96] In effect, using a reasoning that seems to come straight from the royal hunting grounds of Europe, they argued for wildlife preserves that would be entirely constructed – species that had been exterminated would be reintroduced, animals that were considered good for the hunt would be encouraged to reproduce, and the way hunting was carried out would have to be changed from a livelihood to a sport (see Plate 3).

Sportsmanship, for the club, meant that the hunter was to kill only males and avoid females of any horned species to ensure reproduction. For them, "no harm comes to any species from the destruction of a moderate number of bulls, bucks, or rams."[97] In a report of their annual meeting in 1897, the club passed a resolution to condemn the use of steel traps, and the killing of game animals while helpless in the water or in deep snow.[98] This, they argued, would not be "fair chase." And, as Roderick Nash put it, *how* the hunt was conducted was of central importance to the members of the club: "The purpose of the Boone and Crockett Club was the encouragement of big game hunting, but the *character* of the hunter was the real object of concern."[99] For if hunting was meant to re-enact the experience of the frontier, the importance of that memory gave its practice great seriousness. For the Boone and Crockett Club, the hunt was more than a sport, it held a moral lesson for the hunter, a lesson learned in the perfect moment when man and animal come face-to-face in battle. These men took care to distinguish themselves from hunters who kill for money or food. They killed for love. In *The Century Magazine* in 1884, Julian Hawthorne describes well the sentiments behind club members' love of the hunt:

> The hunter pursues animals because he loves them and sympathizes with them, and kills them as the champions of chivalry used to slay one another – courteously, fairly, and with admiration. To stalk and shoot the grizzly bear is to him what wooing and winning a beloved maiden would be to another man. Far from being the foe or exterminator of the game he follows, he more than anyone else is their friend, vindicator, and confidant. A strange mutual ardor and understanding unites him with his quarry. He loves the mountain sheep and the antelope, because they can escape him; the panther and the bear, because they can destroy him. His relations with them are clean, generous and manly. And on the

other hand, the wild animals, ... seem after they have eluded their pursuer to the utmost or fought him to the death, to yield themselves to him with a sort of wild contentment – as if they were glad to admit the sovereignty of man, though death comes with the admission."[100]

The violence of blood sport is implicitly equated here with the sexual prowess of the hunter. As Donna Haraway says in her analysis of Roosevelt's hunter myth, "this is the effective truth of manhood ... Man is the sex which risks life and in so doing, achieves his existence. In the upside down world of Teddy Bear Patriarchy, it is in the craft of killing that life is constructed."[101] Physically invigorated by the "strenuous life" of the hunt, fortified in courage (numbed to the weaker sentiments of pity), and vindicated by the process of winning the struggle, the hunter for Roosevelt was a man who transcended his physical limitations and would pass these attributes onto future generations of fighters and winners. "A race must be strong and vigorous;" he said, "it must be a race of good fighters and good breeders ... no capacity for building up material prosperity can possibly atone for the lack of the great virile virtues."[102]

The Hunter's Camp on the Wooded Isle, then, represents a technology through which over-civilized elites could rediscover the "natural man" and become stronger, more virile and more aggressive. Accustomed to the comforts and luxury of city life, American elites feared they had lost the native vitality of their frontier ancestors through over-exposure to feminizing civilization.[103] This belief in the benefits to be had from greater contact with wilderness corresponded to an evolution of the masculine ideal in upper-class society. In contrast with mid-nineteenth century society, when Christianity and gentility were viewed as the primary masculine virtues, men in the latter part of the nineteenth century were encouraged to develop their internal vigor and bodily strength.[104] According to a comparative study of magazines of the period, heroes at the turn of the century were admired far more for their strength, size and look of determination that they had been a century earlier.[105] For example, fist fights among boys in prep schools were not frowned upon, but rather were seen as a good preparation for what lay ahead in the increasingly competitive and brutal world of business. Anthony Rotundo, in his study of young men at that period, traces through personal letters and diaries an ideal he calls the "Masculine Primitive." This ideal stressed the notion that civilized men shared with animals the primordial instincts for survival. Consequently, natural passions and impulses began to be seen as a valued part of a man's character. Contact with wilderness would develop and nourish the "natural man" or, in Theodore Roosevelt's words, "make the wolf rise in a man's heart".[106]

The hunter is a "natural aristocrat"

The figure of the hunter also proved useful to the Boone and Crockett Club in justifying the privilege of class in turn of the century America. Under the buckskin of the hunter described in the novels of James Fenimore Cooper, there is always, Richard Slotkin argues, a potential aristocrat. The figure of the hunter-aristocrat greatly attracted Roosevelt and it became a useful trope to justify his notion of leadership through bloodline. In this schema, hunting was a "regeneration through regression," in which the "civilized" white man (someone on the top of the Darwinian pyramid) returned to a more primitive state in order to be reinvigorated.[107] And since status was secured by bloodline, there was no risk of him being trapped at the bottom of the evolutionary ladder. "Regeneration through regression" was not intended for men outside the elite. The untutored and laboring masses – new immigrants, blacks, and aboriginal Americans – were first expected to evolve through the successive stages of civilization. This Darwinian view of social class in a capitalist society provided a justification for the power enjoyed by those at the top of the economic pyramid, while at the same time it provided reasons to despise people of lesser means.

No doubt such antagonism of the wealthy toward the urban poor stemmed from fear. The increasingly political character of labor unrest since the 1870s confirmed that there were real reasons to fear the working class. Roosevelt, like many of his peers, was profoundly impressed by the Haymarket riot and, "as a result of his fear of [class] conflict he almost denied its reality and tried to evolve concepts and techniques which would . . . legislate that conflict out of existence."[108] At each downturn of the economy, as the human costs of unfettered capitalism became increasingly apparent, the theories Darwin elaborated in *The Origin of the Species* (1859) seemed to provide a scientific explanation for why some people benefited from the economy while others were trampled underfoot. Class conflicts, for example, were seen in terms of animal competition in nature. The better animal would survive and pass his traits on to his progeny, while the weaker ones would fall away. For Roosevelt, the "progress" of civilization revealed the process of natural selection: it starts with the more primitive (and weaker) "tribal Indian," who gives way "naturally" to the more advanced types of cowboy, rancher, and farmer. It culminates with the urbanized and industrialized man, the highest stage and one which he, in his view, represented.[109] Roosevelt had no pity for laboring immigrants or for the American Indian; of the latter, he viewed their refusal to become farmers as proof of their trailing behind in the natural evolutionary stages of civilization:

> Give each Indian his little claim; if, as would generally happen, he declined this why, let him share the fate of the thousands of white hunters and trappers who have lived on the game that the settlement of the country has exterminated, and let him, like other whites, who will not work perish from the face of the earth which he cumbers.[110]

The fundamental contributions of the American Indian as farmer or shaper of the Western landscape were ignored in these comments generated from a racist ideology and buttressed by eugenics, the "science" of "clean-species." Genocide, for eugenicists, was as "natural" an occurrence as a flood or earthquake – terrible perhaps, but inevitable.[111] Closely linked in personnel and philosophy, conservationists and eugenicists believed in naturalism; that is, "they recognized the animal origin of human nature."[112] The conservation leaders of the Boone and Crockett Club, like the advocates of eugenics, saw three remedies to "the corruption of man through civilization": first, to limit charity to those worth saving; second, to conserve natural resources, so that in the future they may be available for the "better kind of person"; and third, to keep the "superior" people close to nature so they would remain unpolluted by the decadence of the city and Darwinian natural laws could function. The reproduction of civilized elites had to be encouraged, and that of the "inferior" types discouraged. "Some day," said Roosevelt, "we will realize that the prime duty, the inescapable duty of the good citizen of the right type is to leave his or her blood behind him in the world; and that we have no business to permit the perpetuation of citizens of the wrong type (see Figure 1.24)."[113] For, as Haraway reminds us, "decadence was a venereal disease [of] the organs of social ... reproduction. ... From the point of the view of Teddy Bear Patriarchy, race suicide was a clinical manifestation whose mechanism was the differential reproductive rates of Anglo-Saxon vs. 'non-white' immigrant women."[114] "Natural selection" was given a helping hand with respect to those deemed to be not "worth saving." Famines on Indian reservations were precipitated by withholding provisions agreed to in treaties, and legislation to help the urban poor was frowned on by the elite. "In fact, the eugenicists attacked modern government as being too soft toward the unfortunate. They asserted that the welfare programs of the state ignored the natural laws of the survival of the fittest. According to eugenics dogma, society must emulate nature for the future of the race"[115] – that is, for the future supremacy of Anglo-Saxon or Teutonic Americans. Both conservationists and eugenicists "used natural law not as a means for establishing a democratic society in which all men realized an equitable situation in life, but to defend civilization from the menace of the biologically inadequate."[116] In this latter category were included the physically or mentally deficient, along with deviants of all stripes: political, such as anarchists and socialists, and moral such as murderers, homosexuals and white women reluctant to reproduce.

Together, conservation and eugenics were intended to secure the resurrection of the "natural man." They would also provide the theoretical basis for the National Park idea. We see here a complete transformation of the earlier romantic love of nature. Wilderness no longer provides the transcendental experience described by Thoreau, but rather, wilderness preserves were to become a Noah's Ark for the lucky few. As the spiritual

1.24 "American Standards of Humanity," 1893. "No less than 20,000 individuals of each sex were submitted to calculation for the desired scientific result."

benefits of a wilderness sojourn were re-cast in "scientific" terms, the "preservation of nature and germ plasm all seemed the same sort of work."[117]

"Fair chase" and "free trade"

As a re-enactment of the frontier experience, the hunter's battle with the big game in the wilderness operated as a metaphor for the battle in the workplace. So strong was this metaphor that the naturalist John Burroughs wrote with admiration that Theodore Roosevelt "can stand calm and unflinching in the path of a charging grizzly, and he can confront with equal coolness and determination, the predacious corporations and money powers of the country."[118] The philosophy of naturalism sanctioned aggressiveness, coolness, and lack of compassion for the weak as necessary attributes to succeed in the rarefied world of American business and politics.

The species the hunter confronted were arranged according to a hierarchy which implied an increasing amount of courage. The deer was the lowest in that arrangement, followed by the grizzly bear and finally, the American panther was seen as the most difficult to stalk and kill. But ultimately the "most dangerous" animal was man himself. In the end, hunting was seen as a rehearsal for killing another human being when necessary.[119] This pattern was "laid down by Cooper in *Deerslayer*, one of Roosevelt's favorite books, [in which] the stages of hunting function as preparation for the higher function of the warrior."[120] As chief of police for New York City, the bellicose "rough rider" in Cuba, or the wielder of the "big stick" in the expansionist 1900s, Roosevelt exemplified how this model would be put into action. Many members of the club were, of course, connected to the army: we find in the members' list Civil War generals, veterans of the Indian Wars, and a Secretary of War – all revealing the intimate link between warrior and hunter.

The severe depression of the 1890s, a problem of under-consumption caused by a lack of domestic purchasing power, seemed to the political elite to be intertwined with the closing of the frontier. Because growth and expansion had created the country's wealth, it seemed that only growth and expansion could provide a way out of the economic crisis. And if the domestic frontier was over, then American capital had to move abroad. "Just as the frontier had been essential to Americans becoming who we were as a people," John Mack Faragher comments, "so it would require 'new frontiers' to insure our continued development."[121] This expansion into "new frontiers" found its support both in large companies and in agribusiness. Large commercial farmers, led by populist parties, demanded new markets for their grain. "By 1893, American trade exceeded that of every country in the world except England. Farm products, of course especially in the key tobacco, cotton, and wheat areas depended heavily on international markets for their prosperity. And in the twenty years up to 1895, new investments by American capitalists overseas reached a billion dollars."[122]

In the following decades the new frontier would continue its expansive westward movement across the Pacific Ocean and into the Caribbean, with the help of the US Army, freshly relieved of their task of clearing the American frontier of its native inhabitants. By the end of 1893, American marines had invaded Hawaii; by 1894, Nicaragua. In 1898 the US was engaged in an all-out war with Spain which, by its close, left Cuba, Puerto Rico, Guam, and the Philippines in American hands. Helped by the army, these "new frontiers" created new consumer markets and opened the gate to capital investments abroad – a government/capital venture still familiar to us today.[123]

As we peer into the Hunter's Cabin then, a simple hut, we find a Pandora's box, unleashing its genies and demons across the spread of the globe. The "frontier experience," cast as a site for an encounter between "civilized" and "savage," between "man" and "beast," is a disturbing legacy that shows the ugly side of American mythology. Even conservation, a seemingly neutral term, carries with it a troublesome historical legacy that it cannot shake off. But to stop here, we would underestimate the power of people to recast, reinvent, and rework these seemingly immutable constructions. For although nature and nation, as Raymond Williams has pointed out, share the same root in *natura*, it is in the nature of neither to stay fixed. In the chapters that follow, we will see both reworked. Always turning to its "other," the "nation" will create new ways of representing itself in architecture and landscape, representations that reflect the changing ideals of a constantly changing nation.

Notes

1 Lois Craig, *The Federal Presence, Architecture, Politics and Symbols in United States Government Building*, Cambridge: MIT Press, 1978, p. 212.
2 Craig, *The Federal Presence*, p. 215.
3 *The Columbian Gallery: a Portfolio of Photographs from the World's Fair*, Chicago: The Werner Company, 1894, p. 103.
4 The Act of 1891 in fact only established the reserves but did not yet provide laws for their management.
5 Julie K. Brown, *Contesting Images: Photography and the World's Columbian Exposition*, Tucson: University of Arizona Press, 1994, p. 63.
6 For a remarkable analysis of the relationship between panoramas at World Expositions and European colonial practices, see Timothy Mitchell, *Colonising Egypt*, Cambridge: Cambridge University Press, 1988.
7 *The Columbian Gallery*, 1894, p. 103.
8 "The cartography that so inspired Turner, it turns out, was less a work of science than of the imagination," since "more public land in the trans-Mississippi West was taken up in the years after 1890 than in the years before." Frederick Jackson Turner, *Rereading Frederick Jackson Turner: The Significance of the Frontier in American History and other Essays*, with commentary by John Faraghar, New York: Henry Holt, 1994, p. 6.
9 *Rereading Frederick Jackson Turner*, p. 32.
10 Turner's masculinist construction of the frontier has been critically analyzed by Richard Slotkin, *The Fatal Environment: the Myth of the Frontier in the Age of*

Industrialization, 1800–1890, New York: Harper Perennial, 1985. Annette Kolodny explores the differences between men and women's fantasies about the frontier. Men essentially sexualized the wilderness, seeing it as a fertile land to be conquered and ravished, "paradise with all her virgin beauties." Women, on the other hand, fantasized about homes, communities, and gardens, domesticating the frontier landscape. Annette Kolodny, *The Land Before Her: Fantasy and Experience of the American Frontier, 1630–1860*, Chapel Hill: University of North Carolina Press, 1984.

11   Turner, *Rereading Frederick Jackson Turner*, p. 33.
12   Slotkin, *Fatal Environment*, pp. 58–9.
13   Theodore Roosevelt, letter cited in E. Morisson, *Letters of Theodore Roosevelt*, vol. 1, New York: Scribers and Sons, 1894, p. 191.
14   Christine Boyer, *Dreaming the Rational City: the Myth of American City Planning*, Cambridge: MIT Press, 1983, p. 38.
15   Howard Zinn, *A People's History of the United States, 1492–Present*, New York: Harper Perennial, 1995, p. 277.
16   Boyer, *Dreaming the Rational City*, p. 12.
17   Alan Trachtenberg, *The Incorporation of America: Culture and Society in the Gilded Age*, New York: Hill and Wang, 1982, pp. 88–9.
18   Samuel P. Hays, *Conservation and the Gospel of Efficiency: the Progressive Conservation Movement, 1890–1920*, Cambridge, MA: Harvard University Press, 1959, p. 266.
19   Richard White, "Frederick Jackson Turner and Buffalo Bill" in Richard White and Patricia Nelson Limerick (eds), *The Frontier in American Culture*, Berkeley: University of California Press, 1994. Many scholars have pointed out the connection between the rise of the conservation movement and the close of the frontier. William Cronon, for example, states, "it was no accident that the movement to set aside national parks and wilderness areas began to gain real momentum at precisely the time that laments about the passing frontier reached their peak. To protect wilderness was in a very real sense to protect the nation's most sacred myth of origin." William Cronon "The Trouble with Wilderness; or, getting back to the Wrong Nature," William Cronon (ed.), *Uncommon Ground Rethinking the Human Place in Nature*, New York: W.W. Norton and Company, 1996, p. 76.
20   For a good analysis of the politics of marginalization at the fair, see Robert W. Rydell, "A Cultural Frankenstein? The Chicago World's Columbian Exposition of 1893" in Neil Harris, Wim de Wit, James Gilbert and Robert W. Rydell (eds), *Grand Illusions: Chicago World's Fair of 1893*, Chicago: Chicago Historical Society, 1993, pp. 143–71.
21   The not-so-subliminal message of the "White City" was not lost on African Americans. Frederick Douglass referred to the Chicago Exposition as the "whited sepulcher." Trachtenberg, *Incorporation of America*, p. 220.
22   In addition to Christine Boyer's *Dreaming the Rational City*, see Peter Hall, *Cities of Tomorrow*, Cambridge: Cambridge University Press, 1983 and Norman T. Newton, *Design on the Land: the Development of Landscape Architecture*, Cambridge, MA: The Belknap Press of Harvard University, 1971. Burnham carried forward the city planning ideas embodied in the White City into his urban plans for Chicago, Washington DC, Cleveland, San Francisco,

Manila, and Baguio (Philippines), known collectively as the "City Beautiful" movement.

23   Both Native American and African American requests for representation at the fair were denied. The eventual display of Native Americans occurred only under the paternalistic auspices of the US government, through the Smithsonian Institution and the Department of Indian Affairs. African Americans were refused permission to exhibit at the fair, a goal they achieved only ten years later at the Louisiana Purchase Exposition in 1903. A third example of marginalization at the Columbian Exposition can be seen in the "marginal" location of the Women's Building, at the juncture between the "legitimate," serious portion of the fair and its carnivalesque "other" of the Midway. This in spite of the support of the most powerful women's clubs in Chicago.

24   Frederick Law Olmsted, *Report From Landscape Department*, 1893, Daniel Burnham Collection, Call No. 1943.1, Box 58, File 15, Burnham and Ryerson Library, Chicago Art Institute.

25   "There was nothing original in it [the 1890 plan] except the introduction of the canal, the lagoons and the wooded island; the grand court being the same arrangement as at Paris, with a water basin in the center and a dome at one end, in front of which was to be the great fountain." Daniel H. Burnham, "The Organization of the World's Columbian Exposition," a lecture given at the World's Congress of Architects, and published in *The Inland Architect and News Record* 22 (August) 1893, p. 6.

26   Frederick Law Olmsted, *Civilizing American Cities*, Cambridge, MA: MIT Press, 1971, p. 189.

27   Olmsted, *Report From Landscape Department*.

28   Olmsted, *Civilizing*, p. 190.

29   Frederick Law Olmsted, "Report of the Director of Works, Superintendent of Landscape," Daniel Burnham (ed.), *The Final Report of the Director of Works of the World's Columbian Exposition*, vol. 1, New York: Garland Publishing Company, 1989, p. 8.

30   Peter B. Hales, *Silver Cities: The Photography of American Urbanization, 1839–1915*, Philadelphia: Temple University Press, 1984, p. 145.

31   Hamilton W. Gibson, "Foreground and Vista at the Fair," *Scribner's Magazine* 14 (July–December) 1893, p. 32.

32   Trachtenberg, *Incorporation of America*, p. 108.

33   Boyer, *Dreaming the Rational City*, p. 34.

34   "Public Parks and Playgrounds: a Symposium," *Arena Magazine* 40, 1894, p. 276.

35   An interesting thought when we know that an enormous proportion of children had to work to help sustain the family.

36   A good reference on the parks movement in the United States is Galen Cranz, *The Politics of Park Design: a History of Urban Parks in America*, Cambridge, MA: MIT Press, 1982.

37   Cronon, "The Trouble with Wilderness," p. 89.

38   Horace H. Albright, *The Birth of the National Park Service, The Founding Years, 1913–1933*, Salt Lake City: Howe Bros., 1985, p. 5.

39   "American Game Park, The 'Forest and Stream's' Third Annual Report on Game Preserves," *Forest and Stream* (July 11 1896), p. 23.

40 Mary Belle Sherman (the president of the Federation) was so dedicated to the cause of National Parks that she became known as the National Park Lady. See Polly Welts Kaufman, *National Parks and the Women's Voice, a History*, Albuquerque: University of New Mexico Press, 1996, p. 32.
41 Black Elk, *Black Elk Speaks: being the life story of a holy man of the Oglala Sioux*, as told to John G. Neihardt (Flaming Rainbow); introduction by Vine Deloria Jr., Lincoln: University of Nebraska Press, 1988.
42 Mitchell, *Colonising Egypt*.
43 *Columbian Gallery*.
44 Ibid.
45 The same logic of isolation and purification is practiced today in the establishment of wilderness parks in developing countries. Governments anxious to attract tourism do not hesitate to forcibly remove entire villages living in these remote areas, destroying local cultures as well as livelihoods.
46 Richard White, "Are You an Environmentalist or Do You Work for a Living?" Cronon, *Uncommon Ground*, p. 175.
47 Letter from Theodore Roosevelt to D.H. Burnham, dated 8 June 1893. Daniel Burnham Collection, 1943.1, WCE, Box 59, File Folder 42, Burnham and Ryerson Library, The Art Institute of Chicago.
48 Hofer was hired by Roosevelt to serve as an "interpreter" of the Hunter's Camp during the summer of the Chicago Exposition.
49 A description of the Hunter's Camp exhibit can be found in the first publication of the Boone and Crockett Club, which appeared the year of the Chicago Exposition. See Theodore Roosevelt and George Bird Grinnell (eds), *American Big-Game Hunting: the Book of the Boone and Crockett Club*, Edinburgh: David Douglas, 1893, p. 334. Roosevelt founded the club at his home in New York City in 1887.
50 Edward A. Renwick, Recollections, unpublished typescript, 1932, p. 171. According to Robert Bruegmann, Renwick's 200+ pp. manuscript has "been around" since mid-1940s, when Frank A. Randall, in his *History of the Development of Building Construction in Chicago* (1949) uses it. Copyright unclear.
51 Letters from Theodore Roosevelt to Elwood Hofer, 15 March 1892, 5 December 1892, and 13 November 1893. Manuscript, Accession no. 92-36. Yellowstone National Park Archives.
52 Obituary of Edward Kemeys, no author, n.p., 1907. Burnham and Ryerson Library, Pamphlet P-13870. Another invitee to the cabin, James W. Ellsworth (a founding member of the Field Museum) had such fond memories of the cabin that he acquired it after the fair and had it moved to his country estate. See letter from W.I. Buchanan (Office of the Director-General of the World's Columbian Exposition) to James W. Ellsworth, 10 November 1893, Box 2, Files 11 and 12, James W. Ellsworth Collections, Incoming Correspondence, Chicago Public Library.
53 Theodore Roosevelt, *Wilderness Hunter*, New York: G.P. Putnam's Sons, 1893.
54 The forestry advocate and future governor of Pennsylvania, Gifford Pinchot, joined later.
55 Frederic Remington later joined the club, and the animal sculptor Edward Kemeys was supported by club members until his death in 1907.

56 "The Boone and Crockett Club," *Forest and Stream* (23 January 1897), p. 66.
57 It is interesting to note that the historic Boone and Crockett held very different attitudes to the frontier and particularly to the American Indian. Boone was a tenacious Indian fighter in Kentucky, while Crockett argued vigorously against the removal of the Cherokee and at one point in his life, had some standing in an Indian community. After his death at the Alamo, his name began to be linked with Boone's in a myth-making process about Indian-fighting and the frontier. See Richard Slotkin, *Gunfighter Nation: The Myth of the Frontier in Twentieth Century America*, New York: Athenaeum, 1992.
58 Daniel Boone quoted in Roderick Nash, *Wilderness and the American Mind*, New Haven: Yale University Press, 1967, p. 63. Boone was not a literary man. His "autobiography," from which this quote is taken, was in fact written in 1784 by a fellow Kentuckian, John Filson. Crockett by contrast participated in the creation of his own myth, through his numerous writings.
59 I am thinking here of men such as Brooke Adams. For an excellent discussion of antimodernism in turn of the century United States, see T.J. Jackson Lears, *No Place of Grace: Antimodernism and the Transformation of American Culture, 1880–1920*, Chicago: University of Chicago Press, 1983.
60 Slotkin, *Gunfighter Nation*, p. 49.
61 Under the nom de plume of "Kata Phusin."
62 Joseph Rykwert, *On Adam's House in Paradise: the Idea of the Primitive Hut in Architectural History*, 2nd edn, Cambridge, MA: MIT Press, 1981.
63 For two excellent studies of the nineteenth century search for "national" identity, see Eric Hobsbawm, *The Invention of Traditions*, Cambridge: Cambridge University Press, 1983 and Benedict Anderson, *Imagined Communities: Reflections on the Origin and Spread of Nationalism*, London: Verso, 1983.
64 Meyer Schapiro suggests instead that the shoes were Van Gogh's own shoes, worn during his ministry to the striking miners of Belgium. Heidegger's reading de-politicizes and de-historicizes Van Gogh's shoes, casting them in an eternal present of "essential" character. See Schapiro, "The Still Life as a Personal Object – A Note on Heidegger and Van Gogh," in Marianne Simmel (ed.), *The Reach of the Mind, Essays in Memory of Kurt Goldstein*, New York: Springer Publishing Company, 1968, pp. 203–9. Klaus Theweleit has presented perhaps the best criticism of the connection between soil and nationalism in his *Männerfantasien*, translated into English under the title *Male Fantasies*, 2 vols, Minneapolis: University of Minnesota Press, 1987.
65 Rykwert, *Adam's House*, p. 36.
66 Rykwert, *Adam's House*, p. 43.
67 Ibid.
68 Rykwert, *Adam's House*, p. 49. Two years before Laugier published his *Essais*, Jean-Jacques Rousseau used the idea of the "natural" man to criticize contemporary civilization. Rousseau employed the primitive hut to make an argument about the degeneration of humanity, from a state of true communion with God into the enactment of shallow rituals.
69 Cited in Rykwert, *Adam's House*, p. 23.
70 Thoreau's cabin on Walden Pond is another American example of Rousseauist ideas in practice.

71 The giant figure of "Columbia" presided over the Court of Honor. Gilded, she referred to the young republic in a direct reference to Phidias' Pallas Athena, which presided over the Athenian city-state.
72 Slotkin, *Gunfighter Nation*, p. 34.
73 See John F. Reiger (ed.), *The Passing of the Great West: the Papers of George Bird Grinnell*, New York: Winchester Press, 1972.
74 Theodore Roosevelt's output by 1893 included *Frontier Life and the West*, New York: G.P. Putnam's Sons, 1888; *The Winning of the West*, New York: G.P. Putnam's Sons, 1889; *The Wilderness Hunter*, New York: G.P. Putnam's Sons, 1893; and *Hunting the Grizzly and Other Sketche*s, New York: The Reviews Company, 1893. This essay was originally presented to the Hamilton Club in Chicago, 10 April 1899.
75 Published as "The Last of the Buffalo," *Scribner's Magazine* 12, no. 3 (September 1892), p. 267, this essay reappears as "In Buffalo Days," in Roosevelt and Grinnell, *American Big-Game Hunting*, p. 155.
76 From an editorial commemorating the tenth anniversary of the club, *Forest and Stream* 48, no. 4 (23 January 1897). The complete constitution of the Boone and Crockett Club is published in Roosevelt and Grinnell, *American Big-Game Hunting*, p. 337.
77 Carl Akeley's work stands out in this regard. His diorama "Indian Warrior on a Mustang," displayed at the Chicago Fair by the Smithsonian Institution, was constructed like a work of taxidermy, over the actual skeletons of both a horse and a Native American man. His "Four Seasons" (now at the Field Museum in Chicago) is the work which, for its scientific exactitude and its breathtaking realism, established taxidermy as a legitimate vehicle for scientific education. For more on the intersection between big game hunting conservationists, taxidermy and the construction of knowledge about the animal world, see Donna Haraway's excellent essay "Teddy Bear Patriarchy in the Garden of Eden," in her major work on primatology, *Primate Visions, Gender, Race, and Nature in the World of Modern Science*, London: Routledge, 1989.
78 He tells how he does it in "Catching Wild Animals," *Forest and Stream* 38, no. 8 (23 February 1892).
79 The Smithsonian Institution acted as a clearing house for these requests, forwarding them to the administration of the Park.
80 In a 261-acre setting in the south Bronx, they hoped to keep the "collection under conditions as nearly like those of their native homes as possible, with abundant room to roam but not so much room as to hide from the visitor." This emphasis on naturalistic settings again reveals the influence of the club, which by the 1890s was not only vocal but also increasingly successful in the political arena in pushing for game and forest preserves. "New York Zoological Society," *Forest and Stream* 48, no. 13 (27 March 1897).
81 Only to be overturned by the Senate a few days later. However, both the scientific justification and the political momentum were there and it was only a matter of time before the reserves were permanently established.
82 Samuel P. Hays, *Conservation and the Gospel of Efficiency, the Progressive Conservation Movement, 1890–1920*, Cambridge, MA: Harvard University Press, 1959, p. 2.

83 Hays, *Conservation and the Gospel*, p. 3.
84 "The Exhibit at the World's Fair," in Roosevelt and Grinnell (eds), *American Big-Game Hunting: the Book of the Boone and Crockett Club*, reprinted New York: Forest and Stream Publishing Co., 1901, pp. 334–6. Ten monumental animal sculptures at the exposition can be definitively attributed to Kemeys. These are the four panthers at the bridge in front of the west entrance to the Manufactures Building (shown standing, striding, crouching and snarling), two grizzly bears on the next bridge south, two buffalo at the east end of the Machinery Building, and two striding panthers south of the Court of Honor. All were enlargements made of staff (stucco mixed with straw) from small originals. Whether Kemeys or A. Phimister Procter sculpted the elks on the bridges from Horticulture and Electricity to the Wooded Island cannot be stated with certainty.
85 Michael Richman, "Edward Kemeys America's First Animal Sculptor," *Fine Art Source Material Newsletter*, p. 106.
86 Charles Moore, cited in Richman, "Kemeys America's First," p. 112.
87 Hamlin Garland, "Edward Kemeys – a Sculptor of Frontier Life and Wild Animals," *McClure's Magazine* 5, no. 2 (July 1895), p. 120.
88 Emerson Hough, "Edward Kemeys – America's First Sculptor of Wild Animals," *Field and Stream* 9 (June 1904), p. 143.
89 "Two Sculptors and Their Work," *The Graphic* 10 (19 May 1894), p. 389.
90 Garland, "Kemeys – a Sculptor," p. 126.
91 Earnest McGaffey, "Edward Kemeys, Sculptor," *Reedy Mirror* 7 (30 May 1907), p. 6.
92 "Edward Kemeys," obituary, pamphlet P-13870, Burnham and Ryerson Library, Chicago Art Institute.
93 After the fair, Kemeys experienced the busiest time of his career, completing the pair of lions flanking the entrance to the Chicago Art Institute and 22 bronze bas-relief portraits of Indians and French explorers for Holabird and Roche's Marquette Building, considered by commentators at the time to be the most magnificent public lobby in Chicago. As other animal sculptors enter the field, Kemeys begins to experience competition in his unusual specialty. His junior colleague, A. Phiminster Proctor completed groupings of panthers for Brooklyn's Prospect Park, and tigers for Princeton University.
94 Hough, cited in Richman, "Kemeys America's First," p. 118.
95 Prentice Gray, *From the Peace to the Fraser*, Forest and Stream, 1900, p. 11.
96 Gray, *From the Peace to the Fraser*, p. 14.
97 "The Boone and Crockett Club," *Forest and Stream* (23 January 1897), p. 66.
98 Nash, *Wilderness and the American Mind*, p. 152. Roosevelt offers his views of sportsmanship:
"True sportsmen, worthy of the name, men who shoot only in season and in moderation, do no harm whatever to game. The most objectionable of all game destroyers is, of course, the kind of game butcher who simply kills for the sake of the record of slaughter, who leaves deer and ducks and prairie-chickens to rot after he has slain them. The professional and market hunter who kills game for hide, or for the feathers, or for the meat, or to sell antlers and other trophies; the market men who put game in cold storage; and the

rich people, who are content to buy what they have not the skill to get by their own exertions – these are the men who are the real enemies of game." Theodore Roosevelt, "Wilderness Reserves," reprinted in Paul Schullery (ed.), *Old Yellowstone Days*, Boulder, CO: Associated Press, 1979, pp. 187–8.
99 Hawthorne, "American Wild Animals in Art," p. 213.
100 Haraway, *Primate Visions*, p. 28.
101 Theodore Roosevelt, "The Duties of American Citizenship," *The Works of Theodore Roosevelt*, vol. 13, New York: The Reviews Company, 1910, p. 281.
102 David E. Shi, *The Simple Life: Plain Living and High Thinking in American Culture*, Oxford: Oxford University Press, 1985, p. 206. Many men of the Victorian era express tender sentiments to a degree that would seem unusual today. The letters of Daniel Burnham, who was writing to his wife daily from the Exposition site, reveal tremendous tenderness and longing for her womanly company. The new emphasis on masculinity had to overcome a substantial societal value placed on sentimentality and polite behavior. The work of Jack London is exemplary in this regard, as is Hemingway in the early 1920s.
103 Shi, *The Simple Life*, p. 195.
104 Anthony Rotundo, "Learning about manhood: gender ideals and the middle class family in nineteenth-century America," in J.A. Mangan and James Walvin (eds), *Manliness and Morality: Middle Class Masculinity in Britain and America*, Manchester: Manchester University Press, 1987, pp. 40–1.
105 Quoted in Rotundo, "Learning about manhood," p. 40.
106 Slotkin, *Gunfighter Nation*, p. 38.
107 Hays, *Conservation and the Gospel*, p. 267.
108 On American versions of the theory of "stages" see Thomas C. Dyer, *Theodore Roosevelt and the Idea of Race*, Baton Rouge: Louisiana State University Press, 1980.
109 Roosevelt, *Hunting Trips*, New York: G.P. Putnam's Sons, pp. 16–17.
110 As an example, the description of a diorama of buffalo and cougar in the US Government Building concludes that animals and Native Indians are bound by the same inevitable phenomenon, "The bison of the American plains ... has been ruthlessly exterminated from the path of civilization. The aboriginal natives of this country are also fading away, and it is easy to perceive the connection of the two facts." *The Columbian Gallery*, 1894, p. 159.
111 Donald K. Pickens, *Eugenics and the Progressives*, Nashville, TN: Vanderbilt University Press, 1968, p. 3. For examples of the overlap between the conservation and eugenics movements, see Haraway, *Primate Visions*, p. 57.
112 Letter from Theodore Roosevelt to the American eugenicist Charles Davenport, 1913, cited in Pickens, *Eugenics and the Progressives*, 1968.
113 Haraway, *Primate Visions*, p. 55.
114 Pickens, *Eugenics*, p. 13.
115 Pickens, *Eugenics*, p. 3.
116 Haraway, Primate Visions, p. 57.
117 Burroughs, "Camping and Tramping with Roosevelt," p. 224.
118 Slotkin, *Gunfighter Nation*, p. 41.

119 Ibid.
120 Faragher, in Turner, *Rereading Frederick Jackson Turner*, p. 5.
121 Ibid.
122 Howard Zinn, *A People's History of the United States, 1492–Present*, New York: Harper Perennial, 1995, p. 293.

2.1 Travel brochure of the Northern Pacific Railway, ca. 1910.

Chapter 2
Accommodating the nature tourist in the national parks, 1903

Just steps away from the main rotunda of the US Government Building at the World's Columbian Exposition, the Department of the Interior exhibited photographs and geological models of western landscapes. The large transparencies by photographer J.K. Hillers were particularly striking, like his *Reflected Tower* of 1873, which showed the Virgin River (in present-day Zion National Park in Utah). This photograph, like many other government-commissioned "survey" photographs, depicted western landscapes unblemished by traces of settlement, mining, logging, or tourism (see Figure 2.2).[1] In pristine depictions like this one, a rapidly transforming west was not only made more "natural," it was constructed as sublime.[2] Such images helped to convince citizens of the benefits of drawing from the public purse to keep these landscapes the way they appeared in the photographs. As an agent for the Northern Pacific Railroad said, "I have visited the World Fair, and we all know something of what that was; but great as it was, that was only the work of simple, powerless men. The Yellowstone Park stands there a marvelous creation, as though God himself were a competitor for first prize for a wonderful production."[3]

The story of the development of the national parks is the story of people who saw such perfect pictures of wilderness and then wanted to go and see the real thing. The more that photographs were reproduced in nature magazines and railroad brochures, the more people wanted to buy train tickets and experience the parks for themselves. In a deeply democratic move, national parks had been set aside for "the enjoyment of the people." And as people began to vacation in them, they became giant playgrounds for urbanites who desired contact with wilderness – a contact that was expected to take place within a safe, controlled and protected setting. Nowhere was this truer than in the western states. Wilderness areas were still unpredictable, with stories of robbery and abduction appearing on the front pages of the local dailies. When pockets of wilderness were established as national parks, they were administered by the US Army, recently freed up from the Indian wars. This military administration was only later replaced with the park rangers. But to accommodate commercial tourism, the parks needed more than just a safe environment. People who wanted to experience "true American wilderness" were also looking for rapid connections to major urban centers, organized travel itineraries and all the comforts that modern life could offer in the 1900s.

2.2 Reflected Tower Rio Virgin, Utah. Photograph by J.K. Hillers.

PROMOTING WESTERN LANDSCAPES

Railroad companies were active supporters of the new national parks. Quick to see their potential for profit, they extended rail lines up to the park borders and promoted the parks in their brochures. They invested heavily in park infrastructure such as accommodation, transportation systems and commercial enterprises, while the government supported road construction and law enforcement. The development of the national parks was the result of a joint effort by government and railroad companies. This private/public venture is significant for our search to reveal a changing attitude toward nature for two reasons. First, because the parks were operated by agents of the federal government, their administration had to be accountable. Their mandate was to keep the park accessible to "the people" which, as we will soon see, meant a specific sector of the population. Similarly, park concessionaires had to prove there was a demand for their services in order to get the coveted franchise with the Department of the Interior. Second, private enterprises like the railroads and their subsidiary hotel companies had to make money, and for that reason they wanted to bring as many people as possible into the parks. The railroads began to understand that their westward-traveling clientele were not only businessmen looking for investment opportunities, but tourists. The combination of private capital and government support meant that an ever-increasing number of people from an increasingly wide range of society traveled west to visit the parks.

A travel brochure for Yellowstone Park published by the Northern Pacific Railroad tells it all (Figure 2.1). The front cover (to the right) depicts a man dressed like a fur trader from the old west, standing with his back to us as he scouts a curious form in the landscape: a steaming waterfall pouring over a sulfuric rock formation, a distinctive feature of Yellowstone. Two Indians sit on either side of him, waiting. The image recalls a time when Native Americans still inhabited the region of the Yellowstone river, and helped to guide those who ventured into these wild and glorious landscapes. But when in 1872 the area was declared a natural reserve, the government decided its Native inhabitants had to leave (see Figure 2.3).[4]

The back cover of the brochure (to the left) brings us to the 1910s. Now emptied of its Native inhabitants, the scene is populated with tourists who gaze at the spectacular landscape formations while a cozy-looking hotel in the distance waits for them. From the western scout to the modern tourist, this brochure takes us from the early explorations of the west into a full-scale consumption of its landscapes. The painting shows a young woman perched on a rock (where the Indian was) as she watches the eruption of the Old Faithful geyser. A man, presumably her husband, leisurely reclines on the ground below. She is dressed for the outdoors, with her feet firmly planted on the ground and a riding crop across her knees. Her figure is almost regal – in fact, she sits in a posture that art historians reserve "for men, or for women of authority: queens, warriors, sibyls."[5] Here, her authority lies in the economic force she and her husband represent. Their commanding view of the landscape shows a couple at ease in their role as nature tourists. They are as relaxed in the western wilderness as they would be in their garden at home.

Every detail of these two images speaks of the transformation of the

2.3 Sheepeater Bannocks. Medicine Lodge Creek Idaho, 1871.

west through tourism at the beginning of the twentieth century. Elite men no longer went hunting for trophies with their friends, they now traveled by train with their wives, daughters, or fiancées to enjoy the natural wonders of the western parks. Spending time in the western wilderness was no longer a courageous, virile and instructive activity – rather, it had become an experience that was safe, fun and visually stimulating for all.

Why Yellowstone Park?

Yellowstone National Park was established in 1872, followed by Yosemite and Sequoia in 1890, and Mount Rainier in 1899. It is in Yellowstone that the "park idea" began – discussed around a campfire in September 1870 by the Washburn–Langford–Doane Expedition. So important was this originary moment that it was re-enacted in subsequent years at the foot of "National Park Mountain" near the confluence of the Gibbon and Firehole rivers in Yellowstone (Figure 2.4). But as Horace Albright recalls, the idea did not catch on quickly: "few people were going to the parks and national monuments. They were hard to get to and had limited accommodations."[6] Yellow-

2.4 Re-enactment of campfire of 19 September, 1870 where "National Park Idea" originated.

stone, as the first park to be commercially developed for large numbers of visitors, experienced a marked improvement in its roads, lunch stations, and hotels in the period from 1883 to 1915.[7] And the Northern Pacific Railroad took care to ensure that their clientele would know the parks were becoming more comfortable, writing in their promotional literature:

> The first appropriation to care for and improve [the park] made in 1878 [amounted] to but $10,000. Now mark the change! In 1902 Congress appropriated $75,000, in immediate and continuing appropriations, to improve and perfect the park and to provide the proper administrative force, and this exclusive of the cost and maintenance of the soldiery quartered there.[8]

In 1903, the improvements of the federal government and the investments of the railroad companies began to transform Yellowstone into a "modern" park. Until that year, tourists were required to disembark several miles north of the park at Cinnabar, Montana, but once a spur line was finally extended to the park boundary at Gardiner, visitors could step off the train at the north entrance to the park into a new rustic-looking station, where a fleet of carriages would pick up those who had booked an organized five-day tour.[9] The excursion into wilderness began in a moment of grandeur as they passed under the monumental arch marking the park entrance – dedicated by President Theodore Roosevelt that year. With the completion of a new hotel in the remote Upper Geyser Basin in the following spring, visitors could complete a five-day tour of the park in comfort: staying in the Fountain Hotel, the luxurious new Old Faithful Inn in the Upper Geyser Basin, the Lake Hotel at Yellowstone Lake and the Canyon Hotel at the Grand Canyon of the Yellowstone, before completing their circuit at Mammoth. The new Old Faithful Inn offered a level of comfort and elegance that was much appreciated by its upper middle class clientele. This is the hotel depicted in the background of Northern Pacific's promotional brochure.

Of course, not everyone who visited the park stayed in expensive hotels. Tent camps set up by a former schoolteacher, William Wylie, offered inexpensive accommodation in fully outfitted tents and meals served under canvas (see Figure 2.5). Bicycling campers were not uncommon, and "sagebrushers" came with horses and mules to camp in the bush. Many of these visitors were from farms or small towns or were slowly traversing the continent from east to west.

So we see how Yellowstone National Park developed as a joint venture between the federal government and capitalist enterprises, particularly the railroad companies and their concessionaires. But as we look closer, we also see that individual personalities played a formative role in defining the new landscape for the park. As we discover the decisions they took along the way, one begins to suspect that the landscape of conservation might have looked quite different had it developed in the hands of other people.

The main players
Superintendent John Pitcher, photographer Frank Jay Haynes and developer Harry Child played crucial roles in transforming a land set aside for conservation in Yellowstone. Major Pitcher was in charge of the park from 1901 to 1907. Although he had been a member of the conservationist Boone and Crockett Club from its inception (when he was stationed in the nation's capitol), Haynes' daughter remembers Pitcher as "a typical military man whose heart was not really in his work. He could not be drunk down."[10] But, as Pitcher reminded his superiors, because "the object for which the troops are here is to guard the park, it is necessary to use [the men] more as mounted police than as soldiers, and if they perform their duties properly in this connection, they will have about all they can attend to."[11]

2.5 A Wylie two-compartment tent interior, postcard. Photograph by F.J. Haynes.

Within the US Army, the Yellowstone assignment was not a welcome job. These men had made a career out of the Indian Wars; they were a tough set of soldiers who suddenly found themselves as caretakers of a "park" – an area that was no longer wilderness and that was populated with tourists rather than settlers. When superintendent Captain Moses Harris arrived in August 1886, he reported the conditions he confronted. Placing squads of troops in strategic places, he "gave notice to those who were illegally doing business in the park to vacate, which they did. He forbade grazing of stock in the vicinity of the hot springs and geysers."[12] Regarding all the fires that needed to be extinguished in different places, "'a stringent law, vigorously enforced' was his slogan. . . . None of the geysers had escaped mutilation. The formations were covered with names, and sticks and logs had been thrust into the pools and craters."[13] Like his predecessors, Major Pitcher enforced rules of behavior in the park. He advanced bridge and road building to make the park accessible, but he also took decisions that held fast to conservationist principles in the face of pressures to get more visitors into the park. He refused, for example, to let in automobiles, delaying their entrance into the park until 1915 when the superintendent at that time agreed to upgrade the roads for automobile traffic.[14]

While Pitcher enforced its laws, built its roads, and literally constructed the park as a landscape, F. Jay Haynes helped to shape how people saw the park, in his role as Yellowstone photographer. He was first hired by the Northern Pacific Railroad to produce high-quality views along the railroad line for documentary and promotional purposes. With a permanent railroad pass and salary of $1.50 for each view he produced, he was in business.[15] One of these expeditions for the company was into Yellowstone Park in the early fall of 1881. He returned in 1882 and in 1883 as the official photographer for the visit of President Chester A. Arthur through the Yellowstone. Understanding the potential of the park for selling his photographs, Haynes secured early on the position of sole photography concessionaire. In 1890, he was commissioned to write a guidebook for the park and the next year bought a controlling interest in it, publishing revised editions thereafter. Physically courageous and tenacious, Haynes toted his heavy photographic equipment to remote locations in the park to find the best point of view for a panorama. While other photographers like William Henry Jackson were better artists and better interpreters of the American west, Haynes's achievement was to set up a business that ultimately controlled all the images that were sold to tourists within the boundaries of the park – in the form of prints, postcards and guidebooks.

The third key figure in the development of the Yellowstone landscape was Harry Child (Figure 2.6). A former superintendent of the park, Edmund G. Rogers, called him a "typical robber baron." Child was a western businessman in the grand style, who wintered in La Jolla, California, summered in Montana and operated many ventures in the Yellowstone area, including his successful stud farm with 15,000 to 20,000 head of cattle. His Flying-D Ranch was one of the largest in the country. A 1923 biography of *Men Who are Making the West* tells us, "The health authorities of New York, or Chicago, or San Francisco would have no hesitation in O.K.ing the milk coming from the Child Shorthorns. His cattle, as they say in Montana, are 'shaved and shampooed.'"[16] Child's interest in Yellowstone Park was in developing it as a luxury destination for upper class visitors. An avid sportsman and a storyteller, Child entertained and toured a great number of captains of industries and Presidents such as Roosevelt, Taft, Harding and Coolidge, as well as European royalty.[17]

As the president of the Yellowstone Park Hotel and Transportation Company – a concessionaire with the Northern Pacific Railroad – Child renovated and built hotels in the park and developed the company that took visitors on tours until he owned 800 horses and 500 coaches.[18] Park superintendent Horace Albright remembers that Child's motto was "never to be in debt to a railroad for less than a million dollars."[19] Through the years, Child played politics with Congress, the President, and especially the Department of the Interior in order to gain the most profitable concessions.[20] In choosing an architect for his new hotel, he hired Robert Reamer – a man who would, in the course of his work for Child, become the architect for all the

2.6 Harry W. Child (left) and Acting Supt. Capt. George Anderson with trout at Yellowstone Lake, 1894. Photograph by F.J. Haynes.

new buildings in the park. Reamer developed an architectural language that spoke of the conservation of nature and at the same time constructed wilderness as a place of leisure.

THE ARCHITECTURE OF THE OLD FAITHFUL INN

Robert Reamer was not the first architect to design a hotel for the Upper Geyser Basin. In 1898, when Child was still a partner in the Yellowstone Park Association, the Department of the Interior approved a Queen Anne style hotel designed by A.W. Spalding. This design, with its modest entrance overwhelmed by the two conical cupolas at each end of the building, was comparable to many generic wood frame railroad hotels built at the time (see Figure 2.7).

On assuming the presidency of the Yellowstone Park Association, Child was able to pursue his own vision for the new hotel: a grand showpiece in the most modern style, a building that would bring national attention to

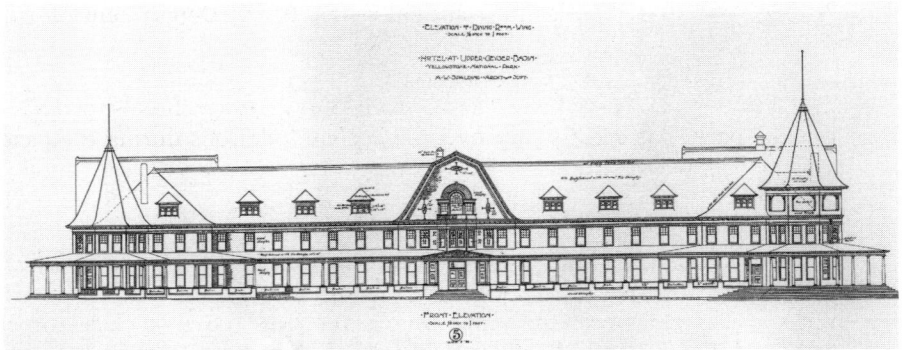

2.7 Proposal for a new hotel on the Upper Geyser Basin, Architect A.W. Spalding, 1898.

Yellowstone and turn a profit for himself.[21] Recognizing the growing appreciation among Americans for the wilderness and for regional styles, he knew the Queen Anne or plain clapboard designs of the other hotels in the park were old-fashioned and inappropriate.[22] He found his architect in San Diego, where Robert Reamer had set up a partnership under the name of Zimmer and Reamer. Child befriended the young architect, invited him to Yellowstone and introduced him to his family, eventually taking him on a European tour in 1909.[23] According to T.J. Hallin, the foreman of the Old Faithful Inn, Child gave Reamer free rein in the design (see Figure 2.8).[24]

He required the latest conveniences such as electricity and hot water, and a spectacular design that would reflect the magnificent setting of the park and draw an upper class clientele. The design seemed to please Superinten-

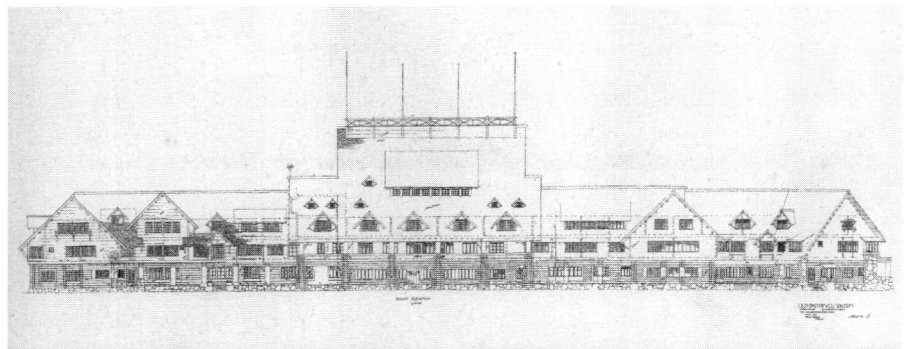

2.8 Elevation of Old Faithful Inn. Architect Robert Reamer, 1903.

dent Pitcher, who described it in his annual report to the Department of the Interior:

> The Yellowstone Park Association, which runs all of the hotels throughout the park, has greatly improved its accommodations during the past season. The new hotel at the Upper Geyser Basin known as "Old Faithful Inn" is a remarkably beautiful and comfortable establishment. It is constructed chiefly of stones and logs, and while rustic in appearance, it contains all of the modern conveniences which the traveler of today is accustomed to, such as electric lights, baths, etc. This establishment is great improvement on the tents which were used at this place for a number of years ... the Old Faithful Inn has 140 rooms and can accommodate 316 guests.[25]

The carpenters who built the hotel experienced the site with some intensity as they had to work through the winter in order to meet the targeted opening date in the spring of 1904 (see Figure 2.9). That winter saw record low

2.9 At work building the Old Faithful Inn, 1903.

temperatures of −40°F and snowdrifts up to 20 feet high, while the building site on the geyser plateau was peppered with geothermal hot spots. A message found in 1954 inside the finial of a flagpole lining the widow's walk of the Old Faithful Inn gives us a sense of that life: "April 1904. Remarks – snowed like hell drank 4 quarts of booze can see about 118 poles." The message was signed by workmen H. Buller, Chas. Lerman, W. High and F. Carmody.[26]

In the architecture of the Old Faithful Inn, Reamer used boulders and logs to create an ensemble that speaks of rusticity in a wilderness setting. While the foundations of the hotel were in fact built of concrete and its walls made with conventional light wood framing, the foundations seemed as if they were made of raw boulders and its walls of rough logs culled from the immediate setting. The massive base of boulders and stones, its piers of stacked timbers, and its brackets of peeled branches suggested the romantic notion of a rustic cabin enlarged to gigantic proportions. The inn's main feature was a huge gabled roof surmounted by a "widow's walk," so that visitors could view the surrounding landscape of geysers and fumaroles. By combining the "Shingle Style" that evoked the great camps of the Adirondacks with ideas from the contemporary Arts and Crafts movement, Reamer elaborated a design for park architecture that became a model for future buildings erected in the national parks across the United States.[27]

With its construction materials seemingly gathered from its immediate surroundings, its handcrafted details, uncluttered living arrangements and general aesthetic of simplicity, the architecture of the inn intensely structured the experience of the visitors to the park (see Plate 4). "There is one man-made structure in the Park," writes Charles Francis Adams, "that looks as though it grew there ... and that is the 'Old Faithful Inn.' All I can say is that the greatest travelers in the world say, 'There is nothing in the world like it or to compare with Old Faithful Inn.'"[28] Letters and diaries in the Yellowstone archives attest that many who experienced the inn were transported by its sophisticated integration of rusticity and fantasy. Its immediate popular success suggests that its design touched people's imagination in a way that earlier hotels built by the Northern Pacific Railroad and its concessionaires did not. The appeal of Reamer's design also transcended class boundaries. Andy Stuart, for example, who worked as a "pack rat" at one of Wylie's camps on the Upper Geyser Basin, remembers the summer of 1909 when he was 16 years of age and the Old Faithful Inn was the draw:

> Frequently on Saturday night we got dressed up and went to Old Faithful Inn for a dance. The only transportation was on foot and it was a mile each way. I imagine we were an odd looking group on the dance floor because it is not easy to look one's best on the rare occasional transition from working slacks to the rumpled suitcase-stored blue serge. I must admit the girls looked much better because they had

pressed their dresses and had slicked themselves up generally. The management of the Hotel deserved a lot of credit for admitting us because we were *not* heavy spenders.²⁹

The overwhelmingly positive response to Reamer's design and the lack of enthusiasm for the more traditional hotels in Yellowstone Park revealed a change in American taste. "Most Americans no longer wanted to pretend the west could be molded into a European landscape," says the historian Anne Hyde. "Because the unique features of the wild landscape now attracted them, tourists wanted to experience it [directly]. They came to Yellowstone to see thermal formations, great chasms in the earth, wild animals, and a safe version of American wilderness. Most visitors demanded a resort that highlighted this experience rather than one that denied it. Old Faithful Inn, ... met these new requirements admirably."³⁰ How did this hotel "highlight" the wilderness experience? How did it help "construct" the tourist's understanding of what the national park represented?

A $200,000 log cabin
From the moment it opened its doors to the public, the Old Faithful Inn was understood to be a spectacular version of a log cabin. A local newspaper, commenting on the new accommodations, described it as a "$200,000 log-cabin."³¹ A young tourist from 1911, who was touring the park with her family in a covered wagon, stopped at the inn to see the view from its widow's walk. She wrote in her diary, "We visited the Old Faithful Inn which is the most extensive log structure yet constructed."³²

The log cabin had long been an icon of frontier life. These primitive dwellings were built by men and women as their first shelter before constructing additional outbuildings for animals or feed. Images from the middle of the nineteenth century depicting log cabins often showed a woman standing at the door, presenting the simple building as a home of a family soon to become prosperous. "Most of all," historian Richard White says, "the [log] cabin had come to represent progress."³³ This was by no means an inevitable reading, and it remained unstable, as we will see in the next chapter, when Appalachian log cabins represented backwardness and poverty rather than progress and prosperity. White continues, "only when it was associated with wealth, or power to follow would it proclaim great achievement from small beginnings."³⁴ This association was used in political propaganda from the middle of the century onward, when the rustic birthplaces of Presidents like Abraham Lincoln or William Henry Harrison were enshrined as proof of humble origins and as examples of the national path to progress and glory. When paired with images of progress, the cabin worked into a "narrative of national progress accomplished through self-reliance and individual energy."³⁵

The ideal of the "simple life," expressed in the rustic architecture of the

Old Faithful Inn, assumes that the most fundamental values and ambitions of American culture would be achieved by a return to the primitive. The continuous experience of frontier life was seen as a major force in shaping the American character. By the turn of the century, log cabins were promoted as instruments for the reinvigoration of the country and its people. Wealthy men flocked to retreats in rustic lodges or hunter's cabins – San Francisco had its Bohemian Grove, Chicago its lodges in the woods of Michigan and Wisconsin, and New York its Adirondacks escapes.[36] Among the middle classes, young couples who wanted to build their own dream cabin could turn to the "how to" manuals published by *Home and Garden* magazine or the many books on the topic (see Figure 2.10). In short, by the early 1900s, the log cabin worked on the American popular imagination on several levels: as a way to reconnect with pioneer life, as an invigorating experience of the outdoors, and as a general appeal for a simpler, less cluttered living environment.

By taking the *image* of the log cabin, the Old Faithful Inn celebrates the final conquest of the west, and because it is a very large building, it reaffirms the validity of this conquest. But it turns inside out the metaphor of the pioneer hard at work to transform "wilderness" into productive land.

Because the national park has been legally pulled out of a productive relation to the land – because it cannot be farmed, logged or mined – the

2.10 "How to Furnish a Log Cabin." From William Wicks, *Log Cabins and Cottages, How to Build and Furnish Them*, 1900.

image of the log cabin is left to signify nothing but leisure, or in other words, non-productive and recreational activities. Like any luxurious resort, the Old Faithful Inn requires the work of many people to keep it running; what is unique is that its architecture speaks about the hard work of pioneer life while it is situated in a landscape reserved solely for leisure. But tensions from its frontier associations remain. They have simply been transferred onto class tensions between hotel patrons and the independent campers known as "sagebrushers." For example, when Charles Francis Adams stayed at the inn he – like many other visitors – climbed to the widow's walk at night to survey the spectacle of geysers illuminated by the searchlight at night. Hearing voices and laughter in the distance, he turned the high-powered beam onto a couple necking in the woods (in Yellowstone rhyming slang not "snogging" but "rotten-logging"), until they decided to leave their private pleasures. Chasing the couple away, Adams aggressively asserted his sense of class privilege. Although he couched it as a joke, *who* was in the wilderness and *how* one behaved was still a subject of conflict.

Reamer took these references associated with the log cabin and transformed them to create a rustic yet comfortable hotel that corresponded to the conservationist ideology of the national park and catered to the wealthy nature tourist. "The Old Faithful Inn presented the comforts of civilization packaged in a primitive container,"[37] Hyde says. But in order to do that, Reamer had to modify the exclusively masculine attributes of the hunter's cabin so that women visitors would feel welcome in the park, and he had to transform a two-room simple building into a large, complex hotel. Both issues open promising avenues to decipher the modern landscape of nature tourism. Let us first explore the way in which the masculine attributes of the hunter's cabin were feminized.

Gender and architecture
Gender has had a long history in architecture, beginning with Vitruvius' gendering of the orders: the Doric being masculine, the Ionic matronly, and the Corinthian maidenly. Adrian Forty tells us that in the eighteenth century, when the terms masculine and feminine were applied to building styles, the former was unquestionably superior to the latter. The architectural theorist Jean-François Blondel strictly distinguished between "masculine," "firm" or "virile" architecture on the one hand and "feminine" on the other. Masculine architectural styles were resolute and expressive, certain in their effects, imposing, simple and solid. A feminine architecture, on the other hand, "generally lacked any specific qualities of its own."[38] It was the "other," the complement to the masculine, and it found its expression in interior decorations and smaller, precious buildings.

That this schematization continued into the nineteenth century is evident from even a cursory examination of the commentary on Sophia Hayden's design for the Women's Building in the Chicago Expo of 1893 – a building doubly feminized by its purpose as the pavilion for women in the Columbian Exposition and by the fact that its architect was a woman:

> It is eminently proper that the exposition of woman's work should be housed in a building in which a certain delicacy and elegance of general treatment, a smaller limit of dimension, a finer scale of detail, and a certain quality of sentiment, which might be designated, in no derogatory sense, as graceful timidity or gentleness, combined however with evident technical knowledge at once differentiate it from its colossal neighbors, and reveal the sex of its author. . . . The design is lyric rather than epic in character, and it takes its place on the Exposition grounds with a certain modest grace of manner not inappropriate to its uses and to its authorship.[39]

Even in domestic interiors of the nineteenth century, gender coding found its way into every room. For example, dining rooms (coded as masculine spaces) were expected to be fitted out in massive and dark woodwork and sparsely decorated, while drawing rooms (coded as feminine) were to be brightly painted, gaily decorated and furnished with light and airy furniture.

At the time Reamer was designing the inn, architecture was seen as an important vehicle for developing a national identity, and the gendering of nascent American architecture as masculine was a way to assert its worth. In the later part of the nineteenth century, "the architect H.H. Richardson was widely regarded as having achieved this state: his work was described by the architect and critic Henry van Brunt, for example, as having a 'large, manly vigor.'"[40] Louis Sullivan was most explicit about the superiority of a "masculine" architecture in his adoring review of Richardson's Marshall Field Store in Chicago:

> I mean, here is a man for you to look at. A man that walks on two legs instead of four, has active muscles, heart, lungs and other viscera; a man that lives and breathes, that has red blood; a real man, a manly man; a virile force – broad, vigorous and with a whelm of energy – an entire male.[41]

Richardson's use of heavy rusticated masonry, solid volumes and deep relief in his architecture was thus interpreted simultaneously as distinctively American in the way it spoke eloquently about the greatness of American landscapes, and as reassuringly masculine. The historian David Leavengood brings precisely this kind of reading to the Old Faithful Inn when he says that "in the American west, the design of resort hotels became fortresses of protection against the awe-inspiring range of natural forces, they embodied in physical form the anti-urban sentiment and a need to escape an increasingly confined and 'feminized' Victorian middle class."[42]

Yet at the time the Old Faithful Inn was built, such gendered notions of materials and space were beginning to be consciously manipulated and at times even subverted in the "progressive" aesthetic of Arts and Crafts designs.[43] According to the design historian Pat Kirkham, the Arts and Crafts movement significantly altered Victorian conventions of gendered interiors.[44] An intellectual of the time, W.B. Yeats, felt that "society was entering one of those rare periods of unity of being, and mutual interpenetration of the sexes, which would find expression in a bisexual art."[45] We can see an example of this subversion in a landmark Arts and Crafts building, the Glasgow School of Art designed by Charles Rennie Mackintosh. The boardroom was designed as an airy space, where all the walls and ceiling were painted a light cream, brightly lit by large vertical windows. When the school opened, its board members refused to meet there. They moved to the darkest room of the building, which was decorated with oak paneling, while the original boardroom was converted into a "flower painting studio" for female students.[46] Clearly, such challenges to the conventional coding of rooms encountered resistance. Because the Old Faithful Inn is also an Arts and Crafts building, it becomes an intriguing proposition to investigate how this building played with the Victorian codes of gendered rooms and spaces to create an architecture in which both men and women would feel comfortable.

The design of the Old Faithful Inn includes many qualities that are either feminine or cut across the expectations for a masculine architecture. First, guests are not led into the lobby on axis with the straightforward certitude expected of a masculine architecture. Rather, they approach the hotel along the side facing the Old Faithful geyser – a reminder that nature, not the hotel, is the goal of the journey. A comparison of the lobby of the Old Faithful Inn with that of Glacier National Park Hotel (also built in the rustic style about ten years later), shows that in Glacier the visitor enters at one end of a long, narrow lobby and descends past two rows of massive tree trunks which serve as columns (see Figure 2.11). This space is modeled on the forestry building built for Seattle's world's fair of 1905 and in its rough outlines, is derived from Greek temples. Everything about this space reaffirms its masculine qualities: the strong axiality of its interior space gives it direction and purpose, its peristyle of columns underlines its upward thrust, its massive timber posts lend a sense of permanence, and the fact that decorations are kept to a minimum corresponds to the bare simplicity deemed masculine.[47]

The lobby of the Old Faithful Inn, on the other hand, is more ambiguous and complex. While it also has bare timbers, rough and rustic materials and no plaster or applied decoration, its vertical supports are intertwined with its horizontal beams and the lacy network of brace and cantilever is virtually impossible to untangle with the eye. The timbers are more slender than at the Glacier Park Hotel and they are kinked and curvy where the posts branch out to meet the beams (Figure 2.12). While the hearth at Glacier reinforces the dominant central axis of the lodge, at the Old Faithful it is set

2.11 The "Forest Lobby" of Glacier Park Lodge.

off-axis and ensconced within a lowered seating area that is almost intimate in scale, where guests could make popcorn or chat in rocking chairs. The exterior shingles of the Old Faithful are cut into decorative shapes – and decoration is a "feminine attribute." In short, in the Old Faithful Inn the rough and refined, the vigorous and the delicate coexist. Thus, the imagery of the log cabin designed for the conservation agenda of the Boone and Crockett Club at the Chicago World Columbian Exposition has been dramatically feminized.

Stepping into the inn from the outside, one is struck by the darkness of the interior. The Yellowstone historian Aubrey Haines described the main lobby as "a great, balconied cavern, open to the roof, with all the supporting beams and braces exposed to view like the skeleton of some enormous mammal seen from within."[48] A dark, cavernous retreat from the open landscape of the Upper Geyser Basin, the space encloses its visitors and transports them into another world. Such darkness was understood at the turn of the century to reinforce the masculine character of a space. Saloons, smoking rooms, libraries, hunting camps – each of these masculine spaces was expected to be darkly painted and dimly lit. So in this sense, the main lobby of the inn expresses a masculine space, a kind of hunter's cabin made large.

As a reviewer commented in *Western Architect* in 1904, "the building was a product of the forest, built with ax, saw, and hammer and containing not a yard of plaster."[49] Yet the structure supporting the roof brings with it another sensibility. It is not made of trusses or giant beams, simple monolithic architectural elements, but rather it is supported by hundreds of small timbers interlaced and stepped up in tiers. It is an embroidery of beams and posts, like a nest – in fact, it houses a "crow's nest," a small stage high up among the rafters for evening orchestral performances for the dancing guests below (see Plate 5). Walkways and balconies criss-cross this space, allowing guests to conceal themselves in innumerable small aeries and overlooks. By counterbalancing the dark and monumental volume of the lobby with the lacy woodwork which supports the roof lit by small-paned windows, Reamer again achieves a space that cannot be easily read. Is it masculine or feminine? Is it a bit of both?

Even the configuration of balconies illustrates an overlap of spaces that are gendered in different ways. Because the balconies surround the lobby, they are an ideal place to look at other people across the space and below. The gaze, as in a theater, is understood to be male. Men look, women parade and pose.[50] But lining the back walls of the balconies are writing desks, each one with its own lamp and a comfortable chair. Such desks were for the lady of the house, they were not the desks of doctors or lawyers. These writing tables were highly charged for women at the turn of the century, who saw in travel writing and diaries one of the few avenues available to express themselves.[51] Again, the masculinity of the theatrical balconies is altered by the femininity of the writing nooks.

The reworking of gender codes in the rustic architecture of the Old Faithful Inn should not give us the illusion that architecture alone structured the development of the modern "nature tourist" in Yellowstone Park. As we saw earlier, nature tourism was vigorously promoted by railroad companies looking to develop new markets. Nevertheless, the playfulness with which the Old Faithful Inn subverted established Victorian codes destabilized assumptions and created a space for the imaginary in this new landscape of leisure. It is clear that this new hotel was more attractive to upper class women touring Yellowstone than had been most accommodations available in the late nineteenth century west. Before the Old Faithful Inn, park hotels were simple wood-frame structures, occasionally adorned with a few columns to give them an air of gentility (Figure 2.13). The sleeping quarters were often rough, especially by the standards of lady visitors. O.S.T. Drake describes her trip to Yellowstone in 1887 in an article published in *Every Girl's Annual*. She says that on her first night, "The Mammoth Springs Hotel turned out to be a huge wooden structure, with an imposing exterior, which the unfinished bare walls, unplastered ceilings, and air of general discomfort did not carry out within. As to the cookery and attendance, the less said the better."[52] Her stay at Firehole rest station the next day was even worse. "The hotel was primitive,

2.12 Lobby of the Old Faithful Inn, 1904. Photograph by F.J. Haynes.

being an unfinished log-hut, the daylight peering through every plank. My room was about six feet square sufficiently filled with two beds. The walls are stretched over with canvas. It could not be described as luxurious, and every snore was audible."[53] Seventeen years later, another visitor described the Old Faithful Inn in her diary and it seems clear that she was satisfied with the accommodations:

> Constructed out of boulders and logs, its architect seems to never have lost sight of the fact that this was to be a purely rustic structure. Indeed, the inn seems not lacking in any detail, for its furnishings are in harmony with the character of the structure. It is the only hotel in the Park that appeals to my fancy.[54]

A coordination between architecture and interior design was one of the main ideas advocated by the Arts and Crafts movement. Many of the clientele coming to the Old Faithful Inn were readers of the *Ladies' Home Journal* and would have been familiar with the "lessons" of interior design put forward

2.13 The Fountain Hotel, Lower Geyser Basin, ca. 1895. Photograph by F.J. Haynes.

by its editor, Edward Bok.[55] The magazine promoted the new Arts and Crafts aesthetic to its female readership but with a conservative slant that distinguished it from Gustave Stickley's socially progressive *The Craftsman*. As David Shi rightly suggests, the influence of the *Ladies' Home Journal* in making the Arts and Crafts movement a success helped to turn "the lure of the rough edge into another form of conspicuous consumption."[56]

A comparison of the interior shown in the 1901 booklet *The Garden of a Commuter's Wife* with a bedroom of the Old Faithful Inn reveals similarities but also some significant differences (Figure 2.14). Haynes' photograph depicts a choice corner bedroom in the Old Faithful Inn, one located on the ground floor with a direct view of the Old Faithful geyser (Figure 2.15). In its details and choice of materials, this room expresses interior design as a "bisexual" exercise. Rough log walls, electric "candles" on wrought iron brackets, and a rustic washstand of stained wood and copper provide a setting that is both wild and civilized. Fine cotton bed linens and window curtains give a delicate touch of domesticity. But in contrast to the refined room shown in *The Garden of a Commuter's Wife*, the bedroom in

2.14 "Below Lies the Moonlit Garden." From Mabel Osgood Wright, *The Garden of a Commuter's Wife*, 1901.

the Old Faithful Inn plays with extremes: there are rough logs and cotton lace, electrical candles and a copper washstand. In this space, couples are supposed to enjoy sex as "a natural act" in which the woman can be spontaneous and the man a "healthy animal."[57] The architecture is addressed to both sexes by being rustic and refined, a playful retreat dedicated to leisure activities in the bower of nature.

2.15 Bedroom at the Old Faithful Inn, 1904. Photograph by F.J. Haynes.

A grand hotel in the regional style

The next issue is one of scale. If, as Anne Hyde claims, "Reamer was one of the first to adapt the entirely domestic rustic style to a large public building," we might ask how a log building can still speak of nature and conservation when it has expanded to the size of a 140-room hotel?[58] First, it can express in its architecture that it is integrated in the landscape. Leavengood sees the Old Faithful as a building whose "geometry and materials respond to the grand scale of the Rocky Mountains."[59] Its facade folds like a mountain chain with buttes and crevasses, as dormers project out for bedroom windows and balconies are recessed in to create outdoor sitting areas (Figure 2.16). Early visitors often commented on the affinity of the Old Faithful Inn to its setting, like this young tourist writing to his father in 1907:

> A fine big rustic hotel is located near there known as the "Old Faithful Inn." This inn is a wonderful place of works of nature transformed into a building by the hand of man. The formation of the trees and limbs are matched in their symmetry and made to correspond into beams, rafters,

2.16 Approach to Old Faithful Inn, 1904. Photograph by F.J. Haynes.

gables in a most wonderful manner. The inside as well as the outside of the inn is the rustic style. An immense fireplace is built in the center of the lobby with a large old fashioned clock over it with a dial of about eight feet and large hundred pound weights attached to it.[60]

A closer reading of the inn would reveal a more complex and potentially contradictory expression of rusticity. For example, the stones used at the base of the building convey a sense of deep geological time, yet they are merely a veneer over modern concrete foundations. Similarly, the exposed logs of the walls conceal the balloon frame construction necessary for such a large building. And the finished interior siding and manufactured windows could only suggest sawmills or even mass production. Yet Reamer's architecture of Yellowstone Park carefully constructed an image of an Arcadian landscape and its use of the Arts and Crafts aesthetic reinforced this, because it was a movement that rejected industrialization and advocated a return to an ideal craft utopia (Plate 6). And in the Arts and Crafts movement it was a moral imperative to show the nature of things. In the words of Gustave Stickley:

> Just as we should be truthful, real and frank ourselves, and look for these same moral qualities in those whom we select for our friends, so should we choose the things with which we surround ourselves in our homes be truthful, real and frank. We are influenced by our surroundings more than we imagine.[61]

In the promotional literature for the Old Faithful inn, then as now, visitors are told that the building materials come from the immediate surroundings: the stone from a quarry near Black Sand Basin, and the logs and gnarled lodgepole pines from the forest on the road to Yellowstone Lake. This is a good thing, we are reassured, even if it means that trees are felled or rock excavated from a conservation area. The main thing is that the building emerges from its landscape (see Figure 2.17).

The architecture of the Inn was also "regional" in ways that are not mentioned in the tourist brochures. Both the washstands in the bedrooms and the electrical "candles" that lit the darkened corners of the building used copper, rustically hammered into sheets or drawn into filaments for incandescent lights. This was the primary product of nearby Butte, Montana. "With the invention of Morse's telegraph in the 1840s, Bell's telephone and Edison's incandescent lamp in the 1870s," a historian of Butte tells us, "the demand for copper wiring and conductors mushroomed dramatically. Before this time, copper had been valued chiefly for its resistance to corrosion and as an alloy with zinc to form brass."[62] Digging what will become the largest open air mine in the world, known as the Berkeley Pit, Butte's "copper kings" were moving fast to satisfy the demand for this metal. As Edwin Dobb says, "too busy digging ore to worry about appearances, Butte has never fit well in the gallery of wholesome outdoor portraits that makes postcards of Montana."[63] It was a cosmopolitan town, with tall office buildings using the new skyscraper technologies developed in Chicago, and a large foreign-born population working in the diggings. It was the birthplace of organized labor in the west, as the International Workers of the World, also known as the

2.17 Tree incorporated in the architecture.

"wobblies," founded by Joe Hill, brought socialist ideals to the landscapes of western enterprise. The years that the Old Faithful was being planned and built saw some of the most militant and combative battles between capitalists (backed by government) and organized labor in the history of the country. The juxtaposition of this highly industrial landscape with a romantic hotel worshipping craft and wilderness was the real context for tourism in the national parks at the turn of the century. Samuel Hays sees the conservation movement allied with big capital in this struggle, saying "the conservation movement did not involve a reaction against large-scale corporate business, but in fact, shared its views in mutual revulsion against unrestrained competition and undirected economic development. Both groups placed a premium on large-scale capital organization, technology, and industry-wide cooperation and planning to abolish the uncertainties and waste of competitive resource use."[64] And in the Old Faithful Inn, business interests developed the look of conservation.

The inn as a moral lesson

Putting aside questions of architectural interpretation for a moment, the design of the Old Faithful Inn also embodies a lesson about how one conducts oneself in a national park. We have mentioned the implicit morality of the Arts and Crafts movement that associated natural materials with "truth" and simple living arrangements with "health." But perhaps the strongest lesson of the Old Faithful Inn was communicated not by what was there, but by what was missing from the hotel. If we think back to the Boone and Crockett Club cabin there were hunting trophies everywhere, from the bison skull over the fireplace to the bearskins on the floor. The same was true with the lobby of Glacier Hotel. That kind of decoration was found in most mountain resorts and lodges. At the Old Faithful Inn there is none of this. When animals are depicted, they are shown alive. There is a bear series in sandblasted glass panels, originally in the bar, now in the restaurant, and the only stuffed animal is a fish mounted on a frame, decorating the lobby. Fishing was permitted in the park.

In the Old Faithful Inn, the nature tourist was put into an environment that promoted a hands-off *visual* enjoyment of nature, not the more interactive model promoted by hunting trophies and images of hunting scenes. It is a purely recreational enjoyment of wilderness that is being pushed here, a perfect translation of Thorstein Veblen's idea of "conspicuous consumption" onto the world of nature and wilderness.[65] A large terrace makes it easy for hotel clients to watch the Old Faithful geyser from a distance, and a giant clock on the chimney allows one to calculate the time until the next eruption. Searchlights mounted on the roof of the inn ensure the spectacle continues throughout the night. In place of the conventional hunting trophies, the walls are decorated with Navajo rugs (that can be purchased). Nature, at the Old Faithful Inn, is a place of no work, a place of leisure that is also a moral space. The next section will explore how people were expected to behave in such a space and what resistance they put up to this indoctrination.

THE LANDSCAPE OF THE TOUR

The architecture of the Old Faithful Inn did not create a discourse about conservation on its own. It was part of a larger landscape that stretched to the boundaries of the park. For this reason, it is important to look at the park as a whole. The transformation of the land around the Yellowstone River into the landscape we know as Yellowstone National Park occurred through the building of roads, hotels and railroad stations and also through representations. We will next explore how paintings, photographs, railroad brochures and postcards helped to create a discourse about the park even before visitors came to see the real thing.[66]

The construction of the park through images

The artist Thomas Moran was the first person to paint features of the Yellowstone region. As a member of the 1871 Hayden survey expedition, Moran executed a series of watercolors that can be seen today at the Yellowstone Park museum. He used these field studies (and photographs taken at the same time by the expedition photographer William Henry Jackson) to compose a set of monumental oil paintings of Yellowstone. These idealized landscapes served to "convey the impression of an epic countenance for America's western geography," and met the aspirations of many Americans to possess and boast of something that was distinctively American.[67] The Protestant theology of the American elite had rejected pilgrimage as a religious rite and we find no pilgrim shrines in Protestant culture. But as Victor and Edith Turner suggest, "some form of deliberate travel to a far place intimately associated with the deepest, most cherished, axiomatic values of the traveler seems to be a 'cultural universal.'"[68] Travel to the natural monuments that grace the American landscape seemed to fulfill that need in the white Protestant culture of the 1900s.

Moran's paintings depicting landscapes as national monuments were instrumental in gaining political and financial support for the park. As John Sears explains, "'The Grand Canyon of the Yellowstone,' which measured seven feet by twelve feet and rivaled Albert Bierstadt's Yosemite canvases, was purchased by Congress in 1872 and hung in the capitol in Washington."[69] Moran's ability to paint western landscapes in this "nationalistic" style deepened with successive journeys, including trips to Yosemite, the Grand Canyon (with explorer John Wesley Powell), and the area of Utah that is now Zion National Park.[70]

Yet ultimately, it was not painting but photography that did most to construct the landscapes of Yellowstone. Early on, William Henry Jackson's photographs helped to gain congressional approval for the bill establishing the national park and his subsequent "Detroit Publishing Company" sold thousands of Yellowstone photos, many in stereoscopic views.[71] Twenty years later, the "park photographer" F. Jay Haynes became nearly obsessed with capturing the perfect representation of each site in Yellowstone Park. The thousands of prints in the Haynes archives bear witness to his practice of taking many views of the same place: more than one hundred views, for example, of the Grand Canyon of the Yellowstone, taken in all seasons and at all hours of the day, showing subtle differences in light. "He purposefully produced many of these ... in stereo views or in large size ($20" \times 24"$). Both formats were meant to impress the viewer with an image larger than one's field of vision, they thereby approximate the experience of personally beholding the Canyon."[72]

Haynes' landscape photographs often included figures standing erect and looking out. These figures gave scale to the landscape and placed the tourist into the representation. According to Carol Crawshaw and John Urry, in this kind of photographic work, the photographer, and then the viewer are seen to be above and dominant over a static and subordinate landscape, which lies beyond us inert and inviting our inspection. Such photographic practices thus demonstrate how nature was to be viewed, as dominated by humans and subject to their mastery; the mode of viewing being taken as emblematic of the relationship of domination of humans over nature.[73]

Most of Haynes's panoramas that include such a "tourist" show a man standing alone regarding the scenery beyond. His posture is stiff and he is dressed like a city-dweller, not a hunter or a "sagebrusher." These photographs showed tourists how to behave – how to "look right" in the landscape.

In a more humorous vein, Haynes gave a visual form to some of Davy Crockett's "tall tales" about the park (like his story of seeing "petrified birds on petrified trees"). Bears were always a prime target for a laugh. Postcards like *Feeding the Bear* or *Bear on a Log* showed these animals as anthropomorphic and cute (Figure 2.18). Other postcards displayed nature as a source of entertainment. The *Handkerchief Pool*, for example, shows a soldier holding a white piece of cloth over a bubbling geyser. The geyser would suck the handkerchief down into unknown regions and keep it for a few minutes

2.18 Feeding wild bears, postcard.

before spitting it up, freshly "laundered." The Yellowstone landscape offered the visitor strange experiences that stood regular conventions on their head. *Fishing Cone* shows a man and a woman fishing on a geyser cone near Yellowstone Lake, reeling in their catch from the cold lake and then cooking it in the bubbling waters of the geyser while it is still on the line (Figure 2.19).

At first, Sears tells us, Yellowstone Park was seen as an enormous "cabinet of curiosities," a series of strange natural phenomena.[74] Even its grand canyon had "lurid" colors and "grotesque" rock formations. This is perhaps why the park was called Wonderland, after Lewis Carroll's immensely popular *Alice in Wonderland* published in 1865. The term was first given by a local newspaper, *The Helena Daily Herald*, in 1872 and then adopted by the Northern Pacific for their advertisement campaigns. Alice, the heroine of Carroll's book, appeared in a number of railroad brochures advertising Yellowstone Park and other Northern Pacific destinations. In one of them, Alice is shown holding binoculars and dressed in hiking clothes ready for her tour of the park (Plate 7). This image carries a double message: on the one hand "wonderland" is a place that promises surprising natural phenomena, on the other, this clever independent girl will be our guide. To cross over to the other side of the mirror, we must follow a girl.

2.19 Fishing Cone, Yellowstone Lake, postcard.

Experiencing the space of the park

Touring the park was an education. A highly structured experience, the tour helped turn a would-be wilderness explorer into a modern nature tourist. Places were chosen to represent certain ideas about wilderness and about Yellowstone. In the tour, the "couponers" who had bought a package tour traveled in old-fashioned "tally-ho" stagecoaches taking 28 passengers pulled by teams of six horses or smaller ones carrying seven to eleven passengers. This slowed down the pace of travel and played into romantic notions of the west as a frontier. Yellowstone chronicler Olin Wheeler praised this anomaly, "the stagecoach, like the buffalo, has ceased to be a feature of the western landscape. ... The stage of romance and of reality a dozen years ago cannot be found in any part of the West except in the National Park [of Yellowstone]."[75]

The tour could be completed a number of ways: visitors coming with the Union Pacific railroad could enter through the west entrance at Monida, while those coming up from the Colorado and Southern line (a subsidiary of the Burlington Railroad) could enter at the east entrance near Cody, Wyoming. But the most popular way to tour the park was a five-day loop that began and ended at the north entrance near Gardiner, Montana (Figure 2.20). It did not take long before the tours focused on major areas of interest

2.20 Disembarking at the Gardiner train station at the north entrance to the Park.

that were varied enough to keep the visitors entertained and at the right distance from each other to keep up the pace. Visitors taken in by the experience felt that nature had perfectly arranged the sites for their enjoyment. Stephen Dale, who toured the park in 1904, recounts his experience in an article published in *Ladies' Home Journal*:

> The six days of the journey are all differentiated, each one by its special kind of spectacle. This happens to be because of two most fortunate, though wholly accidental, circumstances: first, the more striking phenomena, although of five different kinds, are grouped roughly, each kind in a different district of its own – a district of only a couple of miles radius ... and second, the order of these groups' succession is an order of progressive excellence. Each day presents, not only a new but also a more engaging spectacle than the day before ... swelling all the while until it reaches its denouement in the roar of the Lower Falls and goes off dying in reverberation down the cañon.[76]

A typical five-day tour left Gardiner Station at 11:30 in the morning with a first stop at Mammoth Hot Springs for touring the calcified terraces, followed by Devil's Kitchen and the Obsidian Cliffs, arriving at the Fountain Hotel for the first night. The next day featured the Lower and Upper Geyser Basins, with an overnight stay at the Old Faithful Inn. The third day took the visitors to Yellowstone Lake, where they could ride a steamer and overnight at the Lake Hotel. The fourth day was spent visiting the Upper and Lower Falls and finished at the Canyon Hotel.[77] A visit to the Grand Canyon of the Yellowstone on the next day was the climax of the tour, before returning to Gardiner Station for a 7 pm departure on the evening of the fifth day (see Figure 2.21).[78]

From this itinerary, one gets the sense that the tourist was expected to visit as many sights as possible within the five-day period. This sense of urgency was understandable at a time when there were no paid vacations and those with moderate incomes could not afford to take off more than a week at a time. Organized tours seemed safe and, according to historian Cindy Aron, allowed middle class tourists "indulging in their own forms of self-improvement, [... to] feel they had turned their vacations into useful and productive endeavor."[79] As tours became the norm, the collection of "sights" began to dominate the very pattern of travel, which was often "organized to facilitate fleeting views of spectacular landscapes."[80] In Yellowstone, these were grouped according to themes: Mammoth Hot Springs Hotel – facing the barracks, the practice grounds, the administration buildings of Fort Yellowstone and Haynes' photo shop – was the urban complex of the park, while the Upper and Lower Geyser Basins were the "cabinets of curiosity," where visitors marveled at the grotesque rock formations and erratically erupting geysers and were alternately entertained and repulsed by the bubbling "paint

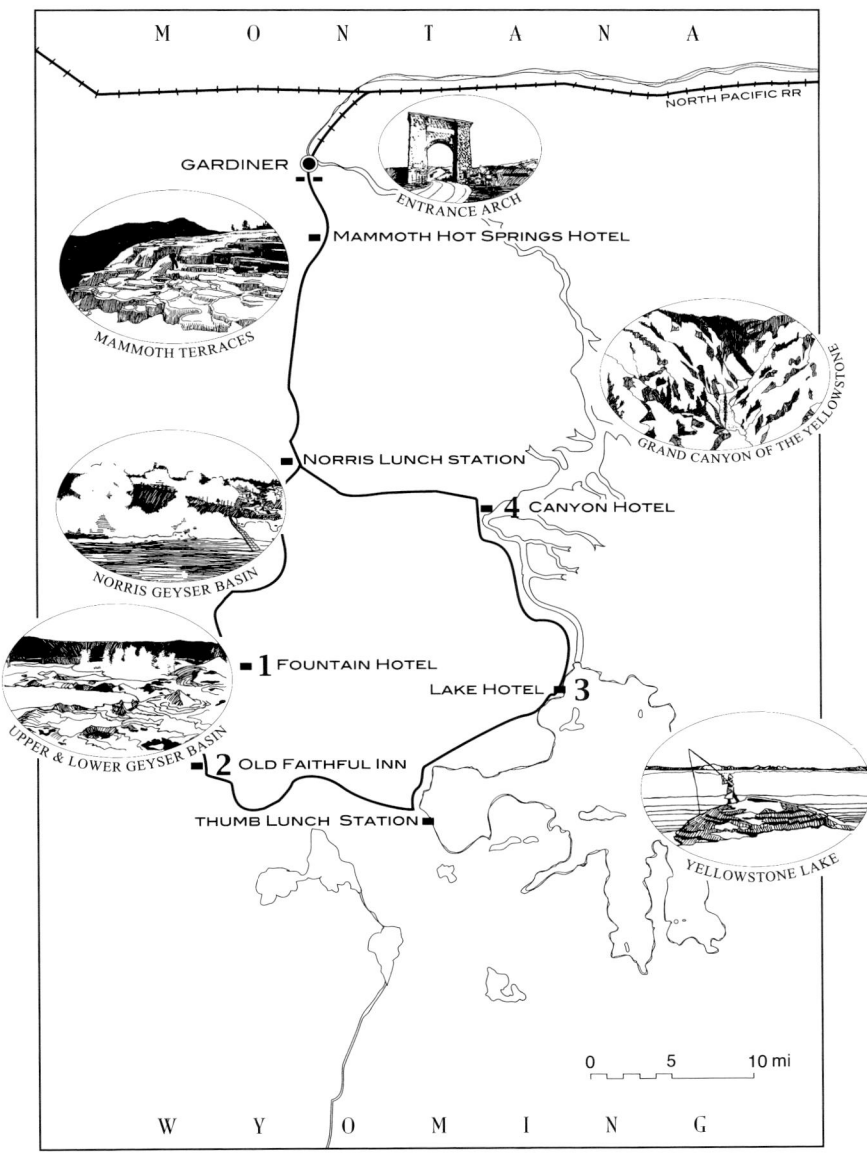

2.21 Map of a typical tour of Yellowstone Park.

pots." (see Plate 8).⁸¹ Yellowstone Lake was compared to lakes in the Swiss Alps, and the Grand Canyon of the Yellowstone was a sublime panoramic landscape of extraordinary colors, its dramatic impact reinforced by the height of the nearby Tower Falls.

A precursor to Disneyland's "Magic Kingdom," Yellowstone Park's circular itinerary with well-defined thematic experiences was a way for the park's early concessionaires to guide people around an attraction. Not only did this itinerary present different aspects of the American landscape, it carried a moral fable about the power of the park to transform the citizen. It is a story about leaving the known world behind (represented by the settlement at Mammoth), venturing into the strange and curious "hell" of the Upper and Lower Geyser Basins, before being rewarded with the sublime beauty of the Canyon of the Yellowstone and the spiritual high of the Falls. Coming "home" to Gardiner Station, one is a transformed person.⁸² Tourists were just as critical then as they are now. They were expected, one traveler wrote, "to squeeze in among men in yellow dusters and women in gray dusters and red Shaker bonnets, and drive along ... in a chaos of alkali dust ... until the fifth day brings him back to his starting point a wiser and dustier man."⁸³ There was no choice of where to go or what to do, but one could look forward to the pleasures to come and rest assured the trip would be enjoyable. By comparison with the "sagebrushers" who camped out and set their own itineraries, the "couponers" who took the stagecoach tour purchased a sense of security in exchange for a chance to see the park on their own terms. The tour structured the park experience as a sequence of stations, with activities to do and landscapes to admire from specific viewpoints. Tourists were directed to look at features of the landscape and their interaction with it was limited to a set of permitted behaviors: taking the temperatures of the hot waters, collecting samples of colored earth in little boxes and having fun with the geysers by throwing objects into their cones. But in general, the tour was designed to keep visitors as separate as possible from what they were looking at and have them move through quickly.

Learning to become a modern tourist

As Yellowstone Park became commercialized, two developments helped to transform the traveler into a nature tourist: the invention of the hand-held camera and the establishment of zones of preserved wilderness. In general, tourism and photography evolved hand in hand. Urry and Crawshaw tell us, "the shift from a scholastic pursuit to a visual pleasure, from the traveler's ear to the traveler's eye, began at the end of the eighteenth century," and "sight became increasingly significant in the ordering of tourist and travel discourse."⁸⁴ In Yellowstone, images were crucial to the construction of tourist memories. The emphasis on images became so significant that by the 1920s many tourists were buying postcards as a substitute for venturing into the wild. Marjorie Albertson, who worked at the Old Faithful Inn postal station, bluntly said, "Most tourists from the East spend their vacations seeing Yellowstone from the back of picture post cards."[85]

The role of hand-held cameras in shaping how people saw nature is another matter. On the one hand, tourists who took pictures reinforced established aesthetic notions of how nature should look. But on the other, photography seemed to have played an important role in the constitution of tourists' subjectivity.[86] Photo albums stored in the Yellowstone Park archives serve as testimony that both are true. Many personal photographs collected in these scrapbooks replicated the dominant visual conceptions of the Yellowstone landscape; they show views already known. These snapshots were taken when the carriage stopped and everyone was told to admire a landscape from a particular vantage point. They represent the "essence" of Yellowstone. But other photographs, often including family and friends, are more personal interpretations – as the comments written below them in the albums reveal (Figure 2.22). For example, the scrapbook on one young woman who worked for the Wylie camp pokes fun at the tourists she served and complains about work she was asked to do (building a barn) that was not part of her job description.

2.22 Billings group at the Opal Terraces. Photograph by F.J. Haynes.

Such personal pictorial interpretations were not possible before Kodak developed the hand-held cameras. The empowerment this new activity – which came to be called "kodaking" – gave women should not be underestimated (Figure 2.23). When the young tourist Aline Tieche discovered the joy of catching wild animals in action, she writes:

> We had already seen hot springs and geysers, but not a real, live bear, and as we are told they are feeding on the garbage on the mountain side at the rear of the hotel – perhaps 40 rods away – we hasten, Kodak in hand not be "hugged" or taken, but to "take" the bears. There were six in the group at another time the mother and two cubs. We saw others at some of the hotels, where they were chained to trees, and quite tame. I touched one.[87]

2.23 Woman "kodaking" at Old Faithful Geyser, 1896.

Taking a picture, Susan Sontag says, "is reassuring." It enables people "to take possession of the space in which they are insecure."[88] And Yellowstone was a strange environment – theatrical and seemingly artificial – as we can see in the language visitors used to describe what they saw. Geysers "perform," bears "act" and colors of the Canyon are "painted." Photography was one way visitors could control this imposing and at times aggressive theatricality. Certainly, photography gave tourists a language through which they could describe and appreciate the environment surrounding them. Photographs and the albums in which they were assembled also gave visitors a way to recollect stories and adventures – to explain, even justify, how and why they visited a particular place.

The interactions of visitors with nature became increasingly structured as Yellowstone Park developed. But tourists of the 1900s took more liberties than they would today. They regularly collected "souvenir" pieces from petrified trees, measured the temperatures of geysers, timed their eruptions, "washed" clothes in them and threw items into them. They fished and fed bears. "Front stage" and "back stage" were not clearly separated, although both the army and the Yellowstone Transportation Company understood the necessity of creating zones for visitors that were separate from places of work. On the front stage, visitors were presented with a landscape that was "wild" and without work. Back stage was meant to be invisible. At times, this distinction led to ridiculous situations, as when bears were fed with kitchen garbage from a cart or buffalo were fenced in a corral near Mammoth Hot Springs.[89] Although milk cows were permitted, they had to be kept on back roads and hidden behind tents. The situation was not always clear and many people were surprised at the seemingly arbitrary distinction between wildlife and livestock. A young man who worked for the Wylie camps recalls bringing cows for milking into the park only to be stopped by a soldier:

> I failed to notice the sign prohibiting loose stock to go through the Golden Gate. When the cows were through the gate a soldier came along and called my attention to this mistake. I told him how sorry I was ... being so absorbed in the wonders of the scenery, since this was my first trip. He first thought he should take me to Fort Yellowstone, which now is called Mammoth, but he finally said he would overlook it for this time, which was much appreciated by me.[90]

At that time, neither "nature" nor "wilderness" were the rarefied notions operating in national parks today. For example, when the superintendent of Sequoia and General Grant National Parks sent seedlings to be planted in Yellowstone Park, the fact that they came from the Sierras was seen as part of their attraction. He requested in his letter, "the trees in question [should] be properly labeled with the correct name of: *Sequoia Gigantea*, coupled with the statement that they came from the Giant Forest in Sequoia National Park."[91] Black spotted trout were raised by the Bureau of Fisheries at West Thumb to be "planted in the waters of the National Park."[92] Grass was seeded and sprinklers installed at great cost near Mammoth Hotel to attract elks. They then got skin diseases and had to be captured and treated.[93] When mountain sheep were introduced, they had to be fed in the winter with hay brought in by the cartload.[94]

The distinction between front stage and back stage created a space in which nature tourists were given the illusion of a pristine "original" wilderness. In exchange, they had to perform their role as visitors. The army was there to ensure that took place. Today, we think of the nature tourist as someone who has internalized "ecological" behavior, a process Michel Foucault has described as the internalization of the controlling gaze. Under the watchful eye of the army, tourists in Yellowstone National Park had to behave according to rules and regulations that were often new to them. Fishing was allowed but not hunting, bathing in the hot waters was permitted only when it took place in little shacks dotting the landscape. Wild animals could be trapped, but only by licensed hunters working for zoos or taxidermists, while others who did the same thing were criminalized as poachers. And the most important rule, the one that affected migrant groups the most, was that camping was allowed only as a form of recreation – making illegal the presence of Native Americans in the park.

Resistance

There was resistance to these new codes of behavior. Lining up to register at the hotel, which seems so natural today in the United States, was greatly resisted. "I tried to get them to stand in a line instead of crowding around the registration desk," Marge Albertson recalls. "Did you ever try to line up a crowd? I even drew chalk lines on the floor, and tried pushing them onto it! Some would take a look at the line and deliberately, or otherwise, step out about five feet, and then complain they lost their turn to register."[95] With limited success, soldiers were constantly reminding people not to look down a geyser for they could get burned by a sudden eruption. A seasonal worker tells a story about having fun by enticing a tourist to bend the rules:

> Several Savages [seasonal workers] had been hiking in the region of the Lone Star Geyser one afternoon, when one of them discovered an old water pitcher that had been discarded by some tourist camp. He immediately grasped this fact as an opportunity to have some fun by fooling the horseback party that was due in a few minutes from the inn. Taking a pen from his pocket he wrote in large letters, "To be used in priming geyser." Then he hung the pitcher on the sign telling of the habits of the Lone Star, and joined the rest of the fellows to fish. When they returned later that afternoon, to their utmost delight, they saw a man who had climbed the fifteen foot cone of the geyser, and was expectantly pouring river water into the vent![96]

On the whole, those involved in creating a landscape of tourism in Yellowstone were remarkably effective in getting visitors through the park quickly, packaging problematic and at times unattractive nature through representation and humor, and ultimately in controlling the behavior of visitors to turn them into modern nature tourists.

NATIONAL PARKS GROW INTO A NATIONAL LANDSCAPE OF LEISURE

In the early 1900s the national parks were still administered as separate entities, each one independent of the others. Although they were nominally the responsibility of the Secretary of the Interior, there was little personnel or money allocated for their development or administration. But as new national parks were added and the number of visitors increased, pressure began to mount for a government agency dedicated solely to the parks. In 1916, the National Park Service was established as a branch of the Department of the Interior, and it has remained the administrative center ever since. That year, 365,000 visitors entered the parks. Seven years later, the number was 3,500,000 – nearly ten times as many.[97] For these people and those who followed them, the national park system began to represent "American wilderness." These were a set of spaces distributed across the country that were set aside from work and constructed as places of leisure. They were part of a system, but each featured a unique aspect of the American landscape.

In retrospect, we can see a constant tension in the National Park Service between the desire to create a unified system out of the disparate parks and a desire to differentiate one park from another so that each reflects the unique qualities of its region. One of the strategies for unification was the establishment of a uniform set of rules and regulations in all the parks – from standardized entry fees to regulations regarding hunting and fishing, garbage disposal, making fires, where and when to use hiking trails, how long one could camp and where, the removal of natural objects such as flowers and rocks, and so forth. These rules were meant to guarantee visitors a certain predictable experience of nature but also to normalize their behavior – turning curious energetic urbanites into well-behaved nature tourists.

By contrast, the promotional material of the parks went to great lengths to highlight regional differences. The official NPS souvenir booklet from Arizona's Grand Canyon bursts with reds and oranges, while the same kind of booklet from Yosemite radiates greens and blues. Also in the built landscape, the park architecture of cabins, lookouts and information centers shows an attempt to differentiate one park from another. In effect, the tension between the creation of a unified system and the articulation of regional differences underlie the development of the parks.

Strategies of unification

The transition from army to NPS administration is one of the clearest expressions of unification in the national parks. Originally, Horace Albright recalls, "the military presence shielded the park from poaching and prevented vandalism, but it did not do the natural resources much good. The officers who served as superintendents over the years had no real understanding of wildlife management."[98] But while the new park rangers replaced the soldiers, they retained some attributes of military life. Rangers wore uniforms, passed entrance examinations, satisfied restrictions as to age and gender, and needed to be physically fit and "a good shot." They also inherited a bit of the woodsman: the Department of the Interior first hired forest rangers to take the place of troops guarding forest reserves. These men had to know how to fight forest fires, ride and care for horses and have some knowledge of trail construction. A set of regulations from 1915 governing rangers in national parks makes it clear that the ranger was paid to protect national resources and do so in an organized and systematic manner. They were expected to wear a standard uniform and write a monthly report of their daily duties, their travels, the conditions of game, any unlawful trespass, and any other activities (see Figure 2.24).[99] Again following the model of the army, NPS regulations allowed rangers to stay only a few years in each park before they were required to move to another. As a result, rangers' knowledge of each park

2.24 Rangers with Horace Albright in Yellowstone Park, ca. 1920.

remained relatively superficial and it was especially difficult for those who had strong family ties in the area to advance in the park service. The mandatory nomadic life of the park service was and still is a deterrent to rangers who have strong attachments to their local communities.[100]

But unlike the soldier, the park ranger was encouraged to educate the tourist "to make them understand what they see." It was assumed that park visitors came from urban environments and had little knowledge of nature or the local region and therefore required instruction in the form of evening lectures and guided walks (Figure 2.25). The historian John Ise explains:

> for some years the word "education" was used, and the work was "educational" in the sense of imparting information, enlarging the knowledge of visitors through pamphlets, lectures and in various other ways. Later the Service turned more and more to the word and the concept of "interpretation." [It was described as] "an educational activity which aims to reveal meanings and relationships through the use of original objects, by first hand experience, and by illustrative media, rather than simply to communicated factual information." It is "the revelation of larger truth that lies behind any statement," its chief aim "is not instruction, but provocation," and it "should aim to present the whole rather than the part."[101]

2.25 Ranger giving an evening lecture.

When it came to the historical interpretation of the tribal cultures the "larger truth that lies behind" was more often than not ill-informed and at times entirely incorrect. In Yellowstone for example, the myth that Native Americans were fearful of the geysers was a useful justification for excluding them from the park.

The Park-to-Park highway

The frontstage/backstage split that structured the tour of Yellowstone was recapitulated nationwide in the regulations regarding access roads to parks and in the design of parkways. As the national parks were established one by one, businesses sprang up on roads near park entrances. In an effort to "clean up" these roadsides, the park service passed regulations to close down businesses and remove buildings they considered to be eyesores. The intention was to present a natural façade to the park that would be unpolluted by commerce. This cleaning-up strategy frequently removed the only means for local people to make a living, generating a ready workforce for the low-paying menial tasks in the park. Designed naturalism extended to the roads inside the parks as well. At the Grand Canyon of the Yellowstone, for example, "the park roads and a system of paths and scenic over-looks brought park visitors on foot or horseback to the edge of the cañon. Concern for the encroachment led to the cañon's designation as a unique area in the 1930s and the eventual removal of the hotel and campground."[102] This hotel, designed by Robert Reamer in 1911, was, by all accounts, the most impressive architectural feature of the park.

The idea that roads leading to the parks should be bordered by a natural-looking landscape led to arguments for a Park-to-Park highway. Such a highway would link all the national parks into a cross-country tour of leisure spaces – recreating the Yellowstone tour at the scale of the nation! In this vision, park visitors would be able to travel along a continuous ribbon of verdant nature for hundreds of miles. A number of Park-to-Park highways were proposed at different times. The first one, planned in 1915, was meant to link all the western parks in a loop. It would begin at Denver, ascend to Rocky Mountain National Park, Yellowstone and Glacier, cross west over to Mount Rainier and descend through Crater Lake, Yosemite and Sequoia, before cutting back across the Rockies to Salt Lake City and down to Denver, creating a circular tour of 3,500 miles.[103] As historian Keller Easterling explains:

> Some [of the Park-to-Park highways] were privately funded by tourism while others were proposed as part of the national park system. For instance, in 1930, Congress entertained a proposal for an Eastern Park-to-Park Highway connecting Washington, Shenandoah National Park, the Great Smoky Mountains, and Mammoth Cave, near Louisville, Kentucky. Another Park-to-Park highway bill, proposed in the House of Representatives in 1934 described four parkways that would link

national parks across the entire continental United States. The interstices of these networks were not major US cities, as they would later be in the interstate networks, but were rather locations like Grand Canyon National Park, Boulder Dam, Yosemite, or Niagara Falls.[104]

Feeling the wind shift from the railroad to the motor car, Harry Child was an active supporter of the idea of a Park-to-Park highway. In his obituary, the local paper recalls that in order to support the "See America First" program that began during World War I, "Mr. Child drove his own car on a 6,000 mile tour from national park to national park, stirring up what promises to be a thoroughly successful movement to construct good roads to link the nation's pleasure grounds so that automobile tourists can 'See America First' in comfort; a movement in which Mr. Child has the most cordial backing of the federal government."[105]

In the early designs for parkways, roads followed the contours and were integrated into the surrounding landscapes by the use of rock work and native vegetation in their abutments. The interest in naturalistic landscaping came from advances made in gardening design and landscape theory.[106] But while early designers saw the road as a means of accessing and experiencing a diverse set of regional landscapes by car, Easterling suggests that "it was eventually designed as a hermetic system that created its own channel of surrounding traffic-engineered landscape contours."[107] The traffic engineers designed everything from the path and dimension of the roads to the turning radius of the driveways and landscaping on either side, further emphasizing the homogeneous character of the road.

Most people who chose to drive and camp did so because it was more affordable. Car camping also "supplied a masculine remedy for the feminized resort vacation."[108] Referring to a certain class of woman visitor who would otherwise be frequenting the high-end watering holes and seaside resorts of the urbanized elite, Cindy Aron argues that the spread of the automobile made it more acceptable for these women to camp and exercise skills that were associated with men.[109] The author of a 1902 article entitled "The People at Play" describes an encounter with two women teachers from San Francisco who were camping in Yosemite. Aron comments, "unlike twenty years earlier these women brought no cook nor driver, no doubt sparing considerable expense. They also revealed that, by [then] some women felt comfortable embarking on a camping venture without the assistance of men."[110] In time, the entire space of the national parks became an acceptable area for middle and upper middle class women to frequent, even when they were not chaperoned.[111] The New York socialite Emily Post, who refused to camp on her first cross-country trip, reflected on the experience after it was over:

> Some day we are going back. When we go again, we are going in two cars – one to help the other in case of need, and if possible, a third car

to carry camping outfit – and camp! [Alice] and I both hate camping, so this proves the change that can come over you as you go out into the West.... Why difficulties seem to disappear; and why that magic land leaves you afterwards with a persistent longing to go back, I can't explain; I only know that it is true.[112]

Through the last three decades of the nineteenth century, magazines and newspapers advocated the restorative possibilities of camping. With automobiles becoming more affordable and the national parks paved with asphalt roads, camping became an increasingly popular form of vacationing. Car camping in the national parks touched a deep chord in the American psyche. It corresponded to a pioneer spirit of individualism that evoked the covered wagon and outdoor life. And increasingly, institutionalized forms of camping grew in all the national parks (Figure 2.26). Special cleared and flattened areas were set aside as campgrounds. These offered drinking water and latrines, but also contained visitors in a limited area so that fires, the pollution of freshwater streams and garbage could be controlled. In exchange for predictable amenities provided by the National Parks Service, campers had to

2.26 "Fishing Bridge" public auto camp, Yellowstone National Park. Photograph by F.J. Haynes.

behave according to a set of uniform rules. The campgrounds rapidly became a standard, unifying experience of wilderness.

Regional differentiation

If the rangers and the roads helped to unify the disparate national parks, the architecture of their hotels, cabins, lookouts and information centers were intended to blend into their distinctive settings. The first policy put forth to regulate the landscape architecture in the national parks dates from 1918, when Steven Mather wrote that "in the construction of roads, trails, buildings and other improvements, a particular attention must be devoted always to the harmonizing of these improvements with the landscape."[113] This directive suggested that engineers and architects should look to the specific regional landscapes.

Returning to Yellowstone for a moment, let us look at the range of buildings designed over the years by Robert Reamer for the park. Carefully sited to harmonize with the surrounding landscape, Reamer's early park architecture used local materials and handcrafted details. Because the Yellowstone Park Company wanted each of their hotels to correspond to the unique character of its site (the featured attraction for the day's tour), the result was distinctive architectural styles for the three major areas of the park, in a sort of miniature "regionalism." Reamer's proposal for a redesign of Mammoth Hot Springs Hotel shows a series of massive stone piers along the front of the building. These towering pillars and the floors "hanging" between them echo the strange calcified "hoodoos" and horizontal terraces of Mammoth Hot Springs (Plate 9). The rusticated logs and gnarled wooden lace work of Old Faithful Inn evoked the forests surrounding the Upper Geyser Basin. The new Canyon Hotel of 1911 had cantilevered huge terraces and low roof lines to mirror the horizontal stratification of Yellowstone's Grand Canyon. When asked about the Canyon Hotel, Reamer answered in characteristically humble manner, "I built it in keeping with the place where it stands. Nobody could improve upon that. To be at discord with the landscape would almost be a crime. To try to improve upon it would be an impertinence."[114] The designs for Yellowstone had a lasting impact on the development of subsequent park architecture, not only because Yellowstone was the prime jewel of the National Park System, but because it was the training ground for the longest-serving director of the National Park System, Horace Albright, who was superintendent at Yellowstone from 1919 to 1928. The success of the Old Faithful Inn set a standard by which park architecture should be measured as appropriate to its magnificent settings.

In 1938, the National Park Service published a two-volume compendium of park architecture – inspired possibly by the contemporaneous Historic American Buildings Survey and the WPA travel guides to the regions of the country. This massive compilation includes examples of architecture from national and state parks across the United States. All the structures share a certain aesthetic – stonework is rustic and cyclopean, the buildings use unmilled timber rather than lumber, pitched roofs are shingled. A drinking fountain is fashioned from a large boulder with the top hollowed out to form a basin. Fallen trees are recycled into footbridges and handrails, reducing the number of trees felled. The rustic aesthetic has an exaggerated sense of naturalism. But as one looks closer, this normative handbook of how to create a "park architecture" is made more complex by its attempts to reflect the specific cultural geography of each region. The section on "one-room cabins" for example, tells us that "these cabins carry special interest for the fact that each is so characteristic of locality and tradition. The *Letchworth* cabin is our old friend, the Adirondack shelter, enclosed. The *Kentucky* cabin is certainly something of a southern mansion in miniature. The *Palo Duro* cabin is typed at a glance as of the Southwest."[115] Hundreds of other examples in this two-volume series display regional characteristics: in a Florida cabin, a gap is left between logs in a wall to allow wind to pass through (Figure 2.27). In Texas, the buildings rely on solid masonry and flat roofs to maintain dark and cool interiors. In Illinois, wide overhangs and low horizontals offer summer shade and protection from winter snowdrifts and echo the long line of the prairie (Figure 2.28). Such park architecture interprets not only the physical characteristics of each area (its raw materials and

2.27 Cabin in Myakka State Park, FL.

2.28 Picnic shelter in I&M Canal State Park, Marseilles, Illinois.

weather conditions), but begins to evoke the cultural landscape of the regions too.[116]

The architects and landscape architects who worked for the National Park Service generally developed a distinctive idiom for each region of the country. The architecture of the mountainous western parks like Yellowstone, Yosemite and Glacier adopted the rustic look of unmilled timber and cyclopean masonry developed by Reamer in the Old Faithful Inn. In the arid south-west, Grand Canyon National Park and neighboring national parks and monuments drew from the rich architectural traditions of Native Americans in those regions. The establishment of a category of national monuments was itself a tacit recognition that culture, as well as nature, had a key role to play in the formation of a national identity. National monuments were a curious mixture of Civil War battlegrounds, prehistoric settlements like Chaco Canyon and Montezuma's Castle, and Spanish buildings such as the Tumacácori and Grand Quivira National Monuments. Visitors were drawn from one park to the next by advertisements that emphasized the uniqueness of each.

Originally, Weigle and White explain, "the Santa Fe Railway had not featured Indians in its advertising until the turn of the century, in part because trains were still equipped with Winchester rifles against raids as late as the 1880s, and in part because the metaphor (of Native American = nature) and means of marketing had not been developed."[117] But with the end of the Indian wars and the success of novels like Helen Hunt Jackson's *Ramona*, which depicted a romantic image of Indians and Spanish colonials, the commodification of tribal culture through architecture and craft became part of the discourse on American wilderness. Both tourists and workers participated in the idea of regionalism through their respective activities. Caucasian women learned to behave like tourists, looking at the distant horizon through a telescope, while Hopi women of the same age found themselves weaving baskets for the tourist trade outside the luxury hotel El Tovar (Figures 2.29 and 2.30). The basket will be sold and her weaving captured as

2.29 Hopi basket-weaver at El Tovar, Grand Canyon National Park, 1914. Photograph by Herbert J. Cowling.

2.30 Tourists at the "lookout," Grand Canyon National Park, 1914. Photograph by Herbert J. Cowling.

a souvenir of the "Grand Canyon experience." While one of these women is learning how to be a tourist, and the other is teaching Indian traditions, they are two faces of the same process, connected in the modern economy of leisure and tourism.

In terms of park architecture, one of the better-known examples of integrating Native American traditions can be found in the designs of architect Mary Colter. Colter began her work as an interior designer for Fred Harvey, who was the main concessionaire in Grand Canyon National Park. In 1905, she designed a souvenir shop on the south rim of the canyon, directly across from Hotel El Tovar. Known as Hopi House, the shop was in the style of the Hopi dwellings at Oraibi, Arizona.[118] Although Hopi communities were more than 80 miles east of the park, the flat-topped terraces of their dwellings were a distinctive architectural feature of the region and one considered by eastern tourists to be more picturesque than the hogans of the Navajo.[119] Colter's building featured terraces made of local stones with steps and ladders connecting one rooftop to another, each rooftop forming a terrace for the apartment above (Figure 2.31).

Reinforcing the link between nature and culture, every aspect of

2.31 "Hopi House," Grand Canyon National Park, 1948. Photograph by Virgil Gipson.

Colter's design spoke of the way natural materials were used by Native Americans: the floors looked as if they were made of packed earth but were in fact cement. Baskets and pots were displayed on hand-hewn tables and Navajo rugs decorated the rooms.[120] The main room was decorated with a sand painting and a Hopi ceremonial altar. Members of the Hopi nation were hired to construct the building, and once it was opened, others came to weave rugs and baskets and make jewelry in the "workroom" for visitors to purchase in the shop. But the performance did not stop there: "in the evening, the Hopi sang traditional songs, and their dancing on the patio at five eventually became a daily event."[121]

A quarter of a century later, when Colter was in her sixties, she designed the "Desert View Watchtower and Kiva" – a panoramic lookout, rest station and gift shop at the eastern end of the South Rim of the canyon, which opened in 1932. It was intended, Colter said, "to bring about better understanding of the American Indian."[122] Made of stones artfully assembled to give the impression of a tower in ruin, it evoked the architecture of ancient settlements like Mesa Verde, which are widely distributed throughout the region. Working like an archeologist, Colter chartered a small plane and "after she had located the remains of a tower from the air, she would go overland by Harvey car to photograph and sketch it. For more than six months she studied the construction and masonry techniques of these prehistoric towers" (see Figure 2.32).¹²³ She claimed not to be making a copy of these ancient structures but rather a "re-creation," thus justifying her radical

2.32 Mesa Verde ruins. Photograph by Ansel Adams.

changes to their scale and context. Colter's Watchtower was 70 feet high, much taller than the originals it was modeled after and with a much greater diameter at its base (Figure 2.33). It sat on a concrete foundation and was reinforced with a steel framework that was covered by carefully selected stones found in the area. It contained a large observation room on the ground floor modeled after a kiva that was entered from the top with a ladder. From the "kiva," visitors ascended to the first floor of the tower, the Hopi Room. There Fred Kobotie, a Hopi artist who worked as a guide for the park, decorated the room with large paintings describing the Snake Legend. Tens of thousands of tourists visited the Watchtower each year to get a glimpse of "Hopi culture."

2.33 "The Watchtower" and "Kiva" at the Grand Canyon National Park, 1932.

The galleries above the Hopi Room were reached by a stair that curved along the inner wall of the tower, past walls richly decorated with frescoes. These were adapted from ethnographic drawings from ancient kivas, caves and cliff walls from the Abo caves in central New Mexico.[124] The roof of the tower provided a panorama with "reflectoscopes" that allowed visitors to get a better view of the canyon.[125] To the side of the tower, Colter constructed a "village" in ruin. The intention was to show how the ruin "simulated the sort of remains from which archeologists work to piece together knowledge about past civilizations."[126] For the Hopi, this strange representation of prehistoric architecture still needs more discussion. Leigh Jenkins, appointed in 1989 by the tribal council as the director of a new cultural preservation program, says of the Watchtower, "they designed it in isolation. Maybe they talked to a few individuals, but they did not consult the tribe or the elders."[127] Certainly, a tower in ruins was an evocative and romantic attraction for North American tourists in the 1930s, evoking long-gone civilizations on the continent or even, as Walter Benjamin has suggested so beautifully, such ruins express architecture returning to nature.[128]

As a rule though, the place for Native Americans in the representations of conservation was very restricted – generally taking the form of "bygone" cultures or folk entertainment and craft. There are many instances of Native Americans being hired by the National Park Service but the case of Glacier National Park stands out as particularly exploitative. Louis Hill, the major concessionaire for Glacier, used members of the Blackfeet tribe as bait to lure tourists to the Park. Robert Keller and Michael Turek explain:

> Louis Hill employed Blackfeet Indians as official hosts at his chalets and hotels. The tribe became known, even to themselves, as "the Glacier Park Indians." Hill promoted a Plains Indian mystique on the railway's advertisements, calendars, and resort decor. The tribe drummed, danced and signed postcards on the sprawling estate of a hotel, then conducted naming ceremonies in the crowded lobby. Indians "passed the tom-tom" for tips and sold miniature bows, arrows, and teepees. Between 1914 and 1919 hardier tourists slept in real teepees on the lawn of East Glacier Hotel. When the popularity of such camping declined, the railroad hired Blackfeet to live on display in teepees (see Figures 2.34 and 2.35).[129]

After World War II, the tribe began to question their role and members of the younger generation entirely lost interest in performing for tourists. In general, the park's mandate was to "freeze Indians as an idea and artifact, a static and quaint people who have few economic needs."[130] The difficulty that the park service had in recognizing the economic needs of the tribes living near (or in) the parks led to constant conflicts and tensions between the service and Native American communities:

2.34 "Indian Camp near St. Mary's Lake," Glacier National Park.

Of the 367 Park Service units in 1992, at least 85 had some relationship with Indian tribes. If one subtracts the Civil War sites, fossil beds, presidential homes, famous buildings, malls and parkways, the ratio becomes much thinner; look only at the "crown jewels" of the system and the figure reaches 100 percent. We found parks totally inside Indian

2.35 "Medicine Elk Ceremony," Glacier National Park.

reservations and Indian reservations totally inside parks. There are parks sharing a common border with one tribe, parks surrounded by half-dozen or more different tribes, and tribes encircled by the National Park Service. In places a tribe may have title to park land. Elsewhere Indians may lease land to the National Park Service, or the service may lease land to Indians.[131]

The list of conflicts and disputes between the National Park Service and Native American tribes is long: "boundary lines, land claims, rights-of-way, hunting and wildlife management, grazing permits, water rights, employment preference, craft sales, cultural interpretation, sacred sites and the disposition of cultural artifacts, entrance fees, dams, the promotion of tourism, commercial regulation, 'squatting' in parks, relations with tribal parks, and resentment over past injustices."[132] When conflicts arose, the park service, caught by surprise, often reacted in a patronizing or defensive manner. Native Americans, on the other hand, usually identified the National Park Service as just another cog in the federal bureaucracy.

The national parks were created as conservationists were able to argue for the preservation of certain landscapes. It is perhaps not surprising that the landscapes Anglo-Americans felt were extraordinary or worth conserving already held a deep significance for their original inhabitants. In fact, the most spectacular or unique landscapes had been long integrated into Native American religious practices. NPS director Russell Dickinson admits that he doesn't know "of a single major national park or monument today in the western part of the US that doesn't have some sort of Indian sacred area."[133] We might say then that the sacred has been doubly recognized in wilderness areas: first within the framework of Native American beliefs and practices, and secondly as instances of what John Sears has called the "sacred places" of American national tourism.[134] This second reading is further complexified by a more recent sacralization of wilderness areas by ecological activists.

The parks become imbedded in the national psyche

As we have seen, the national park was a complex cultural landscape. A landscape created in the first place by Native American husbandry, it was subsequently set apart from the rest of the country and transformed into an archetype of untouched nature. It was also made safe, opened to some people, closed to others, commercialized, packaged for the elite and the middle class, made available to women and to men, furnished with leisure activities and regulated in its finest details. The National Park system has remained an enduring "construction of nature" that has been experienced by many generations of citizens (Figure 2.36). As parents went to parks to show their children what American wilderness looked like and the children did the same with their own, these parks acquired an ever stronger status as monuments in the American collective memory. These monuments have remained isolated and protected but they have also been constantly threatened as the country continues to industrialize. By accepting tourists into the pockets of wilderness, the conservationists planted the seeds for what would become a major national industry – nature tourism. In the 1930s, the federal government under Franklin Delano Roosevelt saw a value in integrating people into conservation landscapes – not only as tourists but as inhabitants. This led to a new model for nature that was played out at a regional scale in the Tennessee Valley but had a national influence. This is the subject of the next chapter.

2.36 "The Lookout" near Bright Angel Trail, Grand Canyon National Park, 1914. Photograph by Herbert J. Cowling.

Notes

1 Julie K. Brown, *Contesting Images, Photography and the World's Columbian Exposition*, Tucson, AZ: University of Arizona Press, 1994, pp. 62–3. Brown continues, "J.K. Hillers played a key role in the photographic section of the survey, dividing his time and work between it and the Bureau of Ethnology, both of which were under the direction of John Wesley Powell."
2 See also Peter Bacon Hales, "American Views and the Romance of Modernization," in Martha A. Sandweiss (ed.), *Photography in Nineteenth Century America*, Ft. Worth and New York: Amon Carter Museum/Harry N. Abrams, 1991, pp. 204–57.
3 Olin D. Wheeler, *Wonderland 1903: Descriptive of the Country Contiguous to the Northern Pacific Railway*, St. Paul, MN: Northern Pacific Railway, 1903, p. 57.
4 In the 1870s the Nez Percé periodically traversed the region, while the Bannock,

Shoshone, and Crow nations lived in the Yellowstone area. (Robert H. Keller and Michael F. Turek, *American Indians and National Parks*, Tucson: University of Arizona Press, 1998.)

5   Susan Sidlauskas, "Contesting Femininity: Vuillard's Family Pictures," *The Art Bulletin* 79, no. 1 (March 1997), p. 91.
6   Horace Albright, *The Birth of the National Park Service: the Founding Years 1913–33*, Salt Lake City: Howe Brothers, 1985.
7   Richard A. Bartlett, *Yellowstone: A Wilderness Besieged*, Tucson: University of Arizona Press, 1989, p. 63.
8   Wheeler, *Wonderland 1903*, p. 39.
9   Alfred Runte, *Trains of Discovery: Western Railroads and National Parks*, New York: Roberts Rinehart, 1990.
10 Bartlett, *Yellowstone*, p. 262. Mrs. Arnold was F. Jay Haynes' daughter, who had married an army officer stationed in the park.
11 John Pitcher quoted in Bartlett, *Yellowstone*, p. 262.
12 James M. Hamilton, *History of Yellowstone National Park (previous to 1895)*, Yellowstone National Park, WY: Yellowstone Library Museum Association, 1964, p. 165.
13 Hamilton, *History of Yellowstone*, p. 165.
14 Bill and Doris Whithorn, *Photo History from Yellowstone Park*, Livingston, MT: Park County News, 1970.
15 Montana Historical Society, *F. Jay Haynes, Photographer*, Helena, MT: Montana Historical Society Press, 1981.
16 B.C. Forbes, *Men Who Are Making the West*, New York: B.C. Forbes Publishing, 1923, p. 333.
17 *The Livingston Enterprise*, 6 February 1931.
18 The Yellowstone Park Hotel Company was organized in the early 1880s and began building at Mammoth Hot Springs, but soon entered bankruptcy and was taken over by the Northern Pacific Railroad. In 1891 another company, the Yellowstone Park Transportation Company, was organized by Silas S. Huntley to operate the transportation facilities throughout the park. Huntley's two partners, Harry Child and Edmund Bach, were family: the wives of Huntley and Child were sisters, and Bach was Child's brother-in-law. Child put up the money for the company and in 1901, when Huntley died unexpectedly, he assumed control. Over the next several years, he also came to control the hotel company, the camping company and the filling stations. In later years, all of Child's operations were combined under one organization, the Yellowstone Park Company. Yellowstone Park Company Papers 1892–1963, K. Ross Toole Archives, No. 20, University of Montana Mansfield Library Collection.
19 Personal interview, cited in Bartlett, *Yellowstone*, p. 175.
20 Richard Bartlett, correspondence with the authors, 5 March 2002.
21 With the inauguration of the "trust-busting" President Theodore Roosevelt in 1900, the large railroad companies began to divest themselves of their subsidiaries, and the Northern Pacific Railroad decided to sell their Yellowstone Park Association to the owners of the Yellowstone Park Transport Company. In late December 1900, Harry Child and Edmund Bach, two of the three Transportation Company owners, met with Charles Mellen, the Northern Pacific president, to begin negotiations to purchase the Association. Information drawn

from A. Berle Clemensen, *Historic Structure Report, Historical Data Section, Old Faithful Inn, Yellowstone National Park*, Denver, CO: Denver Service Center, Historic Preservation Branch, Midwest/Rocky Mountain Team, National Park Service, US Department of Interior, 1982.

22   Anne Farrar Hyde, *An American Vision, Far Western Landscape and National Culture, 1820–1920*, New York: New York University Press, 1990, p. 253.
23   Chronology written in 1970 by Reamer's daughter Jane Reamer White. Personal archives of Richard Bartlett.
24   Telephone interview with T.J. Hallin at his home in Livingstone, Montana. Hallin was a good friend of Reamer and his mother was Child's secretary.
25   Report of the Acting Superintendent of Yellowstone National Park to the Secretary of the Interior, Washington DC: Government Printing Office, 1904.
26   Yellowstone National Park Archives.
27   That the Old Faithful Inn became a major reference for subsequent buildings constructed in western national parks is an argument found in a number of books and articles on the subject, including Hyde, *An American Vision*; James C. Massey and Shirley Maxwell, *Arts and Crafts Design in America*, San Francisco: Archetype Press/Chronicle Books, 1998; Christine Barnes, *Great Lodges of the West*, Bend, OR: W.W. West, 1997; and David Leavengood, "The Mountain Architecture of R.C. Reamer," *Mountain Gazette* 46, 1975. For a discussion of the roots of the "rustic" in eighteenth century Britain, see Mark Leslie Brack, *The Nature of Architecture: the Origins of the Rustic Tradition in Eighteenth-Century British Architecture*, PhD dissertation, UC Berkeley, 1999. For the rustic architecture of the Adirondacks see Harvey H. Kaiser, *Great Camps of the Adirondacks*, Boston: D.R. Godine, 1982.
28   *What Jim Bridger and I Saw in Yellowstone Park* (n.p., 1912–14?), pp. 12–18. Ayer Collection, Newberry Library, Chicago.
29   Andy Stuart, "Win, Place Show," Diary Manuscript File, Acc. File No. 92-49, Yellowstone National Park Archives.
30   Hyde, *An American Vision*, p. 265.
31   "A $200,000 Log Cabin," *Indoors and Out* 4 (May 1907), pp. 73–6.
32   Edith Hewes, "Diary of trip through Yellowstone" (1911), Letters and diaries section, Yellowstone National Park Archives, 10.
33   Richard White, "Frederick Jackson Turner and Buffalo Bill," in James R. Grossman (ed.), *The Frontier in American Culture*, Berkeley: University of California Press, 1994, p. 21.
34   White, "Frederick Jackson Turner and Buffalo Bill," p. 21.
35   Ibid. Also see Harold Robert, *The Log Cabin Myth: a Study of Early Dwellings of the English Colonists in North America*, Cambridge: Harvard University Press, 1939 and Edward Pessen, *The Log Cabin Myth: the Social Backgrounds of the Presidents*, New Haven: Yale University Press, 1984.
36   For retreats near Chicago see Robert Bruegmann, *The Architects and the City: Holabird and Roche of Chicago, 1880–1918*, Chicago: University of Chicago Press, 1996. For retreats near San Francisco see G. William Domhoff, *The Bohemian Grove and Other Retreats: a Study in Ruling-class Cohesiveness*, New York: Harper and Row, 1974.
37   Hyde, *An American Vision*, p. 260.
38   Adrian Forty, "Masculine, Feminine or Neuter?" in Duncan McCorquodale,

Katerina Rüedi and Sarah Wigglesworth (eds), *Desiring Practices: Architecture, Gender and the Interdisciplinary*, London: Black Dog Publishing, 1996, p. 146.
39   Henry van Brunt, "Architecture at the World's Columbian Exposition – IV," *Scribner's Magazine* (1893): 729, 731. Van Brunt was one of the most complementary critics of Hayden's work, far more common were the dismissive comments. "As women's work it 'goes,' of course, … it is simply weak and commonplace." (*The American Architect and Building News* 38, no. 880 (5 November 1892), p. 86. And in the words of a French critic, "of the building constructed by the women [. . .] I will confine myself for the moment to repeating to you, without comment, an epigram I heard at Jackson Park; 'The Women's Building, destined to prove to the world and to America the equality of the two sexes, is a monument erected by female hands to masculine superiority'." Marquis de Chasseloup-Laubat, *The American Architect and Building News* 39, no. 892 (28 January 1893), p. 59.
40   Forty, "Masculine, Feminine or Neuter?" p. 147.
41   Sullivan quoted in Forty, "Masculine, Feminine or Neuter?" p. 148.
42   David Leavengood, "A Sense of Shelter: Robert C. Reamer in Yellowstone National Park," *Pacific Historical Review* 3, 1980, p. 500.
43   Forty places the end of gender metaphors as a common way to talk about architecture at around the mid-1920s, therefore Reamer would have been fully emerged in this way of thinking about design but would have also experienced the beginning of a shift.
44   Pat Kirkham (ed.), *The Gendered Object*, New York: Manchester University Press, 1996.
45   Juliet Kinchin, "Interiors: Nineteenth-Century Essays on the 'Masculine' and the 'Feminine' Room," in Kirkham, *Gendered Object*, p. 26.
46   These anecdotes are related as a part of present-day tours through the Glasgow School of Art.
47   Forty points out that while gendered language has disappeared from contemporary architectural criticism, that does not mean that gender distinctions have ceased to operate. He suggests that the notion of "form," as it is used by most modern architects and critics, is a masculine ideal, and he traces its descent from Heinrich Wölfflin's concept of form in architecture in relation to the (male) body. Forty, "Masculine, Feminine or Neuter?" p. 150.
48   Aubrey L. Haines, *The Yellowstone Story: A History of Our First National Park*, vol. 2, Yellowstone National Park, WY: Yellowstone Library Museum Association, 1977, p. 120.
49   Quoted in Jeffrey Limerick, Nancy Ferguson and Richard Oliver, *America's Grand Resort Hotels*, New York: Pantheon/Random House, 1976, p. 133.
50   Griselda Pollock, *Vision and Difference: Femininity, Feminism and the History of Art*, London: Routledge, 1988.
51   Of course a key reference here is Virginia Woolf, *A Room of One's Own*, London: Hogarth Press, 1929. For contemporary analyses of the importance of travel writing in the nineteenth century, see for example, Alison Blunt and Gillian Rose, *Writing Women and Space: Colonial and Postcolonial Geographies*, London: Guilford Press, 1994 and Caren Kaplan, *Questions of Travel: Postmodern Discourses of Displacement*, London: Duke University Press, 1996.
52   O.S.T. Drake, "A Lady's Trip to the Yellowstone National Park," *Every Girl's*

Annual, London: Hatchard's 1887, p. 346. Yellowstone National Park Archives.
53 Drake, "A Lady's Trip," p. 346.
54 Dorothy Brown Pardo, "Dorothy in Wonderland," (1906 or 1911), Journals and diaries section, Yellowstone National Park Archives, 25. According to Emerson Hough, by 1919, 60 percent of park visitors were women and a large percentage of them traveled unescorted. Emerson Hough, *An Appreciation of Yellowstone National Park*, St. Paul, MN: Northern Pacific Railroad, 1925, p. 26. (Earlier edition published in 1919 as a part of the US Railroad Administration National Park Series.)
55 With a readership of one million people, *Ladies Home Journal* had the largest circulation of any of the Arts and Crafts oriented magazines. *The Craftsman* had a circulation of 15,000 and *House Beautiful* 45,000. Number taken from Massey and Maxwell, *Arts and Crafts Design in America*, San Francisco: Chronicle Books, 1998, p. 11.
56 David Shi, *The Simple Life: Plain Living and High Thinking in American Culture*, New York: Oxford University Press, 1985, p. 192.
57 Christina Simmons, "Modern Sexuality and the Myth of Victorian Repression," in Barbara Melosh (ed.), *Gender and American History*, New York: Routledge, 1992, pp. 20–30.
58 Hyde, *An American Vision*, p. 260. This rustic style had antecedants that have been traced back to Andrew Jackson Downing and his picturesque designs. See Vincent J. Scully, *The Shingle Style and Stick Style: Architecture Theory and Design from Downing to the Origins of Wright*, New Haven: Yale University Press, 1955.
59 Leavengood, "Mountain Architecture of Reamer," p. 7.
60 George Warren Widmayer, Manuscript Section, Acc. File No. 91-134, Yellowstone National Park Archives, 6. The wrought iron door handles, hanging light fixtures and fireplace clock were designed by Reamer and made by blacksmith George Wellington Colpitts.
61 Stickley quoted in Leslie Greene Bowman, *American Arts and Crafts: Virtue in Design. A Catalogue of the Palevsky/Evans Collection and Related Works*, Los Angeles: Los Angeles County Museum of Art, 1990, p. 35.
62 Michael P. Malone, *The Battle for Butte*, Seattle: University of Washington Press, 1981, p. 35.
63 Edwin Dobb, "Pennies from Hell," *Harper's Magazine* (October 1996), p. 40.
64 Samuel Hays, *Conservation and the Gospel of Efficiency: the Progressive Conservation Movement 1890–1920*, Cambridge: Harvard University Press, 1959.
65 Thorstein Veblen, *The Theory of the Leisure Class* (1899), reprinted New York: Dover Publications, 1994.
66 The transformation of the landscape occurred in two ways. First, *in situ*, by being physically transfomed by roads, buildings and railroads. The second influence is *in visu*, mediated through representation. See Alain Corbin, *L'homme dans le paysage*, Paris: Les éditions textuel, 2001.
67 Patricia Trenton, *The Rocky Mountains: A Vision for Artists in Nineteenth Century*, Norman: University of Oklahoma Press, 1983.
68 Victor Turner, *Image and Pilgrimage in Christian Culture: Anthropological Perspectives*, New York: Columbia University Press, 1978.

69 John Sears, *Sacred Places: American Tourist Attractions in the Nineteenth Century*, New York: Oxford University Press, 1989, p. 163.
70 Although Moran's work was exhibited a number of times, only a small percentage of Americans would have seen his paintings. The paintings most turn-of-the-century tourists saw were by Abby Hill. When the Northern Pacific put out a call to exchange travel passes for landscape paintings, women were the first to respond and Hill was one of them. Hired to paint views of Yellowstone in 1905–6, she came to the park with her children and camped out in different areas to get the best views. Her presence in the park became legendary. These paintings were reproduced by the hundreds as posters to be displayed in train stations and travel agencies throughout the country.
71 I would like to thank Richard Bartlett for attracting our attention to Jackson's contribution.
72 Montana Historical Society, *F. Jay Haynes Photographer*, p. 169.
73 Carol Crawshaw and John Urry, "Tourism and the Photographic Eye," in Chris Rojek and John Urry (eds), *Touring Cultures*, London: Routledge, 1977, p. 183.
74 Sears, *Sacred Places*, p. 164.
75 Wheeler, *Wonderland*, p. 34
76 Stephen M. Dale, "Through the Yellowstone on a Coach," *Ladies Home Journal* (August) 1904, p. 5. The Spanish spelling of canyon emphasized the exotic nature of the journey.
77 In 1904, we are talking about a very simple hotel, not the Grand Canyon Hotel designed by Robert Reamer in 1911 (now destroyed).
78 To give a point of comparison, in 1919 a five-day tour including transport, meals and hotel lodging cost $52 for an adult and the same with lodging in tents would cost $43. A ticket for a child cost $39.50 and $21.50 respectively.
79 Cindy S. Aron, *Working at Play, A History of Vacation in the United States*, Oxford: Oxford University Press, 1999, p. 128.
80 Crawshaw and Urry, "Tourism and the Photographic Eye," p. 178.
81 Cabinets of curiosity were antiquarian collections by the European elite.
82 See Roland Barthes, "Structural Analysis of Narratives," *Image-Music-Text*, trans. Stephen Heath, New York: Hill and Wang, 1977. Annmarie Adams suggests that the circular route in English picturesque gardens like Stourhead and Stowe may have functioned as models for continental travel. Such gardens were of course also anti-urban and romantic. Letter by Annmarie Adams to the authors, 12 March 2002.
83 Quoted in Richard Bartlett, *Yellowstone Besieged*, p. 65.
84 Paraphrased from Crawshaw and Urry, "Tourism and the Photographic Eye," p. 178.
85 Marjorie Albertson, "Savage Summers," Yellowstone National Park Archives, Manuscript file Acc. No. 93-104 (no date).
86 An example of the first notion can be found in Dean McCannell, *The Tourist: a New Theory of the Leisure Class*, New York: Schocken, 1976. A later reaction is the influential article by Georges van den Abbeele, "Sightseers: the tourist as theorist," *Diacritics* (December 1980) and subsequent field studies by John Urry published as *The Tourist Gaze: Leisure and Travel in Contemporary Societies*, London: Sage Publications, 1990.

87 Letter by Aliene E. Tieche, no date, letters and diaries section, Yellowstone National Park Archives, 2.
88 Quoted in Crawshaw and Urry, "Tourism and the Photographic Eye," p. 183.
89 Letter from the Department of the Interior, 25 November 1902. Yellowstone National Park Archives Item No. 5089.
90 Edward H. Moorman, *Journal of Years of Work Spent in Yellowstone National Park, 1899–1948*, 2 vols, Yellowstone National Park Archives.
91 Letter from acting secretary Mr Hoslyan, Department of the Interior, Washington DC, 21 September 1905. Yellowstone National Park Archives, Letter Box 21, Item No. 5572.
92 Letter from the Department of Commerce and Labor, Bureau of Fisheries, 10 September 1906. Yellowstone Park Archives, Item No. 5924.
93 Letter from the Department of Agriculture, Office of the Secretary, Washington DC, 13 April 1903. Yellowstone Park Archives, Item No. 5076.
94 Letter requesting authorization to purchase ten tons of hay to feed sheep ranging in the park, Yellowstone Park Archives, 17 December 1902, Item No. 5109.
95 Albertson, "Savage Summers," p. 8.
96 Albertson, "Savage Summers," p. 12.
97 Much of this increase can be attributed to the popularity of the car. Automobile traffic was permitted into Yellowstone National Park in 1913.
98 Albright, *The Birth of the National Park Service*, p. 94.
99 Albright, *Birth of the National Park Service*, p. 139.
100 See Keller and Turek, *American Indians and National Parks*.
101 John Ise, *Our National Park Policy, A Critical History*, Baltimore: John Hopkins Press, 1961, p. 201.
102 Linda Flint McClelland, *Building the National Parks, Historic Landscape Design and Construction*, Baltimore: John Hopkins University Press, 1988, p. 3. "The hotel was slated for demolition in 1959 but mysteriously burned in 1960." Barnes, *Great Lodges of the West*, p. 20.
103 Albright, *Birth of the National Park Service*, p. 39.
104 Keller Easterling, *Organization of Space: Landscapes, Highways, and Houses in America*, Cambridge, MA: MIT Press, 1999, p. 86.
105 *Livingstone Enterprise*, "Prominent Men Express Regret When Informed of Death of Harry W. Child, Pioneer Montana Businessman, Was Known over Entire Nation," 7 February 1931, p. 3.
106 A key figure in the use of naturalistic effects in parkways was Samuel Parsons, superintendent of New York City's Central Park for many years. See McClelland, *Building*, p. 3.
107 Easterling, *Organization of Space*, p. 76.
108 Cindy S. Aron, *Working at Play: A History of Vacations in the United States*, Oxford: Oxford University Press, 1999, p. 175.
109 This is not to say that upper class men actually practiced these skills. Aron describes a number of instances when the ladies' maids are the only ones who know how to fish for trout, cook on an open fire, or find a camping spot free of insects.
110 Aron, *Working at Play*, p. 171.
111 Camping was certainly an empowering experience for many women, not just ladies

of the high society. This should be seen within a larger discussion (that cannot occur here) of women and wilderness in the west. See Glenda Riley, *Women and Nature Saving the Wild West*, Lincoln: University of Nebraska, 1999.
112 Emily Post quoted in Drake Hokanson, *The Lincoln Highway: Main Street Across America*, Iowa City: University of Iowa Press, 1988, p. 30.
113 Mather quoted in Regula Campbell, "Grand Hotels in National Parks," *Arts & Architecture* 1, no. 4 (1982), p. 32.
114 J.H. Raftery, *A Miracle in Hotel Building, The Dramatic Story of the Building of the New Cañon Hotel in Yellowstone Park*, Wyoming: Yellowstone Park Company, n.d., p. 7.
115 Albert H. Good, *Park and Recreation Structures, Part I: Administration and Basic Service Facilities*, Washington DC: US Department of the Interior, National Park Service, 1938, p. 21 (our italics).
116 In the 1920s and 1930s, as the aesthetic of park architecture was developing, it fit squarely within emerging modernist predilections among young park architects for honesty in craft and materials, regional character and so forth. Similar work was carried out by Frank Lloyd Wright ("Prairie Style"), Irving Gill in San Diego and Bernard Maybeck in the San Francisco Bay area. In the post-war period, however, regional architecture was tarred with the brush of historicism and young architects favored the uninflected "International Style" and mass production. The Park Service followed suit, resulting in some disappointing additions to the national parks. See William Tweed, *National Park Service Rustic Architecture: 1916–1942*, National Park Service Western Regional Office, Division of Cultural Resource Management, 1977 and McClelland, *Building the National Parks*.
117 Martha Weigle and Peter White, *The Lore of New Mexico*, Albuquerque: University of New Mexico Press, 1988, p. 57.
118 Virginia L. Grattan, *Mary Colter: Builder Upon the Red Earth*, Flagstaff, AZ: Northland Press, 1980, p. 15. Also see Barbara J. Morehouse, *A Place Called Grand Canyon, Contested Geographies*, Tucson: University of Arizona Press, 1996.
119 In the popular imagination at the turn of the century, the ancient ruins at Mesa Verde in Colorado and the inhabited settlements of the Hopi were often conflated. The "Cliff Dwellers" exhibit at the 1893 Chicago Exposition was near the "Ruins of Yucatan" adjacent to the Anthropology Building on the southern edge of the Expo grounds. Also, Henry Blake Fuller's popular novel *The Cliff Dwellers* metaphorically aligned the settlements of "savages" to the new wilderness of Chicago skyscrapers. Henry B. Fuller, *The Cliff Dwellers, a novel*, New York: Harper and Brothers, 1893.
120 Grattan, *Mary Colter*, p. 19.
121 Grattan, *Mary Colter*, p. 19.
122 Quoted in Keller, *American Indians*, p. 80.
123 Grattan, *Mary Colter*, p. 69.
124 Grattan, *Mary Colter*, p. 78.
125 "Claude Lorrain, a seventeenth century French landscape painter, had invented the device, which consisted of a sheet of black glass hinged to a window frame like a shutter. The glass could be moved back and forth to reflect different views; the black mirror reduced the intensity of the daylight and decreased eye-

strain. In the dark glass, the colors of the canyon appeared more vivid, and since the glass reflected only a small portion of the panorama, one could enjoy the beauty of the canyon a segment at a time." Grattan, *Mary Colter*, p. 78.
126 Grattan, *Mary Colter*, p. 80.
127 Keller and Turek, *American Indians*, p. 154.
128 Susan Buck-Morss, *The Dialectics of Seeing: Walter Benjamin and the Arcades Project*, Cambridge, MA: MIT Press, 1989, p. 159.
129 Keller and Turek, *American Indians*, p. 57.
130 Keller and Turek, *American Indians*, p. 178.
131 Keller and Turek, *American Indians*, p. xiii.
132 Keller and Turek, *American Indians*, p. xiv.
133 Ibid.
134 Sears, *Sacred Places*.

3.1 Norris Dam in its "natural" setting.

Chapter 3
Putting nature to work with the Tennessee Valley Authority, 1933

It took a lot of men and machines to rebuild the Tennessee Valley. This vast area of eroded hillsides and exhausted land, stretching from the Blue Ridge Mountains of Tennessee to the flat lands of Alabama, had suffered years of rapacious forestry and over-farming over the course of the nineteenth century. But in ten short years, from 1933 to 1943, in the midst of the Great Depression, 40,000 square miles of worn out land in seven southern states were replanted with trees and seeded with demonstration farms, nurseries and fish hatcheries. Seven mainstream and eleven tributary hydroelectric dams were built, turning 650 miles of wild river into stillwater lakes.[1] Transmission wires were stretched far beyond the reach of the river, to carry electricity – or as the farmers of the time called it, "light" – to the farms and households of one of the most rural regions of the United States. Tens of thousands of people were moved off low-lying farms and resettled into existing towns and new model communities. Navigable waterways allowed goods to circulate up and down the river. New "freeways" threading through the valley brought in visitors to witness the incredible transformation of a devastated land into a productive modern landscape.

This frenzy of activity was the result of an initiative called the Tennessee Valley Authority (TVA). Established by the United States government in 1933 as a project of dam building and power generation, by the eve of World War II the TVA had expanded, in the words of President Franklin Roosevelt, to touch "all manners of human concerns."[2] As the first and most ambitious project of the New Deal, the TVA attracted conservationists, agronomists, nutrition specialists, social theorists, public policy lawyers, planners, engineers and architects, who leapt at the opportunity to put their own visions into practice. Looking back at the early years of the TVA, we cannot help but feel their excitement at trying out such ambitious and experimental plans on a scale unparalleled before or since. It had its contradictions, to be sure: it was a centralized planning effort, directed by the federal government in Washington, that declared itself an example of "grass-roots democracy," and while its driving aim in the early years was to re-establish a "natural" equilibrium in the region, it ultimately became a center for wartime atomic research and a significant producer of nuclear power. But even with all its flaws and contradictions, the TVA offers to us the legacy of a regional plan that envisioned modern technology, water, land, plants, animals and people as part of one interdependent and productive landscape. So we ask ourselves how was this new and daring vision expressed in the architecture of the new towns, hydroelectric dams, and the landscape architecture of public parks and motorways? In other words, how was such a project made visible in the landscapes of the Tennessee River?

At its core, the TVA was a conservation project. It built on the work of early twentieth century conservationists such as Gifford Pinchot, who linked flood control to reforestation and advocated the "scientific" management of government lands so they would yield lumber and minerals over the long term. For scientific conservationists, nature was not seen as a place of recreation and leisure as, for example, in the national parks such as Yellowstone, but as a natural resource to be productively managed under the supervision of government. In the Tennessee Valley settlements and industry had taken their toll on the landscape and people, leaving marginal farms, eroded hillsides and a river prone to floods. This presented a sorry contrast to the image Americans had of their country as a prosperous agricultural nation. The TVA aimed to harness the river with dams, contain its floodwaters and generate electricity to modernize the region. It sought to set up model towns, farms and industries that could be sustained in a system of flows and would ensure an optimal use of the valley's natural resources over the long term, while enabling its people to live much as they always had, on farms and in small towns. Perhaps the best description of the radical transformation of the Tennessee Valley can be found in the words of one of the planners, when he said the valley had become "one unified machine, one organic whole."[3] Linked by the Tennessee River into one interconnected system, the entire valley – its farms and forests, hamlets and towns, dams and industries, spaces of recreation and leisure – had begun to work together as one "organic machine" (see Figure 3.2).[4]

It all began in January 1933, when the newly elected President Franklin Roosevelt faced a nation that was suffering from four years of agricultural, industrial and financial collapse, known to us as the Great Depression. Even before his inauguration, Roosevelt was hard at work planning initiatives that would lead the way to a national recovery. En route to his winter home in Warm Springs, Georgia, Roosevelt stopped at Wilson Dam on the Tennessee River. This site had been the topic of heated debate in Congress ever since its construction in 1915 as a dam and munitions plant for the First World War. Senator George Norris, "the fighting liberal," had argued for 11 years that the dam and the power that it produced should be managed as a public utility and not sold to a private industry or power corporation. The President-elect expanded on Norris's program for public ownership of the power produced at the dam. He suggested that 200,000 men could be put to work on similar hydroelectric projects up and down the Tennessee River, with up to 70,000 working on reforestation. He foresaw long-distance transmission wires carrying hydroelectric power from the dams to decentralized industries, which in

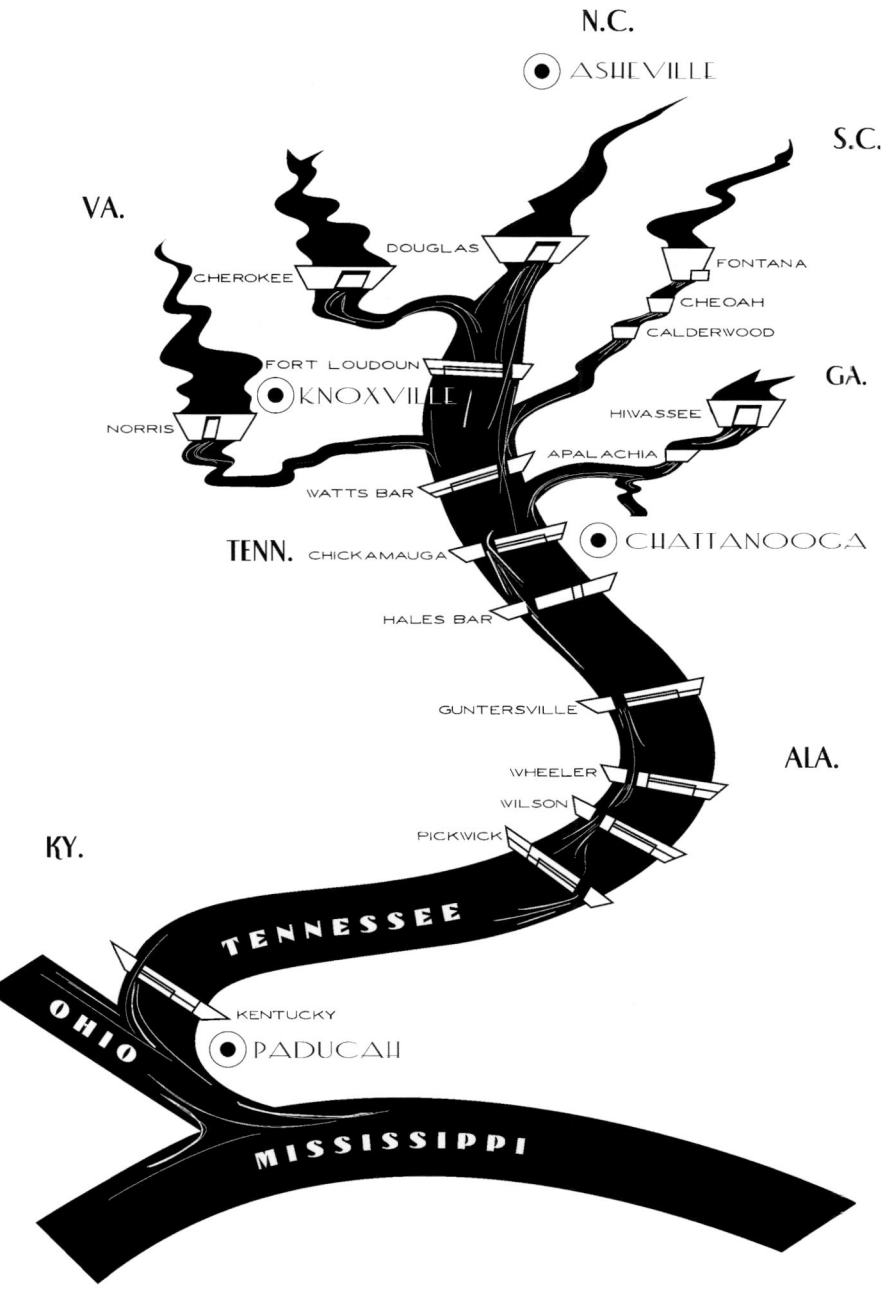

3.2 Diagram of TVA water control system.

turn would contribute to employment in all the rural communities of Appalachia.[5] Passed by Congress within its mandate of regulating interstate commerce, George Norris's TVA Act focused narrowly on flood control, inland navigation and hydroelectric power. But as Roosevelt put his support behind Norris's bill, the TVA became inseparably linked to a much grander vision that became a symbol for national regeneration.[6] As one of the first initiatives of Roosevelt's "Hundred Days" in office, the TVA became the prime example of how planning could heal a nation in crisis. The TVA found its place among other New Deal initiatives that represented an all-encompassing scheme for relief and economic recovery. These included the Federal Emergency Relief Administration, which distributed relief monies; the Resettlement Administration and Subsistence Homestead Act, which built model greenbelt towns and homestead communities; the Works Progress Administration and Civilian Conservation Corps, which employed out-of-work city dwellers on projects that benefited the public realm; the Rural Electrification Administration, which brought electricity to isolated rural areas; and the Public Work Administration, which built the infrastructure for an expanding government.[7]

Despite all these initiatives, the economic effects of the Great Depression in the Tennessee River basin and in rural Appalachia made the ambitious vision of the TVA even more difficult to realize. One of the most striking achievements of the TVA, at least in its early years, was its ability to effectively mold public opinion in its favor. The hyperbole found throughout the early press coverage of the TVA, generated to a good degree by the authority itself and handed over to the press, was a key factor in garnering public support, justifying expenditure to Congress and countering conservative critics who felt that government was unnecessarily expanding into realms better left to the private sector. The TVA leadership recognized that if the project were to be understood and adopted by the public as a model for national regeneration, it had to rework the fundamental myths Americans held about their relationship to nature. In the TVA, we see the American myths of the frontiersman and the farmer layered onto governmental discourses of conservation and regional planning. For example, while visiting the authority's first construction site in November of 1934, Roosevelt evoked the frontier metaphor in supporting the new project:

> I have called those of us that are here today the pioneers of 1934. The accustomed order of our formerly established lives does not suffice to meet the perils and the problems which today we are compelled to face. Mere survival calls for new pioneering on our part.[8]

Henry Wallace, Roosevelt's farm expert, went even further in explaining what the "new pioneering" would require. "The keynote of the new frontier is cooperation," he said, "just as that of the old frontier was individualistic competition."⁹ In these statements, both Roosevelt and Wallace are trying to build support for regional planning and the orchestrated management of natural resources, while suggesting that this seemingly tedious task might share in the romance of the frontier. They both stress that individualism and competition have become a thing of the past. The scientific management of natural resources would supplant the frontier heritage of farming and mining for short-term gain – and it would do so with gusto. For example, Charles Krutch, who later became a director of the authority, reminisced about the pioneering spirit the young agency evoked for him:

> It wasn't merely an agency created by an Act of Congress that was at work here. It was the genius of a nation. But the genius was being expressed in new forms, here in the Valley. It was like seeing the pioneers cutting down trees in New England and Ohio. It was like watching the first plows moving across the unbroken land of Kansas. It was like coming on the first wagons moving over the South Pass. It was like history. It was like epic poetry. It was like music.¹⁰

While they were cloaking their enterprise in the myth of the frontier, the TVA was critical of what the frontier had actually wrought in the Tennessee Valley. In the words of David Lilienthal, one of the authority's first directors, "Here is a tale of fields grown old and barren with the years . . . ; of forests that were hacked and despoiled."¹¹ The popular press, such as this caricature from the *Atlanta Constitution* of 1935, picked up the idea that the people of the Tennessee Valley were now paying the bill for the exploitative practices of earlier frontiersmen (Figure 3.3). Where Daniel Boone and Davy Crockett had once "blazed the way into wilderness for civilization to follow," the frontier had come full circle, its promise, mind, reaped and hewn. What was once a "promised land" now held little more than eroded homesteads and tired people. As Harold Ickes, Roosevelt's Secretary of the Interior, said, "We venerate our ancestors and they never planned. When they cut down one forest, they moved onto the next. When they exhausted one farm, there was always another one a little further on. Like I said, they never planned. They were satisfied to exploit" (see Figure 3.4).¹² If the frontier as glorified by Frederick Jackson Turner was the metaphor *par excellence* for the expansionism of the 1890s, the Arcadian farmer and a landscape in equilibrium represented the New Dealer's ideal for American life.

The TVA was conceived as an experiment in implementing this new vision of the American landscape. Its watchword was regional planning – planning a landscape and managing its resources – to establish an equilibrium between people and nature. This went beyond conservation, although TVA shared some aspects of the earlier conservation movement, such as the integrated management of natural resources and the establishment of a common, nationally-defined good above individual or corporate self-interest. But where

3.3 "Paying the Penalty." Political cartoon, 1935.

the conservation movement under the influence of Gifford Pinchot had looked to manage the largely undeveloped lands of the west, putting them aside or wisely using their resources, the TVA had as its domain a landscape long since settled. If a new Arcadia were to be established, it was going to be a peopled landscape. As Walter Creese puts it, "what was so daring about the TVA . . . was the persuasion that human beings rightfully belonged in the midst of their reconditioned earth."[13]

3.4 Area devasted by logging, Great Smoky Mountains.

The farmer was a central figure in this renewed landscape. It was the farmer that was among the first to suffer from the Depression, his markets failing and his banker foreclosing, but the farmer would also be the first to benefit from the TVA. The mythic figure of the farmer on the frontier, working the land that he has laboriously cleared and cultivated, has reappeared periodically in the national imagination over the century – most recently, in the back-to-the-land movement of the 1960s. The early years of the New Deal were one such time, and we find the importance of the farmer very much recognized, especially in the speeches of Roosevelt:

> In all our plans we are guided and will continue to be guided by the fundamental belief that the American farmer, living on his own land, remains our ideal of self-reliance and spiritual balance – the source from which the reservoirs of the nation's strength are constantly renewed.[14]

That people could, or should, return to the land was an appealing proposition for a President confronting unprecedented levels of unemployment, food lines in urban centers and emergency relief. But the Jeffersonian ideal of self-reliant farmers dispersed over the landscape needed to be reworked for the modern, technological era. For it to contribute to a more productive nation, the landscape of small-scale farms had to be integrated into a cycle of flows – of energy, goods, and commerce – which extended beyond regional boundaries.[15] The attempt of the TVA to reconcile the myth of the farmer with the imperative of modernization may well come closest to an American version of socialism. It is indebted to earlier efforts in rural collectivism and co-operation, such as the Grange and Social Credit movements, yet as a government initiative, the TVA was not a grass roots organization in any sense.[16] As we will later see, the careful grafting of American myths onto a progressive agenda limited the possibilities for social change as much as it served to implement the project.

Ultimately, the TVA created a myth of its own – that nature could be regenerated through human endeavor. The scientific view of the river and its watershed as an interrelated whole led inexorably to a new way of planning in which nature, technology, and people had to be considered and accommodated. It is this trilogy of technology, people and nature that is significant for us here. Nature set the parameters for the scope of the project; from the beginning the TVA realized that the unit of planning would be set by the Tennessee watershed. Technology, in the forms of dams and highways, could be designed to fit in seamlessly with the surrounding landscape. Working the valves and conduits of a system of flows, technology enabled nature itself to create the power that would help people work the land more effectively with irrigation pumps, milking machines or incubators. And the people of the valley would have a place in this renewed natural environment. The new Arcadia would reunite people and technology with nature. The success of the project would be measured in inches of topsoil regained, the number of cows milked, the number of trees planted. Even the advances in industry, such as the tonnage passing through the locks and the kilowatts generated by the dams, were measured in terms of men employed or farming families aided in their efforts.

TECHNOLOGY

Pioneer and farmer		Industrial power
PAST ———————	TENNESSEE VALLEY	——————— FUTURE
Damaged frontier		"Heavenly Valley"

NATURE

We have focused our analysis on the first TVA project because it was the most ambitious in scope and also the most complete realization of the overall plan. In Norris, all of the essential elements of the Tennessee Valley Authority idea come together, allowing us to investigate the relationships between technology, people and nature in each aspect of the project, from the technology of the dam and the architecture of the town to the landscape that connects and surrounds them. In later dams, power generation assumes greater prominence and the town planning efforts are abandoned, victims of disagreements among the TVA directors and the pressure of the war efforts. But in Norris, each of the built components – the dam, town, freeway, and park – was designed to be an interrelated part of a unified plan for the valley.

Norris Dam, a modernist jewel set in the rolling uplands of Tennessee, modulated the erratic flow of the river for the benefit of the larger system. One node in what would soon include many others, it was linked to other systems of flow by electric transmission wires, the river and the roadway. Between these nodes and networks, the once scarred land resprouted with dairy cattle fattening on contoured hillsides, newly planted forests caught rain and anchored topsoil to the ground, and schools of fish were seeded in the "stillwater lakes." Sprouting up out of the rolling hills, the new rustic-looking houses of Norris Town were designed to house people displaced from farms flooded under the rising waters. The sinuous ribbon of Norris freeway, winding through the countryside, completed the transformation of the reconstructed valley as a "scenic resource," allowing goods and people to circulate through the very heart of the "organic machine" and learn about their renewed place on Earth.

The architecture of the TVA – the dams, houses and designed landscapes of parks and freeways – presents to us the many facets of a new relationship to nature, a relationship that does not set modern technology in opposition to conservation, but that integrates it fully in its vision of renewal. Because the hydroelectric dam is where it all started, let us now turn our attention to Norris Dam.

A TECHNOLOGICAL SUBLIME: THE MACHINE NATURALIZED

Norris was the first dam built by the TVA. It stood on the Clinch River, one of the headwaters of the Tennessee. But before the waters even began to rise behind it, construction had already begun further downstream, on Wheeler Dam, then Guntersville, and Pickwick, and Chickamauga, "a series of great barriers that eventually will transform the Tennessee into a series of freshwater pools, locks and dams, regulated and controlled, down 650 miles to Paducah," where the Tennessee River meets the Ohio before it merges into the Mississippi.[17] The main river dams were long, low structures, stretching across the valley lowlands and fitted with locks for river traffic and bridges for cars to cross the waterway. The upstream, or tributary, dams like Norris were dramatic and lofty structures in mountainous territory, serving to hold back floodwaters and generate electricity. To reach Norris Dam, you leave Knoxville on a winding road that takes you into the rolling farms and fields of the Tennessee Valley. The curving road hugs the Clinch River and gradually the river valley narrows as you begin to ascend a gorge. Around a bend, the view begins to open up and you come, suddenly, upon the downstream face of the dam:

> you see the flat implacable slab of its downstream face growing larger and more impressive as you approach, until finally you are overwhelmed by the sheer architectonic scale.... You park your car and re-submit yourself to those mighty architectural forces.[18]

The dams are as impressive today as they were when Frederick Gutheim wrote these words for *Magazine of Art* in 1940 (Figure 3.5). He, like many other first-time visitors to the TVA dams, felt that he was "in the presence of the most impressive symbol of ultimate force the age has produced."[19]

3.5 Close-up view of Norris Dam.

For Gutheim, as for many others visiting in the 1930s, Norris Dam was a manifestation of the technological sublime. This term has been used by David Nye to explain that Americans viewed their technological achievements as if they were spectacular natural landscapes.[20] Leo Marx first coined the term in his classic *Machine in the Garden*, where he charts out a shift in American views on the relationship between technology and nature. While in the eighteenth century they still saw technology as a defacement of nature, by the nineteenth century they began to see it as a "mechanized sublime."[21] From Walt Whitman to Hart Crane, American men of letters praised the technological works of the young country, marveled at their ability to transform nature and saw in them proof of national greatness, much as the giant sequoias or the monumental landscapes of the west served as premonitions of a national destiny. Since their first appearance at the turn of the century, hydroelectric projects were seen as awesome constructions, testimonials to the power of concentrated human effort that could harness mighty natural forces. A critic wrote enthusiastically in 1929 of the "feeling of grandeur and of poetry and of beauty in the orderly assembly of this modern, efficient and economical equipment."[22] Henry Adams saw the central feature of the electric power plant – the dynamo – as an "overwhelming force" that captivated all who experienced it (see Figure 3.6).[23]

Yet while critics of the early twentieth century may have been willing to revel in the new technologies of turbine and dynamo, the dams built in the first years of the twentieth century still employed nineteenth century techniques of architectural ornamentation for their exteriors. Lewis Mumford, writing in the 1930s, felt that new technologies were being forced into the ill-fitting clothes of older ones. As carriage roads became motorways and modern industries sited themselves cheek by jowl with older ones, he lamented that the "habits and life" of the older forms of technology still prevailed, even though the machines of the new had arrived.[24] His *Technics and Civilization* of 1933 was a call for planners and architects to bring present-day practices and patterns of living into the new, "neotechnic," era. The question for designers was what would these new forms look like? In the newly formed TVA, this question was hotly debated.

The making of Norris Dam

The director in charge of the TVA building program, Arthur E. Morgan, had made his name as the creative engineer of the Miami River Conservancy Project, a series of earth dams for the unpredictable Miami River in Ohio that were designed to hold back waters in times of flood but otherwise leave the intensively-farmed land undisturbed. In asking him to head up the new authority, Franklin Roosevelt recognized Morgan's ability to integrate such giant water projects into a densely settled landscape.[25] Yet the first dam design put forward by the newly-formed TVA did not reflect Morgan's reputation for innovative engineering. Under pressure to begin work on Norris

3.6 The visitors' gallery at Boulder Dam.

Dam immediately, Morgan adopted a scheme that had been drawn up a number of years earlier by the Army Corps of Engineers for the site on the Clinch River. In engineering terms, this design was already dated by 1930; it was a gravity structure that used the sheer weight of the concrete to retain the water. Its architectural treatment was also traditional. Like Wilson Dam further downstream and the Aluminum Company of America dams in the foothills of the Smoky Mountains, the Corps of Engineers' design used classical motifs on the crest of the dam and the powerhouse to lend a measure of dignity and civic purpose to this otherwise utilitarian structure. In other words, the design that looked as if it were to be pressed into service as the inaugural project of the TVA embodied everything that Mumford had feared. Far from breaking new ground as an example of modern thinking, it perpetuated outdated aesthetic and engineering formulas (Figure 3.7).

The TVA, however, had attracted the best and most idealistic young men of a new generation, men who were fired up with the promise of contributing to a project that would have unprecedented scope and influence. Like Mumford, they wanted to put into practice the most modern ideas and

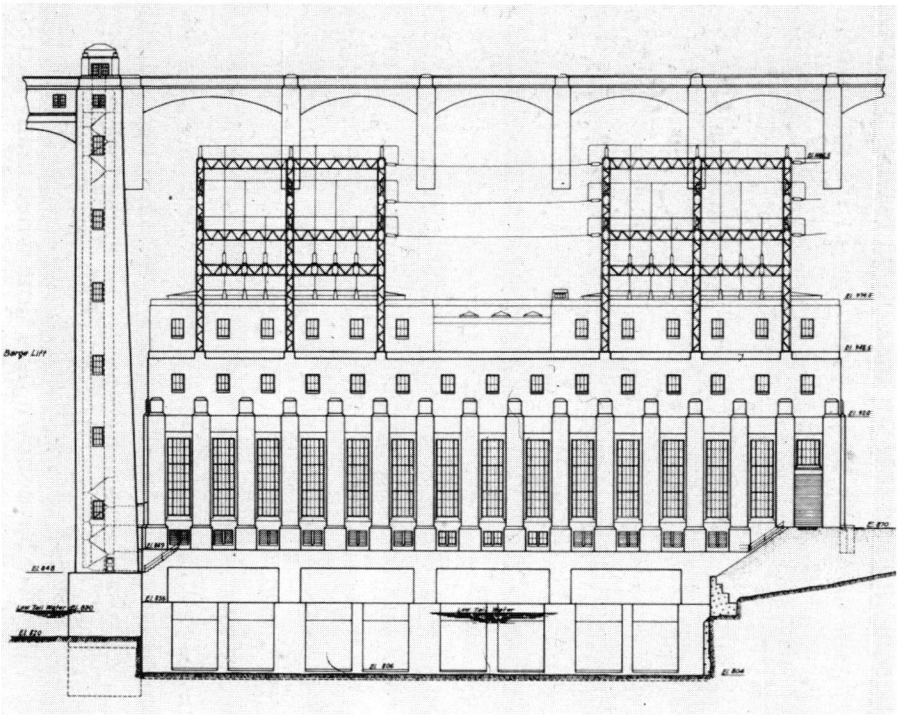

3.7 Detail, Clinch River Dam. Design by Army Corps of Engineers.

indeed most of the young architects in the TVA's land planning and design division, responsible for the design of Norris Town, were advocates of the modern movement in architecture. The head of the architecture section, a young Hungarian named Roland Wank, was perhaps the most fervent and certainly the most outspoken advocate of modernism in the group. While working for the New York firm of Fellheimer and Wagner, Wank had designed low-cost workers' housing in Manhattan and been the lead designer on the streamlined Union Station in Cincinnati. Hired by the TVA in October 1933, he was assigned to work in the housing division, planning Norris township. His modernist convictions led him on a collision course with his supervisor, the regional planner Earle S. Draper.[26]

An interview with Wank in December 1933 shows him excited about the possibilities for entirely rethinking how people should live in the new town, and suggests his frustration with the traditional, "folksy" housing styles advocated by his superior.[27] The day after the interview was published in the *Knoxville News Sentinel*, Wank wrote a fourteen-page letter to chairman A.E. Morgan, setting out his vision for what the TVA should be. Describing the TVA staff as "bearers of the torch," he argued that mass production of prefabricated housing was the appropriate architectural solution to the social renewal promised by the new authority.[28] Although Draper resisted Wank's agitation for "modernistic" designs for the houses in Norris, Wank's objections to the classically ornamented dam design (that had circulated from the engineering division over to land planning) came to the attention of Chairman Morgan.[29] Morgan responded by asking this young and energetic architect to draw up his suggestions for how he felt the dam should look. Wank recomposed the elements of the downstream face of the dam, pulling the building volumes closer together, studying their proportional relationships and removing all ornament. He rearranged the spillway so the water overflow would cascade down the steepest face of the dam, rather than flow gradually down the adjacent hillside. The sheer wall of the dam was emphasized and its junction with the adjacent rock hillside was made more visible. The result was a composition sculpted as a whole ensemble, as if from a solid block of concrete (see Figures 3.8 and 3.9).[30]

When the chief engineer objected to this interference, Morgan referred the matter to Albert Kahn who, as the designer of Ford's River Rouge plant, had gained the respect of both architects and engineers at that time. Kahn preferred Wank's composition to the Army Corps design, and consequently Morgan decided that all issues of overall composition, external appearances and siting would be sketched by architects before being developed by the engineers. This anecdote reveals the importance placed within the TVA on the artistic composition of these dams, and on the centrality of architectural modernism to the public image of these structures.[31]

It is important not to see this simply as a case of a lone modernist pushing his ideas through the resistance of backward-thinking people.

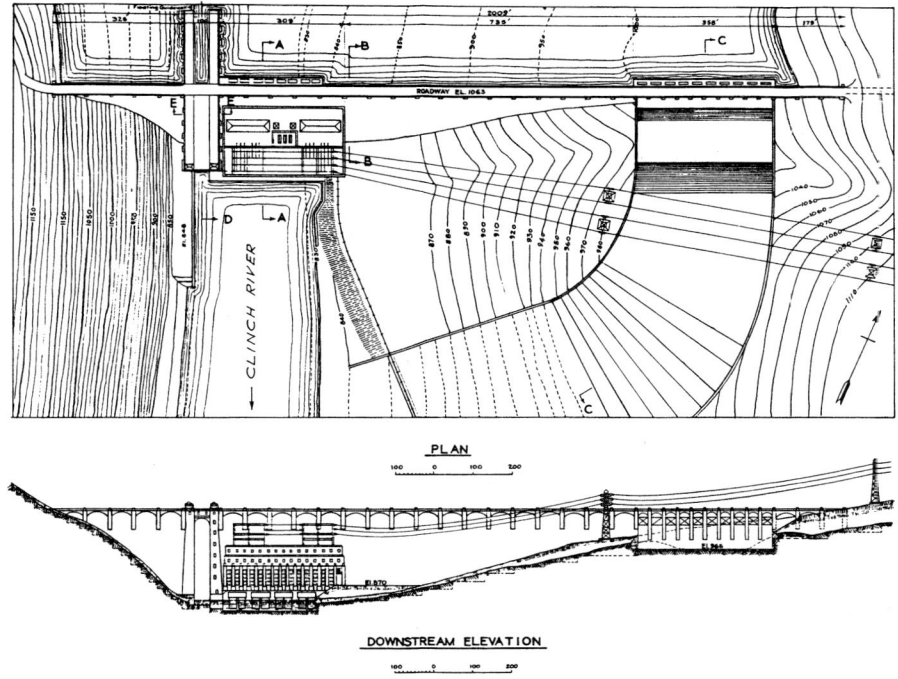

3.8 Clinch River Dam. Design by Army Corps of Engineers.

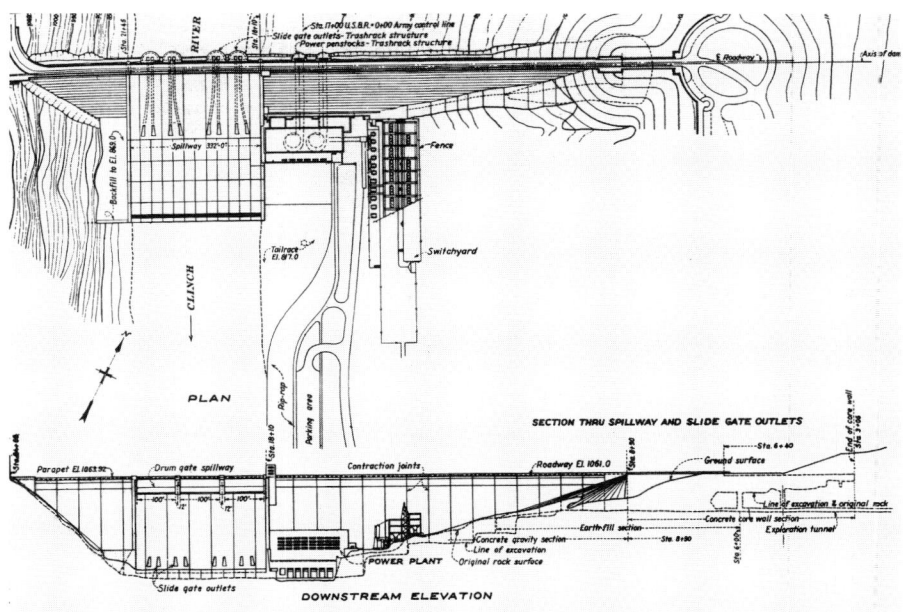

3.9 Revised design for a dam on the Clinch River (Norris Dam).

Morgan, like the other directors, recognized the strategic role that design would play in promoting the public profile of the project. Departing from the usual practice, in which architects worked under the project engineer and were restricted to decorating and detailing ancillary buildings, Morgan set up an architectural design group answerable directly to him, which was empowered to rearrange the project components, as long as their proposals didn't interfere with the functioning of the dam. The architects were also given primary responsibility for designing the visible details of the project. Wank headed this group. He continued to approach the directors – first Morgan and later David Lilienthal – directly with architectural issues he felt strongly about, a practice that irritated his supervisor Earle Draper to no end.[32] In short, as Reyner Banham suggests, this incident set a precedent for the primacy of design issues in the project.[33]

An American modernism

The TVA opted for the modern aesthetic in the dams. What did they expect to gain from this? Recognizing that in the early years the TVA was as much an "architecture of public relations" as the producer of concrete benefits, the TVA directors sensed that the modernist aesthetic might be the most appropriate style for constructions that were to usher in a new age.[34] Certainly the clean smooth lines of Boulder Dam, well captured by photographers of the time, had caught the attention of the public in the Depression years. Hundreds of thousands of visitors had made the trek to that remote location, en route to Los Angeles or the Grand Canyon (Figure 3.10).

To understand the importance of modernism in this American project, we cannot ignore the discussions of the architectural avant-garde during this period. And this avant-garde was in Europe. While the Europeans looked to America for exciting examples of new building forms and technologies, such as the skyscraper, the steel frame, suspension bridge and concrete grain silos, they were highly conscious that they were appropriating these "anonymous" American constructions and turning them into "modern architecture" (see Figure 3.11). As grain elevators from Buffalo and skyscrapers from Chicago were reproduced and admired in European architectural circles, Le Corbusier, like Walter Gropius, doubted that the Americans had the discernment to appreciate what they had invented – proof of this was to be found in the fact that American architects were still dressing their innovative constructions in the outdated fashions of Europe. In his *Vers une Architecture*, Le Corbusier warns, "Let us believe the words of the American engineers, but let us beware the American architects!"[35]

The TVA dams therefore represented a moment when American architects and critics reclaimed modernism as an indigenous invention. Lewis Mumford, writing a review of the Museum of Modern Art's 1941 show, drove this home when he said, "in these dams and power stations the largely unconscious precedents of our grain elevators ... and coal bins reach the

153 | Putting nature to work

3.10 View of Boulder Dam. Photograph by Ansel Adams.

final mark of a conscious aesthetic expression."[36] Mumford's attempt to wrest back American "ownership" of modern architecture was directed toward a small audience, one knowledgeable about architecture and conversant with the latest trends. Yet the modern aesthetic in the TVA appealed to a much wider audience as well – and, we would argue, contributed to the huge media success of the dams. One must keep in mind that the architectural coverage, although quite substantial once it took off in 1939, was just a small fraction of the coverage the dams received in the popular press. The TVA dams became tourist destinations and they were covered in documentaries and international newsreels.[37] As heads of state toured the Tennessee Valley, the dams became models for hydroelectric projects in Iran and India, Europe and China. It seems the directors' gamble in supporting a modern aesthetic for the dams paid off handsomely in capturing the public imagination and garnering support for the young authority.

Architectural modernism seemed to enhance the quality of the dam as a technological marvel while it also helped to knit the dam into its natural setting. Stripped of architectural ornament, the dam could more easily be

3.11 Grain silos.

read as a natural wonder. Geoffrey Baker, writing for the *New York Times*, recognized that the stripped-down functional aesthetic expressed the powerful natural forces contained within the dam, "the Tennessee River ... sets the scale and even dictates the forms. The force of flowing water ... has determined these clean shapes," as if the river itself had carved the face of the dam.[38] In this way, the modernist dam appeared to fit into its natural surroundings, as if it were grafted onto a landscape of valley and forest:

> The entire area [is] so homogeneously treated that there could be no reason for confining the term "architecture" to the one part where the materials used happened to be concrete and steel instead of soil, trees, water surfaces, or rock. Here all the elements conveyed the same theme – of nature tended and controlled so as to yield nourishment, power, and enjoyment all together (see Figure 3.12).[39]

The scar in the rocky outcropping behind Norris Dam, the result of mining the aggregate used in the dam's construction, was carefully sculpted into a boat landing to serve the flooded reservoir. Hills that were cut to make clear-

3.12 Aerial view of Norris Dam.

ance for the dam were contoured and reforested as if gently framing the giant project. The spillway at the center of the dam, designed only for the emergency release of floodwater (because it would circumvent the turbines and generate no electricity), was frequently photographed in use to show the dam as a spectacular waterfall.

In its doctrine of functionalism, modernism expressed not only the flow of water through the dam (see Figure 3.13)[40] but also embraced the flow of people through the buildings and explored how people might see and feel the functioning of the dam.

> From the conception of the scheme to its final execution you feel that each decision has been made in the light of the fact that the public would come, look, and judge by what it saw....[40] There were almost as many problems with people as there were with water pressures and flow in these buildings. They had to be so designed that the thousands of visitors could be welcomed, directed, and shown easily through the powerhouses and around the dams with no interruption of the efficient working of the entire plant.... The designers have somehow, through subtle design and human planning, set human beings as the center of the whole scheme.[42]

Wank's redesign centered on the flow of visitors through the dam. He developed an *architectural promenade* to lead visitors through all the key features of the dam, from the narrow crest overlooking the giant spillway and the downstream river, to the massive battered walls of the foot of the dam and the powerhouse of humming turbines. Curvilinear roadways carried motorists up the steep mountainous terrain effortlessly; contoured parking lots at the panoramic viewpoint encouraged them to step out for an overlook and into an information center and gift shop where they might buy some local crafts or sip a soda at the fountain (Figure 3.14). Choreographing the movement of visitors in and through the dams, Wank was able to manipulate the sensory experience of being there, so that people were able to see and even feel the power of the dams. The carefully orchestrated flow of visitors through the various components of the dam allowed them to vicariously experience the force of the water contained by the dam as they crossed its spine and craned their necks over the guardrail to watch the water descending over the spillway into the churning maelstrom below. Visitors could feel in their bodies the vibrations of spinning turbines as they entered the large cathedral-like gallery of the powerhouse (Figure 3.15), and the raised hairs on their arms pointed to the crackling wires of the transformer grid as they returned to their cars, circling back up the hill, like birds in flight, high above the hive of activity.

Within the powerhouse, Wank integrated a visitors' lobby and linked it with glass doors to the turbine room. Concealed soffit lighting lent a mysterious

3.13 Inside the turbine.

3.14 Norris gift shop and visitors' center.

3.15 Interior view of powerhouse, Norris Dam.

and ethereal glow to the visitors' lobby and glassed-in control room beyond. Didactic display panels explained the functioning of the dam, while even the glass, aluminum and plastic of the lobby evoked the electric age (Figure 3.16), for electricity, in the words of Lewis Mumford,

> brings into wide industrial use its own specific materials: ... new alloys, rare earths and lighter metals. At the same time, it creates a new series of synthetic compounds that supplement paper, glass and wood: celluloid, vulcanite, bakelite and the synthetic resins.[43]

Wank embraced these "materials of the twentieth century – steel, concrete, aluminum, glass, cork, rubber, [and] resin composition" in this monument to the neotechnic era.[44] His team of architects reveled in the electricity produced by the dam, inventing lighting fixtures such as hovering disks that magically lit up the roadway. With its stark surfaces stripped of ornament and its massive diagonals dramatically floodlit, Norris Dam appeared simple and majestic (Figure 3.17):

3.16 Visitors' lobby in the Norris Dam powerhouse.

3.17 Norris Dam illuminated at night.

> The grand scale was not frittered away. The usual American dam is a giant with Lilliputian scholars and clowns posturing all over his back in togas or cap and bells. The ruggedness at TVA, the blocky big simplicity ... may seem to casual visitors to be a natural consequence or purely "functional." This is not so. It is carefully evoked, a matter of design having to do with proportion, craftsmanship with materials, placing, scale and a sense of drama in the whole thing.[45]

The modernist aesthetic worked to express the grandeur of the engineering enterprise behind it. According to Roland Wank, "we aimed to make the TVA *look* as efficient as it is."[46] In fact, the redesign may have made the building appear more modern than it was, because the fundamental design of Norris Dam remained an outdated engineering solution. Its modernist styling however, in the words of Lewis Mumford, "entitled us to a little collective strutting and crowing."[47]

By the time the Museum of Modern Art opened an exhibit on the architecture of the TVA in 1940, Norris Dam had been canonized as a fixture in the American technological sublime, in which built work and natural setting are fused into a harmonious ensemble, and the whole is associated with national greatness. Reviewing the show, Mumford enthused,

> the actual buildings, as I saw them recently in their natural setting of hill and woodland and quarry and boat basin and river, are even more breathtaking than the photographs indicate. These structures are as close to perfection as our age has come.[48] A new architecture, bold as the engineering from which it springs, is rising in the valley. . . . Look at it and be proud that you are an American.[49]

By describing the settings of the dam as *natural*, after the rocks had been blasted to make the quarry and boat basin, the hills had been cut and contoured to meet the dam, and the forests had been planted with trees just seven years earlier, Mumford recognizes the perfect fit between engineering and nature accomplished by the dams. The architecture in turn becomes animate, "springing" from engineering and "rising" in the valley. In these sentences, we can see how architectural modernism had succeeded in naturalizing Norris Dam as a part of the landscape. It had knit the precinct of highest technology into the rhetoric of a natural system, as if it were a giant tool fitted to the arm of the river. Again and again, the press coverage emphasized how well the dams fit into their settings of park and lake, both of which were sculpted just as carefully as the dam itself. As Raymond Unwin said, after visiting several of the completed TVA projects, the Authority was indeed fortunate in being able to locate their dams in such lovely settings of park and lake,[50] not realizing that park and lake, like the dam, were designed to fit each other, creating a new, third landscape that looked natural but functioned like a machine.

The look of power

When we look at the press coverage of the early TVA, it is striking how little was written about the dams during the first years of the federal agency, from 1933 (when the TVA was established) to 1939 (when six dams had been completed). This is not to say that the press didn't write about the TVA – on the contrary, countless articles discussed the aspirations and achievements of the young Authority, and architectural and planning journals devoted many pages to its housing and town planning efforts. But the dams themselves were strangely invisible until 1939 when – in the space of a year – two architectural journals devoted entire issues to TVA architecture, followed by a show at the Museum of Modern Art in New York in 1941 and uninterrupted coverage until the United States entered the war in 1942.[51]

We might conjecture with some confidence that the onset of war in

Europe contributed to this rise in interest in the TVA as an impressive example of an American public works project. The language used to describe the architecture of the TVA also changes in character, as the focus moves from town planning to dam building. One notable attribute of this new coverage is the abundant use of masculine metaphors. For example, "in plain, brute size, measured by any yardstick, ... [the dams are] tremendous," they are a "stripped architecture, endowed with the grace and the beauty of excellent proportion," they display "unbroken simplicity and majesty" and "more power, more vivid and gorgeous scale."[52] This shift in interpretation raises the question of the role played by such masculine metaphors in the press coverage of the dams at a time when the United States was being pulled into an escalating global conflict. It also reveals that architectural critics writing about modernist design in the 1930s relied on nineteenth century tropes of gendered building in order to convince their publics of the virtues of modernist aesthetics.

To understand why masculine metaphors were useful to the press coverage of TVA architecture, we must underline the political context within which these public works were received. From 1939 to 1941 the United States remained a non-combatant in a war that had spread to most European and Asian powers. Belligerent Germany, and to a somewhat lesser degree the Soviet Union, awed American audiences with their mobilized workforce and industry and their ability to mass manufacture the infrastructure of the modern world: not only armaments but *autobahns*, cultural festivals, and highly impressive large-scale public works. One can see then that the escalating press coverage of the TVA and of its dams was a way of positioning the United States in relation to Europe – as an industrial power, as a modern democratic state capable of mobilizing huge amounts of manpower, and as a government able to exert its influence over industrial capital to accomplish political as well as economic aims.

In 1940 Frederick Gutheim, writing for the *Magazine of Art*, compared Norris Dam to a pyramid (Figure 3.18). "The work has the solid dignity of a pyramid. You park your car, get out, and resubmit yourself to these mighty architectural forces."[53] Gutheim was not the only architectural critic to make this curious juxtaposition of the most modern and the most ancient architecture. Here is Lewis Mumford writing about the opening of the Museum of Modern Art's 1941 show on the TVA: "there is something in the mere cant of a dam, seen from below, that makes one think of the Pyramids of Egypt. ... Here is modern architecture at its mightiest and its best. The Pharaohs did not do any better."[54] Both Gutheim and Mumford arrive at the pyramid, in their search for words to express the overwhelming impression the new TVA dams made on them. While they may be paraphrasing Walter Gropius, who was the first critic to compare the severe and impressive constructions of American industry to the "work of the ancient Egyptians," it is perhaps not accidental in this context that "modern architecture at its mightiest and its best" is also modern architecture at its most solid.[55]

3.18 View of Norris from below.

According to the early twentieth century Austrian architect and critic Adolf Loos, the only true works of architecture are the monument and the tombstone. Both are permanent and both solid.[56] The tombstone rises above the transitory life putrefying beneath it, while the coffin below is hollow and even when the body inside is collapsing, the tombstone remains inviolate. The monument also outlasts time. At its core, the monument houses no activity, it too is solid. Perhaps the best example of a perfectly solid architecture in the United States is found in the work of Henry Hobson Richardson, in his Ames monument: a massive pillar of rock built to honor the founders of the Union Pacific Railroad (see Figure 3.19).[57] When it was built, this monument was seen as the ultimate expression of the American west. If Richardson's Marshall Field men's wholesale warehouse formed one of the "canyons" of Chicago, his Ames monument was a butte on the Great Plains – both monument and tombstone to the failed political dreams of the Ames dynasty.

3.19 Ames Monument, Sherman, Wyoming. Architect Henry Hobson Richardson.

According to Catherine Ingraham, the supremely masculine landscape of the American frontier "is a landscape of solid monumental forms (buttes, mesas) seen against a horizon."[58] Talking about western films, Ingraham reminds us that "to become a [western] man . . . must be finally to attain the solidity and self-containment of an object."[59] We see, then, both in architectural discourse and the discourse of the American west, that the "rock-solid" object is completely masculine and purely architectural.

In her recent essay on bodybuilding, Marcia Ian links solidity and masculinity. She suggests the bodily ideal of the hypermasculine bodybuilder is a pillar or column of pure, solid muscle. She says, "what he [the bodybuilder] is building is ... a thing made entirely of dense, hard muscle. A male bodybuilding body ideally has no interior. It is to contain no space, but be solid, lean meat.... Insofar as space denotes interiority, it is feminine because it denotes the negative of the masculine."[60] According to Ingraham, this dilemma of the void, this *horror vacuui*, troubles all modern architecture.[61] Is it object or is it hollow (Figure 3.20)? There is no such ambiguity with the

3.20 Entry to Chicago Tribune Tower competition, 1927. Architect Adolf Loos.

dams. Like the pyramids, with their narrow chambers for the circulation of high priests, the dams contain passages for the circulation of technicians and water – such seminal vesicles allow the machinery to function (see Figure 3.13). As the hollow space within is shrunk down to a minimum, reduced to penstocks full of thundering water and spinning turbines, the dams outstrip skyscrapers as the ultimate architectural expressions of American masculinity. Even Rockefeller Center, thrusting upward to fantastic heights, still carries voids within its towers. The dams, free of such anxiety, are the perfect expression of a solid and therefore masculine architecture.

Lastly, the solidity of the dams figures in their very function. If, as Ian suggests, "the potentially unpredictable and threatening fluidity (an ocean capable of eroding male identity) must be plugged up by the rigid Phallus, and subjected to ... the ontological ground of Western self-knowledge," there could be no better expression of masculinity than the final containment and ordering of this tributary of the "Big Muddy."[62] The sheer weight and mass of dam – in the words of one architectural critic, its "plain brute size," in the words of another, "an amount of architectural structure that would have made a Roman emperor gasp ... a whopper" – holds back the unpredictable, fluid Tennessee, controls it and puts it to work.[63] The flood, the mud, the malaria, the raging torrent are replaced by well-regulated pools and locks that men control with the flick of a switch. "I have seen the area behind Norris Dam both before and after it was flooded ... Not only has water been brought under beneficent control, but in the process a new kind of beauty has been introduced into the region."[64]

A second metaphor of masculinity used to describe the modernist dams had to do with their unornamented exteriors and the application of "functionalist" principles in their design. In the words of one critic, "this is stripped architecture to suit the most puritanical functionalist, but it is a stripped architecture with the grace and the beauty of excellent proportion."[65] According to another, these are "forms honest and direct and, as a result, beautiful."[66] At first glance, the relation between a "stripped architecture" and "grace and beauty of excellent proportion" clearly calls on the Beaux Arts tradition in which students studied the male nude as an example of physical perfection. In architecture schools, like in fine art schools of the nineteenth century, only male students were allowed to view and draw nude models from life, an essential prerequisite to appreciating classical, Greek (and necessarily male) beauty. If we pursue this idea even a bit, we can find much corroboration for the notion that a nude body of excellent proportion is a masculine body.[67] The male body has nothing to be ashamed of, and in fact might be even more honest and more healthy when he exposes himself. Isn't Clark Gable all the more admirable man as he strips off his shirt in the 1933 movie *It Happened One Night*, revealing his nude and muscled chest unencumbered by a tee shirt? According to Mark Wigley, modernist architects promoted the truth of structure and material by stripping off the superfluous dissimulating veneer of fashion.⁶⁸ He says that Siegfried Giedeon felt that the clothes of the building were adopted to conceal anxieties about industrialization and nervousness about the new technologies. For Giedeon, to remove the clothes is to revel in the new technologies. When the US dams can do this, it shows that Americans have come to terms with their possession of power – that they can finally accept their position on the world stage. Atlas and Hercules have no need of the "togas and bells" of historicist ornament (see Figure 3.21).⁶⁹

In the opinion of Adrian Forty, the very notion of architectural "form" as it has been used by most modernist architects represents a masculine ideal. He argues that the modernist preference for strong diagonals, planes, and volumes was based on a conviction that a building should represent on its exterior the conflict of forces within the building: be these gravity or the movement of people or light inside. "The notion that architecture represents implied movement within forms that are not themselves in motion has been a conventional part of modernist thinking, and still seems to be taken for granted." He continues, "the entire notion of form as a static representation of a conflict of internal forces relies on an ideal of the male anatomy, for it is in the male body that the closest correspondence of external form to muscular effort is to be found."⁷⁰ The angular lines of bones and muscle visible on the outside of the male body was understood to reveal the internal forces at work in the body. The female body could not reveal this – it was sign, not

3.21 Hiwassee Dam elevation study.

signifier. It was represented, it did not represent. When the Museum of Modern Art wrote that "the bold diagonals of the huge dam, the sober rectangles of the reinforced concrete powerhouse and the finely etched lines of the transformers combine to form one of the monuments of our civilization,"[71] we see that (as Forty says), "seemingly neuter, 'form' is, in the way it is generally conceived and discussed in twentieth century architecture, a masculine ideal."[72]

Curiously, we find as many references to the smooth and streamlined agile body as to the bulky massive body in the press coverage of the TVA. For example, a description of the TVA's gradual refinement of crane design is couched as an evolutionary metamorphosis creating a light insectile body, "the first crane at Wheeler is 'raw engineering', heavy, brutal, unrefined. The second crane at Pickwick shows 'industrial design', structure and machinery rationalized and encased in smart overcoat. The third crane at Hiwassee shows refined machine form, overcoat discarded, asserting its structural elegance and delicacy."[73] We could say the same of the crane at Kentucky Dam, which shows its structural logic while expressing a streamlined sculpted silhouette (Figure 3.22). The old, outdated body is clad in an aluminum chrysalis before being reborn as a new and vigorous, elegant and delicate machine.[74] It is as if the portly gentleman of the nineteenth century, formerly the embodiment of wealth and power, becomes a wasteful and even ugly extravagance in a modern machine age. The lean, healthy body functions like a well-oiled machine and is ideally nude.

Where clothing, or architectural "cladding," is still present in the TVA dams, it is the clothing of modern men who are (as Adolf Loos suggested) ideally "well dressed" rather than "richly dressed," that is to say they are dressed severely and soberly but in materials of quality. In his designs, Wank avoids the sumptuous surfaces of stone, marble, brass, and gilt. He brushes bare aluminum, sandblasts glass and raises the relief of raw concrete, accentuating the surface qualities of each material. Lewis Mumford praised Wank,

> for the masterful way in which he ... used concrete. Engineers and architects have used concrete for a long time without thinking of anything better to do with it than to sheathe it in stone, as the Romans did. Wank strove for a new effect; instead of obliterating the delicate pattern impressed in the concrete by the grain of the wood ... he made the effect all the bolder by contrasting horizontal with vertical patterns (see Figure 3.23).[75]

In this way, as Talbot Hamlin says, "the walls have life."[76] Indeed, sometimes it seems these bare buildings – powerhouses and dams – appeared to reporters of the 1930s and 1940s to be living things themselves. In this excerpt from his article for the *Magazine of Art*, Frederick Gutheim describes his feelings inside a TVA powerhouse:

169 | Putting nature to work

3.22 Gantry crane at Kentucky Dam.

Above the floor rise the cylindrical generator housings beneath which you sense the powerful operations of the dynamos. It is a hypnotic experience. Your ears are filled with the insistent hum of the powerful generators, your eyes are filled with the impression of strong mechanical and structural forms, you touch the solid concrete, the tile, the aluminum hand-rail, you sniff the faint odor of ever-present oil – the total impression is complete, everything contributes to the one major effect. Your are in the presence of the most impressive symbol of ultimate force the age has produced.[77]

Touching on each of the senses in turn – first his ears, and then his eyes filled, touching solid materials, sniffing odors – Gutheim gradually increases the intimacy felt by the reader with the nude, exposed and operating interior of

3.23 Detail of concrete at powerhouse, Norris Dam.

the powerhouse, until one feels almost an erotic as well as a spiritual communion with its architecture. The press coverage of the TVA stands out in the early modernist canon for its explicit adoption of masculine tropes – of power, size, and stripped and excellent proportion. These tropes tapped into earlier categories employed in the architectural criticism of ornamented buildings, to justify the raw materials and simple geometries of a nascent modernism.

Insemination

The central function of the dams, of course, was to contain the floodwaters of the Tennessee and to generate electricity. That being said, the TVA quickly escalated into a much more ambitious plan for the regeneration of a region. Here, we'd like to look at the metaphors of regeneration as a part of the popular success of these dams. Everyone knew that before the TVA built dams and reforested hillsides, the topsoil of Appalachia made the river run red. Floods in Chattanooga and barren hillsides in Appalachia were familiar sights in Depression-era newsreels.

In his 1938 documentary *The River*, Pare Lorentz intoned a litany of loss to flooding and frontier exploitation: "a million miles of lumber, a million bales of cotton, and a million cubic yards of topsoil flowed down the river." Once the TVA has plugged up the river and restrained it, no longer does the wasted seed of the frontier spirit flow downstream. If the self-serving ethic of frontier capitalism is associated with wasted seed flowing downstream, a biblical sin in this Bible belt region, the collective spirit of New Deal cooperation was to fertilize and renew the American garden. As Douglas Haskell put it, "the dams are merely the climaxes" – they are the virile members that produce the juice (fertilizer and electricity) that will inseminate the barren earth.

From the dams, we are told in the press, flows power. As water is restrained, power is generated. And this is what makes the TVA so important to the American press on the eve of war. "What is there about a building project such as the TVA that puts it so entirely apart from other large ... ventures such as Rockefeller Center?" Douglas Haskell asks, answering, "the difference lies in the sense of something being done for literally everybody, of unbounded power used with unreserved magnanimity."[78] R.L. Duffus described this spreading of power from the dams to the region almost as if it were the tongues of fire at a religious revival:

> I have visited the dams from time to time, always drawn by an irresistible fascination, seeing dams in all stages of construction, watching the waters back up behind them, feeling the throb of power in the great transmission towers that began to stride across the country, and aware, also, that this majestic enterprise was stirring towns, cities and people to a new and vigorous activity.[79]

As power infuses the region, it will make it productive. In the form of electricity or fertilizer generated with the nitrates of the Tennessee River basin, "power" stands in for the potent juices of the natural world, retained and turned back on itself to inseminate and irrigate so that forests will sprout, fish will hatch, dairy cattle will multiply on newly-verdant hillsides, and farmers and townsfolk will prosper in this new Eden.

AN AUTHENTIC FOLK: THE PEOPLE NATURALIZED

Describing the dam-building projects of the New Deal, the historian Richard White says, "the lust for growth the dams unleashed seemed almost elemental, and to control it the progressives needed a social vision of the same raw strength. What some of them embraced instead was a pious, essentially backward-looking nostalgia."[80] While White quite rightly recognizes the dams as a phenomenal achievement, he, like many other critics, dismisses the "social vision" that accompanied the dambuilding project. The 1930s was after all a time of visionary urban plans and social engineering schemes. On the one hand we find projects such as Le Corbusier's "radiant city," a paean to corporate statism that glorified high-rises as machines for living and promoted the wholesale demolition of Europe's "unhealthy" urban inheritance. On the more progressive end of the political spectrum, the massive public works that had been realized a decade earlier in social democratic Vienna and Weimar Germany had effectively reinvented the European city to give pride of place to workers' housing and garden city planning.[81] The United States, in contrast, had realized little in the way of visionary urbanism by the 1930s – the most notable achievement being Clarence Stein and Henry Wright's Radburn, a "garden city for the motor age" made palatable to Americans in being stripped of the collectivist principles that underlie the first garden cities in England.[82]

But the town planning efforts of the TVA attract our attention here not because they championed modernist housing design because, indeed, they did not – at least not at first glance. What we find instead in the first town planned by the TVA is a vision of modernity in which modern technology is used as a servant to help people realize a way of life that is in many respects pre-industrial and that is also seen as fundamental to the American character. In the 1930s, the United States still imagined itself as an agricultural society of small landowners and farmers. As thousands of people returned to their family farms with the collapse of urban employment in the wake of the stock market crash of 1929, this view seemed all the more justified. The TVA then, rather than shoehorning people into "machines for living," sought a town-planning model and a domestic architecture that would reconcile modernization and an improved quality of life with the enduring myth of an agrarian society nestled in a landscape of rolling hills. We are intrigued here with the way in which the TVA's town planning recuperated the past as a way to usher in the future. The TVA aimed to integrate modernity in this rural landscape.

Charles Colby, writing to TVA's head planner Earle S. Draper in 1934, recognized the seductive power of Norris's town planning when he said,

> People are interested in both the works and the plans of the Authority. Up to the present they have been more interested in the works than the plans, but I believe that they are becoming more interested in the plans than in the works. The Norris Dam excites people's imagination, and they want to see it just as they want to see the Boulder Dam. They have higher expectations, however, of the results of the former than of the latter. On the whole not much is expected of Boulder Dam. As one man put it, "we know that Boulder Dam is a Los Angeles scheme to promote a land boom so that folks can unload their real estate – it reeks of the pork barrel."[83]

Colby did not overstate popular interest in the social and town planning of the TVA. Journals such as *Business Week*, *Literary Digest*, *Collier's*, *New York Times Magazine*, and *Christian Century* wondered if the Tennessee Valley was just a "guinea pig valley," or would it become "a promised land?" Described as a "vast setting of a power age dream," was the Tennessee Valley also "a prevision of utopia"? If "revivifying the psychology of an ancient people" was to be achieved by "America's most gigantic technical task," they could then ask "what will TVA do to the USA?"[84]

As the TVA dams unleashed the dynamic of modernization in the valley, it was its inhabitants who were ultimately meant to show the ensuing benefits. The people, after all, were the ultimate justification for the effort expended to rebuild a landscape out of balance. Their malarial-ridden and malnourished bodies, eloquently photographed by Lewis Hines and Walker Evans, had been displayed at TVA press conferences as proof that the old frontier ethos had led to wasted resources and wasted lives. And if the American people were to be convinced that the TVA's project of regional renewal and revitalization was a success, it would once again be the people of rural Appalachia that would serve as evidence. They had to be well fed and contented, housed in snug homes and busy on prosperous farms and in clean industries. They had to become "model" citizens living in model towns. The "promised land" and the "heavenly valley" described by Lorena Hickok in her tours of the country could not be populated by footloose unemployed exiles from the industrial centers of the North, striking miners of coal country Appalachia, or share-cropping farmers of the rural South.

If the entire valley were to function as a model for a perfected and renewed nature, not only did the technology of the dams have to be knit back into a renewed landscape, but the inhabitants of the valley had to be knit back into the land. Instead of representing Appalachian hill-dwellers as the historical victims of frontier capitalism, the TVA reinvented them as the American "folk" who were to populate a new Arcadia. In other words, the people of the Tennessee Valley – like its dams – had to be naturalized, reinvented as a part of a larger system of flows and cycles, growth, regeneration and renewal (Figures 3.24 and 3.25).

3.24 Miners at work in Appalachia, ca. 1933. Photograph by Lewis Hine.

175 | Putting nature to work

Recasting the inhabitants as folk built on earlier discourses about the people of Appalachia. In the nineteenth century, the putative primitivism of rural populations was a cause for Victorian hostility. Arnold Toynbee's statement that "the neo-barbarism of the Appalachian people traces back to their adoption of traits from the savages they eradicated," and an editorial in the

3.25 "Mountaineer" at tan-bark mill, near Great Smoky Mountains National Park, 1930s.

New York Times of 1912 that equated mountain people with "red Indians" who "must be educated or exterminated," are only two examples of a much more widespread hostility to the primitivism that supposedly characterized Appalachia.[85] A recent documentary film *Strangers and Kin* tries to explain such attitudes: "it became easier to carry [industrial] progress forward if you could say that the people who were being hurt by progress were worthless to begin with."[86] In the first years of the twentieth century, we see the beginnings of a change in this attitude, in which the mountain people are presented as a purer sort of American, untouched by modernism. The president of Berea College, a settlement school in the Appalachian Mountains, called them "diamonds in the rough," "our noble ancestors."[87] This shift must be seen in the larger context of increasing hostility to immigrants and agitation for eugenics, which advocated selective breeding to ensure the survival of a "truly American" stock. So the "folk" in Appalachia came to be seen as a valuable repository of cultural essence and the "right" gene pool.[88] The "pioneer farmer" and the "common folk" were useful symbols of self-reliance and national pride in a time of retrenchment and uncertainty. Thus we can see that the transformation of Norris residents into a folk enabled them to stand for all Americans, and the model town of Norris in the center of a renewed landscape could function as a microcosm of a renewed nation.

It is vital to see this characterization as a cultural construction – a process of *naturalizing* a population that was in fact heterogeneous and radically uprooted. To turn the people of Appalachia into a "folk" is to pull them out of their historic context, which is a precondition, in the Marxist sense, for class consciousness and collective action. We can then explore what possibilities for social transformation were shut down through this process and what forms were set more firmly into place as part of the "natural order." Critical of the folk ideal, the historian Ian McKay argues that it erases an awareness of class struggle and closes down the possibilities for economic and political emancipation. The "good and simple life" replaces memories of starvation, mercantile exploitation and impoverishment:[89]

> To visit the Folk and enjoy their songs and tales was to transcend class divisions and to live ... a pastoral vision of society – in which rich and poor were bound together by ties of love and understanding.... The Folk repertoire [of handicraft and folk music] ... could unite people of a common national culture and of a common "race" – it testified to the deep organic solidarities which modernity had not succeeded in eliminating.... Workers and socialists, those deracinated products of the coalfields and cities, could not be a true Folk, ... because in their emphasis on politics based on class, they violated the vital nucleus of the Folk idea: the essential and unchanging solidarity of traditional society (see Figures 3.26 and 3.27).[90]

3.26 Mrs Jacob Stookesbury's family, Loyston, TN, 1933. Photograph by Lewis Hine.

3.27 Family at fireside in TN, 1933. Photograph by Lewis Hine.

In terms of race, this construction assumes that a traditional society is an all-white society. The history of slavery is erased from the "usable past" and (like in Rockefeller's Colonial Williamsburg) Norris is established as an all-white town, even though 4.5 percent of the population in the fourteen counties surrounding the dam was black.[91] Black laborers were denied permanent accommodation at Norris, and set up instead in temporary collective quarters, effectively excluding their wives and dependents, or forced to find their own dwellings elsewhere. When J. Max Bond, the "supervisor of Negro training," criticized chairman Morgan for his support for Jim Crow policies in a federal project, Morgan equivocated.[92] He denied that black employees wanted houses in the town, while at the same time he used economic arguments against allowing them to live there, pointing to the additional costs of creating the separate schools, facilities and meeting rooms required by Tennessee state law.[93] Although black labor, like Cherokee labor, was welcomed in limited roles in the dam-building projects (especially once the war broke out), these people had no place in the social planning of the young Authority. Accusations of racism in the planning of the town of Norris beset the TVA long after the town was complete.

The town of Norris

Chairman Morgan had scarcely received his brief from Roosevelt before he set to work with vigorous activity. In the first few months of his appointment to the TVA, Morgan set up employment policies for the new Authority that were progressive for the time, including support for unions, hiring and promotion policies based on merit, a 33-hour work week and a living wage (see Figure 3.28).[94] He brought similar progressive ambitions to the design of the workers' living quarters. From his experience managing large construction sites in the Miami River Conservancy District, Morgan knew that construction camps were usually flung up cheaply and hastily and provided poor living conditions for the workers. He was determined to provide good accommodations. He was also convinced that if long-term economies were factored in, a permanent settlement at Norris would cost less than a temporary one. But mostly, he saw the design of the workers' town at Norris as an opportunity to put into practice a model planned community, a community that would represent everything the TVA stood for. Morgan wanted the scientific planning and management exercised in flood control and land reclamation to extend to the design of human settlements. In this, he had an ally in Roosevelt, who expected "all forms of human concerns" to be touched by the TVA.

Visiting Norris today, it looks like any small suburban community, although the houses are spaced somewhat further apart and situated in a lovely region of rolling hills and deciduous forest. The modest bungalows, curving streets and culs-de-sac are well within the vernacular of the Anglo-American suburb. But if you went back in time, you would see a town that was very different from other small American towns. It was called a town of

3.28 Interviewing applicants for the TVA, 1933. Photograph by Lewis Hine.

the electric age and accused of being communist because of its cooperatives and godless because it had only one non-denominational church.[95] Because it was the property of the US government, the houses in Norris were not owned by residents; in this sense, it followed the example of the first garden city Letchworth (built in England in 1907), in preventing speculation.[96] For the United States, Norris was innovative because it housed a number of collective enterprises and provided services to its residents that encouraged a renewed sense of "community." Residents of Norris had access to adult education and training. There was a collective dairy, experimental farms, cooperative workshops, an innovative school for children, a community store run on cooperative principles and a meeting hall.

The town was built around three centers (Figure 3.29). The "town square" at the heart of the community contained a public hall and administration buildings clustered around a New England-style village green. This center supported most of the social life of the town with its stores, a public market, a post office, and a telephone exchange, providing a place for the exchange of pleasantries, gossip and social interactions so important to a small community. The bus station and a small hotel provided novel comings and goings, while the men could discuss events at the gas station with its

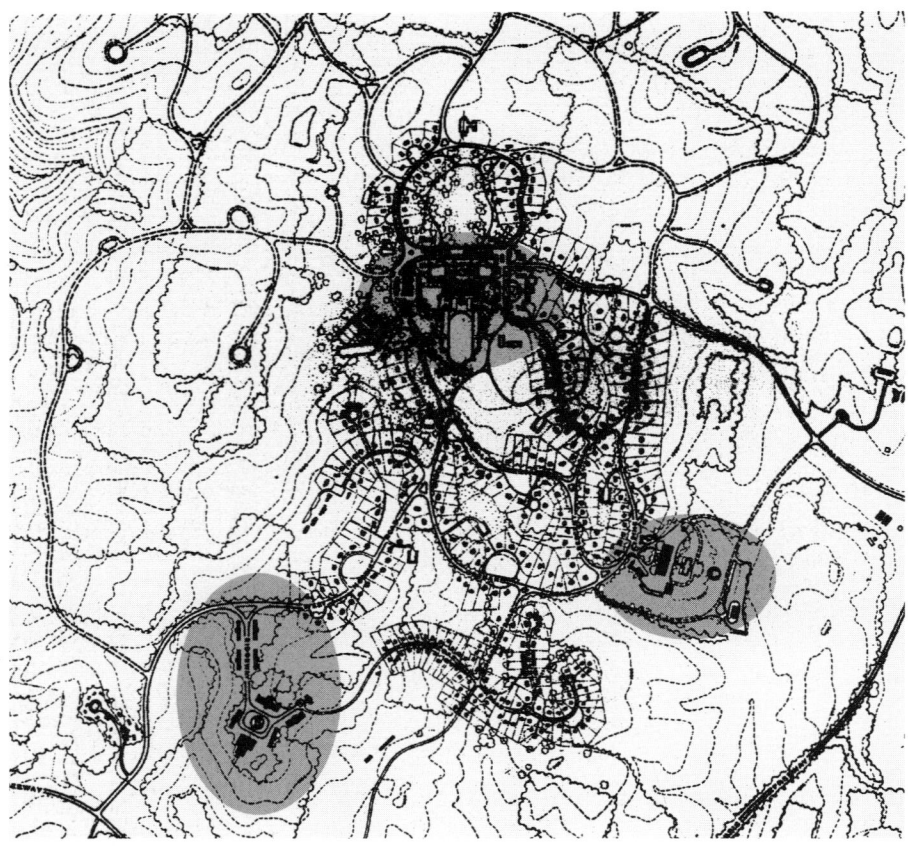

3.29 Town plan of Norris.

adjacent garage for car repair. The grade school and high school were near this center, as was the hospital. A second center was located on the road toward the dam site. This area was designed to accommodate the thousand unmarried construction workers in denser housing than was provided for in the scattered family houses that made up most of the town. Close to the Civilian Conservation Corps campsite, this center also held a collective kitchen and commissary, a library and a gymnasium and auditorium. In the other direction and near the freeway, a third center contained repair shops, light industry and the budding manufacturing enterprises.

Most of the houses in Norris were spaced widely apart, set back from curving streets and culs-de-sac, and nestled in the woods, accommodating sloped sites with split-level foundations. Like in the garden city of Radburn, New Jersey, pedestrian paths were clearly separated from vehicular roads,

1 With the close of the twentieth century, Americans began to see the wilderness as an important resource – not to be exploited but to be preserved and cherished. In his design for Columbian Exposition of 1893, Frederick Law Olmsted placed a wooded isle in the center of the "civilized" White City.
"The Afterglow in the Lagoon," Charles Caryl Coleman, 1893. Oil on wood panel.

2 In front of Louis Sullivan's Transportation Building, sculptures of big game like these elk guarded the bridges to the wooded isle. These were the first artistic depictions of indigenous American big game.
"The Golden Doorway of the Transportation Building," Frank Russell Green, 1893. Oil on canvas.

3 The early conservationists saw hunting as an education in manliness and citizenship and as a training ground for future leaders. Members of the Boone and Crockett Club depicted here were influential advocates for national parks and forest reserves and they helped to define the "look" of the wilderness in paintings, sculpture, landscape design and rustic architecture.
"The Life I Love," Irving R. Bacon, 1887. Buffalo Bill Historical Center, Cody, WY.

4 The rustic look of national park architecture was first developed by Robert Reamer in Yellowstone National Park in the 1900s. Tourism in western parks created rules which taught people how to behave in the wilderness.
Old Faithful Inn and Geyser, Yellowstone National Park.

5 The Old Faithful Inn was a shrine to nature. Rustic and welcoming to women, it combined tropes of the pioneer life with the new Arts and Crafts aesthetic.

6 Wrought iron door hardware, Old Faithful Inn.

7 The commercial development of national parks in the early twentieth century was a joint venture between business and the US government. The railroad companies encouraged women to see these spaces not as dangerous frontier regions but as safe and enjoyable spaces of leisure. The Northern Pacific Railroad adopted the curious Alice in Wonderland as their mascot.

"Alice's Adventures in the New Wonderland." Northern Pacific Railroad advertisement, 1885. National Park Service, Yellowstone National Park.

8 The natural features of Yellowstone Park seemed strange and at times repellent. Guidebooks and tour operators went to great lengths to balance the scenic with the comic, and the strange with the sublime.
"The Sponge," postcard.

9 Reamer's designs for the hotel entrepreneur Harry Child developed a different look for each area of Yellowstone Park. This unbuilt proposal for Mammoth Hot Springs echoes the calcified formations of the mineral springs in its vertical pillars. This regionalism was repeated across the country, as the many new national parks tried to create distinctive evocations of their local spectacular nature.
Proposal for Mammoth Hot Springs Hotel. Architect Robert Reamer, n.d. Watercolor.

10 The hydroelectric dams of the Tennessee Valley Authority allowed water levels to be raised and lowered with the flip of a switch. Fish hatcheries, contoured hillsides and replanted forests completes the engineering of nature.
Fontana Dam reservoir at "draw down."

11 The Tennessee Valley Authority, in Stuart Chase's words, was an "organic machine" to transform a seven-state watershed into a productive modern landscape that integrated people, nature and technology. In the process, farming families were resettled, cemeteries were dug up and moved, and thousands of miles of electric lines were strung across the region.
View from visitor center at Watts Bar Dam.

12 Foreign visitors to the Tennessee Valley commented on the beautiful park-like settings for these monuments to high technology, not realizing this was the result of careful and coordinated design. Distant view of Fontana Dam, powerhouse and visitor centre.

13 The movement of visitors was seamlessly choreographed, from the gently curving motorways to dramatically situated public outlooks. The visitor centre at Fontana is poised above the 480 foot sheer face of the dam, the highest east of the Rockies. The road continues accross the dam to join the Appalachian Trail as it winds toward Maine, knitting this modernist masterpiece into a national network of leisure spaces.
Fontana visitor center overlook.

14 This image shows an artificial "farm" constructed as camouflage on the roof of the Douglas Aircraft plant in Santa Monica, California during the Second World War. The young architects of the Case Study House program were surrounded by a landscape that was simultaneously industrial and (as this photograph suggests) rural. Camouflage farm atop Douglas Aircraft plant, Santa Monica, California, 1943.

15 While the architects Buff, Straub and Hensman did not design a home office for biochemist Dr. Ruth Bass, they acknowledged that her kitchen was "as precisely planned as a laboratory." Her husband however, the designer Saul Bass, had a room of his own. Here Dr. Bass poses in glamorous pumps for the photographer Julius Shulman.
Dr. Ruth Bass in her kitchen, Case Study House 20, 1958. Architects Buff, Straub and Hensman.

climbing up and over hills while the roads followed the lower contours. Small parks and playgrounds were scattered through the town, as were collective parking garages. The whole town was surrounded by a permanent green belt to restrict unplanned expansion – in this zone were located the demonstration farm and dairy, subsistence farms and recreational areas. In Norris then, we see the seeds for how the whole regional plan was meant to work: the fertilized and electrified farms, light industry, cooperative workshops, and stores represented the modern world being ushered in by the TVA, while the rural-looking houses provided a reassuring anchor to the past (Figure 3.30).

As we sifted through the TVA's archives in Norris, it became clear to us that the TVA architects and planners were excited to have the opportunity to design a truly modern town – modern, like the neotechnic society Mumford was advocating – powered by electricity, using modern technology, and promising modern social engineering as well. Wank communicated some of his excitement in his December 1933 letter to Morgan. Passing quickly over "engineering projects which are already being considered by better qualified members of the force," Wank outlined his detailed recommendations for the workplace in the new town, including the seizure of existing industries by the government and the establishment of nationwide cooperatives. Calling the Subsistence Homestead preference for small land holdings a "medieval subsistence," he argued that large parcels of land should be cooperatively farmed using the most modern machinery. He envisioned the shops in town

3.30 Conceptual sketch of Norris, 1933.

operating 24-hour days in four shifts (like the construction site for the dam), making products for export, and that all other public services would follow cooperative lines. In the realm of housing, Wank advocated total government control of production, which would consist entirely of prefabricated units. He closed his letter with the confident comment that "quite a few members on the force are thinking along the same lines – an illustration of the fact that advanced thought is more prevalent than generally suspected."[97] In this, Wank's ideas for the TVA seem more in line with Konstantin Milyutin's socialist city of *Sotsgorod*, than any Jeffersonian Arcadian dream. Indeed, the early press coverage to TVA was quick to compare it with the Soviet system, often pejoratively as an example of dangerous "collectivism," but other times favorably, as in an article in *Scribner's* titled "A Revolution in Electricity," which compared the TVA to the Soviet *piatletka*, or five-year plan.[98] Such comparisons served as fodder for arguments to undermine or support the young Authority, but shed little light on the actual practices of either experiment. For example, the USSR's reinvention of communal life under Stalin stressed modernization at the expense of all traditional practices. Craft and artisanal manufacture were forbidden, and the peasantry was redefined strictly as an agricultural workforce. In the TVA by contrast, the promotion of light industry (and the electrified industry that would follow), craft and farming as activities that supplemented the construction work on the dam attempted to create a hybrid between modern and traditional ways of life.

Community life at Norris
While eager to experiment with many aspects of the new community, Morgan stressed in his public speeches that the innovations of Norris were pragmatic and common-sense. He affirmed TVA's opposition to Soviet-style social and economic planning, and insisted that there was no five- or ten-year plan for the valley.[99] In fact, his vision of the future owed more to nineteenth century communitarian utopianism than twentieth century socialism. He was a great admirer of Edward Bellamy, whose *Looking Backward* (1888) had spawned many hundreds of "Bellamy clubs" across the country at the turn of the century. These clubs promoted Bellamy's utopia of a perfectly planned society in which economic competition and conflict are replaced by expert planning and cooperation. In the town of Norris, Morgan wanted to avoid competition in the shops and between churches. There was to be one dispensary, rather than several shops that might cut quality or exploit labor to compete. There would be one ecumenical house of worship, rather than several faiths, which could drain the community's resources and fracture its social solidarity. As an innovative educator, coming to the TVA from his position as head of Antioch College, where he instituted cooperative education (alternating classes with work experience), Morgan stressed the importance of both children and adult education. The children's school in Norris was renowned for its innovative programming.

There was not much thought put into the role of women in this ideal new community. Morgan reserved his communitarian ambitions for the realm of production, not reproduction. He was eager to experiment with collective farming and cooperative industry for the men who were employed in dam construction, but possibilities for collective enterprise on the part of women were ignored, as women were brought into the social plan only insofar as they were part of a nuclear family. One must keep in mind that there had been a great deal of experimentation in the first two decades of the century in collective child-rearing, cooking, cleaning and other domestic tasks, that represented concrete examples Morgan could have drawn upon.[100] Nineteenth century extended families relied on sisterly or motherly bonds across the chasm of marriage to help combat the inevitable isolation produced by the heterosexual coupling, and the Tennessee Valley was no exception to this pattern. In fact, kinship bonds across families were particularly strong and helped to create what even the TVA anthropologists realized were the tightly knit communities of the Clinch River basin. The TVA's emphasis on *nuclear* families as the fundamental building block of Norris town exacerbated the upheaval caused by relocation and left women even more isolated from family and kin. In this policy, Morgan followed in the footsteps of his fellow Quaker Herbert Hoover, who had advocated the single family house as the natural model for American domestic life, and thus the only one deserving of governmental mortgage assistance and tax relief.[101]

Yet for men, Norris offered a unique access to community activities. Morgan actively promoted small-scale cooperative enterprises that were inventive or experimental, such as demonstration farms using new fertilizers and contour farming techniques espoused by TVA agronomists, porcelain pottery made from local kaolin clay, and an experimental dairy that took advantage of new refrigeration techniques. Adult education focused on the kind of practical skills that would contribute to effective householding or small farming: carpentry, blacksmithing, repair of automobiles and small farm machinery.[102] While the dam was still under construction, these activities were meant to fill the hours remaining to workers after a $5\frac{1}{2}$-hour day at the job site. Once the dam was completed, these small industries were to become the basis for an independent economy.

Craft at Norris

According to Walter Creese, "the craft approach, joined with the technological, was included at the beginning."[103] It is as if the seeds of *industrialization* were to be first sown as *industriousness* and indeed, craft is a pillar of Morgan's plan for Norris Town. Requiring little investment, handicraft could be done at home or in a collective setting, and it occupied both the body and mind. Craft was seen as a gentle way to bring the mountaineer into a modern economy. It was the perfect activity for a people who were meant to embody the Folk.

The promotion of handicraft had already been given a head start by the Quakers in their relief work among impoverished and striking miners in the coal fields of Tennessee.[104] There, "the Quakers proved that the people turn naturally to handicrafts" in a time of economic and social turmoil.[105] Craft, for them, was a form of relief. Along with the food they distributed to starving miners and their families, they set up schools to teach people "traditional" handicrafts. They brought in experts from the region to train unemployed miners, their wives and children in crafts like whittling, quilting, furniture- and doll-making. This was meant to help raise the self-esteem of the unemployed and generate a small cash income. But mostly, the Quakers succeeded in raising the profile of the crafts movement in southern Appalachia, expanding on its origins in the settlement schools that followed in the wake of the coal mining industries.

In his book *All That is Native and Fine*, David Whisnant shows that the craft movement in Appalachia was built on a movement that had already begun in the late nineteenth century.[106] At that time, educated, urban, middle and upper class "culture workers," fanning out from the urbanized centers of the Eastern seaboard, searched for repositories of "authentic" American culture, first in the mountains of Vermont and New Hampshire, and then in the more remote hills of Appalachia. He shows how they defined, preserved, transformed, revived and promoted this "folk" culture through institutions such as settlement schools, training camps and folk festivals (Figure 3.31). This movement in Appalachia was indebted both to the social reform movements of the urbanized north-east and to a larger strain of anti-modernism felt by urban elites in the late nineteenth century, which took the form of a search for a "simple life."[107]

Ironically, the seeds of the craft movement in southern Appalachia were sown only after the industrialization of the region, as northern "missionaries" such as the Russell Sage Foundation followed in the footsteps of northern capitalists like Andrew Carnegie and John D. Rockefeller who came for coal. The early song collectors used the metaphor of mining treasure, but handicraft promoters had to "educate people to see the natural forms around them," all too often obscured by such polluting modern influences as Tin Pan Alley, radio, automobiles and high heels.[108] By the 1930s, craft had taken off as a commercial success and Southern Appalachia joined New Hampshire, Quebec and Mexico in a full-fledged craft renaissance. The craft movement was given a national profile, with three successive Presidents' wives appearing in public wearing skirts and dresses made of homespun wool. That year, Mrs Coolidge, Mrs Hoover and Mrs Roosevelt sponsored the Southern Mountain Handicraft Guild exhibit at the Corcoran Gallery in Washington DC.[109]

In introducing handicraft production into the new town of Norris, Morgan tapped into the full complexity of the craft discourse. The idea that handicraft was a preventative medicine against the ailments of inadequacy and defeatism appears in Norris in the provision for the cooperative "produc-

3.31 Weaving studio at Berea College, 1930s. Photograph by Doris Ullman.

tion, collection and sale of handicraft products such as knit goods, rugs, bed quilts, and other textiles, pottery, wood carving and furniture."[110] As a training ground for future industrial workers, handicraft was seen as "compensation for unemployment," a "substitute for industrialization," or a "transitional work ethic."[111] Master craftsmen from a furniture factory in Highpoint, North Carolina and teachers from the craft shops of Berea

College, Kentucky were brought into the Norris trade shop to teach residents how to make "early American furniture that was good looking, of good quality and useful in the household."[112] These "products of individuality and character" were, according to Morgan, "preferable to mass-produced items" of the factory.[113] The transitional position held by craft, between modern design and traditional handiwork, could also be seen in the interior design of the major community buildings at Norris. The folding writing tables of the community post office and the built-in undulating wooden shelves of the cooperative grocery surrounded the Norris resident with the tangible benefits of the marriage between craft and design (Figure 3.32).

The popularity of craft in this period also had a commercial underpinning in the growth of the tourism economy during the Depression years, aided by the state-sponsored construction of highways and campgrounds, programs like "See America First!", and the active intervention of government in inventing traditions and monitoring tourism (Figure 3.33). Local crafts were sold in the visitor centers of Norris and Chickamauga Dams and in TVA outlets closer to target urban audiences, such as the Patten Hotel in Chattanooga and even in Rockefeller Center in New York City. Indeed,

3.32 Wooden shelves of co-op grocery, Norris.

187 | Putting nature to work

3.33 Craft signs near Great Smoky Mountains National Park, 1941.

"crafts were socially therapeutic not because they were outside the modern cash nexus, but precisely to the extent that they were embedded in it."[114] Situated at the crest of the Norris Dam, the streamlined visitor center welcomed tourists into an airy space that echoed the modern powerhouse below. Made of wood but clad with smooth marbleized stucco, sporting aluminum light fixtures and a chromed soda bar with padded stools, and focusing on a panoramic window over the dam, this building displayed the baskets, weaving and whittled objects produced in the Norris Town workshops. Here "the handmade object took its proper place in the precinct of the highest technology."[115] Craft in Norris was a symbol of the golden age, the perfect expression of a mountain folk once again industrious, who turned to handicraft "to appease their restless hands" (see Figure 3.34).[116]

The houses in Norris

From the beginning, Norris Town was meant to be inhabited by "mountain folk" – or, more precisely, by workers on the dam whose families had been displaced by land acquisition. In fact, TVA land purchases in the Clinch River basin had displaced over 3,000 rural families. One-third of these small-scale "hog and corn" subsistence farmers were tenants, the rest were landowners.[117] Some had recently returned to the countryside from urban areas, out of work after the crash of 1929. But the fair employment practices of the TVA required that all employees, even construction workers, take civil service exams, which in effect limited town residency to the literate. So very few of the displaced Clinch River families came to live in Norris, being settled

3.34 Gift shop interior, Norris Dam.

instead into several small existing communities in the river basin. In reality, the labor pool for the dam came from the whole region and encompassed a wide group of people from agricultural, industrial, urban and rural backgrounds. A few resettlement cases, families of coal miners from Wilder, Tennessee were included as part of Morgan's strategy to obtain Subsistence Homestead monies. In view of the heterogeneous population that actually inhabited Norris, we are struck all the more by the insistence of the early TVA planners that this was a "mountaineer culture in a period of change."[118] This insistence on folk culture, as we have seen, took the form of creating time and space for craft production and it also influenced the architecture of the houses in Norris. The single family houses were meant to blend with the regional landscape. This led to houses that looked like traditional "dogtrot" cabins and had gently sloping roofs extending over open-air porches (Figure 3.35). The split wood shingles, stone fireplaces, and board-and-batten siding of the houses symbolized the hard-working folk now resettled in their Arcadia (Figure 3.36).

But as the folk ideal was brought into the town plan of Norris, contradictions and complexities abounded and generated many disagreements among the architects and planners. The early TVA planners were aware of the possibilities of contradiction. In an article on the planning of Norris,

3.35 Dog-trot house type D-2 in Norris, 1934.

3.36 Stone house in Norris, 1934.

Tracy Augur wrote, "to the people who have made their homes there . . . it is not new-fangled, but homey. For although Norris is new, it is also old."[119] Walter Creese explains,

> The TVA had been a last effort to resolve a dichotomy between the earlier idealistic vision of an earthy, agrarian, frontier society, to be made prosperous in a particular place; and a succeeding dream of perfecting that same environment through the hygienic influence of a "good" civilian technology.[120]

We see, for example, that while the houses of Norris look as if they were scattered in the forests and hills, they were in fact linked by paved walkways and discreetly hidden roads. Norris was, according to McDonald and Muldowny, a "suburb in the wilderness."[121] Parking was provided in collective lots, but secluded so as not to disturb the rural appearance of the town (Figure 3.37). On the other hand, the farms that were ostensibly meant to supplement the wages of those working on the dam were far from the houses on the outskirts of town, providing a buffer space between residences and forest. Such contradictions run right through the design of the houses at Norris as well.

David Frisby has questioned the view that modernism was ever a unified project with a single aesthetic expression. He suggests that modernism was experienced as discontinuous fragments, only a small portion of which

3.37 Collective parking garages in Norris, 1934.

have been taken up into the written histories of modernism.[122] T. Jackson Lears takes this position even further, arguing that anti-modernism is one thread of modernism, which works to recuperate it.[123] We see the importance of the folk idea to the TVA as a tactic to recuperate what was felt to be the alienating qualities of its larger modernizing agenda. Far from being an opposing or contradictory force to the modernization that was to be realized through the dam building project of the TVA, the folk idea helped to ensure that people would be included in the renewed and productive landscape.

The first press coverage of the houses at Norris shows no evidence that the design of the houses was felt to contradict the larger goal of bringing modernity to the valley. On the contrary, the "naturalness" of the houses was praised in a 1939 *Pencil Points* article, which admired how "the whole purpose of the plan ... was to blend the village as far as possible" with the regional landscape, and saw "a beautiful natural simplicity in the gabled roofs, quiet walls, large windows and protected porches" on the houses.[124] The local population was somewhat less convinced by the blending of the new town with the surrounding landscape, as for example when a woman visiting Norris for the first time said, "I wouldn't live way back there in those woods!"

During the design of the houses, questions about what would be modern and what would be folksy was under constant negotiation by the "modernists" and the "regionalists" of the Community Planning Division. In developing the plans for Norris, the TVA architects studied the houses along the Clinch River basin that were scheduled to be removed to make room for the rising backwaters of the dam (Figure 3.38). They carefully measured and drew all the rooms and furniture. They hired anthropologists to ask "housewives in mountain cabins and industrial towns about their desires."[125] Photographers like Lewis Hines were hired to document the "mountain way of life." This careful documentation found its way into many aspects of the new houses in Norris, in the sloped roofs, open porches, shingled siding and "dog-trot" plans. Yet the modernist agenda made its way into the houses as well: in materials, electrification, Taylorized kitchens and even, more subtly, in bourgeois assumptions about living rooms and separate bedrooms. The kitchen in particular became a flashpoint for disagreements about the incorporation of modern technology. Morgan's wife Lillian insisted that wood or coal stoves be provided so the "mountain women" would feel at home. But in a project that was to serve as a showplace for rural electrification in a region where 96 percent of the surrounding households had no electricity, the view of Roland Wank (backed by director David Lilienthal) prevailed, that modern electric appliances were essential.[126] And in fact, we see "an unusually complete electrification" in the houses at Norris, justified by the low electric rates that were established by the new Authority with energy to sell.[127] They were outfitted with electric ranges, refrigerators and water heaters, electric lights, electric water pumps, humidifiers and "circulating fans." We see then that the folksy-looking regional houses of Norris were completely equipped with the most modern appliances. This was the result of A.E. Morgan's deeply conservative insistence on the traditional archetype of house, coupled with David Lilienthal's passion for developing a consumer market for the dam's electricity. The offspring of this strange union was the single-family homeowner as a consumer – a post-war vision we are familiar with today. So we can see in Norris the traditional form of the single family house, harking back to a rural ideal, coupled with the new appliances that anticipated a consumer culture of the future.

The incorporation of fireplaces in all the homes led the architect responsible for house design, Charles Barber, to admit "it may appear a paradox to find that primitive heating device, the fireplace, side by side with the electric heaters that are so novel as to be almost unknown." In a rational vein, he suggests that "they supplement the electric heaters in keeping the homes comfortable," but he adds "taking off the chill is a mental process as well as a physical one."[128] Clearly an accommodation to the "mountaineer culture," the fireplace evoked Roosevelt's ideal of "the house, the home, the homeplace, the cabin with a family in it."[129]

The folksy exterior of the houses concealed real technical innovations in their construction. In this sense, the houses were the opposite of the dam: they looked old but were modern underneath, while the modern styling of the dam concealed outdated and inefficient engineering design. Wall assemblies, framing assemblies and finishes were all investigated with an eye to mass pro-

193 | Putting nature to work

3.38 Mountain cabin near Norris, 1933.

duction, economy and speed of erection. The architects introduced "dry finishes" on the house interiors, such as plywood for the walls and insulating board on the ceilings, and steel sash with aluminum screens for the windows (Figure 3.39). They explored residential steel frame, but after one prototype it was deemed too expensive and was not pursued (Figure 3.40). The susceptibility of wood floors to termites led to explorations in building masonry floors. Slab on grade required too much cut and fill, so they developed precast concrete joists and pans, with finish floors nailed on top. These were later refined as integrally-colored vibrated polished concrete floors and precast vibrated concrete for shower stalls. This type of floor was used in one of the least expensive building systems, made of concrete block, painted inside and out. With a metal roof, these were advertised as "vermin and termite-proof and fire-resisting."[130] The concrete block house became a model for the Federal Housing Authority and was later exported to England.[131] In such neotechnic interiors, the TVA architects also developed prototypes for the electric appliances like heaters and integrated shower and bath enclosures made of sheet metal (anticipating Buckminster Fuller's Dymaxion tub).

It may be difficult for us today to reconcile the folk imagery of the Norris houses with modern materials used to build them – such a hybrid architecture seems more in keeping with the post-modernism of the 1980s

3.39 Living room, Norris.

3.40 Steel frame house, Norris.

3.41 Bedroom, Norris.

than the regionalism of the 1930s (Figure 3.41). But if we return to Leo Marx, and consider his reading of Emerson, we can see such a move as very much in keeping with the American celebration of technology in the heart of a landscape of forest and farmland. Certainly in using these modern, industrial and experimental materials, the designers of Norris worked with the understanding that the region around Norris was going to be an industrial area. According to Earle Draper, this assumption "was in everybody's mind at the time [it was built]."[132] Roland Wank, for example, took care to design the face of Norris Dam so that it would look good at the epicenter of the future metropolis that he envisioned would grow there. The sustained tension in Norris between industrial future and folk past is more evident if we compare it with a Subsistence Homestead like Crossville, Tennessee, just a short distance from the river downstream. Planned as a completely self-sufficient homestead community, the buildings in Crossville are made exclusively of stone and wood. Rhetorically, these materials signify that the Subsistence Homestead was hewn from the logs of the nearby forests and built up from field stones – it was literally "closer to nature." The "regional" materials of

Norris by contrast are gypsum board and plywood, steel sash, cement block and precast concrete, in other words the products of an industrialized region that is not self-sufficient, but linked to larger networks of production and exchange. Alongside these modern materials in Norris, the hand of the craftsman persisted in the split shingles, stone chimneys and woodwork on the porches.

Farming at Norris

The farms in Norris (from the small vegetable lots near the houses and larger fields on the periphery, to the experimental dairy and demonstration farms) were planned to supplement the dispersed industrial development that was sure to follow in the wake of the hydroelectric projects. Many people in the 1930s, not the least among which was Roosevelt, viewed small-scale farming as compatible with industrial modernization. In the Tennessee Valley, one of the best-known examples was Henry Ford's proposal for the unused Wilson Dam at Muscle Shoals. In 1922, as Senator George Norris was still trying to gain support for a bill that would allow the federal government to generate electricity from the recently constructed but inoperative dam, Henry Ford offered the low sum of $5 million for the whole complex (which had just been completed at a cost of $150 million). Ford laid out an ambitious program explaining why the government should sell him the dam below cost. He would produce automobiles at the Wilson Dam site, using energy from the dam, and help establish small communities all the way up the river for 40 miles. Each community would be centered around a small industry, making one part or another for Ford's car, but – as they would be spread apart and surrounded by farmland – each worker could also till his fields, supporting a family with the produce and earning extra cash (perhaps also justifying lower wages) along the way. The parts would be shipped downstream to the plant, creating a 40-mile assembly line along the Tennessee River. The similarities between Henry Ford's ideal and the new town of Norris were not lost on commentators of the time:

> After you have studied the plans they are making for the villages of the valley for a while, you begin to suspect that Henry Ford, rather than Arthur E. Morgan, must be the real director of the scheme. For this is really Mr. Ford's proposal for decentralized industry on an agricultural base, now to be tried at an enormous scale. Mr. Ford believes that the most stable and rewarding type of industry is that which plants the worker on the land, as a source of food and bodily vigor, and then gives him access to the factory, as a source of supplementary income.[133]

For Ford, farming was not only a strategy to supplement low wages, it was fundamental to his vision of the self-made man. Best expressed in his "Greenfield Village," an open-air museum outside the grounds of his River Rouge

Plant in Detroit, Ford felt that inventive genius – exemplified by the American inventor Thomas Edison, the Wright brothers and, of course, himself – springs from facing everyday problem solving, rather than from a fancy education and abstract theorizing. He felt that it was the fruit of common people and not the exclusive domain of the elite. Industry, in this sense, is viewed not a parasite on the agricultural traditions of the United States, but as literally springing from the soil.[134] So the incorporation of farms in Norris Town was intended to support the "self-reliance and spiritual balance" advocated by Roosevelt, providing the medium out of which the new industry would spring.

As a place of production and consumption, the town of Norris was a microcosm of how the whole valley was meant to operate. The dams were emptied of labor and the town showed the cycle of labor, with people re-integrated into a renewed landscape. Modernization was brought into the archetypal home as a servant of the family, and the folk – aided by electrification and training – were re-integrated into the national economy as consumers (of electric appliances) and producers (of tourist goods). We have now placed the representative pieces of the "organic machine", with its hydroelectric dam, new town and farms, and we can set the machine into motion as we get into the car and drive on the new "freeways" linking one dam to the next, all the way down the Tennessee River.

SETTING THE MACHINE INTO MOTION

Once the dam was completed and the waters started to rise, the turbines began to spin and electricity began to flow out to towns and industries. Industrious folk were able to send their goods to distant markets and visitors from faraway places came to visit the valley, bringing cash into the local economy and linking the valley into a larger national system of production and consumption. And come they did, as Charles Krutch remarked: "at the end of the first years, visitors at Wilson Dam and the Wheeler and Norris sites were coming at the rate of a thousand a day – it was a great show."[135]

These tourists arrived on the budding network of state and interstate highways that were being charted and signposted throughout the country. The road built at Norris began as a conduit to carry materials from Knoxville to Norris and workers from the town to the construction site. But the TVA planners recognized that the Norris road was only one link in a much larger network of roads, linking Knoxville to Cincinnati and creating a new route from the south of the country to the Midwest. As they did with the town and the dam, the TVA planners saw the construction of the road at Norris as an opportunity to rethink what a modern road should be.

The ideal relationship between town and highway had been spelled out more than a decade earlier by Benton MacKaye, beginning with his pamphlet of 1921, "The Appalachian Trail: a Project in Regional Planning" and pursued further in his 1930 essay "The Townless Highway."[136] MacKaye advocated the development of a continuous roadway, bordered on each side by forest and parkland, that would run the entire length of the Appalachian Mountains, from New York to Georgia. He argued this highway would serve as a spine for industrial development, allowing mountain resources such as coal and wood to reach the urban centers of the Eastern Seaboard, while providing recreational access for urbanites up and down the coast to the forests of Appalachia. He did not suggest continuous development along this vehicular spine, on the contrary, MacKaye was one of the most vociferous critics of urban sprawl. He wanted "highwayless towns" to be set slightly apart from the freeway, so that they would be free of dangerous through traffic and unsightly billboards and strips. "Townless highways" in turn would serve as scenic parkways, attractive to tourists.

When invited by Earle S. Draper to join the TVA as a regional planning consultant early in 1934, MacKaye was thrilled by the possibility of applying on a large scale the ideas he had been advocating as a member of the Regional Planning Association of America. He first proposed that the construction access road to the dam be built as a demonstration of a limited access "freeway," allowing for rapid movement (35 mph), curved to follow the contour of the rolling landscape, and provided with a 250-foot right of way to prevent the erection of billboards or unsightly roadside shacks.[137] But most importantly, the freeway was envisioned as a tightly constrained conduit for extending the dynamic of modernization into the landscape (Figure 3.42).

MacKaye's ideas were well received by TVA planners who aimed for the overall economic revitalization of the region, while holding fast to its park-like beauty. The Department of Regional Planning Studies agreed that Norris freeway was "one of the major features of the regional development plan," which set the stage for "the full expansion of the resources and opportunities to be developed in the Valley."[138] Describing Norris knit by roads into a metropolitan cluster of rural trading and manufacturing centers, they saw the freeway as a means of accelerating the economic development of the region.[139] It would allow truck traffic to flow more easily, linking dispersed production to dispersed markets. It would bring tourists into the region, enabling them to consume the scenery and purchase the craft commodities. Contained within arteries, traffic would circulate through the "organic machine" and feed its system of exchanges. In this sense, the freeway was like the river. Both are conduits of modernization. Both irrigate the economy. Both use a technology that does not stand opposed to the landscape, but is inserted into it, so that a seamless continuity is presented to the viewer. MacKaye made the analogy between "the stream of water in the rivers and the stream of development along the highways. [He] wanted the TVA to extend its 'sphere of influence' to 'the flow of water,' 'the flow of products,' and 'the flow of population.'"[140] In this way, the once isolated,

199 | Putting nature to work

3.42 Norris freeway.

underdeveloped region would be knit into a national economy on its way to recovery.

The experience of motoring was also important to MacKaye. He wrote at length of the aesthetic qualities of the freeway that would take motorists through the scenic landscape. The Norris freeway itself was an "aesthetically sublime second nature."[141] It was designed to harmonize with the scenery, allowing nothing to come between drivers and their experience of the landscape. Entering into the system of flows, the motorists on the freeway circulate in the organic machine, becoming a part of the reconstructed nature. Their experience is visual, the motorists *see* the landscape as scenery – indeed, the TVA planners working on the freeway begin to describe the Tennessee Valley as a "scenic resource."[142] As images of the valley roll past the moving vehicle, a landscape of dams and houses, farms and forests is turned into cinema. On the freeway, the valley is transformed from a terrain of production into a site of consumption. In this sense, the freeway continues the operation we first see in the dam, when Morgan recognizes the crucial role the dam's appearance would play in public support for the project. The cinematic narrative unfolding past the motorist on the Norris freeway becomes the story of the Tennessee Valley told *not* to its residents, who are working on the farms and in the industries, but to the visitor from out of state, who grasps the whole project as a picture. Immobilized in their moving vehicles, these motorists are projected into "an idealized natural environment of an earlier pre-industrial past."[143]

As the reconstructed nature rolls by, an American Arcadia is presented like a picture, the farmers at work and the historic sites of the first frontier marked out by helpful roadway signs. Leaving the town of Knoxville behind, motorists advanced on Norris freeway through forests and farms, driving by the past (in the form of a frontier-era water mill dating from 1797, reconstructed and flagged by signs), and onto the future, as they crossed the spine of the dam on their way north to Kentucky and Cincinnati. Other freeways of the era were designed to expose tourists to historic sites being reclaimed in the Depression-era search for a "usable past," like the Mount Vernon Memorial Highway that led from Washington DC to the newly reconstructed birthplace of George Washington, the "father of the nation."[144] Similarly, the Blue Ridge Parkway that ran through the Shenandoah wilderness was built shortly after the National Park Service established the Cumberland Gap Park, commemorating Boone's historic trek through Appalachia in "pioneer" days.[145] Each of these parkways of the 1930s knit together a reconstructed past with a promised future. The modern freeway, as Edward Dimendberg says, "unfolding fresh vistas for the spectator, ... becomes a powerful allegory for continuity and progression, a historical teleology and a vision of the future projected onto the landscape itself."[146] Cast in the terms of popular culture, we might say that the Norris freeway knit frontierland to tomorrowland. The motorist of the neotechnic world, gliding through the ribbon of highway on rubber wheels, retraces the paths of the pioneer of the past and always moves, like the pioneer, to an ever-opening landscape.

A landscape of leisure

Who were these tourists? The TVA visitors' register at the Norris powerhouse tells us that they came from Tennessee, Ohio, Kentucky, Illinois, Indiana and West Virginia.[147] They were part of an overwhelming growth in automobile tourism during the 1930s – a growth that Earle Draper, in writing about the TVA parks in 1937, attributes to a number of factors: a rise in automobile ownership and the spread of highways, shorter working hours as a result of trade unionism, and, most fundamentally, a changing attitude to the Protestant work ethic, so that one no longer needed to be ashamed of "leisure" activities.[148] Not that the typical tourist had to be employed to afford a motor holiday. Traveling down from the Great Lakes into the rolling hills of Pennsylvania, Kentucky and Tennessee, the motor tourist could count on inexpensive lodging at any one of a number of newly-created state parks. In Tennessee alone, the state park system had achieved "twenty five years of progress" in a five-year span, spurred on by demonstration parks set up by the TVA near the dams, with the assistance of the National Park Service and the Civilian Conservation Corps.[149]

While the recreational potential of the artificial lakes created by the dams was overlooked at the outset (the focus of the TVA being on relief, resettlement and retraining), it did not take long before TVA planners recognized the economic potential represented by the thousands of curious visitors to the dams. By 1937, Earle Draper was writing articles about demonstration parks at Norris, Wheeler, Pickwick and Wilson Dams, and the following year he published an inventory of the scenic resources of the Tennessee Valley.[150] When Norris Park opened on 30 May 1936, as many as 3,000 to 5,000 people visited each weekend.

The biggest draw, of course, was Norris Dam. In its tourist literature, the city of Knoxville promoted the dam in the same breath as the newly-created Great Smoky Mountains National Park.[151] To be sure, the scenery of Appalachia was still seen as second-best to the spectacular western landscapes that formed the core of the National Park Movement.[152] Nevertheless, the new TVA dams offered a jaw-dropping spectacle of technology and nature reconciled, their "park-like" settings were verdant and picturesque, and all the recreational activities associated with a park holiday were there: horseback riding, boating, fishing, evening entertainments in an outdoor amphitheater, and a rustic parks architecture. The craft aesthetic and folk architecture that we see in the houses in Norris appears again in an even more rustic version in the log cabins and park pavilions of the Norris and Big Ridge State Parks (Figure 3.43). The demonstration parks of the TVA reflected a park ideal that was being implemented nationwide, with the immense growth in state parks that accompanied CCC park-building efforts. The mandatory woodland setting of these state parks, replete with lake and rustic dwellings, celebrated, as Phoebe Cutler points out, "an earlier, pioneer vision of America ... a simpler, freer past as an antidote to a distressed present. Like the grass lawn before it, the rustic state park format advanced across the nation."[153] The model for these parks may have originated in the Adirondack resorts of turn-of-the-century America, but with the involvement of the National Park Service in helping states to set up their own parks, it is not difficult to discern the influence of Yellowstone's "park architecture" and the formula for blending recreational leisure activities with a sense of "roughing it" in a primeval American wilderness (Figure 3.44).

In the TVA parks, we find a constant tension between the search for an authentic pioneer experience and a desire to accommodate the tourism industry in the provision of leisure infrastructure. While Arthur Morgan exceptionally insisted that Big Ridge Park keep tourist amenities to a minimum so that visitors could have a wilderness experience, in general the TVA was happy to

3.43 Vacation cabin, Norris State Park.

3.44 Open air amphitheater, Norris State Park.

promote and enhance the many commercial enterprises that accompanied parks development. One of the most popular activities in Norris Lake, for example, was the Labor Day speedboat regatta, sponsored by the Dixie Motorboat Association. In his address to the US Senate, reporting on the economic potential of TVA-related recreation, Earle Draper said, "waters of the lake, spouting outboard motors, cruisers and yachts, where bottom lands formerly were devoted to corn, may be the harbinger of a new day."[154]

In this new landscape, earlier categories of natural and artificial are dramatically reworked. In a caption accompanying press copy about TVA tourist attractions, sent to the editor of *Architectural Forum*, Roland Wank tells us, "At each of its projects, the Authority has provided overlook buildings commanding views over the dam and powerhouse. That at Norris Dam is typical. At tables on the curved terrace visitors may enjoy a Coca-Cola while listening to the generators from the powerhouse below."[155] The substitution of sublime technology for spectacular nature here is revealing. After being "vibrated with a view," the tourist can then step into the craft shop at Norris Dam, and purchase a souvenir of the Tennessee folk culture, because, again in Wank's words,

> The mountain people of the Tennessee Valley have always made by hand many of the fabrics, utensils, and household goods for everyday use. Settlement schools and machine workers have encouraged these crafts as a source of supplementary income for mountain homes.

When visiting Yellowstone Park, tourists might return home with an Indian rug, an elk horn souvenir, or a bit of petrified tree, so what better memento – when visiting the "first frontier" of the Tennessee Valley – than the homemade crafts of an "original" folk American? Who would ever imagine that the modern men who had built the dams spent their afternoon hours whittling milking stools? Even the most natural-seeming parks activity concealed an astonishing amount of artifice to ensure that the amateur angler would bring back a string of fish to the campground. Again, Wank writes,

> The Authority's river-development program, changing a swiftly flowing river into a series of deep, still lakes, profoundly affects wildlife associated with the river. In cooperation with the US Bureau of Fisheries from the Biological Survey, the Authority is conducting a cooperative program of biological readjustment. Its lakes are stocked annually with several millions of young fish from hatcheries and rearing pools developed by the Authority in cooperation with these other agencies.

Such "biological re-adjustment," or tinkering with the organic machine, was inevitable before the entire system would function smoothly. The dams' multiple functions of flood control and power generation frequently interfered with the new-found recreational potential of the lakes, as, for example, when "draw down" created problems at the water's edge for the "small fry" seeded in the lakes that would flop around and rot in the summer sun (see Plate 10).[156] Secondary dams were built to secure lake levels for swimmers, but then the waters had to be chlorinated and artificially circulated for public health reasons, concrete bottoms installed at wading depths, and "beaches" of sand and turf provided at the perimeter (see Figure 3.45).[157] Ultimately, part of the magic of visiting the TVA was the seamless fusion of technology and nature. A European visitor commented how fortunate the Americans were to have their technological achievements situated in such beautiful parks.

The visitors' facilities at Norris were just a seed for the spectacular provisions that were made in dams built on the Tennessee in the years to follow. The choreographic procession through the dams grew ever more elaborate. In

3.45 "Beach" at Big Ridge Park, Norris Lake.

Watts Bar Dam, for example, the visitors' center was located on a prominent escarpment with a panoramic view of the dam, road and lock below (Plate 11). Within the circular lobby, a built-in sofa curved around a spiral strip of aluminum set into the terrazzo floor, echoing the flow of water through the spinning turbines far below. The ceiling ventilator in this room also copied the turbine housings, reinforcing the feeling that one had entered the precinct of highest technology (see Figures 3.46 and 3.47).

Fontana Dam, begun in 1942 and finished in 1944, presents perhaps the ultimate visitor experience (Figure 3.48). Because construction on this dam began after the war was under way and it was built under time pressure and with rationed materials, one might expect that little care would have been taken with the visitor amenities. But by the time this dam was designed, both Roland Wank and his assistant Mario Bianculli had developed a sophisticated understanding of the visitors' expectations and the didactic potential of this new architecture. Like in Watts Bar, they placed the visitors' center at the very top of the dam in a cantilevered platform that thrust far over the

3.46 Ceiling of visitor center, Watts Bar Dam.

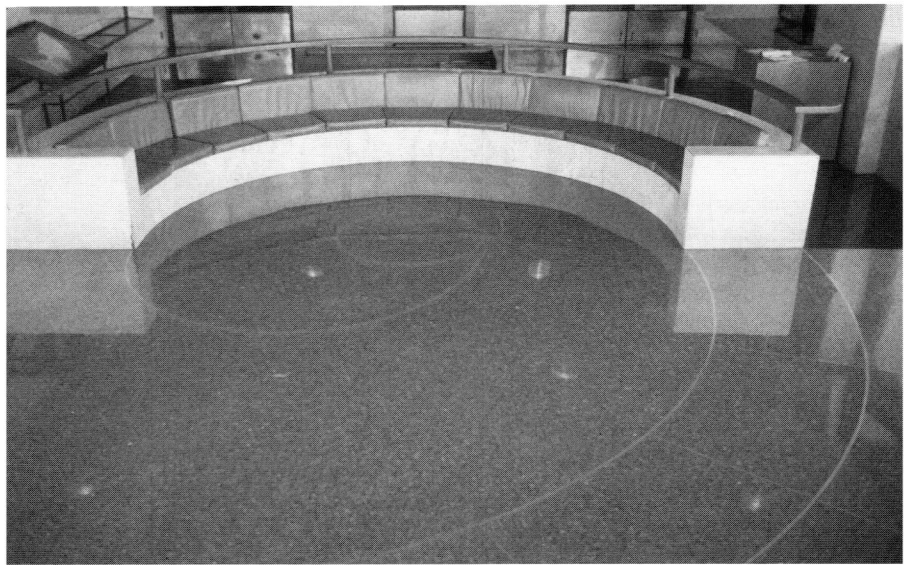

3.47 Floor of visitor center, Watts Bar Dam.

3.48 Aerial view of Fontana Dam.

precipice (Plates 12 and 13). After taking in the view, the visitor was directed down a spiral stair and onto a glass-enclosed funicular railway, which plummeted 300 feet down an inclined plane to the powerhouse before disgorging its passengers among the throbbing turbines. In this dramatic itinerary, the flow of tourists literally mimicked the flow of water thundering through the penstocks of the dam. Arriving at the bottom, they entered the majestic all-concrete powerhouse, welcomed by the words "Built for the People of the United States of America (Figures 3.49 to 3.51)."

The attention paid to the visitors' experience paid off in an annually escalating number of tourists who came to see the miracle of the TVA. The TVA captured the imagination of liberal intellectuals, "as an augury of progressive politics, regional development and the entire panoply of New Deal Reform."[158] Foreign as well as American critics saw the TVA as "an outstanding example of democratic planning, ... the first large-scale regional planning organization which operated ... on the democratic principles of persuasion, consent, and participation."[159] Talbot Hamlin, in *Pencil Points*, enthused,

3.49 Fontana incline car.

3.50 View from inside Fontana incline car.

it is the world's most striking contemporary example that planning – large scale planning – is possible in a democracy; that such false efficiency as that of a dictatorship is necessary to produce great national works, conceived and executed for the benefit of all the people. Perhaps one could go further and even say that, under a dictatorship, that controlling atmosphere which creates the humanity and charm of much of TVA would have been impossible. The designers have somehow, through subtle design and human planning, set human beings as the center of the whole scheme.[160]

The influence of the regional planning experiment that was the TVA extended far beyond the boundaries of the United States. In 1939, Julian Huxley foresaw a Danube Valley Authority and wrote of the possibilities for such authorities in Africa and the Middle East, and in 1944 the idea of a Jewish Valley Authority in Palestine was proposed in *Land Magazine*. In 1944, a contingent of Chinese officials visited Norris Dam, to be followed by Jawaharlal Nehru in 1949 and David Ben Gurion in 1951.

209 | Putting nature to work

3.51 Inside powerhouse at Fontana Dam.

A landscape in equilibrium
When the broad brush strokes of the TVA were completed, no aspect of nature remained untouched. Every lake is artificial, every tree has been planted, every contour has been molded, every stone has been moved and placed. Nestled in its beautiful park, the dam opens and closes its sluice gates, moderating the

wild rhythms of the river, irrigating the fields downstream with water and the homes and industries with electricity, so both fields and folk can produce more easily. Resettled in a community that is neither town nor farm, but a bit of both, the people of Norris were able to balance work and education, learning skills usable in daily life and preparing themselves for the new opportunities opening up in a national economy. The reconstructed region is threaded through with freeways, connecting industry to town and region to nation.

The early years of the TVA presented a plan to achieve an integrated, harmonious, interdependent landscape in balance, in which technology and nature were reconciled in an Emersonian vision recast for the 1930s. The cast of characters charged with developing the plan pulled it in different directions, each stressing their own aims – be they social engineering, architectural modernism, the public ownership of power, liberal or conservative ideals. But what we have looked at here was a certain moment – the period of building Norris – in which the fuller, integrated dimension of the TVA came forth. It is a moment far removed from the alienation proposed by present-day ecologists who see human beings as a stain on a purer, more perfect world from which they are absent. As the quintessential project of the early New Deal, this early phase of the TVA was predicated on the belief that people have a place in the landscape, and they can contribute to its balanced maintenance. It is a productive landscape in which each construction, be it dam or town or highway, is designed to increase production, to accelerate the organic machine. But each built work was also designed to fit into the "natural" system – dams and freeway inserted like prosthetic devices into their verdant settings, the town sprouting from freshly cleared forest to look like it had always been there, its native houses, wooded copses and carefully tended fields evoking an eternal synchrony with the rhythms of nature.

To call on nature as the ultimate reference for a region reaching a state of balance entailed certain costs – to see *people as nature* was to radically de-historicize them and conflate certain mythic constructs with the lived reality. To see *engineering as nature* was a way to advance the myth of a manifest destiny, setting the creation of a productive infrastructure on a par with a landscape of natural monuments that were seen as signs of a unique national mission. To see a *planned landscape as nature* points to what is perhaps the greatest legacy of the TVA – that humans have a place in regenerating a natural landscape that they have damaged (Figure 3.52).

As massive effort in reconstruction, the TVA primed the pump for the war. The Tennessee Valley was integrated in the national networks of wartime production, its hydroelectric dams supplying the seemingly limitless demand for power of the nuclear experiments at Oak Ridge, its fertilizer plants once again supplying nitrates for munitions, and its aluminum plants turning out airplane fuselages. Its director David Lilienthal became head of the new Atomic Energy Commission, and Arthur Morgan's vision for a people at home in their region seemed archaic and remote. After the war, as

3.52 Young man on Appalachian Mountain.

Walter Creese has pointed out, the regionalism of the TVA seemed to offer little to a nation concerned primarily with its global influence.[161] The fundamentally civic and collective ideals of the early TVA atomized into a liberal ideology of single family houses in the suburbs, each garden serving as an icon of the Arcadian agrarian myth, while the rhetoric of pioneering extended to the globe or even into outer space. Yet the early TVA holds a lesson for architects and planners. It represents a moment when the ambitions of these professionals extended beyond the particular building projects they were engaged in, when they eagerly embraced the larger implications of their designs as acts of collective self-definition, and recognized the interdependence of house and town, nature and technology, region and nation.

Notes

1. Wheeler (1933–6), Pickwick (1934–8), Guntersville (1935–9), Chickamauga (1936–40), Kentucky (1938–44), Watts Bar (1939–42) and Fort Loudon (1940–3) were built on the Tennessee River. On the tributaries, the TVA constructed Norris (1933–6), Hiwassee (1936–40), Cherokee (1940–1), Douglas (1942–3), Fontana (1942–4), and Apalachia, Chatuge, Nottely and Ocoee Dams Nos. 1, 2 & 3 (early 1940s).
2. Franklin D. Roosevelt, Message to Congress on Muscle Shoals Development, House Doc. 15, 73rd Congress, 1st Session, 10 April 1933: 7. Cited in numerous popular publications of the time, including Paul Hutchinson, "Revolution by Electricity: the Significance of the Tennessee Valley Experiment," *Scribner's Magazine* 96, no. 4 (October 1934), p. 195.
3. The phrase is the TVA economist Stuart Chase's, quoted in "A Vision in Kilowatts," *Fortune* (April 1933). Chase went on to publish *Rich Land Poor Land: a Study of Waste in the Natural Resources of America*, 1936.
4. We are indebted to Richard White for this term in his analysis of the Columbia River Basin. See Richard White, *The Organic Machine: the Remaking of the Columbia River*, New York: Hill and Wang, 1995.
5. Paul K. Conklin, "Intellectual and Political Roots of the TVA," in Erwin C. Hargrove and Paul K. Conklin (eds), *TVA: Fifty Years of Grassroots Democracy*, Urbana: University of Illinois Press, 1983, p. 23.
6. In the years following the establishment of the TVA, Roosevelt proposed to Congress that seven such authorities be set up in the country. He also suggested that the TVA dams, along with dams on the Colorado, Columbia and St Lawrence rivers, serve as federally owned and run "yardsticks" to gauge the fair cost of power and keep utilities in line. (See Goodwin in Hargrove and Conklin, *TVA: Fifty Years*, p. 265.)
7. For further reading on the vast scope of New Deal initiatives, see William E. Leuchtenberg, *Franklin D. Roosevelt and the New Deal, 1932–1940*, New York: Harper and Row, 1963; William F. MacDonald, *Federal Relief Administration and the Arts*, Columbus, OH: Ohio State University Press, 1969; US, Public Works Administration, *America Builds: the Record of the PWA*, Washington: US Government Printing Office, 1939; Frank Freidel, *The New Deal and the American People*, Englewood Cliffs, NJ: Prentice-Hall, 1965.

8   Ross Spears, *The Electric Valley* (documentary film), Johnson City, TX: James Agee Film Project.
9   Cited in David E. Shi, *The Simple Life: Plain Living and High Thinking in American Culture*, New York and Oxford: Oxford University Press, 1985, p. 233.
10 R.L. Duffus and Charles Krutch, *The Valley and its People: a Portrait of TVA*, New York: Alfred Knopf, 1944, p. 28.
11 David E. Lilienthal, *TVA: Democracy on the March*, New York: Harper & Brothers, 1953, p. 1.
12 Harold L. Ickes, *Why I Favor a Program of Public Works*, Washington, 1936. The quote is taken from Anatole Kopp "Les Racines Européenes de la culture du New Deal," in Jean-Louis Cohen and Hubert Damisch (eds), *Américanisme et Modernité*, Paris: Flammarion, 1993, p. 364.
13 Walter Creese, *TVA's Public Planning: the Vision, the Reality*, Knoxville: University of Tennessee, 1990, p. 342.
14 Cited in Whitney R. Cross, "Ideas in Politics: the Conservation Policies of the Two Roosevelts," *Journal of the History of Ideas* 14 (1953), pp. 421–38.
15 Walter Creese outlines in some detail Franklin Roosevelt's support for regional planning, in particular his sponsorship of the New York Regional Plan and his proposals for damming the Saint Lawrence River and capturing the tidal waters of the Bay of Fundy.
16 David Whisnant discusses the debt of the TVA to the early cooperative movements in his *Modernizing the Mountaineer: People, Power and Planning in Appalachia*, Boone, NC: Appalachian Consortium Press, 1980, p. 13.
17 Pare Lorentz, *The River* (documentary film), Farm Security Administration, 1938.
18 Frederick A. Gutheim, "TVA, a new phase in Architecture," originally published in the *Magazine of Art* 33 (September 1940), pp. 516–31. Reprinted as *TVA Architecture, as shown at the Museum of Modern Art*, New York: Museum of Modern Art, n.d., p. 11.
19 Gutheim, "TVA, a new phase," p. 15.
20 David E. Nye, *American Technological Sublime*, Cambridge, MA: MIT Press, 1994.
21 Leo Marx, *The Machine in the Garden: Technology and the Pastoral Ideal in America*, London: Oxford University Press, 1964, pp. 195, 214.
22 Nye, *American Technological Sublime*, p. 134.
23 Henry Adams, *The Education of Henry Adams*, [1907] New York: Modern Library, 1996, p. 382.
24 Lewis Mumford, *Technics and Civilization*, New York: Harcourt, Brace and Company, 1934, p. 224.
25 The other two directors of the triumvirate Board were David Lilienthal and Harcourt Morgan, responsible for public power and agricultural policy respectively.
26 Interview with Earle S. Draper. TVA Archives, 30–1. Somewhat contradicting this, Draper also recollects that he felt Wank "was a genius" and that he was hired on Draper's recommendation. He adds that he often backed Wank in the face of criticism from higher up in the TVA hierarchy. Letter from Earle S. Draper to his son, date, personal collection of Earle S. Draper, Jr. Draper was well known for his humane town planning in factory towns in the south.

27 John T. Moutoux, "R.A. Wank, TVA Architect, Sees Workers' Housing as Great Challenge of Tennessee Basin's New Deal," *Knoxville News-Sentinel*, 2 December 1933.
28 Letter from Roland A. Wank to Arthur E. Morgan, TVA Archives.
29 Interview with Earle S. Draper. TVA Archives, 29–31.
30 TVA had also hired Gordon Kaufmann as a consultant. Jean-François Lejeune, "Democratic Pyramids: the Works of the Tennessee Valley Authority," *Rassegna, Themes in Architecture: Electricity. United States & USSR, France and Italy*. Quarterly/III, Year 17, no. 63 (1995), p. 48. It is tempting to look for correspondences between Wank's redesign for Norris Dam and the schemes of the Italian futurists, such as Antonio Sant'Elia, who developed a series of visionary schemes for dams in mountainous regions of northern Italy in the years just following the First World War. The emphasis on verticality, the careful composition of dam and its supporting structures, and most of all, the sense that the dam would serve as the heart of a future urbanism that would grow around this power-producing heart, are all there. Also under the sphere of influence of Vienna, the relationship between the Futurists and Otto Wagner's "metropolis" modernity has been well charted. Walter Creese has discussed Wagner's influence on Wank's architecture, but whether that extended to Wank's awareness of the Italian designs is left open for speculation.
31 A fact not lost on commentators of the era, who admired the TVA as much for its management of publicity as for any concrete achievements it had accomplished, especially in the first three years. See Gutheim, "TVA: a new phase," p. 17.
32 Interview with Earle S. Draper, TVA Archives, p. 18.
33 Reyner Banham, "Tennessee Valley Authority: the Engineering of Utopia," *Casabella* 542–3 (January–February 1988), p. 74.
34 Gutheim, "TVA, a New Phase," p. 17. According to Neuse, Lilienthal succeeded "in giving the TVA power program [in the years 1934–7] a substantial image when, in reality, it was no more than a Potemkin village." Steven M. Neuse, *David E. Lilienthal: The Journey of an American Liberal*, Knoxville: University of Tennessee Press, 1996, p. 83.
35 Le Corbusier, *Vers une Architecture*. English translation by Frederick Etchells, *Towards a New Architecture*, 1927, p. 33. See also Cohen and Damisch, *Américanisme et Modernité*, p. 364.
36 Lewis Mumford, "The Architecture of Power," *New Yorker* 17, no. 2 (7 June 1941), p. 58.
37 In 1938, Pare Lorentz's film *The River* won best documentary at the Venice Biennale, and by the eve of the US entry into World War II (1942), up to two million tourists a year were visiting the dams. While these were mostly American, Europeans were writing about the TVA; see, for example, Odette Keun, *A Foreigner Looks at the TVA*, Toronto: Longmans Green, 1937, and Julian S. Huxley, "TVA, an Achievement of Democratic Planning," *Architectural Review* 93, no. 558 (June 1943). TVA continued to exert its attraction on Europeans traveling to the US in the post-war period. Among French architects alone, we find Le Corbusier, Gaston Leclaire, and Marcel Lods visiting the TVA between 1945 and 1948. See Marcel Lods, "Retour d'Amerique," *L'Architecture française* 7, no. 54 (January 1946), and Gaston Leclaire, "Impressions d'Amerique," *L'Architecture française* 75–6 (1948), pp. 66–71.

38 Geoffrey Baker, "Architecture and Design of the TVA," *Journal of the Royal Architectural Institute of Canada* (April 1942), p. 59.
39 Douglas Haskell, "Architecture of the TVA," *Nation* 152 (17 May 1941), p. 592.
40 Frederick Gutheim's article in the *Magazine of Art* devotes several pages to a step-by-step tour through Norris Dam, describing the physical experience of being there.
41 Gutheim, "TVA, a New Phase," p. 17.
42 Talbot Hamlin, "Architecture of the TVA," *Pencil Points* 20 (November 1939), pp. 722, 731.
43 Mumford, *Technics*, 229.
44 Moutoux, "R.A. Wank, TVA Architect."
45 Haskell, "Architecture of the TVA," p. 592.
46 Multiple references to this quote can be found in the early press accounts of TVA architecture. See, for example *Time* 37, no. 19 (12 May 1941), p. 46.
47 Lewis Mumford, "The Architecture of Power," *New Yorker* 17, no. 2 (7 June 1941), p. 58.
48 Mumford, "The Architecture of Power," p. 58.
49 Stuart Chase, in his introductory text to the MOMA TVA exhibit. Cited in Mumford, "The Architecture of Power," p. 58.
50 Marian Moffett and Lawrence Wodehouse, "Noble Structures Set in Handsome Parks: Public Architecture of the TVA," *Modulus* 17 (University of Virginia Architectural Review), 1984, p. 77.
51 In 1939, an entire issue of *Pencil Points* 20 (November) was devoted to the TVA, and a 41-page pictorial essay on the TVA appeared in *Architectural Forum* 71 (August). The following year the *Magazine of Art* 33 (September) ran a 15-page spread by Frederick Gutheim, entitled "Tennessee Valley Authority, A New Phase in Architecture." In 1941, with the opening of the MOMA show, articles on TVA architecture appeared in *Magazine of Art*, *Time Magazine*, *Nation*, and *New Yorker*, as well as continued architectural coverage in *Pencil Points* and *Architectural Forum*.
52 Hamlin, "Architecture of the TVA," pp. 721, 729.
53 Gutheim, "TVA, a New Phase," p. 12.
54 Mumford, "Architecture of Power," p. 58.
55 Walter Gropius, "Die Entwicklung Moderner Industriebaukunst," *Jahrbuch des Deutschen Werkbundes*, 1913. For a developed commentary on how European modernist architects viewed North American industrial construction, see Reyner Banham, *A Concrete Atlantis: US Industrial Building and European Modern Architecture*, Cambridge, MA: MIT Press, 1986.
56 "Insofar as architecture is useful, it is not art.... Only a very small part of architecture belongs to art: the tomb and the monument." Adolf Loos, "Architektur" (1910), reprinted in *Sämtliche Schriften, Adolf Loos*, vol. 1, Vienna: Verlag Harold, 1962, p. 317. Translated in Yehuda Safran and Wilfried Wang (eds), *The Architecture of Adolf Loos: an Arts Council Exhibition*, London, 1987, p. 108. Loos here adopts Kant's argument that the appreciation of beauty and thus art requires a beholder disinterested in the utility of the object. A useless architecture then, one which cannot be entered and does not contain, can most closely approach pure beauty and pure architectural signification.

57 The Ames were long-term patrons of Richardson. His Ames Gate Lodge in Easton, MA is one of the earliest instances of his "geologic" architecture, using simple, monumental forms and cyclopean masonry.
58 Catherine Ingraham, "Missing Objects," in Diana Agrest, Patricia Conway and Leslie Kanes Weisman (eds), *The Sex of Architecture*, New York: Harry N. Abrams, 1996, p. 38.
59 Ingraham, "Missing Objects," p. 36.
60 Marcia Ian, "When is a Body not a Body? When it's a Building," in Joel Sanders (ed.), *STUD: Architectures of Masculinity*, New York: Princeton Architectural Press, 1996, p. 191.
61 "The Architecture of Architects is Hollow Inside, Not Dense, Not Solid." Ingraham, "Missing Objects," p. 38.
62 Ian, "When is a Body?," p. 198.
63 Hamlin, "Architecture of the TVA," p. 724; *Time Magazine* (1941), p. 46.
64 Huxley, "TVA, an Achievement," p. 141.
65 Hamlin, "Architecture of the TVA," p. 729.
66 Gutheim, "TVA, a New Phase." He continues, "What you see when you look at these vast engineering accomplishments is architecture. And it is not the accidental architecture of a rock formation, nor the naked architecture of a grain elevator; it is as calculated and as controlled a piece of construction as a temple. You know that it is architecture because it is beautiful – beautiful in a way that other dams where there is merely sincere construction are not."
67 Clothing itself, identified with dissimulation and falsity, is a necessary attribute of the "naturally" modest woman.
68 Mark Wigley, "White Out, Fashioning the Modern," in Deborah Fausch, *et al.* (eds), *Architecture in Fashion*, New York: Princeton Architectural Press, 1994, p. 157.
69 "The grand scale was not frittered away. The usual American dam is a giant with Lilliputian scholars and clowns posturing all over his back in togas or cap and bells. The ruggedness at TVA, the big blocky simplicity ... , may seem to casual visitors to be a natural consequence or "purely functional". This is not so. It is carefully evoked, a matter of design having to do with proportion, craftsmanship with materials, placing, scale, and a sense of drama in the whole thing." Haskell, "Architecture of the TVA," p. 592.
70 Adrian Forty, "Masculine, Feminine or Neuter?" in Duncan McCorquodale, Katerina Rüedi and Sarah Wigglesworth (eds), *Desiring Practices: Architecture, Gender and the Interdisciplinary*, London: Black Dog Publishing, 1996, p. 150.
71 Elizabeth Bauer Mock (ed.), *Built in the USA, 1932–1944*, New York: Museum of Modern Art, 1944, p. 111.
72 Forty, "Masculine, Feminine or Neuter?," p. 153.
73 Gutheim, "TVA, a New Phase," p. 20.
74 Douglas Haskell repeats this strange conflation of crane and insect when he talks about "the steely mechanical beauty of the smooth, insectile cranes." This insect metaphor may call on popular culture of the time – I am thinking of Orson Welles' radio address "War of the Worlds," in which the machines are both animate and frightening, as well as all-powerful.
75 Mumford, "The Architecture of Power," p. 58.
76 Hamlin, "Architecture of the TVA," p. 724.

77 Gutheim, "TVA, a New Phase," p. 16.
78 Haskell, "Architecture of the TVA."
79 R.L. Duffus, "Our River of Power Flowing to War," *New York Times Magazine* (28 March 1943), p. 7.
80 Richard White, *The Organic Machine*, p. 76.
81 See Hilde Heynen's discussion of modernist town planning in Frankfurt in her *Architecture and Modernity*, Cambridge, MA: MIT Press, 1999, and Eve Blau, *The Architecture of Red Vienna*, Cambridge: MIT Press, 1999.
82 Radburn, New Jersey was built in 1928.
83 Letter from Charles Colby to Earle S. Draper, 1935. TVA Archives.
84 "Happy Valley," *Business Week* (15 Feb 1933); Guinea Pig Valley," *Literary Digest* 115, no. 16 (22 April 1933); "The Promised Land," *Collier's Magazine* 91 (3 June 1933); "Vast Setting of a Power Age Dream," *New York Times Magazine* (25 June 1933); "Tennessee Valley, a Prevision of Utopia: revivifying the psychology of an ancient people will be paced by America's most gigantic technical task," *Literary Digest* 117, no. 11 (17 March 1934); "What will TVA do to the USA?," *Christian Century* (11 April 1934).
85 The citations are taken from Herby Smith, *Strangers and Kin* (documentary film), Whitesburg, KY: Appalshop Films, 1984.
86 Ibid.
87 Ibid.
88 "Another potent asset, that should appeal to the lover of America and American institutions, is that these southern Appalachian Mountains are giving to the nation every year 100,000 new citizens of the purest American type, which is no inconsiderable item when we know that fifty per cent increase in many of our large cities is made up of a low type of immigrants from the slums of Europe " *The Carolina Churchman*, March 1910, cited in David E. Whisnant, *All That is Native and Fine: the Politics of Culture in an American Region*, Chapel Hill and London: University of North Carolina, 1983.
89 Ian McKay, *The Quest of the Folk: Antimodernism and Cultural Selection in Twentieth-Century Nova Scotia*, Montreal and Kingston: McGill-Queen's University Press, 1994, p. xvi.
90 McKay, *Quest of the Folk*, p. 12.
91 Nancy L. Grant, *TVA and Black Americans: Planning for the Status Quo*, Philadelphia: Temple University Press, 1990, p. 48.
92 "Jim Crow" is a slang term used to refer to segregation laws that required separate facilities for black and white citizens.
93 Grant, *TVA and Black Americans*, p. 37.
94 Employment across racial lines continued to dog the TVA. TVA made some efforts to hire black employees in proportion to their representation in each region, but job opportunities and advancement were restricted. See Grant, *TVA and Black Americans*.
95 According to McDonald and Muldowny, this accusation of 'Godlessness' stemmed from statements made by a minister in Chicago that were given nationwide distribution by the *Chicago Tribune*. "The controversy centered around charges that Norris had been left without provisions for religious worship." Subsequently, "the TVA authorized the circulation of a petition to determine the religious preferences of people in the town. Almost unanimously,

the townspeople voted in favor of a communal non-denominational church." [Michael J. McDonald and John Muldowny, *TVA and the Dispossessed: the Resettlement of Population in the Norris Dam Area*, Knoxville: University of Tennessee Press, 1982, p. 231.]
96   Letchworth, designed by architects Barry Parker and Raymond Unwin in 1907, was the first realization of the "Garden City" principles that were set out nine years earlier by Ebenezer Howard in his pamphlet, *Tomorrow: the Peaceful Path to Real Reform* (1898). Intended as a middle path between countryside and city, the Garden City was to provide the advantages of both and the disadvantages of neither. Property speculation was discouraged through a system of cooperative ownership, the residents owning shares in the whole society.
97   Letter from Roland A. Wank to Arthur E. Morgan, 14. TVA Archives.
98   Paul Hutchinson, "Revolution by Electricity: the Significance of the Tennessee Valley Experiment," *Scribner's Magazine* 96, no. 4 (October 1934).
99   Grant, *TVA and Black Americans*, p. 10.
100 See Dolores Hayden's significant work on the centrality of feminism to early communitarian social planning in the United States. Dolores Hayden, *Seven American Utopias: the Architecture of Communitarian Socialism, 1790–1975*, Cambridge, MA: MIT Press, 1976.
101 While paid employment of women was not ruled out in TVA towns, it was discouraged in this project like in other New Deal resettlement programs. In Greenhills, Ohio, a Resettlement Administration "greenbelt" town designed by Wank, families in which the mother worked outside the home were denied eligibility for the houses.
102 Visiting Norris, James Agee was fascinated that auto mechanics, plumbing and wrought-iron work were taught. [Creese, *TVA's Public Planning*, p. 259.] Other crafts taught at Norris included pewter-pounding, weaving and leatherwork. [McDonald and Muldowny, *TVA and the Dispossessed*, p. 233.]
103 Creese, *TVA's Public Planning*, p. 245.
104 The American Friends Service Committee, the relief arm of the Quakers, was requested in 1931 by their fellow Quaker President Herbert Hoover, to engage in Appalachian relief work.
105 Allan H. Eaton, *Handicrafts of the Southern Highlands*, New York: Russell Sage Foundation, 1937, p. 237.
106 Whisnant, *All That is Native*.
107 See David E. Shi, *The Simple Life: Plain Living and High Thinking in American Culture*, New York and Oxford: Oxford University Press, 1985.
108 McKay, *Quest of the Folk*, 153, p. 38 and Whisnant, *All That is Native*, p. xiii.
109 Creese, *TVA's Public Planning*, p. 245.
110 Arthur E. Morgan, "Benchmarks in the Tennessee Valley," *Survey Graphic* 23 (November 1934), p. 552.
111 Creese, *TVA's Public Planning*, p. 245.
112 Creese, *TVA's Public Planning*, p. 259.
113 Morgan, "Benchmarks," pp. 551–2.
114 McKay, *Quest of the Folk*, p. 178.
115 Creese, *TVA's Public Planning*.
116 Malcolm Ross, *Machine Age in the Hills*, New York: The Macmillan Company, 1933, p. 237.

117 McDonald and Muldowny, *TVA and the Dispossessed*: 4. The greatest number of any TVA project.
118 According to Earle S. Draper, Norris was "planned specifically to conform to a mountain setting, and, above all, to serve a mountaineer culture during and after a period of measurable change." Quoted in *Architectural Forum* 59, no. 6 (December 1933), p. 519.
119 Tracy B. Augur, "The Planning of the Town of Norris," *American Architect* 148 (April 1936), p. 19.
120 Creese, *TVA's Public Planning*, p. 304.
121 McDonald and Muldowny, *TVA and the Dispossessed*, p. 217.
122 David Frisby, *Fragments of Modernity: Theories of Modernity in the Work of Simmel, Kracauer and Benjamin*, Cambridge, MA: MIT Press, 1986, pp. 4–5. Frisby argues that three key "sociologists" of modernity – Georg Simmel, Siegfried Kracauer and Walter Benjamin – owe little to Max Weber's "classical" theory of modernity centered around rationalization and its consequences for the individual. Rather, these three thinkers were concerned with the new modes of perception and experience set into motion by capitalism. What is specific about their investigations of modernity is that they do not begin from an analysis of society as a whole, or from a structural or institutional analysis. Nor do they start out assuming the totality of modern society. Rather, all three begin with the apparent fragments of social reality. For an architectural analog to Frisby's argument, see Colin St. John Wilson, *The Other Tradition of Modern Architecture: the Uncompleted Project*, London: Academy Editions, 1995. Wilson explores some of the alternative threads of modernist architecture that have been marginalized by the notion of a singular trajectory to architectural modernism.
123 T.J. Jackson Lears, *No Place of Grace: Antimodernism and the Transformation of American Culture, 1880–1920*, Chicago and London: University of Chicago Press, 1983, p. xvii.
124 *Pencil Points* (1939), p. 727. It is only later, as the audience for modern architecture grew larger in the war and post-war periods (and the journals devote more and more coverage to modern designs) that the houses of Norris are increasingly viewed as "old-fashioned." In 1942, Julian Huxley sees them as "labor-saving," but "somewhat nondescript and architecturally uninteresting." By 1970, Frederick Gutheim, writing Wank's obituary, erroneously stated that Wank "did not allow himself to be diverted from the main job, the construction of dams and engineering works, to such trifles as the design of the town of Norris and its housing." (Gutheim, 1970, p. 59.) Just the opposite of course, was true, that Wank not only was initially hired to design houses in Norris, but he continued to consider both house design and town planning an important, if not central part of his work. While still at the TVA, he was "hired out" to the Resettlement Administration as chief architect for the "greenbelt town" of Greenhills, Ohio.
125 Moutoux, "R.A. Wank, TVA Architect". Architects of the TVA Land Planning Division made measured drawings of the furniture in the mountain cabins. [McDonald and Muldowny, *TVA and the Dispossessed*.]
126 McDonald and Muldowny, *TVA and the Dispossessed*.
127 "The TVA's town of Norris will soon be built. No run down outskirts will ever

mar it; nor will through traffic disturb it," *Architectural Forum* 60, no. 1 (January 1934), pp. 77–8.
128 Charles I. Barber, "Architectural Design for the Communities at Norris, Wheeler and Pickwick Landing," *Proceedings on the Conference on Low Cost Housing*, Atlanta, GA: Bulletin, Georgia School of Technology, 1935, p. 21.
129 Creese, *TVA's Public Planning*, p. 247.
130 Augur, "The Planning of the Town of Norris," p. 21.
131 Letter from Earle S. Draper to Forrest Allen, 1936. TVA Archives.
132 Ibid.
133 Hutchinson, "Revolution by Electricity," p. 198.
134 Michael Wallace, "Visiting the Past: History Museums in the United States," *Radical History Review* 25 (1981), pp. 63–96.
135 R.L. Duffus and Charles Krutch, *The Valley and its People: a Portrait of TVA*, New York: Alfred Knopf, 1944, p. 77. Records of visitors in 1937 showed 52,000 from Tennessee, 11,000 from Ohio, 4,000 from Kentucky, 4,000 from Illinois, 4,000 from Indiana, 2,000 from North Carolina, 2,000 from Georgia and 3,600 from West Virginia.
136 Daniel Schaffer, "Benton MacKaye: The TVA Years," *Planning Perspectives* 5, no. 1 (January 1990).
137 Schaffer, "Benton MacKaye," p. 15.
138 Earle S. Draper, "The New TVA Town of Norris, Tennessee," *American City* 48 (December 1933), p. 67.
139 Augur, "The Planning of the Town of Norris," p. 21.
140 Schaffer, "Benton MacKaye," p. 10.
141 This expression is borrowed from Edward Dimendberg in his discussion of the German autobahn in "Cinema, Highways, and Modernity," *October* 73 (Summer 1995), p. 106.
142 MacKaye coined this term while at the TVA, and Earle S. Draper adopted it for the title of the TVA-sponsored survey *The Scenic Resources of the Tennessee Valley*, 1938.
143 Dimendberg, "Cinema," p. 108.
144 Norman T. Newton, *Design on the Land: the Development of Landscape Architecture*, Cambridge, MA and London: Harvard University Press, 1971, p. 254.
145 John Bodnar, *Remaking America: Public Memory, Commemoration and Patriotism in the Twentieth Century*, Princeton: Princeton University Press, 1992, p. 185.
146 Dimendberg, "Cinema," p. 108.
147 J.W. Bradner, Jr, "Tourists at Norris," report prepared for David Lilienthal, 2 December 1937. National Archives East Point, TVA Records Group 142, David Lilienthal, General Correspondence, 1933–46, File 821.2.
148 Earle S. Draper, "Demonstration Parks in the Tennessee Valley, Parks and Recreation, Part One," vol. 20, no. 8 (April), 1937, p. 357.
149 An anonymous National Parks official, cited by Earle S. Draper, in his address to the US Senate on Thursday 2 May 1940, "Recreational Opportunities in the Tennessee Valley," p. 4.
150 *The Scenic Resources of the Tennessee Valley: A Descriptive and Pictorial Inventory*, Knoxville, TN: TVA, Department of Regional Planning Studies, 1938.

151 Roland Wank, Letter to Ruth Goodhue, *Architectural Forum*, 26 December 1939, with accompanying article "Recreational Use of the TVA Lakes," p. 6. National Archives East Point, TVA Records Group 142, Office of Economic and Community Development, General Correspondence, 1940–8.

152 What nature omitted, according to Draper, the TVA provided – in the form of recreational lakes, an "essential component" of park tourism, "the sparkling blue waters" of the storage reservoirs "reflecting the tree-clad slopes of their mountain backgrounds." Draper, address to the US Senate, 2.

153 Phoebe Cutler, "On Recognizing a WPA Rose Garden or a CCC Privy," *Landscape* 20, no. 2 (Winter 1976), p. 7.

154 Draper, address to the US Senate, p. 5. "Personally, I look forward to the day when … recreation supplies the economic base that was lost when coal mining in the … Cumberland Mountains was all but abandoned and the cut-over forest lands of the plateau represented a constantly dwindling source of revenue."

155 These three descriptions are taken from Roland Wank, Letter to Ruth Goodhue, *Architectural Forum*, 26 December 1939. TVA photograph numbers: KX 313, "Overlook Terrace, Norris Dam"; KX 182, "Craft shop at Norris Dam"; KX 596 "String of fish."

156 Draper, "Demonstration Parks," p. 365.

157 Wank, Letter to Ruth Goodhue, 26 December 1939.

158 Dewey Grantham in Hargrove and Conkin, *TVA: Fifty Years*, p. 325.

159 Huxley, "TVA, an Achievement," p. 139.

160 Hamlin, "Architecture of the TVA," p. 731.

161 Creese, *TVA's Public Planning*.

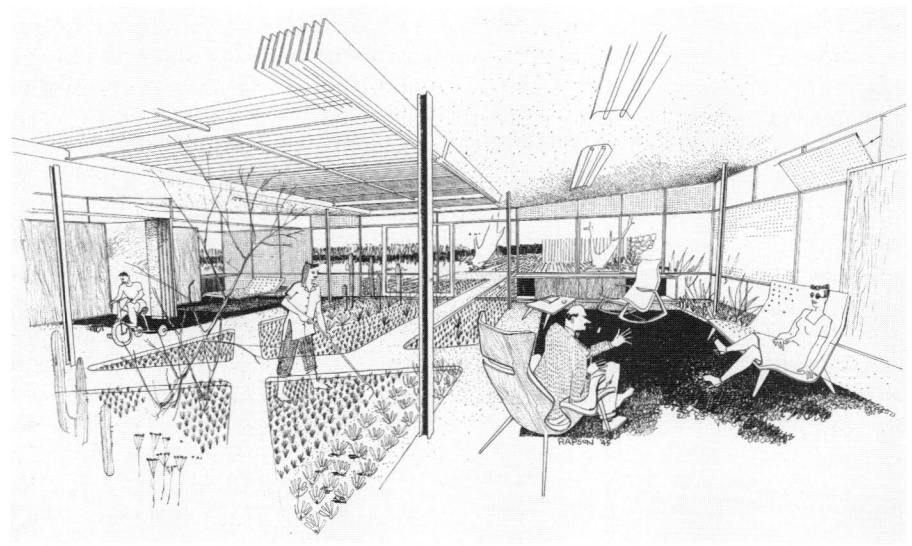

4.1 Hoeing the rows in the Greenbelt House. Architect Ralph Rapson, 1945.

Chapter 4
Nature preserved in the nuclear age:
the Case Study Houses of Los Angeles, 1945

When American soldiers returned home from the Second World War, everyone thought the country would finally get down to reaping the benefits of the "fight for democracy." The tremendous industrial capacity created by the war needed to be adapted to domestic production, and housing was one of the venues for peacetime conversion.[1] Returning GIs read about "their" postwar house in any one of a number of national journals, each of which suggested that domestic life would be changed by the introduction of wartime innovations into everyday life.[2] One of the most fundamental changes in national policy had to do with a new sense of entitlement for the decommissioned soldier. Whatever their background, race or social class, it was expected that returning soldiers had the right to an education and home ownership.[3] This notion alone, that most of the working citizens of the country deserved to own their homes, carried with it huge implications for the radical transformation of the American landscape. And as the government guaranteed millions of home mortgages, suburbs and freeways proliferated.

In that post-war period, it seemed as if the whole country was on the move. In a 1944 article entitled "Cities in Flux," the planner Catherine Bauer estimated that up to a quarter of the nation's population would be moving by the war's end. Fifteen million civilian war workers were preparing to pull up and look for new opportunities elsewhere; eleven million decommissioned soldiers were coming back to re-establish roots, get a college education, or find a new job; newlyweds were looking for starter homes – all of these people were "in a state of flux, physically and psychologically."[4] People who had migrated to cities during the war were once again moving outward into the urban periphery, where the land was cheaper and the houses were new. As people looked for houses outside the built-up industrial centers, many didn't stop at the suburbs but continued outward and westward, re-enacting the movement of the American frontier. Many people "hit the road" in automobiles, bringing the seeds of their nuclear family for planting across these great open landscapes.[5]

This suburbanization was without precedent in its scale and the speed with which it was occurring. It impressed commentators of the time, like William Whyte, who coined the term "urban sprawl" to describe the new landscape being created with the seemingly ceaseless demand for low-rise, single-family homes on the outskirts of the city.[6] It had always been easy to hammer together a house in the United States, but the combination of cheap land, automobiles, and government-guaranteed mortgages for first-time home buyers set up an entirely new relationship to the land. No longer was it necessary to laboriously carve out a homestead or farm; one could simply buy a little piece of paradise, kick up one's feet, and enjoy it.

The suburbs generated a new attitude to the landscape: one that sought for *each citizen* communion with nature in their backyard. Retreating from the big plans with a national reach – plans which led to the national parks system, regional authorities like the Tennessee Valley Authority, and even the marshaling of primary resources under the War Rations Board – the US government in the post-war period effected an enormous transformation through legislation aimed at *individual* homeowners. Each house would contain a bit of nature, and each citizen would have daily contact with it. It is ironic that at a time when America was expanding economically and politically to stretch its reach over much of the globe, its architects and planners focused their attention on the smallest unit of the built environment: the freestanding house on its little plot of land. This intensely private relationship to nature led to a new kind of house design and a new sense of space that encompassed house and garden. As the chapter unfolds, we will see that the privatization of nature in the middle-class home also led to exclusion, isolation, and ultimately paranoia, generating the architectural antithesis of the open house in the garden – the underground concrete bunker.

Sorting through the many post-war homes that fill the magazines of the mid 1940s – "ranch" houses, "dream" houses, and "model" houses – one house in particular stands out for the way it encapsulates this new relationship to the natural landscape. It was commissioned for the Case Study House program, a post-war competition to design modern houses for the average "servantless" new home owner. Drawn up in 1945 by the young Minnesota architect Ralph Rapson, the "Greenbelt House" brought the open landscape of the prairie into the confines of the suburb. Designed for a small suburban lot, this project in one bold move drew the wide open spaces of the American landscape into the house itself. Each room looks onto the central ribbon of landscape, which is both farm and courtyard as it flows through the house. In Rapson's Greenbelt House, nature is *in* the house, not vice versa (Figure 4.1).

The name of the project evokes the government-planned garden cities of the 1930s, such as Greenbelt, Maryland; Greenhills, Ohio, and Greenfields, New Jersey.[7] These schemes with their shared public open spaces and community facilities represented the most progressive urban planning of their time, and were still very much present in the discussions about architecture and planning in the post-war years.[8] But the "greenbelt" that was originally invented to separate cities from industries was, in Rapson's house, put to work to separate bedroom from kitchen and adult from children's spaces. It is a strip of nature brought into the house, while the pre-fabricated modular dwelling that stretches out on either side is extendible, at least in theory, to

4.2 Model, Greenbelt House.

the infinite horizon of the American grid (Figure 4.2). Although this house was never built, it impressed a generation of architects with the way it captured, in one elegant solution, a new attitude to nature, an attitude that greatly influenced other houses to follow (Figure 4.3).

As we look at it closer, it seems that the first lesson it teaches us is that the natural landscape can be appreciated from within the confines of a single family house. But in the process, the landscape is changed. When Rapson brings farmland into the house, he uncouples it from food production. He abstracts it and makes it an object of beauty. His prototypical family may indulge in a little hobby gardening, but the main point of his project, he states, is to provide "a view – a place where children and adults alike might live and play in close association with nature."[9] Thus, the American landscape becomes food for thought and an object of reflection, not a site of production.

The second lesson of Rapson's house is that family life will benefit from contact with nature. Elaine Tyler May has shown that the post-war family was "homeward bound," in both senses of the phrase. Tethered to their acre of land with a mortgage, father, mother and children form a productive and reproductive unit of society; a "natural" unit, it was understood, that would

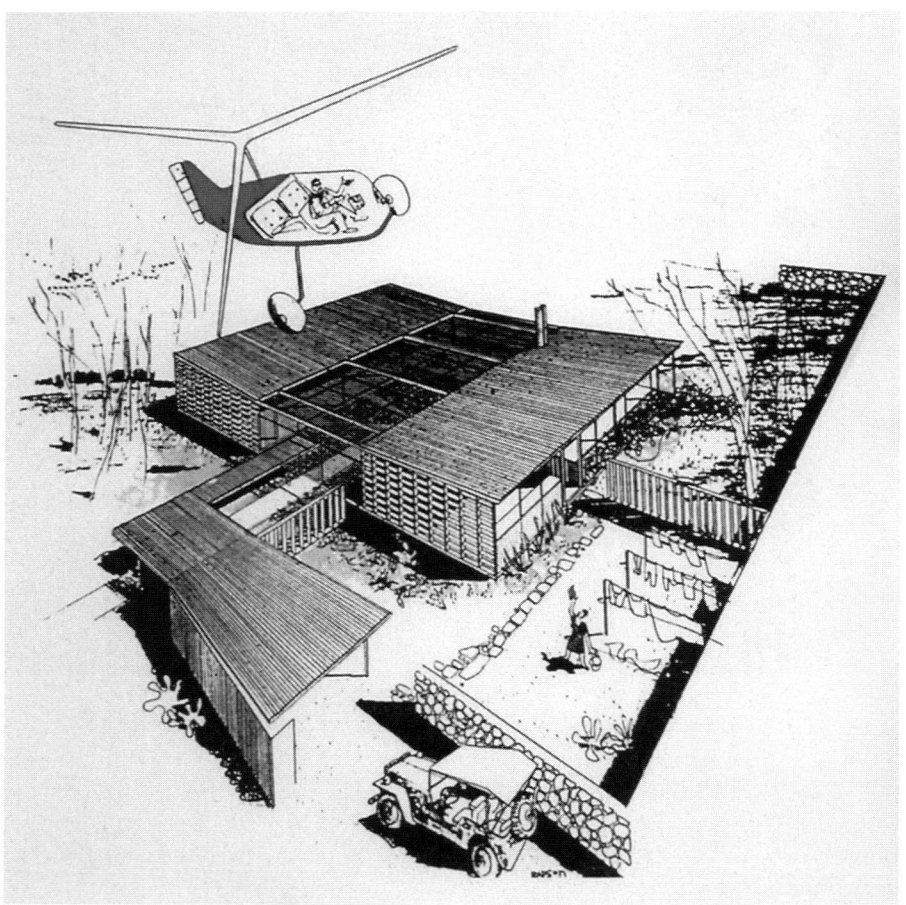

4.3 Axonometric drawing, Greenbelt House, 1945. Architect Ralph Rapson.

be best ensconced in a natural setting where their healthy instincts could be satisfied, free from the constraints and pollution of cities. Women could give free rein to their mothering impulses, tending toddlers and watering plants, and men could get in touch with their natural selves, mowing the lawn and providing for the household (Figure 4.4). Children would thrive, playing in the garden. As the cult of the nuclear family reached a historical high in the post-war period, we find that it serves as ground zero for all of the important national discussions, including the question we look at here – how Americans should live in their vast landscape. Rapson's use of the word "grow" was unequivocal as he says of his house, "here, the individual might grow and develop."[10]

4.4 Mother in the kitchen, Greenbelt House.

The Greenbelt House was one of nine houses commissioned by John Entenza, the editor of *Arts & Architecture* magazine, for his Case Study House program launched in 1945. Rapson's house was almost too extreme for Entenza, who sent it back for several revisions to make it more believable as a model house for the average post-war family. Entenza's goal was to "sell" modern architecture to a middle-class audience. The returning soldier, he argued, expected practicality in a house, and neither needed nor desired the traditional trappings of picket fence, shutters, and a porch. Entenza's conviction that modern design and a contemporary lifestyle would appeal to the new generation of first-time home buyers was proven correct when the Case Study Houses were opened to the public and attracted tens of thousands of new home buyers eager to look at the latest ideas in home design and furnishings. In the years between 1945 and 1961, the Case Study House program was one of the most effective initiatives to promote modern design in the country, encompassing architecture and landscape design as well as product design, furniture and crafts. While war-time shortages in building materials delayed the construction of many of these houses until the end of the 1940s, they were well-documented from the outset with drawings and models in the pages of *Arts & Architecture*. Entenza published these house designs alongside articles about painting and psychoanalysis, avant-garde art and music. The driving aesthetic was modern but casual, and it attracted notice across the country and worldwide as the "California Look." The work of the architects who participated in the Case Study House program – Eero Saarinen,

Charles Eames, Richard Neutra, Pierre Koenig and Ralph Rapson to name but a few – helped to define this aesthetic, and photographers like Julius Shulman and Herbert Matter made it visible with evocative and romantic images that underscored the formal qualities of these modern spaces.

The Case Study Houses not only promoted the "California Look," they also promoted the industrial products of a newly industrialized region. The modern materials and manufacturing techniques used in their construction drew directly from Los Angeles's aviation and shipbuilding industries. And in their packaging and promotion, they benefited from the proximity of the movie industry. Models and actresses pose as inhabitants of these houses that are glamorously lit and beautifully photographed. Part of their enduring allure is no doubt a result of their origins in a city that fabricates myth, seduces the eye, and captures the imagination. Media icons, the Case Study Houses reflected and magnified a mass-market ideal. They were marketing tools to sell modern design. They were trendsetters, style makers. And they helped to promote a new popular attitude to the landscape which turned away from the street and the neighbor and opened onto nature in the garden, the sky and the sun.

A SENSE OF EXPANSION IN THE POST-WAR HOUSE

While the Greenbelt House was a provocative proposal to literally incorporate nature in the suburban house, the general idea of outdoor living captured the imagination of the entire country in the years immediately after the war. Mass-market weeklies like *Time*, *Popular Science* and *Vogue* covered the rage for "Californian living," publicizing the houses of the Case Study program and linking modern architecture to a new way of living out-of-doors. *Sunset Magazine* warned its readers that "someday, someone is going to go too far in this business of outdoor living and forget to build a house."[11]

Indoor–outdoor living

From the beginning of the program, the Case Study architects designed their houses to open up to the outdoors. This was not a new idea in California. On the contrary, modernist architects had been designing outdoor rooms and open air sleeping porches in California since the 1910s – the most famous examples being Rudolf Schindler's house for his family and the Chaces, built on the memory of an outdoor camping trip in Yosemite; and Richard Neutra's "Health House" for the fitness and fresh air buff Dr. Lovell in the Hollywood Hills. Two other California architects, Gordon Drake and Harwell Hamilton Harris, had designed houses in the 1930s and 40s which entirely opened the living spaces to the outside (Figure 4.5). These modernist buildings, in turn, were indebted to the earlier Arts and Crafts promotion of room-sized porches, loggias, terraces and outdoor sleeping porches – stripped-down spaces developed in the search for the simple life.[12] Sleeping

4.5 Drake House, Los Angeles, 1945–7. Architect Gordon Drake.

porches were favored by adherents of the fresh air sleeping movement, such as Robert Baden-Powell, founder of the Boy Scouts and champion of nose-breathing (cleaner! filtered by nose hairs!).[13] But in the post-war modern house, it is not the sleeping room but the dining and "living" areas that are extended to the outside and meant to benefit from the play with nature.

To make house interiors flow seamlessly into gardens, Case Study House architects embraced new building technologies like Kawneer's aluminum storefront (designed by William Lescaze in 1942). Whole walls could be opened up to the outside, both visually and physically on sliding tracks, so that the living spaces of the house could extend into the garden. In Julius Ralph Davidson's CSH 1, for example, the living room floor seems hardly cognizant of the glass envelope as it shoots past it into the space of the terrace and beyond (Figure 4.6). Richard Neutra of course, was the Californian pioneer of the sliding glass wall in his Beard House of 1934, and he subsequently refined this detail until the frame of the glass door was reduced to a minimum such as in the Nesbitt House built in Brentwood in 1942 (see

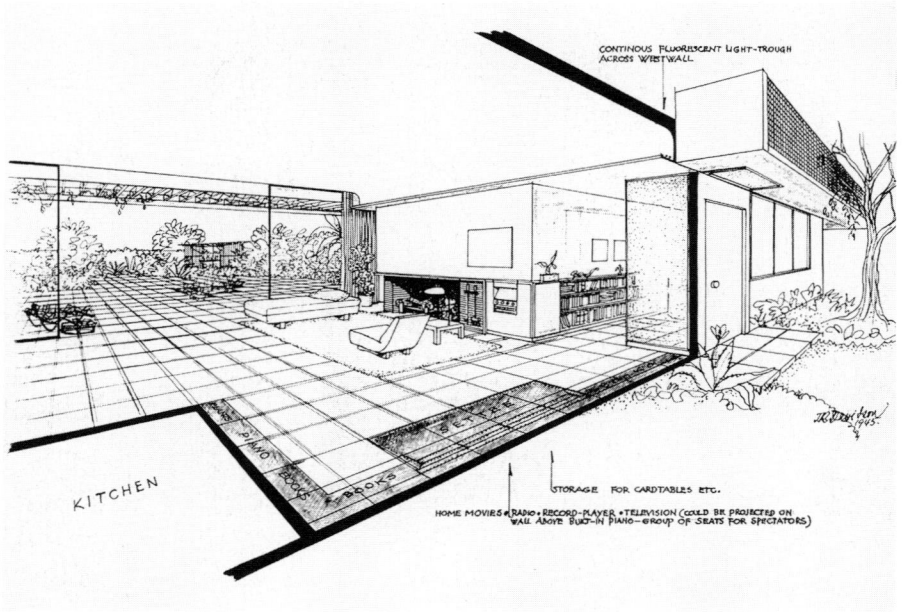

4.6 Perspective drawing, CSH 1. Architect J.R. Davidson.

Figures 4.7 and 4.8).[14] But it was the Case Study House program that essentially canonized the sliding glass wall as an essential feature of 1940s modern, with each of the first nine designs employing this architectural device. The sliding glass wall allowed the Case Study Houses to "borrow" the extra space of the garden and make it part of the living space of the house.

Living terraces, dining terraces, kitchen courtyards and garage patios were all ways of taking advantage of California's mild climate and to increase the usable floor area of the house. Sumner Spaulding's CSH 2 has a number of these terraces, and he also brings the garden inside with a free-form planter that insinuates its way past the glass wall and into the living room. Whitney Smith's CSH 5 is almost as extreme as Rapson's Greenbelt House in the way it managed to suggest that the whole house was a sort of encampment in nature, described by him as "living islands under one roof" (Figures 4.9 and 4.10). Trees and shrubs are sprinkled liberally around this plan, which provided a number of small enclosures linked by an amorphous indoor–outdoor space. This is living space opened up, becoming more aerated and extending into the outside, as if it were necessary to reassure returning war veterans they would not be confined to four walls after years in the field and in the company of men.

4.7 Nesbitt House, Brentwood, 1942. Architect Richard Neutra.

4.8 CSH 20 (Bailey House), 1947. Architect Richard Neutra.

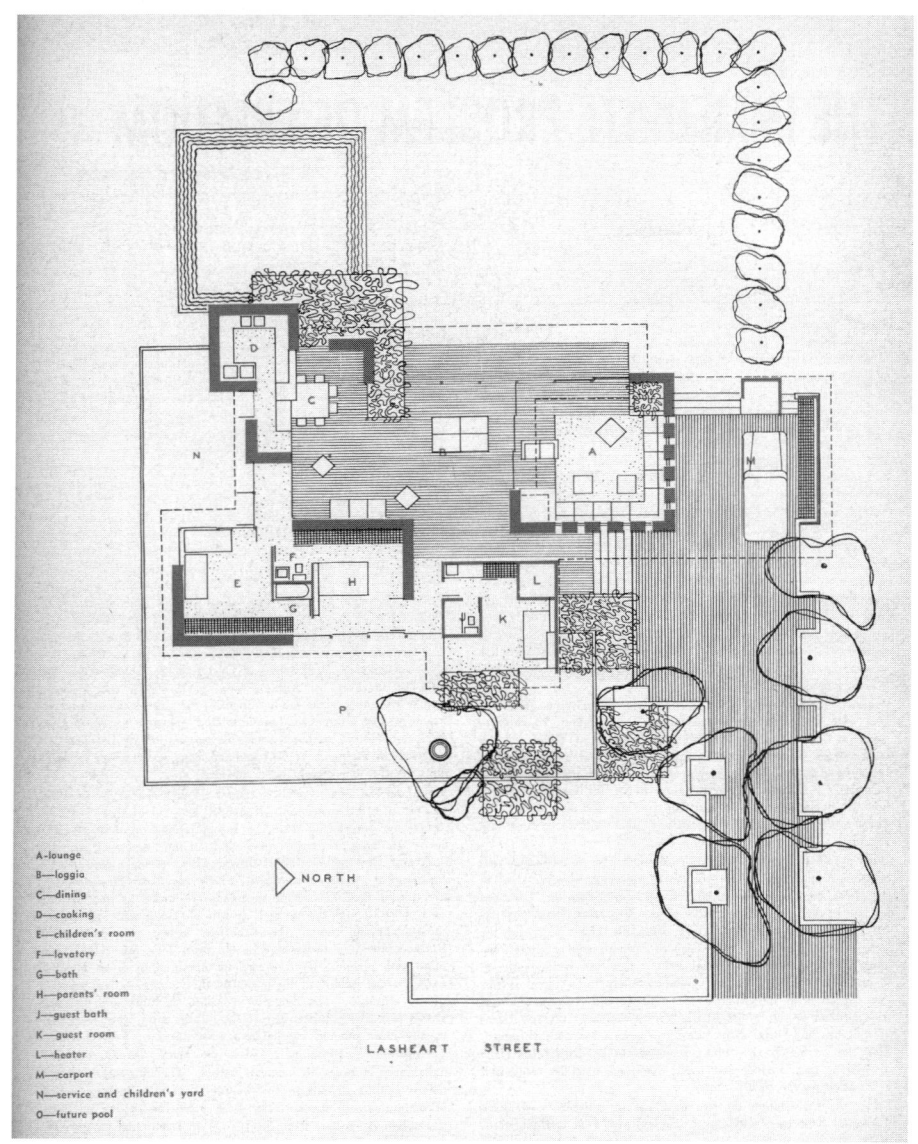

4.9 Plan of CSH 5, 1945. Architect Whitney R. Smith.

4.10 Model of CSH 5.

It was hard to tell sometimes what was indoors and what was outside in the Case Study Houses. While Rapson's Greenbelt House is probably the most extreme expression of this tendency, all of the early Case Study Houses bring greenery inside with potted plants and free-form planters and use outdoor paving materials (like brick pavers and tiles) in the inside spaces. For Rapson, the benefits are visual and therapeutic, "drawing nature inside the house," he believed, "would help overcome the disadvantages of the city lot; it would offer a built-in view while giving a space in which to pursue healthful leisure-time activity."[15] As Beatriz Colomina has noted, gardening was seen as a form of therapy for returning war veterans, but we may well assume that it was generally the housewife rather than the husband who was expected to tend to the indoor plants in her spare time.[16] By bringing nature inside the house, the view of the garden is internalized and the leisure activities that take place there are privatized. At the same time, domestic life is re-invested with the primal experience of communing with nature. The house becomes a glass enclosure around the nurtured kernel of family in nature.

As the living spaces opened up to the outside, gardens also changed. Manicured, artfully arranged and lit, the garden began to be considered a part of the composition of the house. Garrett Eckbo, writing for *Arts & Architecture*, was the foremost proponent of this new style of landscape design. While he designed gardens for only two Case Study houses, his influence as a writer and a designer of hundreds of modernist gardens in the Los Angeles region is evident throughout the Case Study program. For Eckbo, as for the Case Study architects, space was the most important aspect of landscape design. As he later wrote in *Landscape for Living*, "when we purchase a lot, we are actually buying a block of space – why be concerned with only the design of its surface?"[17] According to Eckbo, the modern garden should be designed in the same way the modern house is designed, that is, as a three-dimensional space, the only difference being that "one discipline produce[s] roofed space and the other spaces open to the sky."[18] His garden designs echoed the modernist designs of the houses and extended the "space" of the house to include the whole suburban lot.[19] Is the house-garden relationship one in which "indoor" becomes "outdoor," or is it the other way around? he asked (Figure 4.11). Rejecting the traditional middle-class conception of the backyard as a place of work – a vestige of the farmyard used for hanging laundry, gardening, storage, or car repair – Eckbo's gardens are abstract compositions and also spaces of leisure, peopled with young adults, occupied children, and thriving plants carefully tended by the housewife in her leisure moments.

This indoor–outdoor space of living required furniture that could be easily moved outside and back in again. Van Keppel and Green metal and rope lounge chairs, low-slung patio furniture and all-weather pottery met this need and were just as readily found on outdoor terraces as inside the spacious interiors. Barbecues and hibachis brought cooking outside, while plastic

Outdoors–indoors?

Indoors–outdoors?

4.11 "Outdoor–indoors or indoor–outdoors?"

dinnerware by Russel Wright and casual pottery by Eva Zeisel blurred the traditional distinction between formal table settings and casual picnic ware. These objects not only moved easily between inside and outside, they negotiated with equal facility formal and informal activities and were meant to express the American ideal of the classless society.

But they still cost money. In 1946, *Sunset Magazine* suggested that the home handyman might make his own patio furniture with surplus war materials bought at bargain prices. Leftover artillery cartridge cases could be used as planter boxes and sawed-off bomb casings turned into outdoor ashtrays. With a little cutting and welding, aluminum pistons could be turned into candleholders and aircraft gears into an umbrella stand. One ingenious suggestion showed a stylish low table constructed out of wood fiber strips from airplanes screwed to a plywood top.[20] The use of recycled materials was not limited to furniture. *Sunset* describes a barbecue station built by Gilbert Holidays on his small patio in Santa Barbara, California:

> the spit is placed before a vertical fire cage which burns charcoal. The cage is suspended from a horizontal rod which slides back and forth on angle irons fixed in the brick, thus adjusting the heat to the proper intensity for the spitted meat. Beneath the spit is a cast-iron grilling plate heated by a gas burner from an old oven. The bake oven is gas fired, and came from a commercial bakery; its capacity is enough for the largest party. An automobile jack was used beneath the fire grate for the 48-inch grill. By turning the crank, it can be raised or lowered 16 inches.[21]

One cannot help but wonder what was in the kitchen.

One of the most distinctive strategies used to connect indoors to outdoors in the early modern houses are the large skylights which flooded indoor spaces with daylight. These were supplemented with trellises and open lath work which softened the perennial California sunshine. Departing from the precedents established by the earlier generation of California architects, postwar designers turned away from the massive arcades and loggias of Irving Gill and Bernard Maybeck in favor of delicate steel and wood trellises which filtered the light from above. These trellises are as common as glass walls in the Case Study Houses. To cite just a few examples: Julius Ralph Davidson's CSH 1 continues the living room roof into the garden terrace with a trellis cut into the roof plane. Wurster and Bernardi's CSH 3 places a skylit and trellis-covered "loggia" as an entry hall in the heart of the house (Figure 4.12), while Rapson's Greenbelt House makes the trellis-covered skylit planting area the main feature of the design. In Thornton Abell's CSH 7, a small trellis appears at the junction where the two wings of the house join, but when Abell finally builds this project in a greatly modified scheme three years later, the trellis has grown to cover a large skylit indoor planting area. Much

4.12 Skylight in CSH 3, 1949. Architects Wurster & Bernardi.

of the perimeter of the house is enclosed as a large space of its own, called the "lath house." Rodney Walker designs an exaggeratedly high skylit trellis covered "loggia" as the entry hall for his own house built under the program (CSH 16), while Whitney Smith dubs his entire house the "Lath House" (CSH 12), proposes that it is built for a gardener, and includes two completely lath-enclosed and lath-roofed spaces which are intended to serve as plant nursery and entry (Figure 4.13). One might well ask, what is going on here?

These kind of trellised roof structures were a familiar sight in wartime Los Angeles, but at a completely different scale. To protect the many aircraft and munitions plants from aerial bombardment, huge industrial zones were covered with camouflage netting to give the appearance of being farmland from the air. Decorated with sham agricultural buildings and fake shrubs, acres of building were masked as rural landscapes, while beneath the "ground", war workers took their breaks in the filtered daylight between the industrial sheds (Figure 4.14) We know that architects were fascinated with these industrial buildings and indeed, we find the juxtaposition of "nature" in the roof plane and the lightweight wood and steel shed below in several

4.13 Model of CSH 12 (Lath House), 1946. Architect Whitney R. Smith.

house designs published in this period – most notably Ralph Rapson's entry for *Arts & Architecture* "Design for Post-war Living" competition of 1943. The wartime factories beneath layers of trellis, net and fake shrubbery foreshadow the delicate loggia and lath work of the Case Study Houses. If one can "bury" a whole factory beneath the "landscape," it is not much of a stretch to imagine single family houses nestled in the flowing contours of the land, open to the sky above and linked in this literal way to the expansive horizons of a growing country (Figure 4.15).

For the do-it-yourselfer, trellises, lathhouses and louvered skylights were a way to recreate in one's own home a way of life that many men had experienced first-hand in the Pacific theater of war. In his "Pacific Notebook" column for *Sunset*, Donald Button writes in 1951:

> let us see how the Western home and garden may be influenced by our sons and daughters when they return [Veterans were asked to recall houses in the South Pacific islands that had] green growth, shade, rain protection, an open circulation of air; a view of garden, seashore, or mountains; in short the spot where you talked, lounged, ate, drank, and spent some of your happiest hours in the islands.[22]

4.14 Under the camouflage, Douglas Aircraft plant, Santa Monica, California, 1943.

240 | Nature preserved in the nuclear age

4.15 Indoor trellis in CSH 25, 1962. Architects Killingsworth, Brady & Smith.

The *lanai* – the main outdoor space of the Pacific Islanders – is a recurring theme. "Even though the lanai is not completely practical for all Western localities, it could . . . be modified by the use of screen and glass, to provide an indoor–outdoor living room. . . . We think palm mats have definite possibilities for thatch on a garden house, or as woven walls for windbreaks."[23]

The new suburbanite was exhorted to make the garden usable living space with screens, trellises, lath and garden walls. With these architectural devices, the outdoors was inhabited, and began to host activities that were previously restricted to the inside of the house. Barbecues, "casual entertaining," and gardening activities encouraged people to spend more time outside, as we read in *Sunset*, "Here are six ways a garden living room can erase that 'back-yard' feeling."[24] Clearly, the backyard was out and the outdoor living room was in.

Open space in the house

The integration of indoors and outdoors with sliding glass walls, skylights and trellises is a key feature of post-war modern design. It is as if the open space and freedom associated with the suburb extends into the space of the house itself. Living "space" flowed through the house, linking eating and cooking areas to entertaining and leisure zones. Lynn Spigel points out that "women's home magazines, manuals on interior decor, and books on housing design all idealized the flowing, continuous spaces of California ranch-style architecture which followed the functionalist design principles of 'easy living' by eliminating walls in the central living spaces of the home." She continues,

> This emphasis on continuous space suggested a profound preoccupation with space itself. These rambling domestic interiors appeared not so much as private sanctions which excluded the outside world, but rather as infinite expanses which incorporated the world.... The home magazines spoke constantly of the illusion of spaciousness, advising readers on ways to make the home appear *as if* it included the public domain.[25]

While the average post-war house relied on picture windows or wallpaper of nature scenes to create a sense of spaciousness, the Case Study architects could take advantage of the modernist architectural idea of the "open plan" invented by Frank Lloyd Wright. The open plan was a critique of the notion of separate rooms – instead, Wright proposed that living spaces should flow one into another. The European modernists Mies van der Rohe and Le Corbusier took this idea one step further, asserting that architecture should be concerned with the composition of "space," an entity which extends infinitely in all directions and can be defined through the use of walls, ceilings and floors for visual and kinesthetic effect. Modern architects embraced the understanding that all objects in effect, created space. Space became the primary concern of architectural composition; Wright and Mies for example, were declared the first great architects of "space."[26] In his landmark *Space, Time and Architecture* of 1941, Siegfried Giedeon described the world that opened up for designers as a consequence of this new understanding of space.

> With the cubist's conquest of space, and the abandonment of one predetermined angle of vision which went hand in hand with it, surface acquired a significance it had never known before. Our powers of perception became widened and sharpened in consequence. We discovered the interplay of imponderably floating elements irrationally penetrating or fusing with each other, as also the optical tensions which arise from the contrasts between various textural effects. The human eye awoke to the spectacle of form, line, and color – that is, the whole grammar of composition – reacting to one another within an orbit of hovering planes.[27]

Designer George Nelson, writing in 1950, saw the potential for innovative design that came along with the modern house, suggesting that "because of the new problems presented, all sorts of objects are re-examined and then redesigned so they can stand clear of all walls, whether opaque or transparent. At which point, of course, they become sculpture. The fact that you may still sit in some of them, as in Eero Saarinen's big chair, or park your drinks on others, such as the Noguchi or Armbruster coffee tables, is relatively inconsequential."[28] Furniture, objects, plants and people all float in the expansive spaces of modern architecture. Harry Bertoia said of his steel-wire chairs, "if you will look at these chairs, you will find that they are mostly made of air, just like sculpture. Space passes right through them."[29] This is the space of the Case Study Houses. Solids open up to reveal the spaces within. Rooms virtually disappear, to be replaced with living areas or (to use a favorite word of the period) "zones." Moving away from the wall, furniture and fireplaces, like trees, lawns and pools, become sculptural free-floating objects in the three dimensional space of indoor–outdoor living (Figure 4.16).

This sense that people and objects share a space but are only tenuously related within that space can, according to Thomas Hine, be seen in all sorts of creations of the mid-twentieth century, from philosophy to advertisement graphics.

> It is an expression of social fragmentation, perhaps, of a loss of belief, of the discoveries of science that almost everything that appears to be solid is made up almost entirely of emptiness and of tiny particles bound with immense energy in almost inconceivable motion. It is into this empty landscape that Samuel Beckett puts his tree. Existentialists stood in this nowhere with the resolution to *do something*, absurd as it might be. Beatniks hitchhiked through it; families packed up the Chevrolet and sped through it.[30]

The Case Study program readily embraced the expansive open space of modern architecture. Writing in 1943 for *Arts & Architecture* magazine, Ray

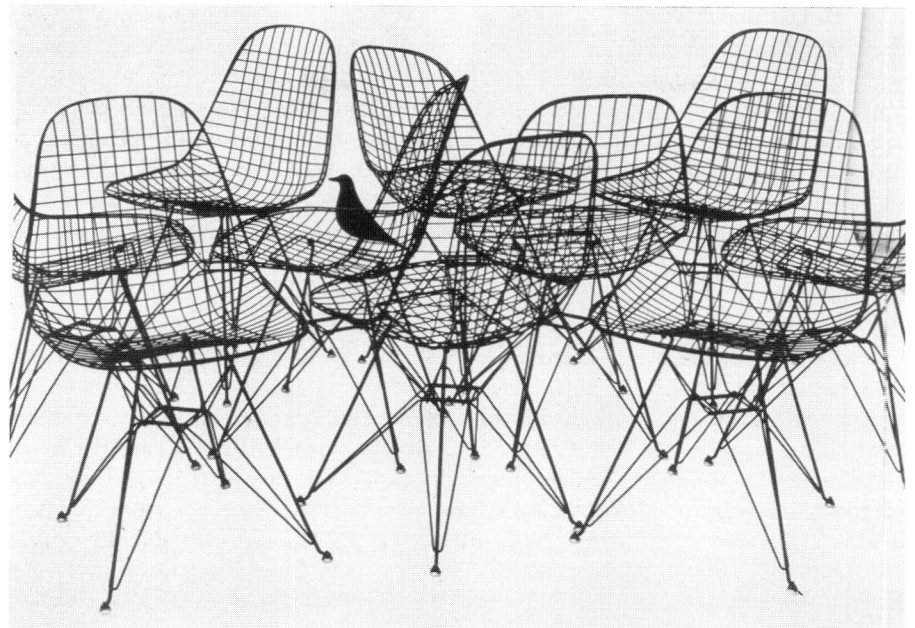

4.16 Wire chairs, Eames Office.

Eames declared that "space and the relationships of spaces become so engulfing, so important, that objects in themselves lose value."[31] Eames doesn't seem disturbed by the prospect of such a devaluation, but rather exhilarated at the liberation it promises. She implies that space itself is valuable; although intangible, it is a quantity to be treasured. Perhaps, as Thomas Hine has suggested, the encounter of Americans with the vast open spaces of their continent predisposes them to accept a new formulation of space itself.[32]

When Edith Farnsworth turned to *House Beautiful* to publicly repudiate her Mies van der Rohe-designed house as "unlivable," her critique struck a chord among many American architects, most notably Wright, who felt that modern buildings should connect to the landscape, use local materials, respond to the local climate, and link inside to outside. Hine astutely calls it the "debate between the American, landscape-based sense of openness versus the international, abstract sense of openness."[33] While Mies saw landscape outside a building as scenery to be framed with the floor and ceiling planes, architects practicing in America were more ready to see the landscape as a continuation of the interior spaces of the house.[34] In the United States, the flow from inside to outside was a horizontal one.

Expansive space

But there was more to the American ideology of space than a sense of expansion. As suburban houses were proliferating across the country, the United States government was expanding its influence to the farthest corners of the globe, supporting its economic ambitions with political, military and cultural initiatives designed to increase the reach of American products into foreign markets. As Hélène Lipstadt, Jane Loeffler, and Serge Guilbaut have shown, modern architecture, like modern art, was promoted by the highest levels of government as a vehicle to express American ideals of democracy and transparency in an era of increasing American political and economic domination.[35]

In many respects, the home was the post-war battleground for American hegemony. According to Elaine Tyler May, the American argument for superiority in the cold war era rested not on weapons, but on the secure and prosperous family life represented by suburbia (Figure 4.17). In the now famous "kitchen debate," Vice President Richard Nixon and Premier Nikita Khrushchev entered into a heated exchange of ideological positions at the model kitchen in the American Exhibition in Moscow, when Nixon called attention to a built-in panel-controlled washing machine.

> "In America," he said, "these are designed to make things easier for our women." Khrushchev countered Nixon's boast of comfortable American housewives with pride in productive Soviet female workers: in his country they did not have that "capitalist attitude toward women." Nixon clearly did not understand that the Communist system had no use for full-time housewives, for he replied, "I think that this attitude toward women is universal. What we want is to make easier the life of our housewives." Nixon's ... verbal bout with the Soviet Premier was his articulation of the American post-war domestic dream: successful breadwinners supporting attractive homemakers in affluent suburban homes.[36]

American expansion was to be a model for worldwide economic growth, and the American way of life in the open spaces of the suburb was its own advertisement – showing the nuclear family surrounded by the products of affluence and nestled in a verdant setting. Cinema and print media glorified the "American way of life" and promoted ideal houses full of consumer goods and ideal families.

ANXIETY – INVISIBLE THREATS SURROUND US

In 1945, at the dawn of the Case Study House program, transparency in the home was still a novel and exciting idea. This was the year that the plastics and chemicals company Rohm and Haas displayed their "Plexiglas Dream

4.17 "Family Utopia." Photograph by Bernard Hoffman.

Suite" in department stores across the country (Figure 4.18). The small exhibit showed how transparent acrylic sheet could be used to enclose a bedroom, bathroom and dressing room so that the whole unit could be air-conditioned "for a cost approximating that of a home refrigerator."[37] The sleeping area was wrapped in a transparent bubble; clothes, hats and shoes in the closet were stored on transparent shelves, making it easy to pick the appropriate headgear or shoes to "best suit the time and occasion"; and the shower stall was wrapped in transparent as well. In this display, the most intimate details of domestic life such as socks and underwear are put on

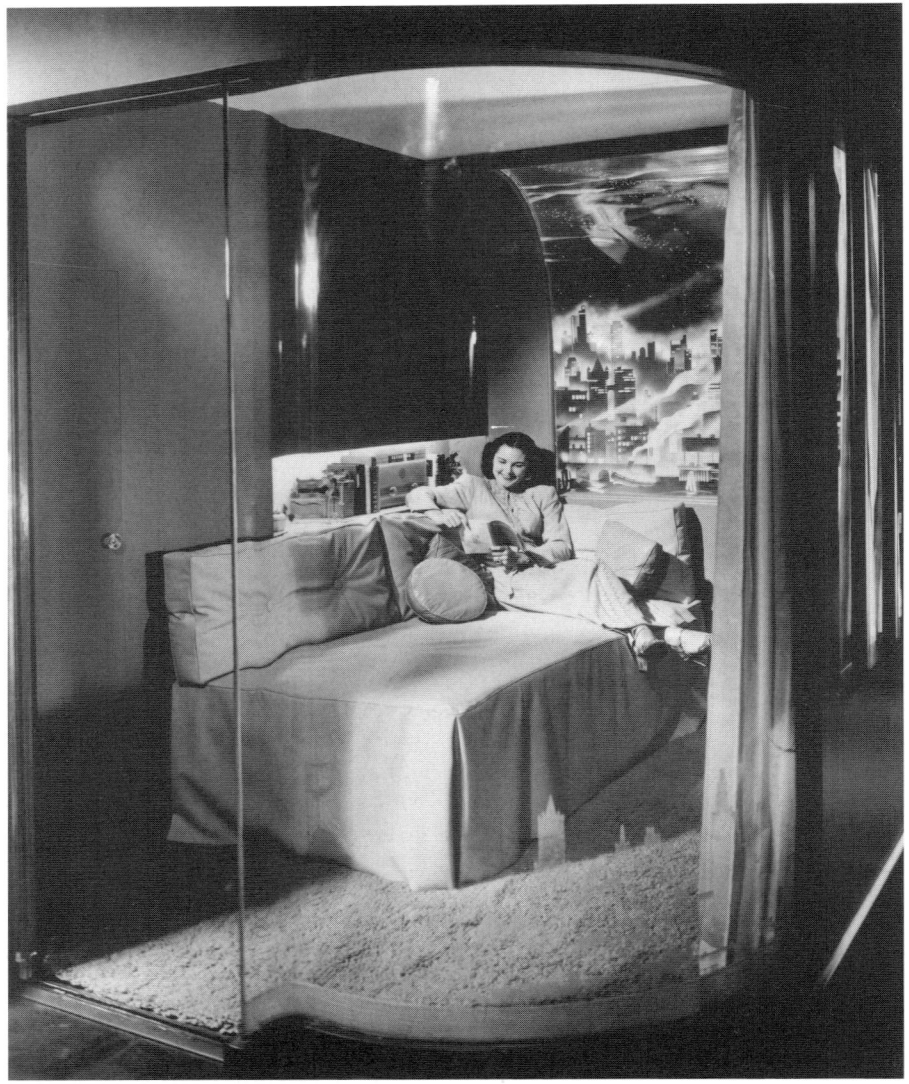

4.18 Plexiglas "Dream Suite," Rohm and Haas, Philadelphia, 1945.

display behind glass – or "plexiglas"! But the point of the exhibit was not to market domestic goods. It was to promote a new technology of visual display in the home. Hundreds of thousands of curious shoppers who gazed at the plexiglas bubble in their local department store imagined how such transparency might be put to use in their crowded apartment or their small starter home. By wrapping a domestic setting in a bubble-like nose cone, the "dream suite" combined the domestic applications of war materials with the commodification of domesticity.

It was one thing to look at a transparent home and dream of owning it. It was another altogether to live in it. Writing in 1946 about an exhibit on the modern house in the Museum of Modern Art, Elizabeth Mock advised aficionados of modern architecture to "think seriously about how much privacy you want from the street and neighbors, as there is a wide range of individual preference. Some people like total seclusion, others feel frustrated if they can't see everything that goes on; and most people seem to like both possibilities."[38]

Transparency and concealment
Two of the Case Study Houses built in 1949 reveal two distinctive and highly personal reactions to the visibility created by large amounts of glass in the house. CSH 9, designed by Charles Eames and Eero Saarinen for John Entenza, is too revealing for this man who valued his privacy. CSH 8, designed by Eames for himself and his wife Ray, becomes an asset in self-promotion for the exhibitionist couple. Even the earliest schemes for these two neighboring houses reveal the dynamic of exposure and concealment which underlies their reciprocal placement on the site. The Eames House is perched high on pilotis and commands the site and a distant view. Entenza's House is doubly buffered from scrutiny by a solid wall facing to the shared greensward and a dense planting which protects the "public" face of his house (Figures 4.19 and 4.20).

Three of the four faces of Entenza's House are completely shielded from view with garden walls, house walls, or service areas like the garage or utility room (Figure 4.21). Only the most social space opens up to the garden and the view, and this face is oriented for maximum privacy. In the first publication of the house, the program brief repeatedly suggests that privacy is the foremost concern. "It [is] a returning place for relaxation and recreation through reading and music and work – a place of reviving and refilling. a place *to be alone* for preparation of work, and with matters and concerns of *personal* choosing. A place for . . . *relaxed privacy* . . . *Intimate conversation* . . . the entertainment of *very close friends*."[39] As a left-leaning homosexual with a public profile living in the nation's media capitol at the dawn of the McCarthy era, Entenza had good reason to guard his privacy. He also, Esther McCoy reminisces, was willing to endure some physical discomfort for the visual pleasure of good design, "a bachelor who hated big parties – [his

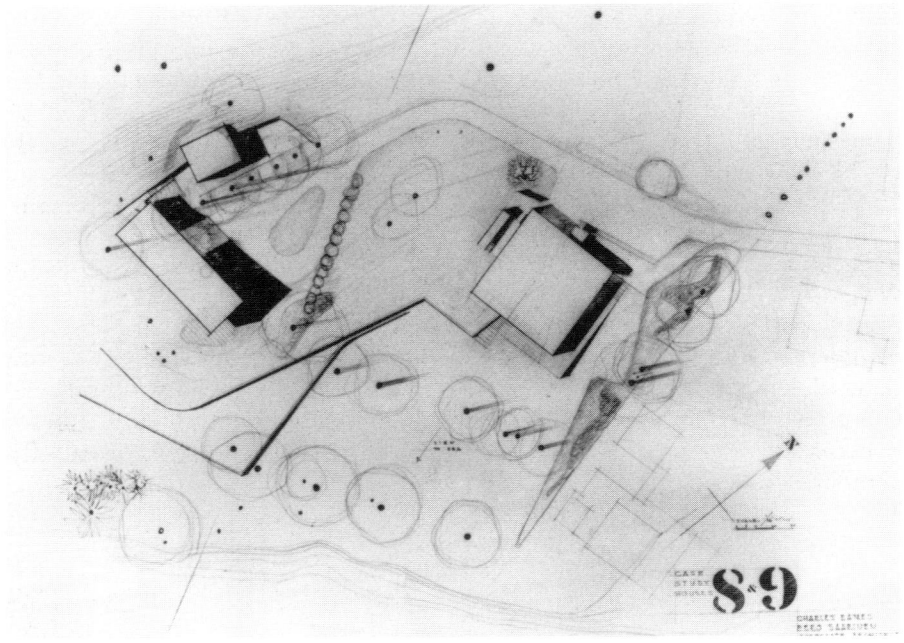

4.19 Site plan of CSH 8 and 9, 1945.

4.20 Model of early scheme for CSH 8 (Eames House). Architect Charles Eames, 1945.

house] had a close to fifty-foot-long living room. Nor was he keen on sunlight, yet light flooded into every room except for a windowless library in the center of the house."[40] As in all the case study houses there was a garden terrace furnished with clipped green plants and chairs overlooked by the Eames terrace above. The house reveals this constant tension between guarding his privacy and advertising the modern design he so strongly believed in. Entenza's most private area, located in the center of the house, was a study with a door – the only complete room in the house apart from a toilet and a utility room. It is completely enclosed, interrupted neither by windows nor by skylights; a hermetically sealed chamber encased in a lighter, larger box of steel frame and cladding (Figure 4.22). The steel framework, signifying modern house design, was drawn and photographed in detail before being clad, while the study was never photographed. Even the social spaces of this house reveal his ambivalence about public viewing of private spaces. CSH 9 is perhaps unique among the famous modern houses for being frequently photographed with the curtains drawn (Figure 4.23). Even in photographs taken from the inside, the outside is rarely revealed. Ultimately, the house

4.21 View from the north-east of CSH 9 (Entenza House), 1949. Architects Charles Eames & Eero Saarinen.

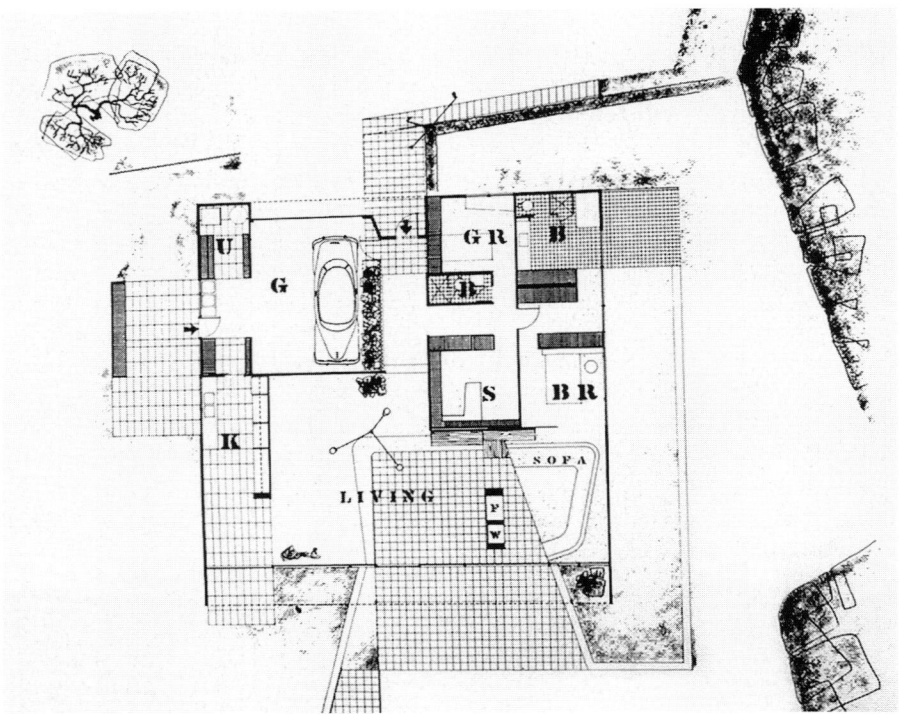

4.22 Plan of CSH 9.

was not private enough. Entenza sold the house shortly after its construction and moved to the Strathmore apartments designed by Neutra in Westwood, which offered the kind of small scale intimate sociability he clearly preferred.

The Eames House, CSH 8, offers a total contrast to Entenza's House. It was designed for visibility and it became a machine for viewing. The house is often discussed in terms of its structure, from a legendary anecdote about how it was re-designed to gain more space for the same amount of steel, to its subsequent iconic status as "something wholly original, wholly American," as the Smithsons put it.[41] Yet, as Ray Eames noted, "the structure long ago ceased to exist. I am not aware of it." If the structural frame was meant to become invisible, one cannot say the same for its inhabitants. They were to become more visible through the technology of the house. The Eameses dealt with the transparency of their house by recognizing their visibility in it and multiplying the images and reflections it produced. They controlled and carefully framed these images. For the Eames, the picture window becomes a kaleidoscope: infinitely multiplying, changing and recombining the images of the inhabitants within.

4.23 Living room with curtains drawn, CSH 9.

Like their "House of Cards," the Eameses House is a playful structure which can be added to and changed as new ideas, products and collectibles come into their working lives. By making a game out of their house, they draw from the energy of the consumer society and its penchant for acquiring and discarding (Figure 4.24). Yet at the same time, their incessant photography of

4.24 Objects in the Eames House.

the house and how they lived in it made them an advertisement for the California lifestyle. From the other side of the Atlantic, Alison and Peter Smithson saw the house as "an Eames-defined territory ... with an Eames content."[42] The content, in other words, was the Eames themselves – how they lived, what they surrounded themselves with, how they worked, what they produced. More precisely though, it was the *images* of these things that captured the imagination of the Smithsons.

There has been much reflection in England on the Eames House. For the Eames House was a cultural gift parcel received here at a particularly useful time. The bright wrapper has made most people ... throw the content away as not sustaining. But we have been brooding on it – working on it – feeding from it.[43]

As Colomina points out, "the Eameses liked to celebrate things. Anything. Everything. Their house became an endless process of celebration over the course of their lives."[44] The Eames House achieves a long-standing dream of Western culture – to live in a building which is totally transparent, concealing nothing, and open to everyone who comes to share with an open heart and mind (Figure 4.25).

Transparency and democracy

The relation between nature, transparency, and democracy concerned the enlightenment philosopher Jean-Jacques Rousseau who, in the mid-eighteenth century, imagined a new "social contract" that would bind together a

4.25 Charles and Ray Eames during construction of their house, 1949.

democratic society. He describes a spontaneous celebration that takes place in a small village in the countryside and he sees in this simple event the potential for a new transparency in human relations,

> The country feast simulates the return to an original state of innocence. ... [It] is in no sense a "ritual." It belongs to no tradition. Nothing is done according to custom. On the contrary, everything appears to be improvised. The feast not only symbolizes a return to the golden age, ... but also represents the efforts of the "very intimate society." ... It is a pure invention, a free creation, unfettered by any pre-established form. ... Here people are not happy because they have come to a feast; rather, the feast is the visible manifestation of the joy they feel in being together. Their happiness runs over into dancing, games, ceremony, and song. This idealized feast is one of the key images in Rousseau's work.[45] The meaning of the feast emerges with even greater clarity in [Rousseau's] Letter to d'Alembert. "Let us not opt for these exclusive spectacles, which sadly enclose a small number of people in a dark cavern; which restrain them, fearful and immobile, in silence and inaction; and which show nothing but walls, steel blades, soldiers, and other distressing images of servitude and inequality. No! Happy nations, these festivals are not yours. It is in the open air, beneath the sky that you ought to gather and give free rein to the sweet sensation of happiness. ... Let the sun shine on your innocent spectacles. You yourselves are one of those spectacles, the worthiest on which the sun can shed its light. But what will the objects of those spectacles be? What will be shown? Nothing, if you will. With freedom, wherever there is affluence there is also well-being."[46]

Rousseau presents the transparency of human relations in the country feast as an allegory for a democratic society. He contrasts the outdoor feast with the dark and enclosed theater, which for him represents the concealment of truth, the exclusion of people and the creation of false hierarchies. Open space on the other hand, suffused with the light of day, exposes people as they really are and puts everyone on an equal footing. In such spaces, people can "give free rein to their happiness, they themselves are one of the spectacles" – free, surrounded by abundance and suffused with a sense of well-being. This democratic ideal was adopted by the founders of the United States in the motto "life, liberty and the pursuit of happiness," and continues to form one of the pillars of American national identity.

What interests us here is the way the Eames House reflects this ideal and by so doing, redeems liberal notions of the free market and the "family of man."[47] The Eames House, like Rousseau's democratic celebration, seems improvised in the open air and under the California sun. Like the country feast, it seems to be about nothing in particular and everything at once. But most of all, it expresses a feeling of freedom, a delight with affluence, the radiant sensation of well-being. It is this ability to communicate a democratic ideal that lies at the root of the Eameses success both in the United States and beyond its borders. By embracing the philosophical construct of transparency in a house that was also physically transparent and very visible in the media, they were able to reassert the fundamental connection between transparency and democratic ideals, and link both of these to "free" markets and liberal ideology.

For Reyner Banham, the Eames House was experienced as an epiphany, as he recalls the dilemma of many British architects and artists in the years immediately after the war.

> Something very weird happened around 1946–1947 when the lines were being drawn for the Cold War. Suddenly there came a moment when it was very difficult to read *Time* or any American magazine at all, simply because of one's political loyalties. In that period there arose a situation where one's natural leanings in the world of entertainment, and so on, were to the States, but one's political philosophy seemed to require one to turn one's back to the States.... This Cold War distinction made, in the forties, a division which runs right through English thinking, and indeed much of American thinking: that to accept, to enjoy, the products of Pop, the products of the entertainment industry, Detroit-styling and such things was to betray one's political position.[48]

The Eames House changed all that. Its attributes of transparency – summarized by Banham as "clarity, honesty, simplicity" – made it acceptable to be seduced by its "wit, too!"[49] In the Eames House there are no barriers to separate one area from another; all activities intermingle with all other activities. The first program brief makes this clear. "Day and night, work and play, concentration, relaxation with friend and foe, all intermingled personally and professionally with mutual interest."[50] In their initial design, curtains, walls, and folding panels open to connect every zone with the adjacent activity. In the redesign, each activity space opens up to the exterior – there are no boundaries and few thresholds. Again, this is the space of Rousseau's feast. All is visible. And all takes place "in the open air, beneath the sky," with the sun shining on the innocent spectacle. Beneath its canopy of eucalyptus trees, and facing the limitless expanse of the Pacific Ocean, the Eames House embodied the freedom, the openness and the plenitude of Rousseau's ideal expression of democracy.[51]

Home alone?

While families that moved to the suburbs expected space to "stretch out" and enjoy the outdoors, the reality of tract houses on fifty feet lots was sobering. The Case Study Houses provided more privacy than most, largely because they were on lots that were larger and more idiosyncratic than the norm. With suburban houses going up cheek by jowl in subdivisions, with no intermediate planting, new residents accustomed to the visual privacy of urban apartment life found that the lack of privacy took some getting used to. For most new suburbanites, getting privacy was an endless battle. The frustration is evident in this article complaining about the "privacy problem,"

> In most cases the enjoyment of the patio depended on the whims of the weather.... Emotionally it didn't feel quite right, either exposed to the sky **or** the neighbor's sight. A six-foot fence around the edge of the lot offers only basic privacy. It still does not block out the sight of other houses or of phone poles, and it offers only the most rudimentary control over the climate.[52]

Expectations of "normal" behaviors began to shape social relations between neighbors. While the fence and the picture window were signs of belonging to this new community, they also began to trigger anxieties about conformity and the associated social pressures and pretense required to fit in. According to the sociologist William Dobriner, the suburb operated according to a new principle he called the "visibility principle," that permitted residents "to observe each other's behavior and general lifestyle far more easily than the central city dweller."[53] Perhaps the best-known dissatisfied inhabitant of a modern house was Edith Farnsworth, who said that living in her Mies-designed home made her feel "like a caged animal." But even the average middle class homemaker in the suburbs had to cope with the increased visibility of domestic spaces that resulted from the open plan and the picture window.

These innovations, adopted by mass-market home builders, added to expectations for a spotless house, since there were no doors to shut and no hiding places for work left undone. The housewife's shortcomings as a homemaker were on display for all to see. The spread of mechanical appliances which operated with the push of a button just made this worse, contributing to rising standards for domestic cleanliness and child care. If, as Mark Wigley has argued, the well-maintained lawn served as a symbol of the well-maintained family, the cleanliness and smooth operation of the house was even more so a sign of social propriety, normalcy and civic order.[54] It was possible to overdo it, of course. People commented on the compulsive behavior of men who spent an unhealthy amount of time trimming and fertilizing the lawn, while women were susceptible to similar pathologies, such as rising at three in the morning to vacuum the carpets.

The widespread acceptance of the open plan corresponded to a strong pressure for family unity. This was not reluctantly accepted but rather, as Elaine Tyler May has pointed out, the roles of breadwinner and homemaker were willingly embraced in post-war America.[55] The 1950s family was not, she says, the last gasp of "traditional" family life. Rather, it was the first wholehearted effort to create a home that would fulfill virtually all its members' personal needs through an energized and expressive personal life.... The new vision of home life ... depended heavily on the staunch commitment of family members.[56]

In the Case Study Houses, we can find many instances where attempts were made to enhance the closeness between husband and wife, as he returns from work and she engages on her evening tasks. Wurster and Bernardi's CSH 3 offers a combined kitchen and workshop space, where the husband can putter alongside his wife as she cooks up dinner (Figure 4.26). Thornton Abell's CSH 7 provided a family work center which connected the living room to the husband's study and darkroom, and adjacent zones where the wife pursued her "interests," including sewing, cooking and gardening. The Eames House, as we have seen, was an exemplary instance of intermingling professional and personal lives.

The ideal was, in fact, to provide at least one area where the whole family could gather together. George Nelson and Henry Wright suggested in 1946 that this "room without a name" could be called the "family room," since it provides "a framework within which members of a family will be better equipped to enjoy each other on the basis of mutual respect and affection."[57] The watchword for the modern family, according to an article in *McCalls Magazine* of 1954, was "togetherness."[58] The television, a focal point for family togetherness, brought examples of well-organized, tidy and contented households into the home, providing the housewife with standards against which she could measure her own performance. The traditional distinction between public appearance and private behavior – still a dominant assumption in this era when people dressed up to be seen in public and

4.26 Kitchen and workroom in CSH 3, 1945. Architects Wurster & Bernardi.

dressed down at home – was eroded with images of the impeccably coifed and crinolined TV "wife" who could whip up dinner and soothe household crises with a perpetual smile on her face. In this sense, the suburban home in the 1950s was increasingly presented as a space of display, a place where one was continually on view. While the open plan provided an architectural expression of family unity, with all the activities of family members visible to all others, it also exposed children's toys, dirty dishes, unswept floors and soiled furniture to the returning husband or the friendly neighbor who dropped over for a casual visit. The state of house (and, by implication, the state of the family) was potentially always visible.

None of the Case Study Houses offered the housewife a "room of her own." One of the most glaring examples of this is CSH 20, built for the graphic designer Saul Bass and his wife Ruth, a biochemist. Mr. Bass was provided with a studio in the "adult wing," separated from the activities of the family by a garden courtyard, while Mrs. Bass made do with a desk in the master bedroom and had the consolation of being provided with a kitchen "as precisely planned as a laboratory," to use the words of the architects Buff, Straub and Hensman (plate 15).

If the interior of the ideal post-war house offered little privacy, from the outside much of the house was visible too. Next-door neighbors could sneak the occasional peek in from a ground level window or through sliding glass doors. Picture windows enjoyed for their view onto the world became "problem windows" that needed to be covered with curtains, blinds or shrubbery to avoid the "fish bowl" effect. Magazines aimed at suburban homeowners were filled with suggestions on how to acquire more privacy: "Fences make an area more intimate. Angles of fence create protected alcoves."[59] When built on the property line, fences "extend the lines of the house" and provide an "effective screen" between the garden and the street. Even the view from the house into one's own garden should be "cleaned up" – a privacy screen was just the thing to hide the garage or the laundry on a line.

The view from the house was ideally a one-way view. Even the television screen, another "window to the world," threatened to turn back on itself, penetrating domestic privacy and monitoring the "dirty little secrets" of family life.

> [Women's home] magazines treated the television set as if it were a problem window through which residents in the home could be seen ... Perhaps this fear was best expressed in 1949 when the *Saturday Evening Post* told its readers, "Be Good! Television's Watching." The article continued, "comes now another invasion of your privacy.... TV's prying eye may well record such personal frailties as the errant husband dining out with his secretary ..." The fear here was that the television camera might record men and women unawares.[60]

By the 1950s, the constant pressure required to keep up appearances began to be recognized as a source of tension, anxiety, possibly even unhappiness for the woman at home. Open plans and glass walls created a uniform and perpetual regime of vision with its attendant expectations for performance. Rousseau's transparent space of democracy led inevitably to an architecture of consensus in which everything is visible, potentially under scrutiny, and exposed to evaluation. As policing becomes internalized in the behavior of family members, the private realm of the house turns into a terrain for the performance of collective norms and standardized routines. While John Keats condemned the stifling conformity felt by housewives who were simultaneously isolated and exposed in the suburbs in his *Crack in the Picture Window* of 1957, Sylvia Plath offers us the most powerful expression of what it was like to be protected, contained and exposed at the same time in her novel *Bell Jar* of 1963.[61] As the nuclear family is put under glass, the biological and reproductive components of society are enshrined as a natural ideal – nurtured and contained, protected and watched over, and pressure is mounting.

Defining those edges

Gardens in the Case Study Houses of the 1950s turn inward, becoming more sheltered and shielded from scrutiny. While the 1945 design for the Eames and Entenza Houses show pavilions sharing a common greensward, the notable Case Study Houses of the 1950s enclose their gardens to protect them from outside views. Two of these houses – Craig Ellwood's CSH 16 and Pierre Koenig's CSH 21 – give us some insights into what happens when both the front and the back yards are completely "domesticated" as a part of the house. The result is a new definition of the public realm of the street and a more intense focus on family life. Neither of these houses has a front yard in the conventional sense. In both of them, the front lawn, with all of its associated social pressures and pretense about conformity, has been replaced by a blank wall to the street. In each, the side and rear yards have been shielded from neighbors, either because of the natural topography as in Ellwood's House, or by carving into the hillside, as Koenig did, to provide a sheltering embankment.

Ellwood's House of 1952 encloses the front garden with a ten foot high fence of translucent glass which presents an uninterrupted wall to the street (Figure 4.27). Although these glass walls are free standing, together with the carport they form the public face of the house. Yet one cannot see in. The front yard is claimed as a private space belonging only to the inhabitants of the house. The activities of children playing in the "bedroom courts" which face the street are hinted at, but not fully visible. Translucent glass then, becomes a device for obstructing vision and enhancing privacy, a technique also used by Raphael Soriano in his Colby Apartments of the same year, and by Killingsworth, Brady and Smith in their three house Case Study complex

4.27 CSH 16, Bel Air, 1953. Architect Craig Ellwood.

of 1961 in La Jolla. Alternately translucent and reflective, this glass enclosure says nature, yes but neighbors, no.

In his Case Study House of 1958, Pierre Koenig also carefully shields his open plan from the neighbors' eyes. The street-facing walls are solid sheets of corrugated steel set apart from the street with a moat, which expands into reflecting pools on the two side yards (Figure 4.28). This house on a very tight site is bordered by a bend in the road on two sides and overlooked by neighbors from a third (Figure 4.29). Koenig places the living terrace on the only side of the site which has a modest outlook and then sites the house in such a way as to screen this terrace from view. Interior spaces, protected by roof and walls from peering neighbors, become private gardens opening onto the exposed outdoor terraces with floor-to-ceiling rolling glass doors, so that "light, water and plant life penetrate its interior."[62] The exterior terraces in turn, have only two functions, both of which are visual: they extend interior space outward and they prevent outside views of the interior. The moat in Koenig's House functions like the glass screen in Ellwood's: it prevents access, it demarcates the territory of the house, and it visually extends the architectural space of the interior into the "semi-public" space of the garden (Plate 16).

261 | Nature preserved in the nuclear age

4.28 Street elevation of CSH 21, Hollywood, 1958. Architect Pierre Koenig.

While it refuses views into the house from the outside, Koenig's CSH 21 makes a fetish of views from the inside. In the center of the house, two bathrooms mirror each other across from a small skylit courtyard. While these intimate spaces are entirely shielded from neighbors' eyes, they are also

4.29 View of CSH 21 from neighbor uphill.

entirely opened to each other (Figure 4.30). Privacy, so prized in relation to the neighbors, is not valued in this conception of the family.

By turning inward around the private gardens and family life, and claiming even the vestigial relics of public street space as part of the private home, these two Case Study Houses of the 1950s represent as well a larger social dynamic of this period – the privatization of the public realm and the creation of a kind of family "hothouse," walling it in, superheating in, and making it the center of focus.

Invisible threats surround us

While the architectural solution to the "visibility problem" is straightforward, requiring that one close off street-facing windows and turn in to the

4.30 Bathroom court, CSH 21.

garden, larger environmental threats could not be warded off so easily. Even the spaces of the suburbs held invisible agents which could be dangerous. From the first great smog attack of 1943, Angelenos throughout the 1940s and '50s started to see the much-vaunted plant life of their gardens and surrounding landscape wither and turn rust brown. By 1949, the effects of smog were widespread in the Los Angeles basin, damaging trees in the San Bernardino Mountains and affecting dozens of commercial crops. While Eckbo was encouraging suburbanites to open up their living spaces to fresh air and sunlight in his article "Landscape for Living" written for *Architectural Record*, the war-boom industries of Los Angeles were spewing 80 tons of zinc and copper and 25 tons of asphalt cement dust into the air daily, along with sulfur emissions from oil refineries and of course the exhausts from an ever-rising number of automobiles. Together with landslides and huge brush fires in the hills, the smog alerts underlined the fragility of the good life in Los Angeles.

Such large-scale environmental problems beyond the control of the homeowner were an ominous sign that the protected garden of the single family house might be vulnerable to destructive influences from the outside. Homeowners tried to keep this in check with vigilant mowing, fertilizing and pesticides. Landscape architects could (and did) find smog-resistant plants. But an even more worrisome and invisible threat was lurking, further creating a sense of personal anxiety about the inviolability of the single family house and the garden. In 1948 David Bradley's *No Place to Hide* voiced what many people felt reading about the atomic bomb tests on Eniwetok atoll in the Pacific. In spite of the cloak of secrecy which surrounded the atomic program, popular press began to express concerns about the effects of fallout from atmospheric testing. John Hersey was the first person to graphically describe what fallout did to the victims of Hiroshima, in his *New Yorker* article of 1948, and *Collier's* magazine cover of the same year showed an atomic bomb exploding over Manhattan. For Los Angelenos, the danger was not so distant or hypothetical. Drinking their morning coffee over *Life* magazine in 1951, they could see a night-time photograph of their own city lit up with a mysterious glow, the result of an above-ground atomic test in Nevada (Figure 4.31). The fear of invisible and omnipresent fallout generated feelings of unease. By the time the Russians tested their own bomb in September of 1949 and the US entered the Korean conflict against the Soviets the following year, unease escalated to a sober assessment of the consequences of atomic war in the United States.

When we consider that the Case Study House program was being realized at a time when atomic anxiety was at its height, it becomes intriguing to explore these open, transparent houses in the leafy suburbs of Los Angeles in juxtaposition to a rising popular awareness of the threat posed by the atomic bomb. The points of comparison are legion – at the urban scale, in terms of home-making, the technologies of home-building, issues around the consensus society during the rise of domestic repression of the McCarthy era.

As early as 1946, Tracy Augur told the American Institute of Planners that the "profession had a crucial role to play in guiding urban dispersal which was widely advocated as a civil-defense measure."[63] "Instead of *There Is No Defense*, one now heard talk – much of it officially inspired – of strat-

4.31 Nuclear test lights up downtown Los Angeles at night, 1951.

egies for protecting a populace against atomic attack. Urban dispersal was proposed with new seriousness."[64] One article, in *American City*, recommended "nucleation," or pockets of concentrated settlement separated by green belts. Another, put together by the mathematician Norbert Wiener of MIT, proposed a program of eight-lane expressways and six-lane railbeds surrounding major urban centers at a distance which would leave them functioning after an atomic blast. The intervening space would be kept as park land in peacetime and, in the event of atomic war, would offer space to erect tent cities and field hospitals for the refugees (Figures 4.32 and 4.33). The Wiener plan, published in *Life* magazine in 1950 under the heading "How US Cities Can Prepare for Atomic War," resurrects the greenbelt idea as tactic for civil defense. In peacetime, it was suggested, such a planning solution "would expand and accelerate the current trend toward suburbs," contributing "to a greater spread of healthy semi-rural life on the urban periphery."[65]

How can one make sense of such seemingly disparate views of suburban life: as a holding pen for atomic refugees on the one hand, and as the ideal environment to raise a family in close proximity to nature, on the other?[66]

4.32 "Nuclear bombing of New York," *Collier's* magazine, 1948.

Perhaps, as the Atomic Energy Commission took some pains to point out, radiation was not a threat at all. Mutation might just strengthen and improve the human organism as it did with a strain of fruit flies, which after 128 generations in highly radioactive containers turned out to be "a much improved race, with greater vigor, hardiness, resistance to disease and with increased reproductive capacity."[67] One did not even have to wait for war to see the benefits of radiation near a "house for a growing family." The desperate search for peacetime uses of this military technology led to experiments in irradiated fields to produce new plant strains – carnations, for example, had been "improved" by removing the last streak of red to produce a pure-white bloom.[68]

If the suburb was being recast as an ideal environment to survive atomic attack, it was the home which remained the "front line" against the fallout from nuclear war. In 1950, President Truman created the Federal Civil Defense Administration, which promoted professionalized home-making for

4.33 "Life belts around cities," *Life* (18 December 1950). Drawing by Alexander Leydenfrost.

the atomic age. What of the house itself? Did the atomic scare have any impact on house design and construction? How did architects and social critics see the house in the light of incipient nuclear holocaust?[69]

When we look at the "media darling" of 1949, the steel and glass house, we are struck by the *hubris* and exuberance these fragile skeletal structures presented to a society transfixed by an apocalyptic sense of imminent destruction. Where does one go to "duck and cover" in a glass house? Is it an act of denial to design and live in one? Or is it daring? The answer may well lie in the discussions surrounding another famous glass house surrounded by nature – the one Philip Johnson built in 1949.

Two buildings make up Johnson's "Glass House" on his large estate in Connecticut (Figure 4.34). Separated by a lawn, one is a steel and glass cage and the other is a nearly windowless brick box. Each is provided with the amenities of domestic life, containing bedroom, study, kitchen, bath, and (a necessity for Johnson the art connoisseur) places to display art. Either house can be inhabited equally easily, and to describe one as a social space and the other as a service space is unnecessary and misleading. The opposition set out by these two buildings is not a functional one, but rather a philosophical opposition, having to do with the nature of transparent and opaque buildings.[70] In the brick box, a bunker of "closet like rooms," human activities are concealed from view (see Figure 4.35).[71] The bedrooms are never photographed. It is a contained vessel, fitted out with portholes and roof hatches, as if it were an ark to ride out the aftermath of war on a desolated landscape. The glass box by contrast, a transparent pavilion, is completely open to view. Yet we do not see how one might live in it, but only *signs* of its inhabitation (Figure 4.36). Comparing it to the Eameses House, which is so full of the

4.34 Glass House at night, New Canaan, CT, 1949. Architect Philip Johnson. Photograph by Ezra Stoller.

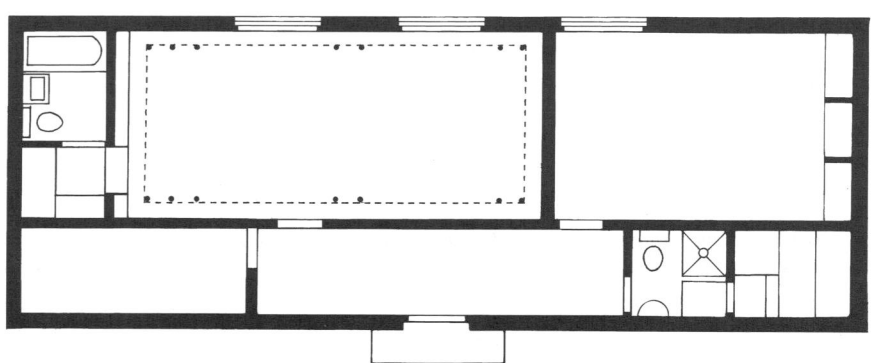

4.35 Plan of guest house opposite Glass House, 1949. Architect Philip Johnson.

Eames themselves living in and using their house, Johnson's Glass House is inhabited by *images* of people and nature that are biological surrogates. Instead of potted plants or indoor planters for example, he suspends a landscape by Poussin, the *Funeral of Phocion*. The spare Mies-designed furniture

4.36 Interior view of Glass House, 1949. Photograph by Ezra Stoller.

is arranged to suggest a social setting or more accurately, as Arthur Drexler suggested in his 1949 review of the building, a theatrical ritual enacting domestic activity. "The dignified proportions of the [kitchen] counter effectively transform it from a mere workspace to the scene of pontifical ceremonies. The mixing of a gin and tonic, or the scrambling of eggs, becomes a luxury which is the significant blend of ritual and necessity."[72]

What intrigues us here is the way this house so clearly expresses an opposition that underlies the paradox of dwelling in the nuclear era. If Johnson's brick block presciently augurs the backyard bunker, his glass pavilion may well be a paean to the impossible paradise promised by a glass house in nature, in a society that possesses weapons of mass destruction. Johnson himself suggests that the house can be seen as an allegory for the destruction of war,

> The cylinder ... forming the main motif of the house, was not derived from Mies, but rather from a burnt-out wooden village I saw once where nothing was left but the foundations and chimneys of brick. Over the chimney I slipped a steel cage with a glass skin, the chimney forms the anchor.[73]

A glass case and a skeletal architecture in a park-like setting makes the "ruins" an object of reflection.[74] In Johnson's glass box, there are also the fleshy remains of bodies: Giacometti's *Night* is a skeletal figure poised in the conversation circle, and Elie Nadleman's organ-like "ladies" hover between the dining area and the kitchen in a vaguely grotesque parody of the marble Maillol nude placed by Mies in his Barcelona Pavilion. An eerie technological glow fills the room, "mechanical moonbeams" which further enhance the theatrical quality of this polemical house.[75]

At the end of his essay in which he revisits the Glass House, Kenneth Frampton muses, "it may well be, as Peter Eisenman has suggested, that the Glass House is Johnson's cryptic monument to the horrors of war; that here beneath the flowers of Xanadu lies the petrified remains of a lost ideal and an elegy for the dead." "Is it not," he continues, "a folding in of humanism upon itself, the state of solipsism raised to unparalleled elegance, the end of a trajectory rather than a beginning?"[76] "The Bomb that fell on America" – wrote the poet Hermann Hagedorn in 1946 – unlike those dropped in Japan,

> Erased no church, vaporized no public building ... did not dissolve their bodies,
> But it dissolved something vitally important to the greatest of them, and the least,
> What it dissolved were their links with the past and with the future, It made the earth, that seemed so solid, Main Street, that seemed so well paved, a kind of vast jelly, quivering and dividing underfoot.[77]

Johnson's House is an essay on the paradox of living in paradise – in a glass house in nature – while one also inhabits a world in which total war is possible. It asks us to reflect on this paradox and it poses, tongue in cheek, two possible solutions: "petrifying" paradise (or perhaps we should say "vitrifying" it) on the one hand, or barricading ourselves in an architectural tomb on the other. The California-based architects of the Case Study Houses were less philosophical than Johnson, and more pragmatic. Looking at the work of Eames and Saarinen, Soriano, Ellwood and Koenig, one does not get a sense that they were concerned with a sophisticated social commentary while they developed their steel and glass structures in the garden landscape of Los Angeles. Yet John Entenza, who commissioned the Case Study Houses, was. In his editorials for *Arts & Architecture* immediately after the war, Entenza cautions his readers that the enemy is no longer foreign nations, but self-serving and reactionary mentalities in all countries including the United States. The cover for the December 1946 issue shows the power of the atom superimposed on a head in profile gazing at a small globe of the planet Earth. Inside, an article entitled "The Brotherhood of Man" makes an appeal for a new post-war order which would transcend the axis and allied blocks of wartime (Figure 4.37).

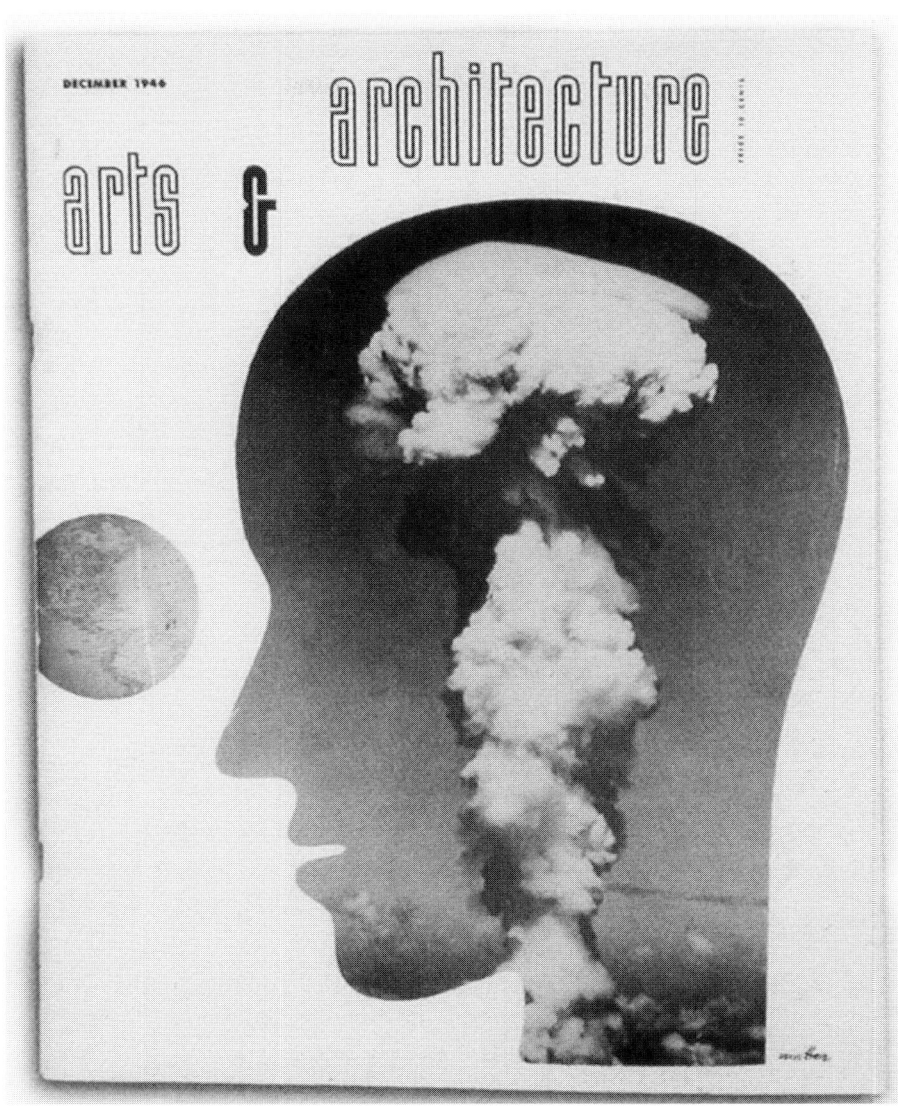

4.37 Cover of *Arts & Architecture* magazine, December 1946. Design by Herbert Matter.

Los Angeles was also unmistakably a landscape created and sustained by military industry. Aerospace factories were the stomping grounds of the Case Study architects as they hunted for new materials and design ideas, they were knee-deep in steel, aluminum and glass, and they embraced an engineer's approach to problem-solving which led to innovative solutions to heating and cooling the modern house, rationalizing its plumbing and exploiting the peacetime uses of military technology. They were also surrounded by the nuclear program, with Vandenburgh Air Force Base to the north, the jet fighter testing grounds of Antelope Valley in the Mojave Desert to the east (where Chuck Yeager and others with the "right stuff" generated sonic booms daily), and the secretive desert tests in Nevada were only a Santa Ana wind away (Plate 17).

The whole idea of building steel and glass houses in arid Los Angeles and its hinterland required technology for cooling interiors. Yet the architectural magazines spoke not of the difficulties of dealing with extreme desert temperatures, but rather of the ways in which nature could be improved by technology. An *Architectural Forum* article of 1949 explains how Neutra's Kaufmann house in Palm Springs pipes water into the pools, ceilings, floors, and outside pavement; turns away the sun with white mica-glazed pavements, granulated-ceramic roofs and heat-reflecting aluminum foil in the walls; and screens the wind with vertical louvers.[78] The electrical power that enables this extraordinary transformation (and in fact lights and irrigates much of the desert surrounding Los Angeles), is generated by Boulder Dam. Another hidden power is even more unmentionable, its eerie glow erupting only sporadically over the desert horizon throughout the early 1950s.[79]

Light and darkness, transparency and opacity, exposure and concealment, expansion and containment – these are the dynamics underlying the social dimension of the atomic bomb as it was experienced in the United States. "Like the shadow of an eclipse of the sun," wrote *Christian Century* magazine, "atomic darkness is racing across the world."[80] In sharp contrast to their initial impulse to contain the atomic threat with a new form of "world government" (which led to the foundation of the United Nations in 1948), by the early 1950s Americans were paralyzed, transfixed with the image of their government testing and stockpiling ever more weapons, and fascinated with their own inactivity. Yet there is little doubt that nuclear war was foremost in the minds of most throughout these years. In 1959, two out of three Americans listed the possibility of nuclear war as the nation's most urgent problem."[81] In his poem *Fall 1961*, the national poet Robert Lowell describes the sensation of paralysis in the face of impending nuclear destruction,

> All autumn, the chafe and jar
> of nuclear war;
> We have talked our extinction to death.
> I swim like a minnow
> behind my studio window.

Our end drifts nearer,
the moon lifts,
radiant with terror
The state
is a diver under a glass bell.

For Lowell, the glass bell is a *leitmotiv* for dwelling in the nuclear era. Busy with the trivial tasks of everyday life, his narrator swims "like a minnow" behind a window watching "our end drift nearer." To be behind glass is to be paralyzed – one can see everything and do nothing.[82] Through glass, the final flash will be visible. Darkened, it becomes the sunglasses worn by spectators of the bomb.[83] Translucent, like in the milky panels of Craig Ellwood's Case Study Houses, it turns bodies into ghosts, much as the atomic flash turns shadows into solids (Figure 4.38). In a story from his popular *Martian Chronicles* of 1950, Ray Bradbury describes a post-apocalyptic Earth seen by horrified humans who return from their colonization of Mars. Automated sprinklers still irrigate the lawn of the now empty house, silently switching on and off; lights still operate on their pre-determined schedules, but "only the shadow images of playing children incised on the

4.38 Sculpture, Claire Falkenstein, *Arts & Architecture* (June 1955).

4.39 Interior view of CSH 16. Architect Greg Ellwood.

scorched walls give evidence that human beings had once been in residence."[84] Like a modern-day Pompeii, humans are captured on the X-ray plate of the glass wall.

When transparent glass turns milky, it is a sign that unseen forces are at work, nature turning malevolent and raining invisible dangers below. During the era of open-air nuclear testing, residents of Seattle started to report a mysterious film, or etching, affecting their car windshields. Many covered their windshields for protection, and the mayor made an appeal to President Eisenhower. Residents of Boise, Idaho also reported pitting on their windshields.[85] This phenomenon was described as a "collective delusion," engendered, no doubt, by the fear of rain-borne fallout. Yet it is telling that clear and crystalline glass reveals the forces of nature as ominous. Glass, which early in the decade promised a home that would open effortlessly onto a benign and tranquil nature, was by the decade's close, an indicator of "over-exposure" – to sun, rain, light, radiation and the ever-present peering neighbors.

The long-standing dream of the glass house as an expression of an open society may have been realized in the Case Study Houses, but in the process transparency itself was revealed as unsettling and anxiety-producing. To see into a Craig Ellwood House from the street is to see something, but one is not sure what. Like the shower scene in the film *Psycho*, we know there are bodies behind the milky glass. But we cannot *see* them, we do not know how they live, they don't *show* themselves (see Figure 4.39). In the nuclear age, our neighbors become strangers; nature, becomes threatening; the single family house discovers a new vulnerability.

CONTAINMENT IN THE BACKYARD BUNKER
A fortress of solitude
If we see the GI Bill and the interstate highway program as elements of a national housing strategy which directed new housing into the suburbs, it is intriguing to explore the next big housing initiative of the Federal government – the home "shelter" program – as both an extension of and a reaction to post-war expansion.

The US developed multi-megaton hydrogen bombs in the mid-1950s that could "take out" any size of city and the Soviets followed suit shortly after.[86] The early scenarios for urban evacuation and the provision of collective underground shelters had been replaced by the idea of the "family fallout shelter," in which every house would be a fortress against the "enemy threat."[87] Well-adapted to the increasing suburbanization of the country, this approach to civil defense also corresponded to the individualism of the suburbs, asking every citizen to invest in a home shelter and provision it for the impending apocalypse. Federal pamphlets such as *By, For and About Women in Civil Defense: Grandma's Pantry belongs in your Kitchen* exhorted responsible citizens to practice the pioneer values of their forefathers, stocking up for adversity, taking responsibility for their own protection and survival.[88] In this sense, the idea of the "family fallout shelter" played directly into the American myth that the suburbs were merely a continuation of a long-standing national tradition of independent, self-reliant homesteaders (Figure 4.40).

Yet the suburbanite of 1961 was not isolated on a rural farmstead. Rather he or she was watching nightly broadcasts and reading newspapers which described escalating Soviet-American hostilities over Berlin and Cuba, practicing Civil Defense drills, listening to radio shows that were interrupted by emergency broadcast system tests. Their houses were equipped with NEAR repeaters plugged into household outlets, which would trigger an alarm the moment the Soviet missiles were determined to be heading toward American soil. On 5 October 1961, President Kennedy went on nation-wide television to exhort every American family to build a home fallout shelter, and authorized FHA home loans to be used for shelter construction. A week later, all commercial and private flights over the US and Canada were banned from 11 am to 11 at night (2,100 flights) and 1,800 NORAD fighter planes,

276 | Nature preserved in the nuclear age

4.40 Backyard fallout shelter under three feet of earth.

250 Strategic Air Command B-47s, B-52s and RAF bombers flew sorties over Eastern seaboard cities simulating bombing runs.[89]

While it was initiated and instigated by the Federal government, the "shelter craze" that swept the country in 1961 revealed an American family feeling exposed and vulnerable to forces beyond their control. We see the mania for building fallout shelters, in part, as a reaction to the expansionism of the post-war period. Margaret Mead made an analysis that goes in this direction in her own attempt to understand the "shelter craze." Writing for the *New York Times Magazine* in 1961, she reminds her readers that "ever since we dropped the first nuclear bomb on Hiroshima, ... we were no longer protected by fixed boundaries. This recognition," she continues, "activated many kinds of expansion," from extended defenses around the world and the exploration of new frontiers in outer space, to support for transnational activities such as the United Nations, bilateral aid programs and the Peace Corps. Mead sees this expansionist activity as a "reaching out into membership in the human race, in a planetary community that existed *de facto* though not yet in theory." She then proposes that "this centrifugal movement" has spawned a countervailing "centripetal pull of fear" – fear of mass destruction, of distant and alien peoples, and suggests that Americans who were "unprepared to take these unexpected giant steps turned inward, ... back in space and time, hiding from the future and the rest of the world, they turned to the green suburb, protected by zoning laws against members of other classes or races or religions, and concentrated on the single, tight, little family."[90]

Certainly, much of the rhetoric about civil defense in the 1950s looked backward "in space and time." For example, a year after establishing the Federal Civil Defense Administration, President Truman gave a short speech which served as an introduction to a training film prepared by the FCDA staff. While recognizing that nuclear war presented a wholly new kind of threat, he suggested that all Americans needed to do was revive "the old American tradition of community self defense." According to Guy Oakes, in his excellent analysis of cold war culture,

> Truman's speech imaginatively reconstructed the early history of the American national experience in Homeric proportions as the epic of the pioneers who had won the West. In this mythology, the old middle class of small-town America and the new middle class of suburbia were identified with their putative ancestors, the pioneer settlers of the frontier. America under the Soviet nuclear gun in the 1950s was identified with the outposts of the new nation under assault by the aboriginal Americans, the "Indians." ... The Cold War would be won by Americans who recovered the ethic of the pioneer forebears: ... optimism, personal responsibility, self-control and solid moral values – these were the key to survival in a nuclear attack.[91]

In this mythology, the suburban house was likened to the pioneer homestead under siege. In the nuclear showdown of 1961, the frontier myth again raised its head in a mass-media discussion about the right of shelter-owners to gun down less-prepared neighbors who might try to enter their shelters in the event of an atomic attack. In an article entitled "Gun Thy Neighbor?", printed in August of 1961, *Time* came down on the side of the rifle-wielders.[92] The following month, *Life* magazine's step-by-step article on how to build home shelters showed Art Carlson, a New York plumbing contractor, and his teenage son Claude, building their basement shelter. The closing image of the sequence depicted Mr. Carlson contentedly settling in to oil his guns (see Figure 4.41).[93] According to *Time* again, 23 "survivalist" groups in California had joined the "Minuteman" vigilantes, swelling its membership to 2,400 people who were enthusiastically training as guerrillas and storing caches of water and ammunition in the California hills for post-holocaust hand-to-hand combat.[94]

The pragmatism, if we can call it that, which soberly prepared to survive a nuclear war was paralleled by a frankly apocalyptic vision of nuclear war as God's retribution on the "evil" of communism.

4.41 "Carlson family settling into their shelter", Life (1961),

For people of a religious inclination, ... atoms, ... like everything in creation should be approached with holy faith.... The connection between bombs and apocalyptic power could take on a precise Christian meaning. A Gospel song of 1950 warned that on the day of judgment, Jesus would "hit like an atomic bomb." Some took that literally. Preachers and religious tracts in the 1950s and 1960s ... said that the Second Coming of Christ would be heralded by nuclear missiles, fulfilling in plain fact the biblical prophecy of falling stars, scorching heat, rivers of blood, and so forth.... The chaos of war and a final Battle are central to Western apocalyptic tradition. Now as throughout history, the preachers and their flocks hoped to be among the remnant of the faithful who would be saved in the Last Judgment. Some millenarian sects moved to remote areas to build fallout shelters, just to make sure. ... This was no minor tendency.[95]

Such millenarians believed that only Communists, as a godless sect, would suffer the wrath of "divine" atomic annihilation, while God-fearing Americans would be saved. Yet for the majority of the population, the only sure outcome was MAD: mutually assured destruction. If, as the government had argued, the suburbs scattered over the face of the land were a strategic advantage in civil defense, Americans began to see the corollary – that it was in the suburbs that they would ultimately encounter the fallout from a nuclear war. Thus, the view from above takes on an additional symbolic importance. Descending on the Angeleno House like industrial smog or the ashes that followed one of the many hillside firestorms of those decades, danger, in the nuclear age, would rain from above.[96] The horizontal expansion of the post-war era, so clearly argued through the early Case Study Houses is replaced by a vertical relation to nature: one which looks up to the sky in terror and down to the ground for salvation. The home no longer relates to nature as a horizon into which one expands, but rather as a vertical axis which must be guarded and fortified in retreat. The home fallout shelter is the ultimate expression of this paranoid protective impulse (Figure 4.42).

Like Superman's isolated Arctic hideout (created during these years), the fallout shelter is an impregnable space dedicated to the preservation of a "super" way of life (see Figure 4.43).[97] Shelters, survival enthusiasts were

4.42 Pre-fab plastic home shelter designed by Arthur Bascomb.

4.43 "Attractive addition in Orlando, FL: Doug Bartholow's concrete block shelter," *Life* (1961). Note that "Mrs. Bartholow tends garden on the roof."

told, had peacetime uses as well: they could serve as a teen hideout, a hobby space, and a second pantry – all suggestions which mirrored Superman's activities in his fortress – "getting away from it all," doing his hobbies like squeezing coal into diamonds and engraving metal with his X-ray vision, and mostly, storing his memories of his earthly achievements and his family origins (the city of Kandor protected under a glass jar).

The shelter is also the final solution to the visibility problem of the overexposed suburban house, replacing the space of the suburb with the security and containment of the shelter. Thus, the open house so prized in the idea of Californian living, engendered, in the short space of fifteen years, an almost complete reversal as the nation scurried into the dark, private and contained underground spaces of the backyard shelters. Writing of that other post-war icon, the flamboyant and media-savvy Howard Hughes, the journalist James Phelan asked, "Why did he let himself become a man that couldn't stand to be seen?"[98]

> At the head of [Hughes's] bed, there was a projector, and on the side near his hand, the control mechanism with which he projected his films, always the same ones, while he always ate the same dishes. We find here a metaphor for vision, the Socratic myth of the cave (a dark chamber), which, carried to its conclusion, required everyone to turn their gaze toward the source of light ... to contemplate the real which is invisible.[99]

Nestled in its shelter, the model family becomes the "real" to be protected, while the world outside is shut out, populated, in the imagination of the shelter dwellers, by demons, threats, and contagion.

Architecture underground

By the end of the 1950s, the decade-long love affair of Americans with the "transparent" suburban house had run its course. One of the last Case Study Houses, CSH 24 by A. Quincy Jones and Frederick Emmons, fuses the containment of the shelter with the indoor–outdoor relationship that had become a hallmark of the Case Study Houses. Published in *Arts & Architecture* the same month that Kennedy gave his fallout speech, this project for a 260-home tract on a former hobby farm near Northridge in the San Fernando Valley was meant to be the Case Study House program's "foremost statement about multiple suburban housing."[100] Working for the developer Joseph Eichler, architects Jones and Emmons developed a master plan and one of five prototype houses that would make up the subdivision (Figure 4.44).

The prototype house, consisting of four bedrooms and a small living area extended by "sun gardens" and "shade gardens" on each side, is almost entirely below grade. Excavated earth is piled on three sides of the house, leaving only the carport easily accessible from the ground plane. The result is a Case Study House that offers total visual privacy. It is ironic that this project,

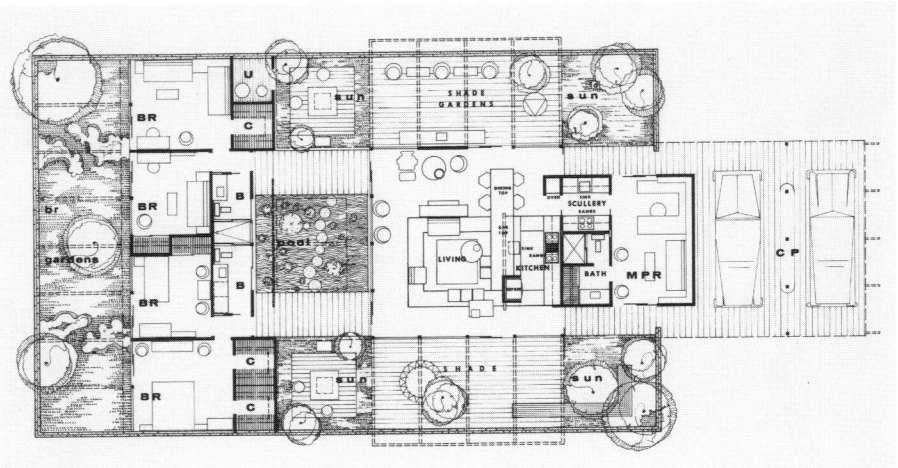

4.44 Plan of CSH 24. Architects A. Quincy Jones and Frederick Emmons, 1961.

which was the program's most ambitious community development, is made up of houses that are completely isolated from each other. Their below-grade "gardens" and earth-bermed walls were meant to visually and acoustically buffer each family from others in the neighborhood. The clerestory windows that surround the house look like they were taken from a page of the FCDA shelter manual.[101] The small living room in the center of the house descends even deeper into the ground, in a conversation pit, mirroring the indoor pool (an emergency reservoir?) (Figure 4.45). There is only one exit from the four bedrooms, and that is past the "multi-purpose room," a surveillance station positioned at the entry which is either a home office or in-law suite. The roof, not incidentally, offers protection from brush fires, especially when it is flooded with water for a cooling system. Even the gardens are buried, and only the roofs hover above an endless sea of the surrounding landscape (Plate 18).

Leftover spaces in a landscape of containment

In the 1960s, we see the process of "containment" carried through all the levels of the American landscape: roads become limited access freeways, shopping streets become limited access "malls," renovated downtowns become inward-looking megastructures (as in Victor Gruen's plan for Dallas-Fort Worth), and neighborhoods are set up as restricted communities according to class, race, and often religion. The psychology of containment begins by protecting the house and garden, but once unleashed, it infects all aspects of public spaces in the landscape. To contain the threat, whatever it may be, one must first identify difference and then isolate one use from another. Like

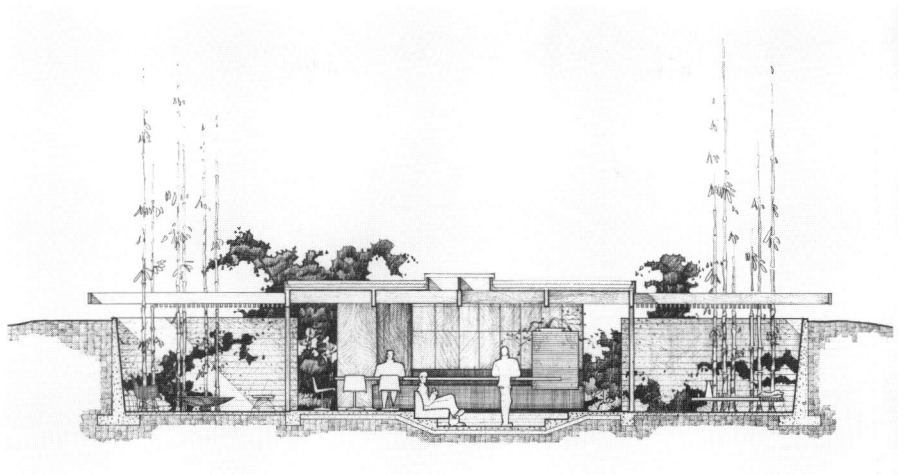

4.45 Section of CSH 24, showing conversation pit and below-grade gardens. A. Quincy Jones and Frederick E. Emmons, Architects.

creating isolated areas for conservation of wilderness, "containment" is a scientific paradigm applied to social values.

In closing, we move up into the air like Charles and Ray Eames did in their film *Powers of Ten*, and look down on the landscape that has been created by "California living." From the air we see each of the many contained and privatized realms of the urban infrastructure – backyard, house, suburb, downtown mall, shopping center, freeway – fed and supported by the proliferating agri-business and military-industrial complex (Figures 4.46 and 4.47). As piece after piece of the public, civic, and national space becomes contained, protected and policed through the 1950s and 1960s, the remainder is abandoned as wasted space; it is once-public space transformed into a no-man's land. In this leftover space we see the consequences on the larger landscape of the abstract and individual relation to nature so well represented by the Case Study Houses. Abandoned and neglected space becomes a site for the proliferation of chemical dumpsites, parking lots, and junk yards. The aerial view allows us to see with a critical eye both the isolation and the environmental consequences of the suburbanization exemplified by post-war Los Angeles. California living had indeed swept across the nation in the 1950s and '60s, and its legacy endures until today. These "left over spaces" will become the playgrounds of the children raised in and around the new suburbs. Their reaction to the rapid and seemingly unstoppable suburbanization of what was recently countryside lays the groundwork for the ascendancy of the ecological movement and sets the stage for our next chapter.

284 | Nature preserved in the nuclear age

4.46 Disneyland from the air, Anaheim, California.

Notes

1 For a good introduction to the influences of wartime technologies on housing design, see Donald Albrecht (ed.), *World War II and the American Dream: How Wartime Building Changed a Nation*, Washington DC: National Building Museum/MIT Press, 1995.

2 In 1942, *Architectural Forum* runs a competition titled "The New House 194X." A year later *Arts & Architecture* followed suit with its "Designs for Postwar Living" competition, *Pencil Points* ran a series on "The Architecture of the Future", and *Women's Home Companion* published "Your Post War Home." In 1944, *Ladies Home Journal* and the MOMA sponsor "Tomorrow's Small House" exhibit, and *Arts & Architecture* holds its second "Designs for Postwar Living" competition. In 1945, *Arts & Architecture* announces the Case Study House program and *Pencil Points* publishes its competition for an average family house. Rohm & Haas's Plexiglas "dream suite" tours department stores, and George Nelson & Henry Wright publish *Tomorrow's House: How to Plan Your Post-War House*. In 1946, *Architectural Forum* showcases the Los Angeles developer Fritz Burns model house on Wilshire Boulevard with 100 ideas for your new house, *House Beautiful* publishes "The First Postwar House," *Los Angeles Builder* writes of "Dream House, Preview of all the things

285 | Nature preserved in the nuclear age

4.47 Fashion Island shopping center, Newport Beach, California.

      Americans may someday have in their homes," and Elizabeth Mock puts out *If You Want to Build a House*, New York: MOMA.
3 However, red-lining practiced by banks and supported by the Federal government at judicial and legislative levels effectively put single-family home ownership in the new suburbs out of reach for black soldiers.
4 Catherine Bauer, "Cities in Flux: A Challenge to Postwar Planners," *The American Scholar* 13, no. 1 (Winter 1943–4), p. 70.
5 The outer fringes of this sense of expansion and liberty was best expressed by Jack Kerouac's classic novel *On The Road*.
6 William H. Whyte, "Urban Sprawl," *Fortune* 57, no. 1 (January 1958), pp. 103–9, 194, 198, 200.
7 These Resettlement Administration projects were designed as suburban model communities for a middle class population with one wage earner and one homemaker.
8 For instance Frederick Gutheim's article "Greenbelt Revisited," *Magazine of Art* (January 1946).
9 CSH 4 by Ralph Rapson, *Arts & Architecture* (August 1945), p. 32.
10 Rapson, *Arts & Architecture* (August 1945), p. 33.

11 *Sunset: the Magazine of Western Living* 108, no. 6 (June 1952), p. 46.
12 See Robert Winter (ed.), *Toward a Simpler Way of Life: The Arts and Crafts Architects of California*, Berkeley: University of California Press, 1997.
13 Schindler designed the beds in the Lovell Beach House to roll from the inside to the outside sleeping porches. Harris did the same in his Lowe House of 1934. See Winter, *Toward a Simpler Way*, p. 279.
14 Sylvia Lavin has analyzed in some depth Neutra's "intense concentration on dismantling conventional barriers between inside and out." See her "The Avant-Garde is Not at Home: Richard Neutra and the American Psychologizing of Modernity," in R.E. Somol (ed.), *Autonomy and Ideology*, Monacelli Press/Canadian Centre for Architecture, 1997, p. 189. Esther McCoy says of Neutra's CSH 20 (Bailey House) that "it was in the vein as the Nesbitt House ... redwood and brick." Esther McCoy, "Arts and Architecture Case Study Houses," in Elizabeth A.T. Smith (ed.), *Blueprints for Modern Living: History and Legacy of the Case Study Houses*, New York and Los Angeles: MoCA/MIT Press, 1989, p. 21.
15 Jane King Hession, Rip Rapson and Bruce N. Wright, *Ralph Rapson: Sixty Years of Modern Design*, Afton, MN: Afton Historical Society Press, 1999, p. 37.
16 Beatriz Colomina, "The Lawn at War," in *The American Lawn*, (ed.), Georges Teyssot, New York: Princeton Architectural Press/Canadian Centre for Architecture, 1999, p. 137.
17 Garrett Eckbo, *Landscape for Living*, p. 17. Or is this his "Landscape for Living" article, *Architectural Record* 105, 1949.
18 Marc Treib and Dorothée Imbert, *Garrett Eckbo: Modern Landscapes for Living*, Berkeley: University of California Press, 1997, p. 21.
19 Esther McCoy says of Eckbo's gardens, "What was exciting at the time about the landscaping was that it looked designed." Esther McCoy, "Arts and Architecture Case Study Houses," *Blueprints*, p. 23.
20 *Sunset: the Magazine of Western Living*, no. 5 (August 1949).
21 "Trends in outdoor cookery," *Sunset* 97, no. 2 (August 1946), p. 45.
22 "Pacific Notebook," *Sunset* 106, no. 2 (April 1951), p. 42.
23 All quotes from "Pacific Notebook," *Sunset* 94, no. 2 (February 1945), p. 2.
24 *Sunset* 108, no. 6 (June 1952), p. 44.
25 Lynn Spigel, "Installing the Television Set: Popular Discourses on Television and Domestic Space, 1948–1955," in Lynn Spigel and Denise Mann (eds), *Private Screenings: Television and the Female Consumer*, Minneapolis: University of Minnesota Press, 1992, p. 6.
26 Peter Collins, *Changing Ideals in Modern Architecture*, Montreal: McGill University Press, 1967, p. 285.
27 Siegfried Giedeon, *Space, Time and Architecture*, Cambridge: Harvard University Press, 1941, p. 462.
28 George H. Marcus, *Design in the Fifties: When Everyone Went Modern*, Munich: Prestel Verlag, 1998, pp. 104–5.
29 Marcus, *Design in the Fifties*, p. 109.
30 Thomas Hine, *Populuxe*, New York: Alfred A. Knopf, p. 148.
31 Ray Eames, *Arts & Architecture* (September 1943).
32 Hine, *Populuxe*, p. 145.

33 Hine, *Populuxe*, p. 144.
34 Richard Neutra is the pre-eminent exponent of an unbounded extension of the house into the garden. Again, see Lavin "The Avant-garde is not at Home."
35 Hélène Lipstadt, "Natural Overlap: Charles and Ray Eames and the Federal Government," in Diane Murphy (ed.), *The Work of Charles and Ray Eames: A Legacy of Invention*, Washington DC: Library of Congress and Vitra Design Museum, 1997, p. 151–75; Jane C. Loeffler, *The Architecture of Diplomacy: Building America's Embassies*, New York: Princeton Architectural Press, 1998; and Serge Guilbaut, *How New York Stole the Idea of Modern Art*, Chicago: University of Chicago Press, 1983. Loeffler reviews the contributions of Case Study House architects to the United States' mid-century program of embassy building, discussing Rapson and van der Meulen's designs for Stockholm and Copenhagen (both 1951–4), and their unbuilt schemes for Oslo, The Hague, Paris and Beirut; also Wurster, Bernardi and Emmons' Hong Kong embassy (1954–7), and Saarinen's winning entry for London (1956–9), and his Oslo design (1959).
36 Elaine Tyler May, *Homeward Bound*, New York: Basic Books, 1988, p. 18.
37 "Transparency in the Home," *Modern Plastics* (October 1945), p. 107.
38 Elizabeth Mock, *If You Want to Build a House*, New York: MOMA, 1946, p. 81.
39 "Case Study Houses #8 and #9, Charles Eames and Eero Saarinen," *Arts & Architecture* (December 1945), p. 44.
40 "He was a man passionately devoted to the new architecture, yet obviously had sensibilities at odds with what the sun-drenched rooms and flowing plans promised." Esther McCoy, "Remembering John Entenza," in Barbara Goldstein (ed.), *Arts & Architecture, The Entenza Years*, Los Angeles: Hennessey and Ingalls, 1998, p. 13.
41 Alison and Peter Smithson, "Phenomenon in Parallel: Eames House, Patio and Pavilion," *Places* 7, no. 3, 1991, p. 20.
42 Smithsons, "Phenomenon in Parallel," 20.
43 Alison and Peter Smithson, "Eames Celebration," *Architectural Design* (September 1966), p. 432.
44 Beatriz Colomina, "Reflections on the Eames House," in Diana Murphy (ed.), *The Work of Charles and Ray Eames: a Legacy of Invention*, Washington DC: Library of Congress/Vitra Design Museum, 1997, p. 127.
45 Jean Starobinsky, *Jean-Jacques Rousseau: Transparency and Obstruction*, Chicago: University of Chicago Press, 1988, pp. 92–3.
46 Starobinsky, *Jean-Jacques Rousseau*, p. 94.
47 The photographic exhibit *The Family of Man* was displayed in the American Exposition in Moscow in 1959 (a geodesic dome designed by Buckminster Fuller containing a slide show by Charles and Ray Eames).
48 Reyner Banham, "The Atavism of the Short-distance Mini-cyclist," in Penny Sparke (ed.), *Design by Choice*, New York: Rizzoli, 1981, pp. 84–9.
49 Reyner Banham, "Klarheit, Ehrlichkeit, Einfachkeit . . . and Wit, too! The Case Study Houses in the World's Eyes," in Smith, *Blueprints for Modern Living*, p. 183.
50 Case Study Houses no. 8 and no. 9, Charles Eames and Eero Saarinen," *Arts & Architecture* (December 1945), p. 44.
51 Writing about Philip Johnson's glass house of the same year, Arthur Drexler makes this relationship between democracy and a glass pavilion set in nature

explicit: "A glass house bespeaks more security than a stone house because the owner can afford to dispense with the safety of stone. The liberty to build openly implies trust, too, in neighbors. In 1930 a young enthusiast declared, 'The greatest architect would be that godlike man who could shelter a space using no materials at all. Architecture without buildings . . . would be paradise. By this last magic of a consummate civilization we should be united in freedom with the most primitive hunter for whom all Nature is home. Our only difficulties – an excess of perfection.'" Arthur Drexler, "Glass house permits its owner to live in nature," *Architectural Forum*, 1949, p. 78.

52 "Western Creation," *Sunset*, p. 44.
53 William Dobriner, *Class in Suburbia*, Englewood Cliffs, NJ: Prentice Hall, 1963.
54 Mark Wigley, "The Electric Lawn," in Teyssot, *The American Lawn*, p. 156.
55 May, *Homeward Bound*, p. 5.
56 May, *Homeward Bound*, pp. 11–16.
57 George Nelson and Henry Wright, *Tomorrow's House: a Complete Guide for the Home Builder*, New York: Simon and Schuster, 1946.
58 Lynn Spigel, "Television in the Family Circle," in Patricia Mellencamp (ed.), *Logics of Television*, Bloomington: Indiana University Press, 1990, p. 75.
59 *Sunset* (January) 1949.
60 Spigel, "Installing the Television Set," p. 26. The mid-1960s television show *Candid Camera* played on this fear of constant unexpected surveillance, by filming "everyday people's" reactions to unexpected (although elaborately staged) events.
61 John Keats, *The Crack in the Picture Window*, Boston: Houghton Mifflin, 1956 and Sylvia Plath, *The Bell Jar*, London: Heinemann, 1963 (published pseudonymously as "Victoria Lucas").
62 Amelia Jones and Elizabeth A.T. Smith, "The Thirty-six Case Study Projects," *Blueprints for Modern Living*, p. 70.
63 Paul Boyer, *By the Bombs Early Light: American Thought and Culture at the Dawn of the Atomic Age*, Chapel Hill: University of North Carolina Press, 1994, p. 51.
64 Boyer, *Bombs Early Light*, p. 320.
65 "How US Cities Can Prepare for Atomic War," *Life* 29, no. 5 (18 December 1950), pp. 76–82, 85–6. The Wiener plan was co-authored by Giorgio di Santillana and Karl Deutsch.
66 Marcel Breuer's 1949 demonstration "house in a garden" built for the Museum of Modern Art was dubbed the "home for the growing family" by *Architectural Forum* (May 1949).
67 "The Facts About A-Bomb Fallout," *Reader's Digest*, condensed from *US News and World Report* (March 25, 1953).
68 Harland Manchester, "The New Age of 'Atomic Crops,'" *Popular Mechanics* (October 1958).
69 In her book *Screening the Body*, Lisa Cartwright explores how radiography was marketed to popular audiences from the 1930s to the 1960s. In *Highlights and Shadows*, a Kodak Research Laboratories promotional film from 1937, Cartwright shows how the iconic death image of the X-ray was transformed into a symbol of community health. As a young, bathing-suit clad woman is

strapped to a table before being X-rayed for signs of tuberculosis, the narrator intones, "this young lady, to whom henceforth a glass house should hold no terrors, will, after an examination of her radiographs, be reassured that she is *indeed* physically fit." Cartwright finds it significant that the interior of the female body is linked in this sequence to the exposed domestic space of the glass house. "Like the occupant of the glass house," she says, "the subject of the X-ray is vulnerable because regions of her body usually kept private are placed on display. But this vulnerability to sight is transformed into a condition of health." The idea of making the interior of her body visible should not frighten her when her swimsuit-clad body is already exposed, and her chest X-ray further confirms "that she is *indeed* physically fit." Lisa Cartwright, *Screening the Body: Tracing Medicine's Visual Culture*, Minneapolis: University of Minnesota Press, 1995, p. 155.

70 Franz Schulz traces an opposition in Johnson's houses between living and representational functions. "Johnson responded to American domesticity in the Wiley House (1953) with a version of Breuer's binuclear living [the reference here is to Breuer's 'House in the Garden,' built for MOMA in 1949, separating living and representational requirements on separate floors. He explains this solution as an attempt to reconcile the (perhaps) irreconcilable: modern architectural purity and the requirements of living American families." Johnson asks, "Why can't people learn to live in the windowless spheres of Ledoux or the pure glass prisms of Mies van der Rohe? No, they need a place for Junior to practice the piano while Mother plays bridge with her neighbors." Franz Schulze, *Philip Johnson, Life and Work*, New York: Knopf, 1994, pp. 157, 214.

71 Arthur Drexler, "Architecture Opaque and Transparent: Philip Johnson's glass and brick houses in Connecticut," *Interiors + Industrial Design* 109, no. 3 (October 1949), p. 96.

72 Drexler, "Architecture Opaque and Transparent", p. 96.

73 Kenneth Frampton, "The Glass House Revisited," *Philip Johnson: Processes, the Glass House, 1949 and the ATT Corporate Headquarters, 1978. Catalogue 9*, New York: Institute for Architecture and Urban Studies, 1978, p. 51.

74 Similarly, Kenzo Tange turned to the pure geometry of the glass box in his memorial to the victims of Hiroshima. Facing the warped steel wreckage of the "A-bomb dome," his severe museum encloses the mute signs of inhabitation (e.g. shadows burned on stone) so evocatively described by John Hersey in his well-known *New Yorker* article of 1948.

75 Drexler describes the "weird light [that] fills the room … mechanical moonbeams" in his "Architecture Opaque and Transparent," pp. 91, 94.

76 Frampton, "Glass House Revisited," p. 51.

77 Hermann Hagedorn, *The Bomb That Fell on America*, Santa Barbara: Pacific Coast Publishing, 1946, pp. 9–11.

78 "House in the Desert," *Architectural Forum* (June 1949), pp. 90–3; and Arthur Drexler, "Glass oasis with cold walls … architect Neutra's improved desert," *Interiors + Industrial Design* 109, no. 2 (September 1949), pp. 80–87.

79 On December 18, 1950, Truman authorized the opening of the Nevada test site and the first atmospheric test took place on 27 January 1951. One hundred and nineteen above ground tests followed until a brief moratorium from 1958–61

(an average of 40 per year), and when testing resumed there was an average of one test per week until the test ban treaty of 5 August 1963. Peter Goin, "Ground Zero: Nevada Test Site," *Landscape* 30, no. 1, 1998, p. 24.
80 "Spreading Atomic Eclipse?" *Christian Century* (18 January 1950), p. 70.
81 Boyer, *By the Bombs Early Light*.
82 In his novel *On The Beach*, Nevil Shute depicts a whole nation in paralysis, as Australians wait for the fallout from global nuclear war to reach their shores.
83 In *The Art of Seeing*, Aldous Huxley wrote, "Wearing dark sunglasses has not only become commonplace but respectable ... dark glasses have ceased to be a sign of infirmity and are nowadays a sign of youth, elegance and sex-appeal. One can wear sunglasses like one takes to cigarettes or alcohol. In the western world, millions of people now wear sunglasses, not only on the beach, but while driving their car, in twilight or in the dark corridors of public buildings. Why then do so many of our contemporaries feel bothered, ill at ease when their eyes are exposed to even a mild light?" Cited in Paul Virilio, *The Aesthetics of Disappearance*, New York: Semiotext(e), 1991, p. 56.
84 Cited in Boyer, *By the Bombs Early Light*, p. 259.
85 Spencer R. Weart, *Nuclear Fear: A History of Images*, Cambridge, MA: Harvard University Press, 1988, pp. 187, 190. Weart cites Nahum Z. Medalia and Otto N. Larsen, "Diffusion and Belief in a Collective Delusion: The Seattle Windshield Pitting Epidemic," *American Sociological Review* (1958), pp. 180–6.
86 The early H-bomb tests were conducted under great secrecy in US overseas territory far from the continental United States: the multi-megaton "Operation Ivy" (1 November 1951) and the 15 megaton "Bravo" 1 March 1954). Of this latter test, the chairman of the Atomic Energy Commission revealed that it could "take out" any size of city, no limits being set on its potential destructive capacity. For the shift in civil defense policy from cities to suburbs, see Guy Oakes, *The Imaginary War: Civil Defense and American Cold War Culture*, Oxford: Oxford University Press, 1994.
87 For early 1950s civil defense scenarios focusing on large cities, see Norbert Wiener's proposal published in *Life* (18 December 1950), and Project East River, published in *New Republic* (21 September 1953). For the notion that every home is a fortress, see Oakes, *Imaginary War*, pp. 129–30.
88 Federal Civil Defense Administration, *By, For and About Women in Civil Defense: Grandma's Pantry Belongs in Your Kitchen*, Washington DC: US Government Printing Office, 1958.
89 The weekend before 20 October 1961.
90 Margaret Mead, "Are Shelters the Answer?" *New York Times Magazine* (26 November 1961), p. 124.
91 Oakes, *The Imaginary War*, pp. 129–30.
92 "Gun Thy Neighbor?" *Time* (18 August 1961).
93 "Fallout Shelters: A New Urgency, Big Things To Do – And What You Must Learn," *Life* (15 September 1961).
94 "The People: Ready to Act," *Time* (29 September 1961).
95 Spencer R. Weart, *Nuclear Fear: A History of Images*, Cambridge: Harvard University Press, 1988, p. 397. See also "Sect Anticipates Atomic Armageddon," *Life* 37 (22 November 1954), pp. 176–7. James Farrell links the bomb's religious dimensions to the development of the Cold War as a religious crusade.

"The 1950s ... was an era of priestly civil religion, in which American mission became identified with God's mission. 'If you would be a true patriot,' advised evangelist Billy Graham, 'then become a Christian. If you would be a loyal American, then become a loyal Christian.' President Eisenhower encouraged this marriage of religion and realpolitik with a series of national prayer breakfasts. Congress added the phrase 'under God' to the Pledge of Allegiance, so that school children could affirm the alliance of America and God in a world where 'the prospect of atomic war' was so prominent. Congress also added a nonsectarian prayer room in 1955, and 'In God We Trust' to coins a year later." James J. Farrell, *The Spirit of the Sixties: The Making of Postwar Radicalism*, London: Routledge, 1997, p. 40.

96 Disastrous summer brush fires blazed through the new suburbs of Los Angeles throughout the 1950s and '60s, aided by large, unprotected windows and wood siding, the lack of clearance between houses and native shrubs, and the narrow streets of the hillside communities. In 1955, the Refugio fire between Santa Barbara and Ojai burned 7,000 acres; in 1956, 44,000 acres burned in Orange and San Diego counties; 1958's Lake Elsinore fire consumed 68,000 acres. In 1961, two fires swept through the most exclusive districts of Los Angeles, destroying 43 houses in Laurel Canyon and the Hollywood Hills and 500 houses in the Santa Monica hills, Bel Air and Brentwood. See Richard Lillard, *Eden in Jeopardy. Man's Prodigal Meddling with his Environment: The Southern California Experience*, New York: Alfred A. Knopf, 1966, p. 109.

97 Mirroring the rise of the US as a "superpower," Superman in the 1960s acquires powers significantly greater than his early abilities to outrun trains, leap an eighth of a mile or withstand any artillery short of a bursting shell. He also gains a family history: in November 1960, *Superman's Return to Krypton* introduces the planet where he was born. Features of Krypton are developed in *The Story of Superman's Life* (July 1961), which reads like a pop culture version of the atomic program. With its core of radioactive uranium, Krypton develops a chain reaction and explodes "like a gigantic atomic bomb." Superman, sent to Earth in a rocket by his parents on the eve of destruction, acquires super powers – invulnerability, super strength and speed, and X-ray vision. Solar radiation hardened his skin. One Kryptonian city was teleported and miniaturized on the eve of destruction, and is preserved by Superman in his Arctic fortress as the "bottle city of Kandor," serving as a link to his past in a glass jar.

98 Journalist James Phelan, cited in Virilio, *The Aesthetics of Disappearance*, New York: Semiotext(e), 1991, p. 28.

99 Virilio, *The Aesthetics*, p. 31.

100 Amelia Jones and Elizabeth A.T. Smith, "The Thirty-six Case Study Projects," in *Blueprints*, p. 75.

101 Indirect daylighting like this would find its most wide-spread application in the California school system a few years later, when the Board of Education stated its preference for "distraction-free" school environments, forcing a generation of California school children to be educated in fluorescent-lit, air conditioned, viewless classrooms in the sunniest state in the nation.

5.1 Moon rising over the US Pavilion, Expo '67.

Chapter 5
Closing the circle:
the geodesic domes and a new ecological consciousness, 1967

The planet Earth was seen in its entirety for the first time in December of 1968 as photographs taken from the Apollo 8 spacecraft were diffused through the television networks and in the press.[1] It was a beautiful thing, floating in the night sky. According to one commentator, the color photograph of the Earth rising over the moon "established our planetary facthood and beauty and rareness and began to bend human consciousness."[2] These images spoke of the oneness of the globe, the interdependency of its systems, and the fragility of the planet. While the space program that produced this photograph used the rhetoric of the frontier, the vision of the Earth as a planet in space became an icon for the emerging ecology movement.[3] On this day, the ecology movement made a quantum leap forward, as millions of people could *see* the idea of global interdependency.

No longer could nature be understood as merely a landscape to be viewed, cultivated, or preserved. Once the whole Earth could be grasped in a single image, it made little sense to think of nature as an area that could be set aside from the rest of the world. Astronaut Russell Schweikart remembers that "many of us, on returning home from space, brought the perspective of a lonely and beautiful planet crying out for a more responsible attitude from its most prolific partner."[4] Rather than speaking of nature, people began to talk about the "environment," a word that refers to the world around us. As the setting for human activity, the word "environment" was a reminder that people and nature share one world and are tied in a web of interdependencies.

It was certainly no coincidence that the work of Buckminster Fuller attracted so much attention in those years. His well-known geodesic domes came with a passionate argument for a more efficient use of the Earth's resources – to do "more with less" was his refrain. Fuller's ethical system seemed to reconcile an ideal of global justice with American values of individual freedom and self-expression; it promised that one could "think globally and act locally" (Figure 5.1).

Fuller's ideas particularly appealed to the younger generation. His extraordinary vitality and idiosyncratic and personal speaking style are legendary. But it was his disdain for "conventional wisdom" and his insistence on "whole world thinking" that struck a chord among an idealistic youth critical of notions of progress and consumer society. Fuller became their

5.2 Playing with the Earth Ball.

prophet, bringing his domes and his vision of technological redemption as he lectured to students in over 300 universities around the world from the 1960s to the 1980s. In short, Fuller's geodesic structures achieved their phenomenal popular success precisely because they seemed to correspond to the emerging insight about the global dimension of life on Earth (Figure 5.2).

The best known of Fuller's domes in this period was the United States Pavilion built for Expo '67 in Montreal. Built at the height of the space program, for an Expo significantly entitled *Man and His World*, it offers us a particularly rich entry point into the role of architecture in the emerging ecological consciousness. Unlike other aspects of '60s activism, the design philosophies that emerged at that time have continued to develop and form the basis for much of what we call sustainable or "green" building today. We will explore the many ways the geodesic dome was interpreted during this period to show that this architecture was generally understood as representing nature in the microcosm and the macrocosm. In the second half of the chapter, we then take a critical look at how the ecological message of Fuller's domes was picked up by the "counterculture," both in back-to-the-land communes and in ecological design theories and experiments of the 1970s.

THE US PAVILION AT EXPO '67

The geodesic dome designed by Fuller and his student Shoji Sadao for the US Pavilion in Montreal's World Expo in 1967 is one of the clearest and most powerful architectural expressions of the emerging ecological discourse in the United States at that time. An enormous structure, 250 feet in diameter and clad in transparent acrylic lenses, the dome brought the environment of the exposition surrounding it into its sphere (Figure 5.3).

And what an environment that was! Canada had pulled out all the stops for their first world exposition, timed to coincide with the country's hundredth anniversary celebration of Confederation. The Expo grounds were created on two islands in the St. Lawrence River. Sainte Hélène, where the American Pavilion stood, was a natural island while Île Notre-Dame was artificial, created by dredging. The islands were linked to one another by a pedestrian walkway and a people-mover and connected to the host city of Montreal by a new rapid transit system and a bridge (Plate 19). The Canadian theme pavilions were gigantic geometric volumes that, according to Reyner Banham, helped make "Montreal the capital city of megastructure in

5.3 Exterior view of US Pavilion at Expo '67.

Expo Year 1967."⁵ Yet even amidst this muscular competition, the enormous American Pavilion could be seen from virtually any point in the Fair. Set against a wooded backdrop, the "American bubble" faced the "flying roof" of its space age rival the Soviet Pavilion across a narrow channel of water bridged by "Cosmos Walk" (see Figure 5.4).⁶

Fuller's initial proposal for the American Pavilion was even grander. His design of 1964 featured a dome nearly twice the size with a massive interior gallery. From this elevated vantage point, the viewer would focus their attention inward to a hundred foot diameter Earth suspended from the ceiling. They would then see this spherical Earth transforming slowly into an icosahedron, before it opens up, unfolding like a flower as it descends to the floor. In this way, Fuller's "geodesic" globe transforms into his "Dymaxion" map of the Earth before the visitors' eyes, displaying the "one world island in one world ocean." And then it would come to life. Wired with tens of thousands of miniature light bulbs, this great map would begin to pulsate with patterns – showing world resources, electricity generation, the flow of trans-

5.4 US Pavilion seen from the Soviet Pavilion.

portation and communication systems across the Earth. This interactive display, this giant bio-feedback device, would be the playing surface of the "World Game." Assembling in teams or playing by themselves, visitors were intended to chart out optimal paths to link resources with industries and population centers, to streamline transportation flows and maximize satellite coverage. The aim, according to Fuller, was to "make the world work successfully for all of humanity ... without anyone gaining advantage at the expense of another."[7]

In short, Fuller's first design for the American Pavilion in the *Man and His World* Expo was a spectacularly didactic exhibit intended to display how the world's resources could be better managed for the well being of everyone on Earth. However he had not been asked to design the centerpiece of Expo '67, but rather to represent the United States and the US Information Agency rejected his proposal. They may have doubted that an orchestrated vision of world resource exploitation might be the best way to, as Fuller suggested, "regain the spontaneous admiration and confidence of the whole world".[8] So while Fuller was kept as the architect for the pavilion, the exhibit design was turned over to the Cambridge Seven, which mounted a politically safe display of American art, popular culture and Americana. The Expo dome that we are familiar with then, is just the shell of Fuller's daring proposal (Figure 5.5).

5.5 Fuller with President Johnson, 1966.

Nevertheless, it was difficult to avoid the symbolism and overwhelming presence of "Bucky's bubble" on the Expo grounds. It seemed to radiate outward infinitely – an apt vision, from the American point of view, representing the United States as a model for democratic government and a global "free market." Like the Eiffel Tower was for the 1889 Universal Exposition in Paris, the geodesic dome came to stand for the whole *Man and his World* Expo of 1967. *Paris Match* filled the front cover of its Expo issue with a close-up of the dome. *Life* magazine likewise. Even the Canadian government used an image of the American Pavilion in its advertisements for the events of its centennial year.[9]

Visitors curious to experience this marvel had to stand in line for hours to pass through the single entry, where they were confronted with a 60 foot wide "American eagle" covered in gold sequins. Then it was up "'the longest escalator in America' [only it was in Canada] – the equivalent of six stories – and you're close to the moon" (see Figure 5.6).[10] In the exhibit *Destination: Moon*, volcanic rubble from Sunset Crater National Monument in Arizona was strewn over 3,000 square feet of the upper deck to simulate the astronaut training terrain developed by the Army Corps of Engineers. The spacecraft Surveyor and a mock-up of the Lunar Module were there, with capsules actually used in the Mercury, Gemini and Apollo missions suspended by parachutes from the ceiling. Giant paintings by American artists were suspended as well; a 2,650 square foot *Cardinal Numbers* by Robert Indiana and 30 foot high canvases by Ellsworth Kelly, Jim Dine and Helen Frankenthaler which dwarfed Robert Motherwell's *Big Painting* #2 (at 13 by 15 feet was the relative runt). Pop art paintings and giant movie stills of Hollywood stars animated the space – James Rosenquist's fireman's legs wrapping a pole, Dietrich's face, Cary Grant's dimple, Roy Lichtenstein's *Big Modern Painting*. Jasper Johns' contribution was a 500 square foot painting of the Dymaxion map, a small token to his friend Fuller's desire to have the map be the centerpiece of the pavilion.[11]

The visitor then descended by foot down a series of platforms showing deep Americana – snippets of Hollywood films, kewpie dolls, quilts, branding irons and duck decoys, mementos from election campaigns, a hat collection. "We're simply trying to create a mood of creative America," said John Hamilton, assistant press officer for the United States Information Agency, "It's a gamble. We may get bombed on it. I don't know."[12] And "bomb" they did, especially by comparison with the dome. "Pure camp," sneered *Newsweek*.[13] Governor George Romney of Michigan was especially critical of the work of his compatriots, "it was pretty on the outside," he said when he got home, "but full of trivia on the inside. When you go through it on the minirail all you see is blown-up pictures of Hollywood actors and actresses. I was bitterly disappointed."[14] The art critic for the *Montreal Sun* was succinct comparing the dome to the exhibits it contained, concluding that "the geodesic dome . . . is perhaps the greatest single work of art at Expo."[15]

299 | Closing the circle

5.6 Escalator to the moon exhibit in the US Pavilion. Photograph by John de Visser.

Eclipsing the displays it enclosed, the dome emerged as one of the most memorable and most talked about events of the Expo year. According to the *Nation*, "the US has now contributed an exhibit hall that is not just a structural gimmick but the prototype of a futuristic 'benign environment' and a sight of undeniable beauty, its multi-faceted skin reflecting the sun or the sky, and at night mysteriously glowing from the interior" (see Plate 20).[16] The Italian semiotician Umberto Eco visited Expo '67, and interpreted the US Pavilion in his book *Travels in Hyperreality*,

> Inside, it was visually open, but the objects and interior structures were still enclosed in a dome of light. Mystical and technical, past and future, open and closed, this dome communicated the possibility of privacy without eliminating the rest of the world, and suggested, even achieved an image of power and expansion.... The only element that did not communicate what we already knew, but added something new, even if intangible and ambiguous, was Fuller's dome. In other words the dome was aesthetically the strongest element of the pavilion, and it was so full of nuance, so open to different interpretations, that it affected the symbols inside and added depth to their easily identifiable, more superficial qualities.[17]

By describing Fuller's dome as adding "something new" to the representation of American expansionism, something "ambiguous" that was "open to different interpretations," Eco is suggesting that it was an example of what he called an "open work" of art. He developed the idea of an "open work" to explain and justify the apparently radical difference in character between modern and traditional art from the point of view of the late 1960s. The aleatory music of Stockhausen, the mobiles of Calder, and Mallarmé's *Livre* are other examples Eco used to illustrate this concept. These artists held in common a decision to leave the arrangement of some of the constituents of their art either to the public or to chance, thus giving not a single definitive order but a multiplicity of possible orders.[18]

The notion of "open work" holds promise as a theoretical handle in our attempt to understand how and why the geodesic dome became significant to the alternative movement in the late 1960s and the 1970s that was based on the idea of breaking down social conventions. From the start, we can say that the deliberate and systematic ambiguity of Fuller's dome, as well as its ability to convey a high degree of meaning, made it rich with metaphors. It could be read as a pop art bubble, the globe of the Earth, a breathing skin, or a garden of Eden. Ultimately, it was an open container into which both Fuller and others could invest ideas of global interdependency and ecological responsibility.

The dome as a living organism

Let us now move closer to the thing itself. Describing his "geodesic skybreak bubble," Fuller says,

> anyone looking at the geodesic dome in Montreal saw a very beautiful piece of mechanics. It did all kinds of things to your intuition. You saw

there were curtains that could articulate by photosynthesis [light sensors] and so forth, could let light in and out. It is possible, as in our own human skin, all of our pores, all of the cells organize, so that some are photo-sensitive and some are sound-sensitive, and they're heat-sensitive, and it would be perfectly possible to create a geodesic of a very high frequency where each of these pores could be circular tangencies, of the same size. One could be a screen, other breathing air, others letting light in, and the whole thing could articulate just as sensitively as a human being's skin.[19]

There is a dialectical movement between nature and technology in this sentence: sunlight is set in relation to artificial "curtains" and organic "pores" are set in relation to the mechanics of "photo-, sound-, and heat-sensitive" cells. Like the membrane of a cell, the skin of an organism, or the biosphere of the Earth, Fuller's thick and mesh-like matrix that enclosed the human activity inside was permeable to light and air. In the words of a German reviewer, "the sun, the moon, the landscape and the sky remain perfectly visible."[20] And it is not static, but dynamic.

Fuller's first exploration with a spatial and climatic skin which regulated the exchange with the environment was in his *Garden of Eden* project (1955). This dome placed two revolving geodesics, each with glass on only one side, inside each other, so they could open to the outside.[21] But the dome in Montreal took the skin metaphor further: its openings designated for climate control are broken down into repetitive components like the pores of the skin. To maintain control over temperature with such a huge amount of glazing, Fuller designed small automated shutters in each cell that would modulate the sun's rays, selectively opening and closing as the sun moved across the sky. "A system of light sensors ... raised and lowered shades in many of the clear panels in response to the amount and direction of the incoming sunlight.... two-hundred and fifty small electric motors connected to a central computer ... would open or close the individual triangular panels in response to weather conditions."[22] The ropes that pull the shades open and closed are like nerves in the body. Unfurled, each triangular shade covers one face of the tetrahedron; retracted, they disappear inside the struts of the space frame. Since each shade opens or closes individually, the patterns they create are infinitely varied (Figure 5.7). It is an architecture operating in four dimensions. It moves as if it were alive.

The animated skin of Fuller's dome leaves the arrangement of some of its constituents to the whims of nature. By integrating movement, the work of architecture becomes a "field of open possibilities."[23] The ever-changing pattern created by the shutters is a display of intrinsic mobility, it has a kaleidoscopic capacity to suggest the infinite permutations we associate with ripples on water or the vibrating shadows of leaves under the trees. As we walk around the exhibits in the Expo dome, the movement of its shades

5.7 Automated shutters creating the "skin" of the dome.

opening and closing combines with the movement of the visitor. The slow motions of the skin and the choreography of the visitors enter into a dance that describes a new relationship between contemplation and utilization of the architecture.

The press were fascinated with the fusion of architecture and nature presented in the dome. It is a "real, breathing if not living skin, composed of nearly 2,000 vari-proportioned acrylic hexagons that throb and change color and keep the sun out or let it in," said the *New York Times*.[24] In the *Nation*, the building is compared to a living creature, "the skin is equipped with vents that permit the bubble to 'breathe' like an animal."[25] Self-contained, dynamic, and internally organized, "the enclosure is an exhibit in itself, demonstrating a completely controlled environment, perhaps a prototype for an enclosed community of the future."[26]

The structures of nature

The popular press were not the only ones to see the connection between architecture and nature in the geodesic dome. Gyorgy Kepes' *The New Landscape* of 1956 and his influential *Vision and Value* series suggested that the new forms of art and architecture drew on the fundamental structures of the natural world, revealed anew through the modern technologies of microscopy.[27] The latticework structure of the geodesic dome glorified this interest and made a monument to the patterns in nature.

The expanded structural mesh of the dome is based on regular repetitive geometries. For Fuller, these geometries exist in the natural world and his work intuited, or divined, the fundamental order which underlay nature. Like the chemist who believes that there are exactly 92 elements from which the world is made because of the rules that direct the placement of electrons and protons, Fuller believed that certain "eternal principles" exist before nature itself and that these are based on geometrical relationships (see Figure 5.8).[28] Speaking to an audience of university students, he explained,

> Today I have given you first some fundamental structural principles and subsequently shown you their use by nature. I did not, however, start by studying these structures of nature seeking to understand their logic. The picture of radiolarian has been available for 100 years, but I didn't happen to see it until after I had produced the geodesic structures from the mathematical sequence of developments which I reviewed for you earlier. In other words I did not copy nature's structural patterns.... The reappearance of these structures as recent scientists' findings at various levels of inquiry are pure coincidence – but excitingly validating coincidence.[29]

For Fuller then, as Oscar Wilde put it, "nature has been found to mirror art."[30]

5.8 Fuller with his models of packing balls and geodesic structure.

In her book *Crystals, Fabrics, and Fields*, Donna Haraway explores the influence of such structuralist ideas on developmental biology. She argues that the idea of form and its transformations is paramount to that world view. Shape is approached not from a sense of static anatomy but from an appreciation of its systematic and dynamic transformations and its capacity to conserve the totality of form.[31] We see these principles at work in the dome as a metaphor for a living organism: its absolute rotational symmetry reinforces its overall form from all perspectives (Fuller called this its "pattern integrity"), and the idea of transformation can be seen in the topological permutations as one geodesic geometry merges into the next to create a three dimensional matrix.

Form reveals a "pattern integrity"

The fascination with form is the first link between biology and art. According to the historian of science Philip Ritterbush, "the sphere was the most ideal of the forms of transcendental morphology and according to that system of beliefs, its shape served to distinguish living nature from crystal growth.... Whatever manifested the spherical form was alive" (see Figure 5.9).[32] Early morphologists saw sphericality as a first principle of life, and they searched for it not only where it was to be found (in animals like sea urchins, microscopic diatoms, and radiolaria), but in globular corpuscles such as cells, where its absence had to be explained. "The attractiveness of the circle and sphere to the early *Naturphilosophen* probably reflected their rotational symmetry. In being rotated around their centers, they are carried unendingly into themselves"[33] – an attribute of living nature, he implies. The closed geometry of the sphere, Ritterbush suggests, gives a sense of finitude and unity. Such "symmetry," he continues, "is a property which figures in almost all serious efforts to explain aesthetic responses and often is used as a synonym for harmony or proportion, but it is also susceptible to rigorous mathematical treatment and is in a strict sense a geometric concept."[34] These regular, repetitive patterns seemed to express a fundamental principle of living nature – its tendency to create order against the physical laws of entropy. While such symmetrical patterns seem artificial or constructed from our perspective today, in the 1960s they represented the very essence of living nature. To understand how the geodesic dome was seen as a "natural" structure, we therefore must turn to its geometry.

While Fuller liked to say that the resemblance between micro-organisms like radiolaria and his domes is a superficial one, it is there (Figures 5.10 and 5.11). And he was not the only architect or engineer of the twentieth century who was fascinated by these little creatures. The German Institute for Lightweight Structures for example, which grew out of the engineer Frei Otto's

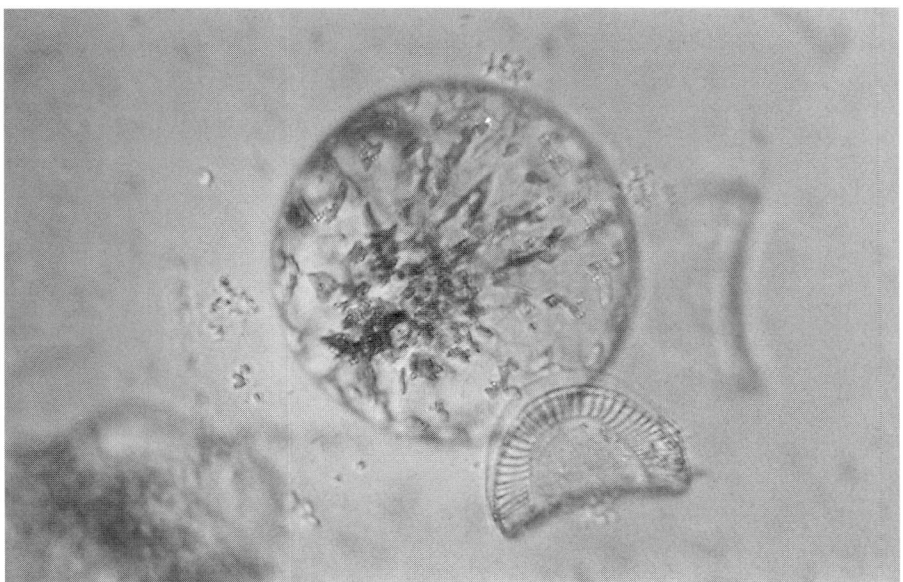

5.9 Living cell (*Campylodiscus-clypeus*).

306 | Closing the circle

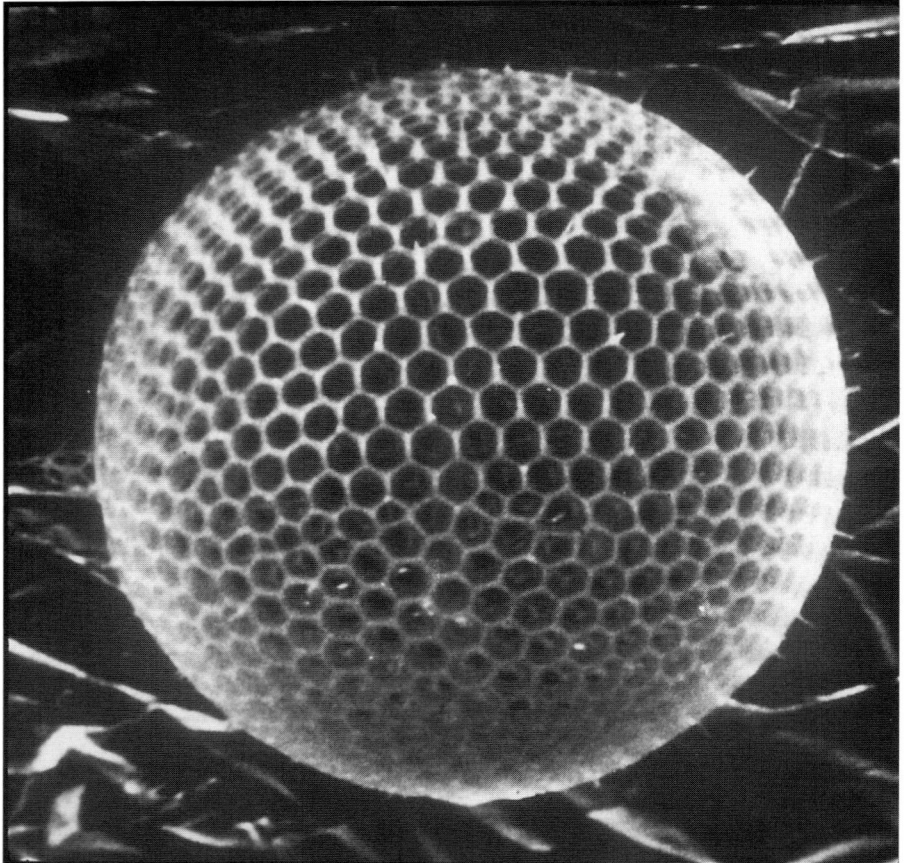

5.10 Radiolaria.

experiments in minimal structures, devoted years to the study of radiolaria and other microscopic creatures that demonstrate regular patterns in their shell structure.[35] D'Arcy Thompson's description of radiolaria remains one of the clearest,

> In its typical form, the radiolarian body consists of a spherical mass of protoplasm, around which, and separated from it by some sort of porous "capsule," lies a frothy protoplasm, bubbled up into a multitude of alveoli or vacuoles, filled with a fluid which can scarcely differ much from sea-water.[36]

The bubbly froth is made of nearly spherical cells and, according to Thomp-

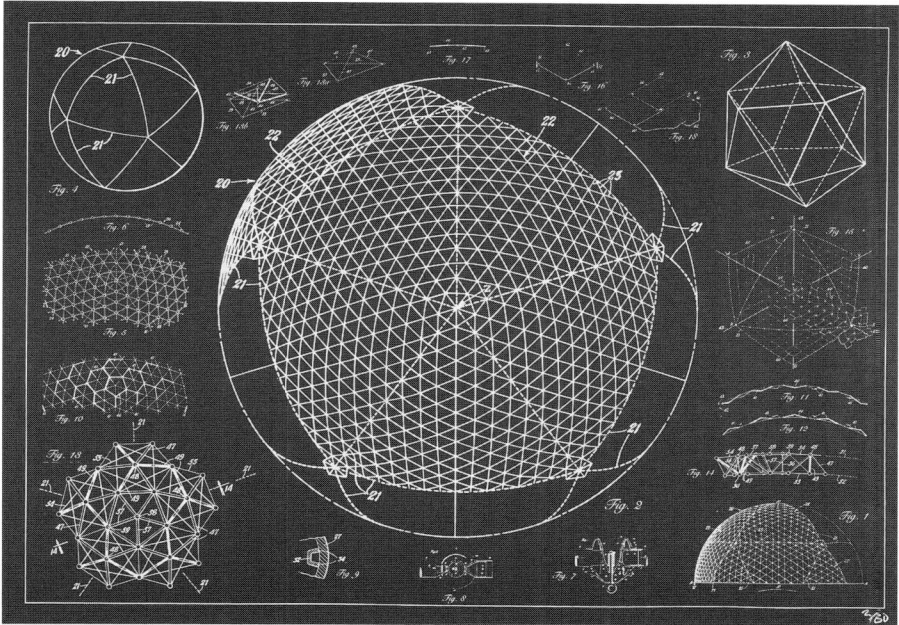

5.11 Regular geometries in Fuller's dome.

son, "the resulting polygonal meshwork [is] beautifully regular." In addition, the outermost layer of the body of certain types "built up of a mass of 'vesicles,' forming a sort of stiff froth" to create a siliceous skeleton. In short, we are dealing with a stiff, interconnected network which resembles a spherical basket or "the finest imaginable Chinese ivory ball."[37]

Most importantly to our work on metaphors, Thompson sees that "the whole arrangement will follow, or tend to follow, the rules of *areae minimae* – the partition walls meeting at co-equal angles, three by three in an edge, and their edges meeting four by four in a corner."[38] These basket-like structures can withstand enormous hydrostatic forces at the bottom of the sea with their three dimensional mesh for a skin. As structural demand increases, the radiolarian expands its mesh-work not as a stiffer crust on the outer surface, but by adding "successive levels, producing a system of concentric spheres."[39] In other words, it increases its strength not by adding mass of silica in its walls and edges, but by creating a system of manifold surfaces and interfaces.[40] The basket-like shell of the radiolarian is its breathing layer. It is made of a series of concentric layers creating an expanded mesh.

When we look at the cross-section of Fuller's dome, we can see such a series of concentric layers. The outermost layer is made of triangular units assembled to create a weave of diamonds. A second, inner, layer made of hexagonal units forms a smaller sphere within the first. The two layers are joined by a filigree network of steel rods which form tetrahedrons, keeping an even distance between the two layers. The result seen from the outside or the inside is a faceted sphere. This sandwich arrangement is created by three different patterns of metal lace: triangular, hexagonal, and three dimensional tetrahedrons. All three patterns maintain the rotational symmetry of the whole (Figures 5.12 and 5.13). "The sphere," Fuller liked to say, "encloses most space with least surface and is strongest against internal pressure; the tetrahedron encloses least space with most surface and is stiffest against

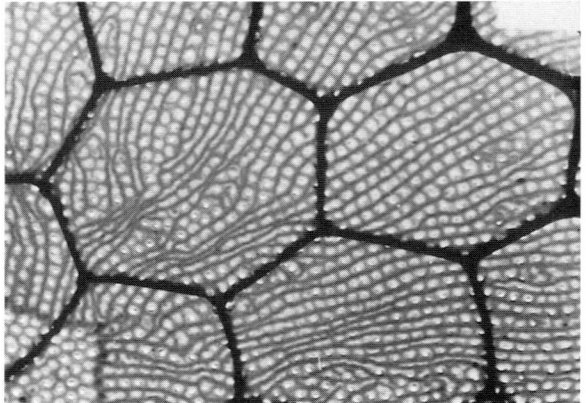

5.12 Flow of hardening fluid starting from the center of a cell.

5.13 Detail of the geodesic geometry of the dome.

16 Steel and glass houses lent a high style to the indoor–outdoor casual living that was promoted as the "California look." To preserve the illusion of a home set in nature, architects maintained privacy and increased the sense of space with careful siting, solid walls to the street, and reflective or transparent surfaces on the interiors. Although it looks as if it were alone in the California hills, this house by Pierre Koenig is surrounded by suburban neighbors on three sides.
Garden court seen from carport, Case Study House 21, 1958.

17 The nuclear tests that left this twisted steel wreckage lit up the night sky in downtown Los Angeles hundreds of miles away. Sun lovers began to look up to the sky with trepidation as fear of fallout tarnished the myth of a natural paradise in the southwest.
Collapsed hangar at Frenchman Lake, Nevada Test Site. Peter Goin, *Nuclear Landscapes*, 1991.

18 This project for a 260-home Eichler tract in San Mateo, California nestles deep into the ground as a water-cooled roof takes on the appearance of a swimming pool. The decade-long obsession with creating private outdoor spaces in the suburbs results here in a landscape of isolated and half-buried houses.
Model of Case Study House 24 (project for Eichler tract in San Mateo, California), 1961. Architects A. Quincy Jones and Frederick Emmons.

19 With its official theme of *Man and His World*, Montreal's Expo '67 was the world's first "environmental" exposition. Cold war rivals USA and USSR faced off with exhibits about their respective space programs. The Americans chose Buckminster Fuller's geodesic dome for their pavillion.
Aerial view of Expo '67.

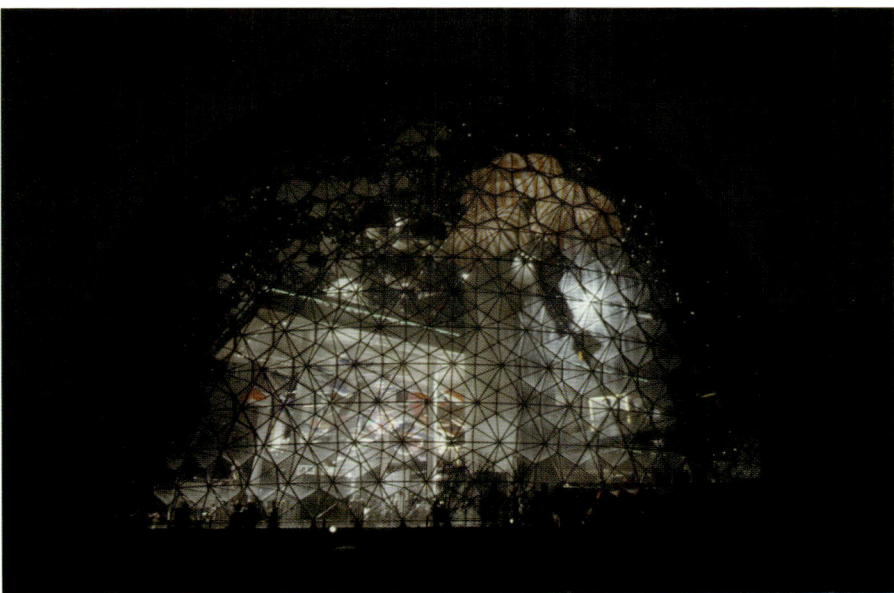

20 Umberto Eco saw the American Pavilion in Expo '67 as an "open work". It was interpreted as a space-age bubble, the planet Earth, and a building that breathed like an animal. Transparent to its natural setting, it corresponded well to an emerging environmental consciousness.
US pavilion seen from outside at night, 1967.

21 Here students at Cornell University are building a Geoscope designed by Buckminster Fuller. This large model of the globe could be experienced from the outside or the inside, and was intended to push people to "think globally" about world resource use. Fuller's ideas found fertile grounds in universities around the world.
Geoscope built at Cornell University, 1952.

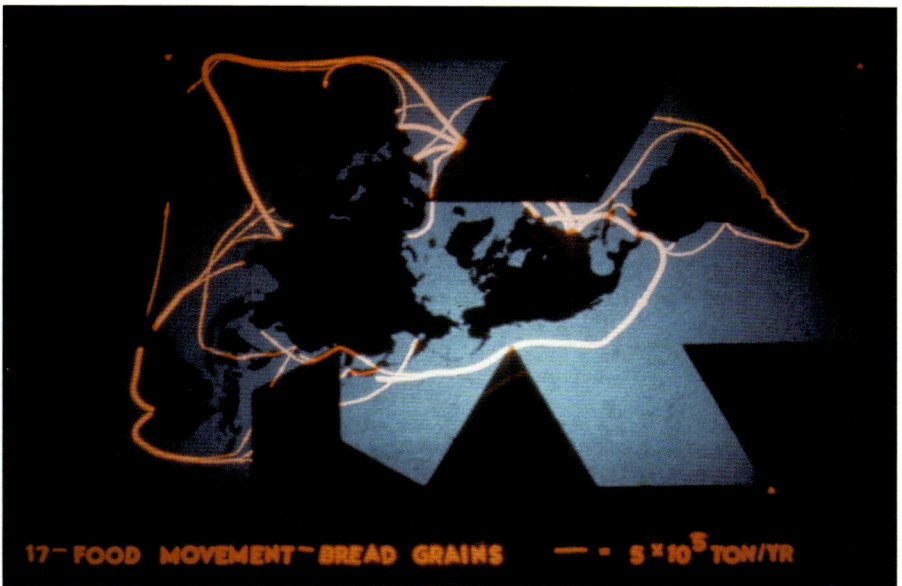
22

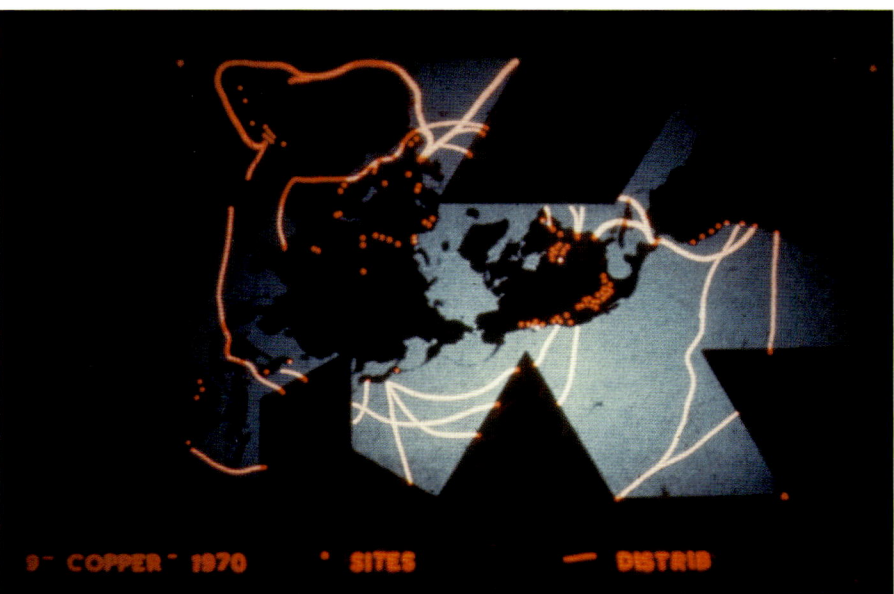
23

22 and **23** Fuller developed the World Game to model, track and predict the flow of resources on the planet. Derived from US military mapping techniques, this was a visualization tool for people to think more ecologically.
World Game Seminar, 1970.

25

24 and **25** Drop City was an artist's community in Colorado founded in 1965 by Gene and Jo Ann Bernofsky and Clark Richert. The architecture used many ideas developed or promoted by Fuller: geodesic domes, the idea of recycling materials and the use of new technologies like wind and solar energy. Minimizing impact on the Earth's resources and creating a natural environment was the aim.

external pressure."⁴¹ Maintaining the integrity of the whole form – what Fuller called a "pattern integrity" – is central to the design.

In this rigid matrix, only the outlines and edges are solid and the rest is a void. As with the radiolaria, the structure of the geodesic dome gets stronger as more elements are used in triangulation. And in both instances, as the frequency of triangulation increases, each element can be more delicate. Here lies a fundamental principle in the search for lightness in construction: voids make a structure strong and light. In fact, as Robert Le Ricolais has shown, the void is a structural principle.⁴²

Young people of the 1960s were excited by the idea of enclosing more space with less material, and by the discovery of what seemed to be fundamental principles underlying the organization of living nature. The geodesic domes were "ecological," light on the earth, and they used materials efficiently. How do they work? To understand this, we turn to the second of Haraway's concepts, the idea of transformation.

Transformations of the sphere

"In a fountain," says Joachim Krausse, "there is a moment of transition between the deceleration during the ascent and the acceleration of the descent. Fuller called this principle [polarity]" and used it in his spherical geodesics to establish an equilibrium in the whole out of the many local forces.⁴³ For scientists, polarity is "an ordering relationship that involves a system of coordinates with directional information."⁴⁴ So, we might ask, how do forces flow through the triangles which are the basis of the geometrical lattice? According to Fuller, "in networks, energy always tries to . . . take the quickest most direct route across. . . . Energy automatically triangulates."⁴⁵ Since the idea is to bring the forces acting on the skin the most efficient way to the ground, these forces follow the lines of the steel struts, creating a regular pattern of energy vectors. But these energy vectors do not simply all flow downward as they would in the ribs of a Renaissance dome. While Brunelleschi made the separation of tension and compression explicit in his design for the cathedral in Florence, with ribs acting in compression and iron chains encircling the dome acting in tension, Fuller's dome created a three dimensional skin working in both tension and compression. Thus, we no longer see Fuller's reticulated structure as a static shell, but as a multitude of short vectors which direct the flow of forces along a web of steel struts.

If we hold on to the image of these rivers of force flowing up and down the reticulated structure, we can see the skin of the dome as a network of capillaries through which the tensile and compressive forces flow. Without these forces being able to flow smoothly back and forth though hundreds of tetrahedrons – if, for example, there were a tear in the fabric mesh or a sudden obstruction in the system – the building would collapse. In other words, the flow of forces represents the life force of the dome.

In his sketch entitled *Noah's Ark 2*, Fuller analyses the flow of stresses in a geodesic grid (Figure 5.14). He shows how they form a figure eight, balancing the forces in this "double-bonded surface," as he writes on the top of the drawing. Each triangle of the figure eight is decomposed into three arrows representing vectors of force. Together, the vectors transform the entire frame into a series of small rivers finding their way around the hexagonal pattern. Seen as a whole, this game of polarities, of on and off, of pluses and minuses, feeds back onto itself. And because geodesics are spherical, they are finite systems. For Fuller, a system must be "a *closed* configuration of vectors – a patterning of forces that returns upon itself in all directions."[46] The figure eight of vectoral forces ultimately envelops the sphere like a reticulated mesh. And like water shedding from a roof, the weight of the structure flows into the foundations and into the earth.[47]

When the dome was completed, stress tests were performed in order to find out how the structure was behaving under wind loads. Using strain gauges, the weight at the foundations was calculated. It turned out to be less than the total weight of the components used to build the dome. How was that possible? Fuller realized that the enclosed space of the dome was so large, it had created an internal climate with a greater air pressure than the outside. The result was a dome that behaved like a hot air balloon, tending to lift the entire structure off its foundations. His domes take to the air. Fuller explains the phenomenon,

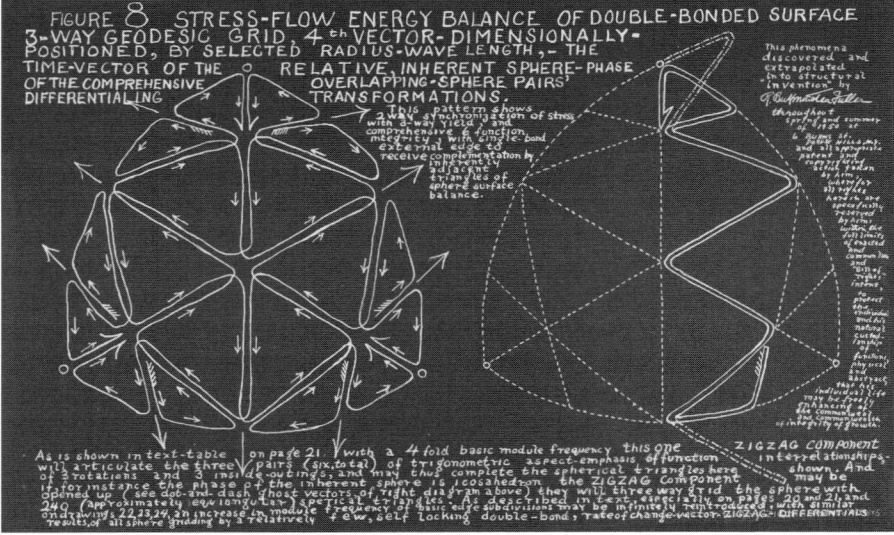

5.14 Stress-flow energy/balance of double-bonded surface.

> When the sun shines on an open frame aluminum geodesic sphere of one-half mile in diameter the sun penetrating through the frame ... gradually heats the interior atmosphere to a mild degree. When the interior temperature of the sphere rises only one degree Fahrenheit, the weight of air pushed out of the sphere is greater than the weight of the spherical frame geodesic structure. This means that the total weight of the interior air, plus the weight to the structure, is much less than the surrounding atmosphere. This means that the total assemblage, of the geodesic sphere and its contained air, will have to float ... into the sky, being displaced by the heavy atmosphere around it.
>
> ... As geodesic spheres get larger than one-half mile in diameter they become floatable cloud structures.... Such sky-floating geodesic spheres may be designed to float at preferred altitudes of thousands of feet. The weight of human beings added to such prefabricated "cloud nines" would be relatively negligible. Many thousands of passengers could be housed aboard one mile diameter and larger cloud structures. The passengers could come and go from cloud to cloud, or cloud to ground, as the clouds float around the earth or are anchored to mountain tops. While the building of such floating clouds is several decades hence, we may foresee that ... man may be able to converge and deploy around earth without its depletion.[48]

Using the logic of nature and applying it to his domes, Fuller envisions whole new environments, gardens of Eden, celestial spheres. He begins to realize how to achieve his dream of forty years earlier, when he wrote "We are leaving the land sphere and progressing ever higher away from it ... despite ever increasing population there is less and less contact with the Earth."[49] No longer do his lightweight geodesics need to be towed around by Marine Corps helicopters or collapsed into shipping packages, they can simply drift to wherever they are required. As the geodesic domes are reborn as floating spheres in Fuller's imagination, they resemble less the eighteenth century *Montgolfier* or the nineteenth century *Zeppelin* than they do the quintessentially twentieth century image of the planet Earth. In his *Cloud Nines* project of 1962, airbound geodesic spheres hover like satellites about the mother planet (Figure 5.15). Thus Fuller's dome itself comes full circle, representing not only the microscopic scale of the micro-organism, but the macroscopic scale of the planets (Figure 5.16).

The dome as a metaphor for the globe

Perhaps the best known image of the dome at Expo '67 was a night photograph that showed only a portion of its curvature with a rising moon behind it (Figure 5.1). This image, widely published at the time, could not but be interpreted in the context of the many photographs beamed back from outer space, showing the Earth floating in the black void of space. Here, the

5.15 "Cloud Nines."

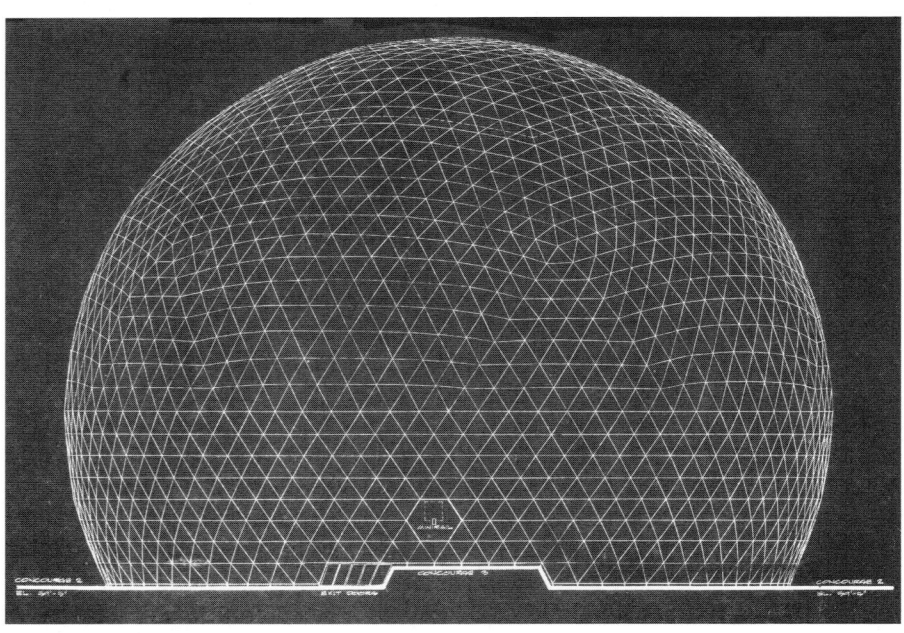

5.16 Elevation of Expo '67 dome.

association of the dome with the Earth is made visually explicit. Like the Moon, it revolves in the vast space of the cosmos.[50]

The similarity between the geodesic dome and planet Earth was not accidental. The geodesic geometry itself was a result of Fuller's long-standing fascination with mapping the Earth. As Joachim Krausse explains, "the Dymaxion world map is the hub, or node, from which all the main lines of his future forty years of work are intermeshed and implicated. Fuller's Dymaxion World [Map] is not only a step to his geodesic domes, ... it is a model for a new image of the world. It is not structural, but conceptual; dealing with a physical configuration, it constructs a consciousness."[51] The consciousness Krausse speaks of here has to do with seeing the Earth not as a collection of nations, but as a geometrical pattern of overlapping circles that reveal new and surprising relationships between regions of the globe. As far back as 1929, Fuller saw the transformation that air travel had wrought in our conception of the world when he said, "suddenly, in the space of a few months, people notice that the planet can be circumnavigated in an unlimited number of ways. The world surprised itself."[52]

As Fuller was working on ever-more accurate ways to translate the spherical shape of the Earth into flat maps, he began to chart the great circles traced by ships or aircraft circumnavigating and connecting the Earth. These *geodesic* lines became the reference for a morphological transformation of the globe. Originating as abstract lines traced around the circumference of a sphere, Fuller realizes they can be seen as the vertices of a polygonal, faceted Earth. This transition from a spherical to a faceted surface can be accomplished with very little deformation, and one can then unfold the facets so they lie flat and be viewed as a map (Figure 5.17). Krausse explains,

> The map and the domes are two sides of the same coin – they frame the problem of projection in the two directions. Map and dome have a common source in the principle of projection.... The image of the world that Fuller developed with the Dymaxion map returns with the geodesic dome in another intermediate scale – in the medio-cosmos, or *oikos* of the house, and then once again in the smallest scale of the microcosmos, in the structural analyses of atoms, molecules and microorganisms.[53]

The geodesic dome then, retains its origins as a map of the Earth in the geometry of its supporting structure.[54] To understand better how geodesic domes contribute to an emerging ecological consciousness, we need to revisit Fuller's idea of the *geoscope*, which he saw as a strategic instrument to show the flow of world resources and their distribution. This was a map of the Earth laid out on the inside of a sphere, so that a viewer standing inside could "take in" more of the Earth's surface in one glance. The precision of the geodesic geometry is crucial both to an accurate mapping and the problem of

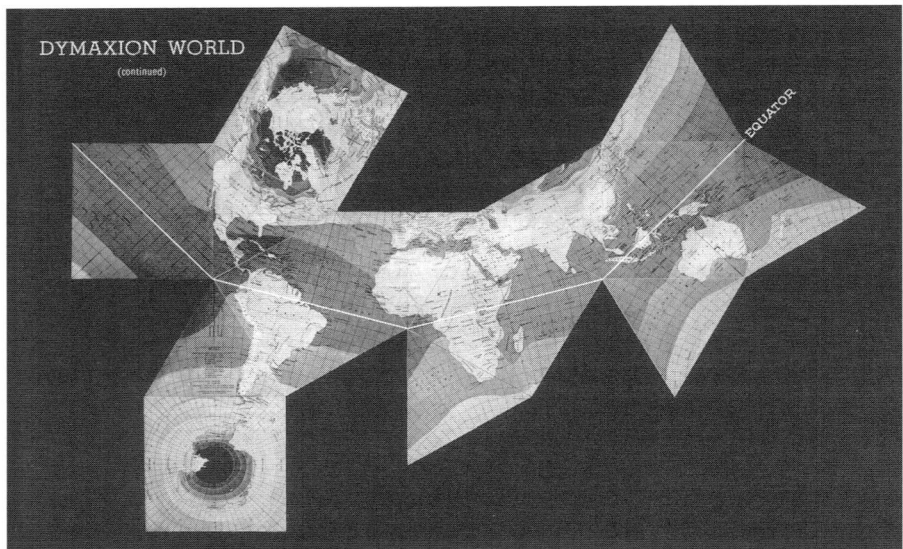

5.17 One of the Dymaxion maps.

structural integrity for a large hollow sphere. As he refined his mathematics, Fuller looks for ever-more public venues for the geoscope: he starts with prototypes built with university students, displays a model in Paris during World Design Science decade, and in 1955 proposes to build a 400-foot diameter geoscope across from the United Nations in New York (Plate 21).

The ideal geoscope would be animated: a perfect mirror of the real-time flows of people and materials around the surface of the globe. It would present all accumulated knowledge about human uses of the Earth at one glance – "all the inventory of human trends, ... needs and fundamental characteristics."[55] The information stored in banks of computers comes from encyclopedias and his *World Resources Inventory* housed at his Southern Illinois University headquarters. Described by Fuller as "an accounting system to examine human evolution," this inventory took him forty years to bring to a state of "high perfection."[56]

The dream of storing all knowledge about the world in one place is far from new. The most famous attempt is the memory theater of Giulio Camillo, a project built for the Valois king François I in 1544, in which all the accumulated knowledge about the world is arrayed in a hemispherical theater. According to David Ruderman, Camillo's theater represented "the order of eternal truth and depicted the various stages of creation, from the first cause through the angels, the planetary spheres, and down to humanity."[57] The images arranged in the tiers and radial sectors of the theater were visible only to the king, who was the only person permitted to occupy the space. These images "were understood to be talismans receiving astral power that could be channeled and operated through the agency of the theater. By mastering the proportions of universal harmony whose memory was preserved in the theater's structure, the operator could harness the magical powers of the cosmos."[58]

Even though its best position was similarly in the center, Fuller imagined his geoscope as a democratic space where many people could stand on the central platform and see all the Earth's resources and its populations at one glance. He believes the data displayed is objective, factual and neutral – that it is a perfect map.[59] This is the end point of Heidegger's world-as-a-picture.

> When Heidegger defines modernity with reference to an "age of the world-picture" he is neither being metaphorical, nor singling out a particular feature of the techno-scientific complex fundamental to modern thinking. Rather, he defines modernity as that epoch in which the world is reduced to – or constituted as – images; not *Weltanschauungen* as value systems and subjective points of view ... but images constructed and verified by science.[60]

Fuller is fascinated with the total trust and confidence that people put into the computerized processing of information – he makes an analogy with the comfort felt traveling on a Boeing 747. One is assured the decisions made are scientific, objective and correct. The process through which they are derived is self-evident and therefore they must be true. According to Gianni Vattimo, "this ideal of self-transparency, according to which social communication and the human sciences are not merely instrumental with regard to the programme of emancipation but in some way concern its very end and substance, is widespread in social theory today."[61] In other words, merely the fact that the globe can be scientifically depicted is in itself liberating.

One can then make decisions about how the Earth's resources might be better used, distributed and administered. It is an updated version of the ideals of the scientific conservation movement of the early part of the century. Nature – in fact, the entire globe – can be managed more efficiently. An end to waste and mismanagement! But as Fuller developed his ideas of world design (as in his promotion of *World Design Decade* in 1967), he turned away from "top-down" decision-making and toward "systems" thinking which aims to predict "trends" and anticipate the behavior of complex living systems. This he takes forward in the World Game.

The World Game
The World Game was an elaborate simulation game intended to model the global use of world resources. Although the data represented on the map of

the world that it uses is statistically precise, the specific configurations showing resource flows would evolve as people played with it. Where Fuller's geoscope was a giant display mechanism to make information available at a single glance, the World Game established a model for collective decision making about the use of the world's resources.[62] The mathematical analog here is the "distributed network," where multiple persons can interact in complex and mutually influential ways, much as his figure-eight flow of forces moves through the network of members around the dome, spreading loads and distributing forces.

If Fuller's Dymaxion Map upsets the conventional Mercator view of the world, exposing new and unexpected relationships as one connects the facets of the globe in various ways, the World Game allows its players to uncover new and surprising relationships between one part of the world and another. The movements of natural resources like copper and the complex circulation of foodstuffs are documented and marked on the constantly evolving map of the World Game. One of the displays showed copper moving across the globe. One could imagine how a metal mined on one side of the globe could serve to make electrical filaments on the other. The same with food resources such as wheat grains (Plates 22 and 23). Essentially, solutions to global ecological problems were sought out by students playing this highly interactive game.[63] While its computer-assisted mapping reassured the player they were seeing a complete and accurate view of the world, by being a *game* it introduced indeterminacy in the form of competition and chance and allowed for the operation of free will, democracy (the will of the majority) and interactive influence (synergy). Another way of seeing the relationship between the total and "transparent" view of the world presented by the geoscope and the interactive and potentially chaotic outcome of the World Game, is the distinction made in Information Theory. "Information theory," Eco argues, "makes a radical distinction between *meaning* and *information*. The meaning of a message is a function of the order, the conventions, and the redundancy of its structure. The more one respects the laws of probability," that the conventions used to convey the message will be used in its interpretation, "the clearer and less ambiguous its meaning will be."[64] The *meaning* of the World Game then, is the data entered in computer banks and displayed on the illuminated surface.

"Conversely," Eco argues, "the more improbable, ambiguous, unpredictable, and disordered the structure, the greater the information – here understood as potential, as the inception of possible orders." The unexpected behavior of people playing the World Game, in other words, adds to the *information* they will get from playing. The playful qualities of the World Game open up new possibilities for interpreting and understanding the world. Participatory, it corresponds with Henri Lefebvre's argument for a re-enchantment of the world, a daring gesture.[65] By reworking the military technology of total global data collection and by recasting it in a spirit of play, the World Game conveyed a strong message about the value of democratic participation.

> Here, the viewer can (indeed, must) choose his own point of view, his own connections, his own directions, and can detect, behind each individual configuration, other possible forms that coexist while excluding one another in an ongoing relationship of mutual exclusion and implication.[66]

For Fuller, the World Game, the geoscope and the geodesic dome are three aspects of a unified vision to orchestrate world development. This ideal resonates widely in the 1960s, as does the vision of nature as a closed system, a complex web of interdependencies in which humanity is enmeshed. The official Expo catalog *Terre des Hommes* represented well this one-world ideology, "Our planet appears henceforth definable as a space ship, with its resources almost completely numbered out. Man stands at the helm and he begins to realize that his prime task is to transform through sheer fraternity and love this drifting raft into an Ark of the Covenant."[67] The image is at once ecological and moral. And it is taken up by the followers of Fuller with a passion over the subsequent decade. According to Fuller acolyte John McHale, "our evolving planetary society must become like a great learning machine in which man's intelligence intervenes and directs the process."[68] And a young biologist named Stewart Brand decides to create a clearing of information to help those who want to consciously affect the evolution of the Earth. Crediting Fuller with its inspiration, he calls it the *Whole Earth Catalog* (1968) and it becomes the pre-eminent reference work for the alternative movement in the United States over the next twenty years.[69]

The dome as a metaphor for the consciousness of the Earth

In the previous section, we have seen the relationship between the shape of the globe and the development of Fuller's geodesic domes. Fuller's technological dream for managing the resources of the Earth (of which his geodesic domes are but one small part) never becomes more than an unrealized Utopian fantasy. But his persistent vision of one world planet suggests yet one more reading of the spherical dome that moves beyond the Earth. This is the relationship between the dome and the human experience of life, or consciousness. Might we read the geodesic dome as a metaphor for "expanding consciousness" – that watchword of the era? This last interpretation of the geodesic dome is in fact taken up enthusiastically by much of the counterculture, as they turn to the "dome home" in search of the ideal expression for a new vision of self and society.

In his *The Metamorphosis of the Circle*, Georges Poulet traces the long history between radial geometries and ideas of consciousness in Western culture.[70] Representing God in the Middle Ages and a human-centered

318 | Closing the circle

5.18 "Earth and its heavenly bodies," Hildegard von Bingen.

universe in the Renaissance, in the eighteenth century the sphere is understood to have a dual orientation outward to the world and inward to the self.[71] A number of artists have put this world view into representation, such as the great mystic of the Middle Ages, Hildegard von Bingen (Figure 5.18). And by the twentieth century, the circle in Western culture becomes a symbol of self in relation to the surrounding world. This insight will become central to the way in which the geodesic domes were embraced by the counterculture of the 1960s: they were interpreted in a *personal* way – in which the spherical shape of the dome expressed the "mind-expanding" self – and in a *global* way – in which the undivided space of the dome expressed community, gathering and sharing. In fact, the dome seemed to express not only the community of the household, but a global community. A letter by one dome-dweller from 1970 encapsulates perfectly how the dome worked its way into the countercultural mentality as a metaphor for ecological and earth-consciousness. It is written to the editor of *Domebook Two*, and entitled "A Reality Gradient to the Geodesic Vision."

> [The first level is] Game Consciousness, the low level awareness of corporate pig consumption. Change their stage props and you'll blow

their reality. Erect a dome and rectilinear thought becomes more obscure, concrete and asphalt become more obscene. No rhetoric of revolution can match the impact of a visible and viable alternative.

Move on to the next grade of Sensory Consciousness. Lying on your back, the translucent skin of your dome registers each energy transformation of the cosmic lightshow. Like a giant retina, the dome scans the heavens. Now it is a tympanic membrane transducing rain into rhythmic meaning. You merge with the dome, its skin becomes your skin, and together you are a creature of tactile delight.

Now on to Cellular Consciousness and the awareness that your shelter follows the blueprint of your own cellular body. There is even a quality of life to the way the dome stretches and heaves with each breath. Above all, there is a niche for your dome in the community of life.

At the Molecular level, you see that you are indeed a respectable member of the community of life. You realize that your dome is a macroscopic molecule evolving out of the DNA spiral. Man, the protein matrix of three trillion DNA body cells, now spins a cellular exoskeleton.

And thus, at each reality, the Geodesic Vision persists. Beyond the reality of games and stage props, your dome is reassuringly real. Beyond any aesthetic notion of what constitutes good architecture, your dome makes sense. And beyond any psychedelic diatribe, such as this, our dome follows the Holy plan of all life.[72]

This is a remarkable variety of metaphorical interpretations for one work of architecture. The dome is a critique of society, a giant retina and a tympanic membrane attuned to natural rhythms. It occupies an ecological niche, it is the cellular exoskeleton of humanity, and it is modeled after the most fundamental patterns of the universe. At each level, the term consciousness is employed.

The *noosphere*

In reflecting on spherical geometries and ideas of consciousness in the twentieth century, a key figure for the alternative communities is surely the Jesuit scientist Pierre Teilhard de Chardin.[73] In his writings, Teilhard de Chardin proposes that "consciousness" emerged on the Earth as the result of the spherical nature of the planet. "One of the most fundamental characteristics of the cosmic structure," he says, is "the roundness of the Earth.[74] Without the involution of matter upon itself . . . there would never have been the biosphere . . . In [its] advent and development, life . . . [is] not only accidentally, but structurally, bound up with the contours and destiny of the terrestrial mass."[75] The spherical shape of the Earth itself forms the basis of Teilhard de Chardin's view that life, spread out in a centripetal extension over the surface of the globe, reaches a "critical point" with the appearance of humanity. With the spread of people around the globe, life begins a centrifugal movement, seeing itself "in the mirror" for the first time. He calls this conscious web of human thought the *noosphere*.

> Man discovers that he is nothing else than evolution become conscious of itself, to borrow Julian Huxley's striking expression.... Having reached the peak, we can now turn round and, looking downwards, take in the pattern of the whole.[76] ... And what is more serious still is that we have become aware that, in the great game that is being played, we are the players as well as being the cards and the stakes.[77]
>
> If there is a future for mankind, it can only be imagined in terms of a harmonious conciliation of what is free with what is planned and totalized. Points involved are: the distribution of the resources of the globe; the control of the trek towards unpopulated areas; the optimum use of the powers set free by mechanization; the physiology of nations and races; geo-economy, geo-politics, geo-demography; the organization of research developing into a reasoned organization of the Earth.... We need and are irresistibly being led to create ... a science of human energetics.[78]

We are struck here by the similarity of Teilhard de Chardin's ideas to Fuller's. For him, human thought wrapping around the globe in the noosphere can and will direct the evolution of the planet (Figure 5.19). For Fuller, humankind must grasp the whole planet in one intuitive glance to be able to orchestrate and manage its resources wisely. Both share a characteristic downward look; both use the term "pattern" and the metaphor of the "game"; both state unequivocally that the future of humanity requires a science of planning and design.

It is perhaps not surprising that Teilhard de Chardin's ideas were embraced within the largest supranational organization engaged in such global planning in the post-war era. Teilhard de Chardin was brought to the United Nations by the evolutionary biologist Julian Huxley, who wrote the introduction to *Phenomenon of Man* and continued throughout his life to be one of the staunchest advocates of Tailhard de Chardin's work. In 1946, when they met for the first time, Huxley was working on the charter for UNESCO – the United Nations Educational, Scientific and Cultural Organization – outlining its plan for advancing a global, scientific and evolutionary humanism. Huxley saw institutions such as the United Nations as the instruments for the *conscious* evolution of life on Earth, where "the struggle for existence that underlines natural selection is increasingly replaced by conscious selection, a struggle between ideas and values in consciousness."[79] As UNESCO's first director general, Huxley brought Teilhard de Chardin into the organization where he influenced several Secretaries General, including

5.19 "World Town Plan," 1927.

Dag Hammerskjold and U Thant.[80] This led to a series of United Nations-sponsored symposia on the state of the Earth's biosphere.[81]

While Fuller never wrote expressly about Teilhard de Chardin's ideas, we cannot help but notice that Fuller's geoscope and World Game were intended as instruments to visualize and plan precisely those "points" that Teilhard de Chardin sees as essential to the "future for mankind." His 1955 proposal for a geoscope across from the United Nations would have presented world leaders with an animated model of the entire planet so large that on it individual houses would be visible.[82] Entering into the structure, elevators would lift people up from ferries, bridges, or tunnels into the center of the structure where they could witness the presentation of stars, satellites, electromagnetic and astrophysical patterns surrounding the Earth, and earthquakes, economic, demographic, and sociological displays of the Earth itself.

Our understanding of what is being represented on this animated model of a globe become more complex in the light of Teilhard de Chardin's thought. The circle thickens. The lacy web of Fuller's illuminated geoscope gives a visual form to Teilhard de Chardin's noosphere. According to Teilhard de Chardin, "the banal fact of the Earth's roundness" was bound to cause an intensification of human thought and "psychosocial activity" – "confined to spreading out over the surface of a sphere, idea will encounter idea, and the result will be an organized web of thought" that envelopes the Earth. If we were to see the Earth from outside for the first time, says Teilhard de Chardin, "the first characterization of our planet would be, not the blue of the sky or the green of the forests, but the phosphorescence of thought."[83] If the hydrosphere, biosphere, and atmosphere are consecutive layers of the Earth that in themselves are the result of the "vitalization of matter" that we call evolution, the noosphere, from the Greek work *nous* or thought, is "yet another membrane in the majestic assembly of telluric layers."[84] Beginning with advances in the technology of transportation, and extended vastly through European colonization, human thought now encounters itself in all directions. And with the development of radio, television, satellite communications and modern transport, "each individual finds himself ... simultaneously present, over land and sea, in every corner of the Earth."[85]

For Teilhard de Chardin, this is not about the dominion of capitalism, or the hegemony of Western instrumentalism. It is a spiritual manifestation of the Earth's evolution. "Zoologically speaking, mankind has achieved something in which all previous species had failed. It has succeeded not only in becoming cosmopolitan, but in stretching a single organized membrane over the Earth without breaking it."[86] With the spread of humanity over the surface of the Earth, "we have the beginning of a new age. The Earth 'gets a new skin.' Better still," he says, "it finds its soul."[87] Fuller echoes the thought,

> You and I
> Are essential functions
> of Universe
> We are exquisite syntropy.[88]

Recalling the tongues of fire that light on the heads of the first evangelicals,

Teilhard de Chardin says, "a glow ripples outward from the first spark of conscious reflection. The point of ignition grows larger. The fire spreads in ever widening circles till finally the whole planet is covered with incandescence."[89] While he never represents the noosphere, Fuller does. Speaking in 1962 of his geoscope project, he says,

> Its interior and exterior surfaces could be ... dotted with ten million small variable intensity light bulbs and the lights controllably connected up with an electronic computer ... At 200 feet minimum distance away from the viewer, the light bulbs' sizes and distance apart would become indistinguishable, as do the size and distances between the points in a fine half tone print. Patterns introduced into the bulb matrix at various light intensities, through the computer, would create an omnidirectional, spherical picture analogous to that of a premium television tube – but a television tube whose picture could be seen all over its surface both from the inside and the outside.[90]

Medard Gabel, the coordinator of the World Game project, describes what he sees when he plays the Game, "Once we started displaying the electrical energy grid and the transportation channels, it became apparent that the world looks like a biological organism."[91] An illuminated icon, it possesses the mesmerizing qualities of a television set, but the image is even more compelling because it is about ourselves. The Game gives a visual form to human self-awareness of life on Earth. It is an elaborate, constantly evolving mirror of our uses and abuses of the planet, our ecological conscience projected on the surface of a sphere. In the words of John McHale, "our evolving planetary society must become like a great learning machine in which man's intelligence intervenes and directs the process."[92] The metaphysical dimension of the geodesic dome is consciousness of the Earth itself.

Teilhard de Chardin's writings recast Fuller's technological utopia in spiritual terms. In the remythologizing of western society that occurs in the 1960s,[93] the idea that people are personally responsible for the health of the Earth spurs new initiatives for realizing on a local scale "whole world thinking." We turn next to the Fuller acolytes that want to spread the message of "treading lightly on the Earth" – the many hundreds of thousands of hippies, communal activists, disaffected youth, back-to-the-landers, and emerging ecologists that contribute to what Theodore Roszak has called the "making of the counterculture."[94]

THE IDEA OF CLOSING THE LOOP IN ARCHITECTURE

In the "summer of love" of 1967, *Time* magazine featured "The Hippies" on its front cover. In among the pages devoted to psychedelia, new life styles and the paraphernalia of the subculture, the article showed photographs of an ephemeral community that had sprung up in the dry landscape of Trinidad, Colorado near the New Mexico border.[95] This was "Drop City" – a small collection of geodesic domes created by a few young artists (Plate 24). With the coverage in *Time*, this small hamlet suddenly found itself at the center of national media attention, becoming – as were the silver boom mining towns of the Comstock Lode ninety years earlier – a powerful magnet for passers-through, adventurers, and people who wanted to leave the cities and forge a new life for themselves in the vast reaches of the west. The original group, Gene and JoAnn Bernofsky and Clark Richert had bought six acres of goat pasture in southern Colorado in 1965. "The idea was to build an artist's community – including many like-minded artists" Richert says. "We were legally incorporated to 'provide food, housing, and studio space for artists.'" A later Dropper, Bill Voyd recalls that "Drop City began as a 'dropping'; like a 'happening,'"

> We heard R. Buckminster Fuller lecture in Boulder, Colorado and decided to build domes. We had little building experience.... We learned how to scrounge materials, tear down abandoned buildings, use the unusable. Culled lumber. Railroad ties. Damaged insulation. Factory-reject plywood. Car tops. The garbage of America. Trapped inside a waste-economy man finds an identity as a consumer. Once outside the trap he finds enormous resources at his disposal – free.... When one stops "owning" things another can begin to use them. Energy is transformed, not lost (see Plate 25).[96]

A few years after its establishment, Peter Rabbit was perhaps the most vocal of the Droppers who saw their domes as an instrument to fight the "establishment" and usher in a new and better world,

> Droppers have learned how to build beautiful houses out of cartops for less than 200 dollars/less than $100/we know how to use solar heating/we're hip to windpower/Droppers know how to best use the government doles & poverty programs/each dollar we use is one less that goes into the making of napalm/every cent that Drop City uses is one less that goes to those insane retarded creeps in Washington.

Soft technologies such as solar energy allowed them to be relatively independent. Richert recalls,

> We had plumbing, hot and cold running water, television, an advanced film workshop complete with 16mm cameras, projectors, and editing equipment. One of our domes, the theater dome, had an under floor projection booth – that projected imagery over the interior surface. On our wish list, way back in 1965, was a computer. Like Fuller, we were

interested in the new, alternative technologies – solar energy, wind energy, and recycling. The first dome we built was eventually heated with passive solar energy – collected via a large flat collector. It worked quite well.

The architecture of the domes used materials in the most reasonable efficient way. Fuller gave Drop City the 1966 Dymaxion Award for poetically economic structural accomplishments. In short, Droppers pursued a more efficient, low cost, healthier ways of living and created a supportive environment to do art. There has been numerous misrepresentations of Drop City over the years, but according to Richert, "the major impetus for the establishment of Drop City was quite simply art."[97] Perhaps because the Droppers were artists, they were able to take ideas such as "recycling" and create an architecture that brought together an American folk aesthetic (the quilt) with ideas of sustainability.

The artists of Drop City were not alone in wanting to practice art as a political and an ecological act. Other artists whose work has been broadly defined as "Land Art," created site-specific interventions that addressed geology, cosmology and the processes of life.[98] In his *Growth House* of 1975 for example, Charles Simmonds created a circular wall of "growth bricks" – sacks of earth containing a large variety of seeds. It began as a shelter over the winter, was destroyed by the sprouting plants in the spring, produced food in the summer and the cycle ended in a harvest. New "bricks" could be made from the mulch to build a new shelter for the following winter.[99] In such work, artists were able to express an emerging understanding that nature and culture were inextricably intertwined. As Herbert Marcuse said, "man's struggle with nature is increasingly a struggle with society."[100] Another example is a 1973 installation by Patrick and Flora Clancy, who "subtly destroyed a rented cement 'garden' by bombarding it with the leftover seeds of their fruits and vegetables. These fragile shoots are parables for the means for which the 'powerless' artist can manipulate space and consciousness."[101] Alan Sondist's *Time Landscape* follows a similar argument. In a 8,000 square feet area of downtown Manhattan, he recreated the history of nature by planting three stages of forest, making "an image of wild pre-colonial land in the midst of a colonized and exploited urban site."[102] It lasted from 1965 to 1978 at the corner of La Guardia Place and Houston Street, when it was destroyed by . . . Such projects speak about healing the earth.

The counterculture rejected the artificial, plastic, and processed products of modern society. The new earth-consciousness called for a return to the organic, the raw and the unprocessed – and for as much local self-reliance as possible. Fuller's idea of "doing more with less" and his global view of world resources struck a responsive chord within the counterculture, who put these ideas into action. The environmental activists frequently cast technology as the villain, and looked for unmechanized technologies. As a

Newsweek writer wryly observed, "On the day two Americans harnessed technology to land on the moon 25 members of New Mexico's New Buffalo commune harvested wheat by hand – 'the way the Babylonians did 3,000 years ago.'"[103]

The back-to-the-land communes were a popular response to a technological age. They were the flip side of the technological and managerial society that put "a man on the moon." And with the spread of communes across the country, the geodesic domes began to spread far beyond anything Fuller could have dreamt of (Figure 5.20). If the major clients for the geodesic domes up to 1965 had been either the United States government, large corporations or universities, after this date Fuller's work began to be appropriated by the counter-culture until it was completely identified with them. The geodesic dome became a symbol of alternative living, "breaking out of the box."

At one level, the popularity of the domes was a return to the "build your own cabin" mythology, so popular at the turn of the century among advocates of the simple life (Figure 5.21). Fuller's pragmatic, do-it-yourself approach inspired how-to books on dome-building, from the early *Popular*

5.20 Domes in the landscape, Pacific High School, California, 1970.

5.21 "The Sixteen Foot Personal Dome," built by Jim Bohlen and Russ Chernoff.

Science "sun domes" to Steve Baer's *Dome Cookbook* which grew out of his work at Drop City. These were soon followed by *Domebooks One and Two*, *The Dome Builders Handbook*, and *How to Build a Dome*.[104] The articles that fill these books testify to the widespread appeal of building your own. They were built in all regions of the country out of an incredible variety of materials, from cardboard to cartops. But certain common experiences emerged: it was learn-as-you-go, a lot of energy was put into calculating chord dimensions and color-coding struts, and working out a strategy for the all-important caulking yet, in spite of that, virtually all of them leaked. All dome builders also expressed, in various ways, a sense of well being and spiritual uplifting from living in circular, domed spaces. Bill Voyd, for example, says that,

All living and non-living units take their form from a balance of energies. On a physical plane, these forces come into nearly perfect balance in the sphere.... To live in a dome is – psychologically – to be in closer harmony with natural structure. Macrocosm and microcosm are recreated, both in the celestial sphere and molecular and crystalline forms. ... Domes break into new dimensions. They help to open man's perception and expand his approaches to creativity.[105]

Recentering the self in the dome home

The domes represented a different way to live, one that could be practiced on the ground and also symbolically in a new kind of architecture (Figure 5.22). Their spherical shape reinforced the idea that each person is the center of their own reality.[106] There is only one center to the dome, and one cannot

5.22 Couple inside Jay Baldwin's dome, 1970.

escape its pull. The "me" generation embraced this insight and its architectural expression. In the words of dome-builder John Premis, "a dome encloses you like an eggshell or a pair of cupped hands – gently, tenderly. In a dome there is an inward focus. You feel that you are at the center of things. There is no way you can be shoved into a corner!"[107] Two contributors to *Domebook One*, Alan and Heath, describe how they feel in their dome home,

> Living in a spherical single unit house makes us wholer people. We feel more whole and have our whole trip around us. We stay more in touch with each other and our friends and also this wholeness has a healthy effect on our possessions, our wants and desires. Feeling whole and centered is crucially important, and domes can surely contribute to this. . . . Domes are such a centering trip. One's eyes can easily center on any of the mandalas formed by the struts. . . . Even our conversations are more centered because we sit in a circle and stay in closer touch with each other. All vibrations – sound, light, heat and all our awareness – begin in the center and radiate outward and rebound back and forth from the center. Consequently, chanting is mind-expanding and all-encompassing.[108]

The geodesic dome then, was understood to be an architecture which fused a sense of self with a sense of the cosmos. Dome enthusiast Lloyd Kahn remembers, "you were somehow in touch with the universe in building a dome" (see Figure 5.23).[109] In a dome, one could feel that perhaps Stewart Brand was right when he stated in his *Whole Earth Catalog* of 1968, "We are as Gods."[110] Novelist Tom Wolfe satirized this sense of personal omnipotence in his *Electric Kool-Aid Acid Test*, as Merry Prankster Ken Kesey is approached by a participant in San Francisco's "Summer of Love,"

> "The thing is, Ken, a lot of people are very concerned about what you've said, or what the newspapers say you've said, about graduating from acid. A lot of people look up to you, Ken, you're one of the heroes of the psychedelic movement . . . and they want to know what you mean. . . . You've got to help us Ken, and not work against."
>
> Kesey looks up . . . out across the gloom of the garage. Then he speaks in a soft, far-off voice, with his eyes in the distance: "If you don't realize that I've been helping you with every fiber in my body . . . if you don't realize that everything I've done, everything I've gone through . . ."
>
> "I know, Ken, but the repression–"
>
> "We're in a period now like St. Paul and the early Christians," Kesey says. "St. Paul said, if they shit on you in one city, move on to another city, and if they shit on you in that city, move on to another city–"

5.23 Lloyd Kahn holding a dodecahedron model inside the geodesic, 1970.

"I know Ken, but you're telling people to stop taking acid and they're not going to stop. They've opened up doors in their minds they never knew existed, and a very beautiful thing, and then they read in the papers that somebody they've looked up to is suddenly telling them to stop."

"There's a lot of things I can't tell the newspapers," says Kesey. His eyes are still focused long-range . . . "One night in Mexico, in Manzanillo, I took some acid and threw the I Ching. And the I Ching . . . said we had reached the end of something, we weren't going anywhere any longer, it was time for a new direction – and I went outside and there was an electrical storm, and there was lightening everywhere and I pointed to the sky and lightning flashed and all of a sudden I had a second skin, of lightning, electricity, like a suit of electricity, and I knew it was in us to be superheroes and that we could become superheroes or nothing."[111]

In this passage, Wolfe neatly outlines a shift in the priorities of the counterculture, from more collectively-oriented political actions (like street protests or communes) to a new sense of *personal* power and responsibility. At one level, this can be seen as a retreat from the progressive view that social change results from mass political action in the public sphere. Yet at another level, it can be understood as a change in tactics. The aim is still global change, but the departure point is the self.

In his book *The Spirit of the Sixties*, the historian James Farrell astutely describes this perspective as a new form of "personalism." Finding common roots between the anti-nuclear activism of the Catholic Workers, the civil rights movement, the anti-establishment activism of the Students for a Democratic Society, and the "communitarian subjectivism" of the counterculture, he argues that all of the major political movements of 1960s America shared a belief that political action emerged from a personal commitment and individual action.[112] In his introduction to the first *Whole Earth Catalog*, Stewart Brand is quite explicit in that regard. "A realm of intimate, personal power is developing," he says, "the power of individuals to conduct their own education, find their own inspiration, shape their own environment, and share the adventure with whoever is interested. Tools that aid this process are sought and promoted by the *Whole Earth Catalog*."[113] For the most part, these "tools" are books explaining how to do organic gardening, harness renewable energy sources, build energy-efficient dwellings, conserve water more effectively and so forth.

Many of the activists of the 1960s embraced Fuller's arguments for a better use of global resources, and they did this with a sense of personal empowerment and responsibility. Some were also critical of Fuller's humanist and technocratic beliefs, proposing instead a more radical position with respect to people and nature. While Fuller said that we should "Reform the environment, not man," Lloyd Kahn asks "Shouldn't that be the other way around?"[114] Peter Warshall adds,

> How much energy that runs the biosphere can be diverted to the support of a single species: man? The question can no longer be treated out there in the biosphere separate from everyday habits of mind. Because we breathe, the question is not a debate between your expanding "inner" consciousness and "outer" awareness of the Earth. Mind process and planet process here become too close, too intermixed, too woven to separate thought and atmosphere, action and ocean, attitude and Earth.[115]

As the novelty of life in a dome began to wear thin, dome enthusiasts pursued a vision of person and globe interconnected – of the circularity of things – in other forms. From this perspective, the ideas embodied in the geodesic dome did not end with the building of thousands of hippie dome homes across the country. Rather, the ecological metaphors that had become associated with the dome were taken up in a much more fundamental and enduring way by the advocates of ecological design. First, in their insistence on the closed ecological system and its corollary propositions that energy circulates in closed loops and that "waste" can be a valuable resource. Technology was seen as a tool to optimize these flows. A second, and equally important principle was the conviction that people are personally responsible for the ecological impacts of their actions, both at the scale of the household and at the scale of the Earth.

The focus shifts from *form* to *flow*, from *material* to *energy*. The result was a whole generation of ecological architecture from the early enthusiasts of geodesic domes, work that has not yet begun to be critically analyzed within the architectural mainstream. The urbanist Peter Calthorpe developed his idea of *Pedestrian Pockets*™ by tracing a walking radius around the house to generate the plan of a community. This proposal aims to reduce dependence on the automobile. The biologist John Todd invented *Living Machines*™, a wastewater treatment system that recreates an ecosystem in miniature (Figure 5.24). The goal is to equilibrate inflows and outflows, so that human beings add no net burden on the environment. Steve Baer (from Drop City) invents and manufactures energy-efficient solar heating and ventilation systems. Dome advocate Lloyd Kahn publishes catalogs of traditional building practices and materials which are "low-energy," recyclable and renewable: earth-sheltered houses, solar houses and straw bale houses.

5.24 "Backyard fish-farm greenhouse" at the New Alchemy Institute, Woods Hole, Mass, 1976.

In other words, the "green architecture" of the 1970s was more than a collection of built experiments. It was a discourse that at times far outstripped the actual events which triggered any particular dome, commune or experimental house. This discourse helped to influence a much wider set of practices and policies in ways that ultimately affected a great number of people. The result today is *things* like solar houses, ecological skyscrapers, "smart" buildings, communities planned as "pedestrian pockets," the folding geometries of tetra paks and self supporting pop-tents. There are also *ideas*, like the notions of embodied energy, sustainable development, "slow" growth and "soft" energy paths. And certain *practices*, such as recycling waste, have become widespread and enshrined in municipal codes.

The Integral Urban House

In Berkeley in 1978, one of these new kinds of ecological dwellings was created on the flatlands of the eastern edge of the San Francisco Bay. Dubbed the "integral urban house" by its creators, Mike and Helga Olkowski and Sim van der Ryn (who was at that time the State Architect of California), this house presented itself as a self-contained "life support system" that was meant to serve as a model for ecological living in an urban environment. Ideas about nature, embodied in this project, are representative of many "self-sufficient" settlements that were built in the 1970s and discussed in alternative journals distributed across the country, like the *Whole Earth Catalog, CoEvolution Quarterly, Mother Earth News* and *Harrowsmith*.[116] In treating the building as a closed ecological system, these projects realized in concrete detail what the Expo dome had presented as an idea.

Premising their argument on a disaster scenario, the Olkowskis ask their reader "what would you do" in your present way of life in the face of a transit strike, a gas shortage (like the "oil scare" of 1973), or a drought (experienced by most Northern Californians in 1977)? As your neighbors drop off like flies from chemical poisoning and cancer, they say, it is only to be expected that "people need to believe in their own ability to create and maintain their basic life-support systems in order to feel at least somewhat in control."[117] While the impulse may be survivalist, the response looks different from the underground shelters advocated during the cold war. The Integral Urban House offers a model self-contained "ecosystem" that can be realized in virtually any suburban setting in the country. It aims to transform "denatured houses into finely tuned, multichanneled, closed-looped, organic instruments for processing nature's flow."[118] The Olkowskis remind their reader there is a moral imperative in this mission. They are not advocating "self-sufficiency," they see that as too isolating. Rather, they are encouraging "self-reliance," that part of the national myth, they say, that is known as "Yankee ingenuity."[119] The house was meant to look (from the exterior) like any others in the neighborhood in order to stand as an example for anyone to follow.

The Integral Urban House does not mimic the forms of nature, as would a dome or spiral house, but seeks to apply "lessons from the biology of natural systems" to the design of human habitats.[120] The goal is human evolution and this is to be carried out on a personal level, not at the level of global planning. "Nature's strategy to achieve stability," they say, is the "closed integral loop." Here, the design of the house starts to get interesting. These loops allows for recycling and self-regulation, in positive and negative feedback systems. "The wastes of one system," they continue, "are the necessary inputs of the other." "Webs" are the connections that comprise living systems, "energy and nutrients flow along these pathways" (see Figure 5.25).[121]

The accompanying diagrams show these loops: the house acted on by the elements, circulating its nutrient and waste flows in a dynamic cross-section that shows the plumbing and heating systems, the plants extracting nutrients from the soil and turned toward the sun to photosynthesize, the bees hovering over their hive, the fish processing gray water, the sun heating up solar tanks. A second diagram called the *Life Support System of an Integral Urban House* shows all the components of a small farm installed on a 50 by 100 foot inner city lot (Figure 5.26). We see insects, fish, small game, vegetable, rooftop and greenhouse gardens; the composting of human and animal wastes and wastewater; a capture of solar radiation in collectors, thermal storage and solar ovens. Everything is linked into systems of flows – "webs" and "loops" – as we can see in the diagram entitled *Energy Flow in a Closed System Habitat* (Figure 5.27). This kind of meticulous planning and design carries forward the idea of the closed circle in countless diagrams. There are nitrogen cycles, a small stock food cycle, a urine/aquatic cycle, a food web of organisms in mulch or soil, heat homeostasis in the body, and many more.

The designers of these self-sufficient systems are far from realizing Fuller's dream of an intuitive response to the flows of energy and goods around the world. While Fuller hoped that people viewing his geoscope would grasp the totality of the planet at one glance, the earnest alchemists of alternative architecture in the 1960s spend an inordinate amount of time on plumbing diagrams which connect one part of the "system" to another, calculating BTUs, detailing instructions for the fertilization and slaughter of small creatures, and meticulously dissecting the cycles of putrefaction. Aesthetics is nowhere to be seen. Rather, we see the earnest morality of the reformer, a religious sensibility directed outward, in practice. If the new age consciousness focuses on the upper *chakras*, this desire for self-mortification corresponds to the lower.

For example, the chapter of *Integral Urban House* dedicated to raising small stock begins with a description of the uses of waste: organic waste from humans is composted in the garden, where food is raised for humans and animals. Chickens are fed organic kitchen wastes, while garden wastes can be

5.25 Front cover of *Integral Urban House*, 1979. Drawing by Gordon Ashby and Bill Wells.

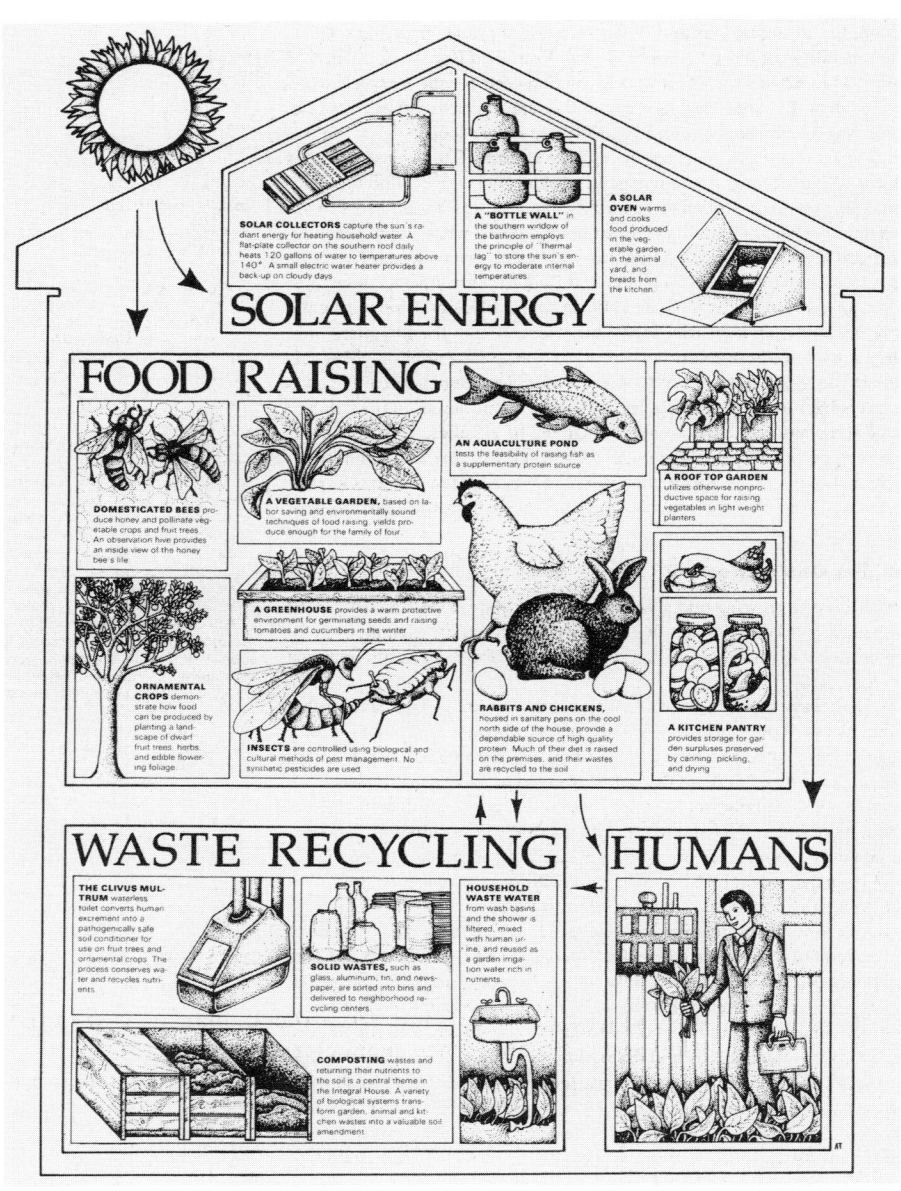

5.26 "Life Support System of an Integral Urban House," 1979. Drawing by Lisa Haderlie Baker.

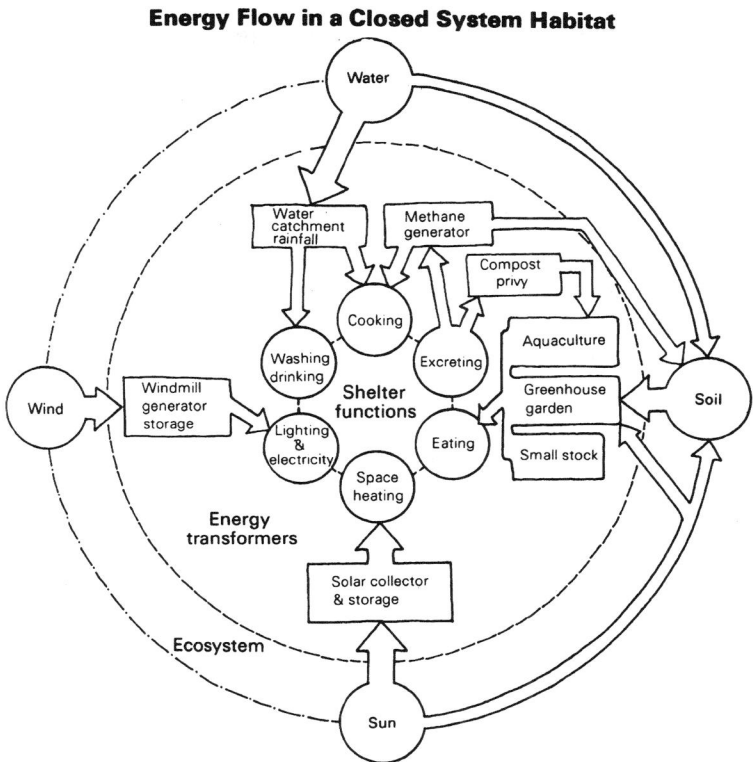

5.27 "Closed System Habitat," 1979. Drawing by Lisa Haderlie Baker.

fed to the rabbits (who are so good at chewing it up that a compost grinder can be dispensed with). Insects, principally flies, may be trapped or raised on wastes and fed to the chickens. The manure from the animals is used in the compost, which helps feed the plants, once again closing the cycle.

As the reader continues on to the raising of chickens, again manure management is key: the best system is the "deep litter" system, in which chickens can pick through their droppings, seeded with garden compost, eating any fly larvae that develop. Cannibalism can be controlled by clipping the horny beaks. In a particularly efficient arrangement, rabbit manure can be combed and raked through by the chickens in a modified version of the deep litter system.[122] No activity is too small for detailed instruction – how to trap flies and how to sterilize them; how much to feed the rabbits; how to determine their sex, breed them, and butcher them; how to tan their pelts. We learn that "mittens, vest and bedspreads are all good possibilities for these useful, pretty skins. Ten to twelve skins, from medium-sized rabbits, will make a man's large warm, wind- and drizzle-proof vest."[123] Just the thing to wear on the new Bay Area Rapid Transit, when hopping over to foggy San Francisco.

The satisfaction is ethical. As the Olkowskis explained, the point is not merely to collect energy-saving tips or grow a backyard garden to help save on food bills. This is, after all, Berkeley, and the participants are college-educated scientists. These goals alone would not make an "integral" urban house.[124] What drives the idea behind this house is a "bioethic," "a system of moral concepts that deal with the relationship of humans to all other living organisms and with the conditions that sustain life and ultimately make continued human survival possible."[125] The last "thrival commandment" states, "respect for self and nature have a common root."

Upon reflection

The alternative architecture of the 1970s may seem to have been too few and too scattered to have had a real impact on the nation's relationship to nature. But these projects were built within an alternative subculture that existed nationwide, and the discussions about alternative ways of building to be more "in touch with nature" were highly articulated and eventually led to a substantial body of knowledge.

But the government had an uneasy relationship with the advocates of green architecture and ecology. During the "oil crisis" of the 1970s, government agencies listened to ecologists and passed laws to reduce oil consumption. This was the era of sub-compact cars, 55 mph speed limits, dedicated bus lanes on highways, and increased funding for public transport. In architecture, new building codes like California's Title 24 regulated the size of windows to reduce heat gain and cut down on energy use for cooling. Its governor Jerry Brown appointed Sim van der Ryn as State Architect, who oversaw "ecological" designs for new government buildings that used passive solar heating and natural ventilation. At a national level, the Carter administration sponsored an architectural competition to bring solar energy to the White House.

But in some instances, the criticism of the status quo embodied in the arguments of ecological activists was too much for governments to accept. Perhaps the most extreme instance of government repression of ecological activism was the 1985 firebombing of MOVE, an African American ecological commune based in Philadelphia. Its members eschewed the killing of any animals and the resulting thriving ecosystem brought media attention and complaints from neighbors. Between police harassment and the argumentative counter-reactions of commune members, the situation escalated to the point where the city sent in SWAT teams and helicopters to launch an all-out assault against the commune. The result was the death of eleven members and the total destruction of sixty neighboring houses. It would be fair to say that issues of race and class influenced government reactions to ecological groups.

And lastly, the 1960s were a time when many people still felt global progress was possible. The "green revolution," the alleviation of world hunger, the spread of democratic states – Fuller's vision of world design science encompassed these global goals. Looking back on this time from the perspective of today, the totalizing view is itself unsustainable. We can no longer conceive of the world, Gianni Vattimo tells us, as one global "transparent" community. And the 1960s helped us to see this. For many people, it is a truism that the activists of the counterculture were earnest, humorless, and self-concerned. The historical record suggests otherwise. We see irony, paradox, and humor on every page of the journals and newsletters produced at this time. We see self-criticism and altruism, pragmatic problem-solving and the most ambitious idealism. In a post-utopian and post-modern age, we are drawn to criticize grand narratives such as globalization and to be suspicious of one-size-fits-all solutions. Yet at the same time today, more than ever, we find that the scale of our many problems and their interdependencies calls for well-organized activism.

History, Louis Althusser says, folds back on itself. That is to say that while people react to recent events, they also look to the past for examples, inspirations, and arguments when thinking through a problem or taking a position. So when we look at Drop City or the Integral Urban House dwellers of the 1970s, we see how they in fact criticized the nineteenth century proposition that nature must be isolated and purified of human activities in order to be protected. Like the hunters of the Boone and Crockett Club, counter-cultural activists wanted a more profound connection to the natural world, but in so doing they also showed an inclusiveness more fitting to a democratic society – arguing for "open land" and respecting Native American knowledge of nature.

By proposing that people should live in equilibrium with nature, the ecologist of the 1970s also recalled the previous wave of the self-conscious homesteaders of the 1930s. Like in that earlier back-to-the-land movement, Arcadian and Utopian imagery abounds. While the TVA was, in spite of its rhetoric, anything but a grass roots movement, the communal and environmental activists of the 1970s were. Elite, perhaps, and mostly white – but a marching pack for new practices, new values, new behaviors and practices. The interesting point here is that with such a grass roots approach, one need not rely on progressive government for change. Although change may be argued from the "margins" of mainstream society, it nonetheless has a voice and a place to accomplish a persistent critique of and present a visible alternative to this mainstream.

Also, the ecology movement of the 1960s grew in the backyards of post-war United States.[126] The privatization of nature in suburbia exposed a huge number of people to the pleasures of nature as a part of daily life – and in the process, raised expectations for nature as a beautiful and picturesque space to be in close proximity. While the ardent youth of the 1960s rejected the consumerism and commodification of the post-war period, they were nonetheless formed with the expectation that nature should be within their reach.

And so the story goes on. The danger now is that this latest shift in the understanding of nature – ecology – could be commodified and marketed much in the same way that the conservation movement found its hard-won achievements commercialized in the development of tourism in the national parks. Perhaps the central lesson we can learn from the 1960s is that if people are to learn to live in harmony with nature, that has to do not only with how buildings are designed, but how we live in them.

Notes

1. The first American photograph of the whole Earth was taken from Apollo 4 in 1967, but received little attention. It showed the Atlantic Ocean with Antarctica just visible at the bottom of a lit crescent – the rest was in shadow. *The Whole Earth Catalog* remarks about the mild reception, "I think it was the shadow which frightened people. There are no shadows on our maps" (1974), p. 1 By contrast, the color image of Earthrise over the arid Moon brought back by Apollo 8 on its lunar orbit became famous. That image "established our planetary facthood and beauty and rareness (dry moon, barren space) and began to bend human consciousness." Harold Morowitz, *Energy, Flow in Biology*, New York: Academic Press, 1968.
2. *The Whole Earth Catalog* recommends a "home movie" to their counterculture readers, "In November 1967 an ATS satellite made a home movie. It was a time lapse film of the Earth rotating, shot from 23,000 miles above South America. Color photographs of the Earth were transmitted by TV every ½ hour to make up a 24 hour sequence. The shots were lap dissolved together to make a movie. You see darkness, then a crescent of dawn, then advancing daylight and immense weather patterns whorling and creeping on the spherical surface, then the full round mandala Earth of noon then gibbous afternoon, crescent twilight, and darkness again." *The Updated Last Whole Earth Catalog*, May 1974, p. 7
3. Denis Cosgrove has explored the nexus of meanings associated with the NASA photographs of Earth from outer space in the context of post-war American geopolitics and the discourses of one-world and whole-earth. See Denis Cosgrove, "Contested Global Visions: *One-World, Whole-Earth* and the Apollo Space Photographs," *Annals of the Association of American Geographers* 84, no. 2, 1994, pp. 270–94.
4. Russell Schweikart quoted in *Coevolution Quarterly* (Spring 1976), p. 6. See also David Steindl-Rast, *CoEvolution Quarterly* (Spring 1976), p. 22.
5. Reyner Banham, "Megacity Montreal," *Megastructures: Urban Futures of the Recent Past*, New York: Harper and Row, 1976, p. 105.
6. Jay Walz, "Expo '67 Will Open Next Friday," *New York Times Magazine* (23 April 1967).
7. R. Buckminster Fuller, "How It Came About," *Fifty Year Design Science Revolution and the World Game*, 1969, p. 111.

8 Fuller, "How It Came About," p. 111. Let us recall that, at that time, the US was heavily involved in the Vietnam War for which they were the target of criticism both internationally and domestically.
9 *Paris Match* (20 May 1967), front cover; *Life* (28 April 1967), front cover; Canada's Centennial Commission, "Share Canada's Exuberance in '67," advertisement (published in *Time*, vol. 89, no. 12 (24 March 1967)).
10 *Bill Bantey's Expo '67* (catalog), Montreal: La Gazette Printing Company, 1967, p. 37.
11 Jasper Johns, *Map*, 32' × 15'-6" canvas, 1967, donated by Leo Castelli Gallery, New York.
12 John M. Lee, "Again the US and USSR are Rivals," *The New York Times* (23 April 1967), p. 5.
13 "Expo '67: the Fairest of All," *Newsweek* (1 May 1967), p. 60.
14 Cited in Robert Fulford, *Remember Expo*, Toronto: McClelland Stewart, 1968, p. 41.
15 Michael Ballantyne, *Expo '67, Art* (catalog), Montreal: Tundra, 1967.
16 Ervin Galantay, "Space/Time in Montreal," *The Nation* (1 May 1967), p. 562.
17 Umberto Eco, "A Theory of Exhibitions," *Travels in Hyperreality*, New York: Harcourt Brace Jovanovich, 1990, p. 301.
18 Umberto Eco, *The Open Work*, Cambridge, MA: Harvard University Press, 1989.
19 Fuller quoted in Joachim Krausse and Claude Lichtenstein (eds), *Your Private Sky: R. Buckminster Fuller, The Art of Design Science*, Baden Switzerland: Lars Müller Publishers, 1999, p. 428.
20 "Der U.S.-Pavillon auf der Weltaustellung in Montreal," *Bauen und Wohnen*, 21. Jahrgang, Heft 10 (October 1967), p. 400.
21 Krausse, *Your Private Sky*, p. 412.
22 Lloyd Steven Sieden, *Buckminster Fuller's Universe*, New York and London: Plenum Press, 1989, p. 363.
23 Eco, *The Open Work*, p. 86.
24 David Jacobs, "An Expo Named Buckminster Fuller," *New York Times Magazine* (23 April 1967), p. 33.
25 Ervin Galantay, "Space/Time in Montreal," *The Nation* (1 May 1967), p. 562
26 *New York Times Magazine* (23 April 1967), p. 33.
27 Gyorgy Kepes, *The New Landscape*, Chicago: Paul Theobald and Company, 1956. We also see a renewed interest in D'Arcy Thompson's classic *On Growth and Form*, 2nd edn, Cambridge, England: The University Press, 1942. See also Peter S. Stevens, *Patterns in Nature*, Boston and Toronto: Little, Brown and Company, 1974.
28 "Intuition," Fuller rhapsodizes, "is the first and utterly unpremeditated event in all discovery, invention and art. It is humanity's *intuitive* awareness of having come unwittingly upon a heretofore unknown truth. A lucidly conceptual, sublimely harmonic, regenerative relationship of a priori Universe – an eternal principle – and then moments later a second *intuitive* awareness regarding what the conceiving individual human must do at once to capture the awareness of and secure the usefulness of that eternally reliable generalized principle for all humanity for now and henceforth." R. Buckminster Fuller, "The Name Intuition," printed in *House and Garden* (May 1972), p. 116.

At this time, the belief in underlying, pre-existing structures also operated in other fields of inquiry that were influenced by structuralism. Structuralist linguists for example, maintain that "the sign systems are grids which we impose upon reality and in this sense pre-exist any uses which we impose upon reality." Robey, "Introduction," *Open Work*, p. xxiii.

29 From a Fuller lecture in Mexico of 1962, cited in Krausse *Your Private Sky*, p. 444.
30 Quoted in Philip C. Ritterbush, *The Art of Organic Forms*, Washington, DC: Smithsonian Institution Press, 1968, p. 40.
31 Donna J. Haraway, *Crystals, Fabrics, and Fields: Metaphors of Organicism in Twentieth-Century Developmental Biology*, New Haven: Yale University Press, 1976, p. 61.
32 Ritterbush, *Art of Organic Forms*, p. 27.
33 Ritterbush, *Art of Organic Forms*, p. 33.
34 Ritterbush, *Art of Organic Forms*, p. 46.
35 *Diatoms, IL 28*, Stuttgart: Institute for Lightweight Structures, 1984.
36 D'Arcy Thompson, *On Growth and Form*, Cambridge University Press, 1961 (first published in 1917), p. 155.
37 Thompson, *On Growth and Form*, p. 155.
38 Thompson, *On Growth and Form*, p. 156.
39 Thompson, *On Growth and Form*, p. 158.
40 Thompson is struggling with the notion that forms could be explained through heredity. Instead he repeatedly suggests that physical forces are of prime importance. Today biologists are inclined to combine the two and say that while genes control shapes, their activities are constrained by the environment. Interestingly, Fuller was a complete believer (like Thompson) in the impact of the environment and also rejected hereditary explanations for deficiencies in human behavior.
41 John McHale, "Buckminster Fuller," *The Architectural Review*, vol. 120, no. 714 (July 1956), p. 19.
42 Marc Mimram, *Structures et forms: étude appliquée à l'oeuvre de Robert Le Ricolais*, Paris: Dumod, Presses Ponts et Chaussées, 1983.
43 Krausse, *Your Private Sky*, p. 401.
44 Haraway, *Crystals, Fabrics, and Fields*, p. 71.
45 McHale, *AD* (July 1961), pp. 290–319.
46 McHale, *AD* (July 1961), pp. 290–319, the italics our ours.
47 But Fuller does not take into account the differences in stress between the upper and lower regions of the dome. Clearly, the lower struts carry a great deal more weight than the upper ones, but this is not reflected in their size.
48 R. Buckminster Fuller, #489.
49 R. Buckminster Fuller, *4-D Time Lock*, 1928. Reprint: Albuquerque: NM Biotechnic Press, 1970, pp. 32–3.
50 Interestingly, the year the Earth was photographed from space for the first time, images of the first indoscopic photographs of the human fetus by Lennart Nillson were being published. Bringing these two images (of human life and planetary life) together leads us to interpret in a different light the floating objects seen through the dome of the Expo '67.
51 Joachim Krausse, "Bauen von Weltbildern: Die Dymaxion-World von R. Buck-

minster Fuller," *ARCH+: Gebaute Weltbilder von Boulée bis Buckminster Fuller*, vol. 116 (March 1993), p. 51. Author's translation.
52 R. Buckminster Fuller, *Fluid Geography*, Private edition, R. Buckminter Fuller, p. 136. Reprint from an article in the *American Reptune*, April 1944.
53 Krause, "Bauen von Weltbildern," p. 63.
54 Fuller's geodesic structures were a direct result of his desire to create large three-dimensional models of the Earth. His early experiments making large-scale models of the Earth began before his well-known work of 1948 at Black Mountain College with Beech Aircraft.
55 Fuller, "How It Came About," p. 111.
56 "Chronology of the Life of RBF," in Sieden, *Buckminster Fuller's Universe*, p. 429.
57 David B. Ruderman, *Kabbalah, Magic, and Science: the Cultural Universe of a Sixteenth-Century Jewish Physician*, Cambridge, MA: Harvard University Press, 1988, p. 113.
58 Ruderman, *Kabbalah, Magic, and Science*, p. 113. Although the theater was short-lived, and Camillo as well, his *Idea del theatro* (Venice, 1550) was published in ten editions by 1584. See the discussion of this and other memory theaters in Frances A. Yates, *The Art of Memory*, Chicago: University of Chicago Press, 1966.
59 According to Reinhold Martin, "For Fuller, progressive ephemeralization means the reduction of... an architectural enclosure to its lightest form: pure information." Reinhold Martin, "Crystal Balls," *ANY 17: Forget Fuller?*, 1997, p. 39.
60 Gianni Vattimo, *The Transparent Society*, trans. David Webb, Baltimore: John Hopkins University Press, 1992, pp. 15–16.
61 Vattimo, *Transparent Society*, p. 18.
62 For a description of the game and images, see John McHale, "The World Game," *AD* (February 1967), p. 93.
63 Some ecologists expressed doubts about the social implications of Fuller's World Game. A letter to the *Whole Earth Catalog* asks, "are we to be Whole Earth technocrats, insuring only our own survival? If you read closely you will note that... Fuller talks about minerals and such, and makes no mention of organic things except what people can eat. Or are we going to be Ecology Action pagans, trying to scramble back to a sense of union with the planet that created us?" *The Updated Last Whole Earth Catalog* (May 1974), p. 28.
64 Eco, *Open Work*, p. 93.
65 In his work criticizing the boredom and ennui prevalent in the French new towns, Lefebvre suggests a reintroduction of the "active ludic element." Henri Lefebvre, "Les nouveaux ensembles urbains," *Revue Française de Sociologie*, vol. 1, no. 1 (1960), p. 190.
66 Eco, *Open Work*, p. 86.
67 Erik Wessberge, Frontispiece to "Terre des Hommes," *Air France*, no. 36 (1966), p. 1.
68 John McHale, "Toward the Future," *Design Quarterly*, vol. 72 (1968), p. 6.
69 Of the origins of his *Whole Earth Catalog*, Stewart Brand says it "got started in a plane over Nebraska in March 1968. I was returning to California from my father's long dying and funeral that morning in Illinois. The sun had set ahead of the plane while I was reading *Spaceship Earth* by Barbara Ward. Between

chapters I gazed out the window into dark nothing and slid into a reverie about my friends who were starting their own civilization hither and yon in the sticks and how I could help ... Amid the fever I was in by this time, I remembered Fuller's admonition that you have about ten minutes to act on an idea before it recedes back into dreamland. I started writing on the end papers of Barbara Ward's book (never did finish reading it)." Cited in Howard Rheingold (ed.), *The Millennium Whole Earth Catalog*, San Francisco: HarperCollins and The Point Foundation, 1994, p. 383.

70 Georges Poulet, *Metamorphoses of the Circle* (trans. by Carley Dawson and Elliott Coleman), Baltimore, MD: Johns Hopkins Press, 1966.

71 According to Martin Bressani, the eighteenth century *philosophe* is forced to recognize that the self mediates experience, making "the cenotaph [for Newton ...] simultaneously a model of the world and of the self." Martin Bressani, "Étienne-Louis Boulée. Empiricism and the Cenotaph for Newton." *Architectura: Journal of the History of Architecture*, 1993, vol. 23, p. 39.

72 Steve Kubby, letter to the editor, Lloyd Kahn, *et al.*, *Domebook Two*, Santa Barbara: Shelter Publications, 1971.

73 According to the *Whole Earth Catalog*, "Reading *The Phenomenon of Man* is a bit unnerving: Teilhard de Chardin manages to say most of the things many of us are trying to say. He said them in 1938. Was no one listening?" *The Last Whole Earth Catalog*, May 1974, p. 31. Paolo Soleri also refers to Teilhard de Chardin in his approach "to man as a cosmic problem by ascending form physics, chemistry, biology and geology ..." ibid, p. 83.

74 Pierre Teilhard de Chardin, *The Phenomenon of Man*, translated by Bernard Wall, with an introduction by Julian Huxley, New York: Harper & Row, 1959, p. 239. [Originally published by Editions du Seuil, 1955.]

75 Teilhard de Chardin, *Phenomenon of Man*, p. 273.

76 Teilhard de Chardin, *Phenomenon of Man*, p. 221.

77 Teilhard de Chardin, *Phenomenon of Man*, p. 230.

78 Teilhard de Chardin, *Phenomenon of Man*, p. 283.

79 Julian S. Huxley, *UNESCO, Its Purpose and Philosophy*, 1946, p. 9.

80 Paul R. Samson and David Pitt (eds), *The Biosphere and Noosphere Reader: Global Environment, Society and Change*, London: Routledge, 1999, p. 53.

81 Samson and Pitt remark that "UNESCO's development was influenced by Teilhard de Chardin's noosphere idea, supported by Huxley, Joseph Needham (Head of the Science Division) and others. A UNESCO international symposium entitled 'Science and Synthesis of Knowledge on Man and the Universe' was convened in Paris in 1965 to mark the fiftieth anniversary of the formulation of the general theory of relativity and the tenth anniversary of the deaths of Albert Einstein and Teilhard de Chardin.... Later still, [in 1971] ... the Man and Biosphere Programme divided the world not into nation-states, but into ecosystems (and 'biosphere reserves') and assembled leading scientists to prepare plans for their best management – an early application of the sustainability idea." Samson, *The Biosphere and Noosphere*, p. 142.

82 Summary of Fuller's work, p. 163.

83 Teilhard de Chardin, *Phenomenon of Man*, p. 183.

84 Teilhard de Chardin, *Phenomenon of Man*, p. 182.

85 Teilhard de Chardin, *Phenomenon of Man*, p. 239.

86 Teilhard de Chardin, *Phenomenon of Man*, p. 241.
87 Teilhard de Chardin, *Phenomenon of Man*, p. 183.
88 R. Buckminster Fuller, cited in Sieden, *Buckminster Fuller's Universe*, p. 418.
89 Teilhard de Chardin, *Phenomenon of Man*, p. 182.
90 Fuller, cited in Mark Wigley, "Planetary Homeboy," *ANY 17*, 1997, p. 17.
91 World Game coordinator Medard Gabel, cited in Hal Aigner, "World Game," *Mother Earth News*, no. 6 (November 1970), p. 66.
92 John McHale, "Toward the Future," *Design Quarterly* 72 (1968), p. 6.
93 Daniel Bell calls this the "re-enchantment" of society, in *Commutarism and its Critics*, Oxford: Oxford University Press, 1993, and Gianni Vattimo "archaic mythologizing." Vattimo, *Transparent Society*, p. 32. See also Christopher Lasch, *The Culture of Narcissism: American life in an age of diminishing expectations*, New York: Norton, 1978.
94 Theodore Roszak, *The Making of a Counter Culture: Reflections on the Technocratic Society and Its Youthful Opposition*, Garden City, NY: Anchor/Doubleday & Company, 1969.
95 "Youth: the Hippies," *Time* (7 July 1967), cover story.
96 Bill Voyd, "Funk Architecture," in Paul Oliver (ed.), *Shelter and Society*, London: Barrie and Jenkins, 1970, pp. 56–8.
97 All quotes from our correspondence with Clark Richert.
98 Robert Smithson's *Spiral Jetty* created in the Great Salt Lake in Utah has become emblematic of that movement. Submerged in water, the earthwork made of black basalt and limestone is coiled like a snake extending 1,500 feet into the lake. The land is cluttered with detritus of abandoned oil drilling and the water is red with algae.
99 Lucy R. Lippard, *Overlay, Contemporary Art and the Art of Prehistory*, New York: New Press, 1983, p. 236.
100 Quoted in Lippard, *Overlay*, p. 230.
101 Lippard, *Overlay*, p. 234.
102 Lippard, *Overlay*, p. 197.
103 "Year of the Commune," *Newsweek*, 18 August 1969, p. 89.
104 "Amazing Sundome," *Popular Science*, May 1966, pp. 108–12; Steve Baer, *The Dome Cookbook*, Corrales, NM: Lama Foundation, 1968; Lloyd Kahn, et al., *Domebook One*, Los Gatos: Pacific Domes, 1970; Kahn, *Domebook Two*; John Premis (ed.), *The Dome Builder's Handbook*, Philadelphia: Running Press, 1973.
105 Voyd, "Funk Architecture," pp. 56–8.
106 "When you live in a dome, you gradually realize that what you've built resembles a living organism. It is a mathematically derived membrane containing life inside." "Sealing," *Domebook One*.
107 John Premis (ed.), *The Dome Builder's Handbook*, Philadelphia: The Running Press, 1973, p. 1.
108 Alan and Heath Schmidt, "Centering," Kahn, *Domebook One*, p. 47.
109 Lloyd Kahn, "Domebook 3," *Shelter* (ed.), Lloyd Kahn, Bolinas, CA: Shelter Publications/Random House, 1973, p. 109.
110 Unintentionally lampooned by the actress Shirley MacLaine when she stated, "I am God. I am God. I am God." Paul Heelas, *The New Age Movement: The Celebration of the Self and the Sacralization of Modernity*, Oxford and Cambridge: Blackwell, 1996, p. 1.

111 Tom Wolfe, *The Electric Kool-aid Acid Test*, New York City: Farrar, Staus and Giroux, 1968, pp. 26–7.
112 James J. Farrell, *The Spirit of the Sixties: the Making of Postwar Radicalism*, London: Routledge, 1997.
113 Cited in Howard Rheingold (ed.), *The Millennium Whole Earth Catalog*, San Francisco: HarperCollins and the Point Foundation, 1994, p. 1. *Playboy* publishes a parody, *The Hole Earth Catalog*, with "Quicksand Houses – cheap, fast shelter for seminomadic types," "Locusts – harnessing locust power for the cause of Good," and "make your own Steel – Tell U.S. Steel to shove it. You will now make your own with a good old-fashioned Bessemer Steel converter." *Playboy*, February 1972, p. 131.
114 Lloyd Kahn, "Technology Review," in Lloyd Kahn (ed.), *Shelter*, Bolinas, CA: Shelter Publications, 1973, p. 87.
115 Peter Warshall, "Earth Shelter," Kahn (ed.), *Shelter*, 1973, p. 87.
116 A good survey of such projects can be found in Gary Coates, (ed.), *Resettling America: Energy, Ecology and Community, the movement towards self-reliance*, Andover, MA: Brick House Publishing Company, 1981.
117 Helga Olkowski, Bill Olkowski, Tom Javits and the Farallones Institute staff, *The Integral Urban House*, introduction by Sim Van der Ryn, San Francisco: Sierra Club Books, 1979.
118 Olkowski, *et al.*, *Integral Urban House*, p. 35.
119 Olkowski, *et al.*, *Integral Urban House*, p. 4.
120 Olkowski, *et al.*, *Integral Urban House*, p. 16.
121 Olkowski, *et al.*, *Integral Urban House*, p. 20.
122 Olkowski, *et al.*, *Integral Urban House*, pp. 253–5.
123 Olkowski, *et al.*, *Integral Urban House*, p. 278.
124 The Integral Urban House was an adaptation of a conventional wood frame Victorian house and once in operation, differed little from its neighbors except for wood chips and shrubberies in place of a lawn. Its architectural normality reinforced that its uniqueness lay in how it *worked on* its inhabitants – changing their behaviors with respect to the environment.
125 Olkowski, *et al.*, *Integral Urban House*, p. 45.
126 Adam Rome, *The Bulldozer in the Countryside: Suburban Sprawl and the Rise of American Environmentalism*, Cambridge: Cambridge University Press, 2001.

Selected bibliography

BOOKS AND ARTICLES

Albrecht, Donald (ed.), *World War II and the American Dream: How Wartime Building Changed a Nation*, Washington DC: National Building Museum/MIT Press, 1995.
Albright, Horace H., *The Birth of the National Park Service, The Founding Years, 1913–1933*, Salt Lake City: Howe Brothers, 1985.
Anderson, Benedict, *Imagined Communities*, London: Verso, 1983.
Anscombe, Isabelle, *A Woman's Touch, Women in Design from 1860 to the Present*, New York: Viking Press, 1984.
Applebaum, Stanley, *Chicago World's Fair of 1893*, New York: Dover, 1980.
Armitage, Susan and Elizabeth Jameson, *The Women's West*, Norman: University of Oklahoma Press, 1987.
Arnold, C.D. and Henry Higinbotham, *Official Views of the World's Columbian Exposition*, Chicago: Chicago Photogravure Company, 1893.
Arnold, Joseph F., *The New Deal in the Suburbs: a History of the Greenbelt Town Program*, Columbus: Ohio State University Press, 1971.
Badger, R. Reid, *The Great American Fair: The World's Columbian Exhibition and American Culture*, Chicago: Nelson Hall, 1979.
Baer, Steve, *The Dome Cookbook*, Corrales, NM: Cookbook Fund – Lama Foundation, 1968.
Baldwin, Jay, *Bucky Works: Buckminster Fuller's Ideas for Today*, New York: John Wiley and Sons, 1996.
Baldwin, Jay and Stewart Brand (eds), *Soft Tech*, Harmondsworth, UK: Penguin, 1978.
Banham, Reyner, "Tennessee Valley Authority: the Engineering of Utopia," *Casabella* 52, nos. 542–3 (Jan–Feb 1988), pp. 74–81.
Banham, Reyner, *Concrete Atlantis: US Industrial Building and European Modern Architecture, 1900–1925*, Cambridge, MA: MIT Press, 1986.
Banham, Reyner, *Los Angeles: Architecture of Four Ecologies*, New York: Harper and Row, 1971.
Banham, Reyner, *Megastructures: Urban Futures of the Recent Past*, New York: Harper and Row, 1976.
Bantey, Bill, *Bill Bantey's Expo '67* (catalog), Montreal: La Gazette Printing Company, 1967.
Bartlett, Richard A., *Yellowstone: A Wilderness Besieged*, Tucson: University of Arizona Press, 1985.
Bauer, Catherine, "Cities in Flux: A Challenge to the Postwar Planners," *American Scholar* 13, no. 1 (Winter 1943–4), pp. 70–84.

Bellamy, Edward, *Looking Backward, 2000–1887*, Boston: Ticknor and Company, 1888.
Berry, Wendell, *The Unsettling of America: Culture and Agriculture*, San Francisco: Sierra Club Books, 1977.
Billington, Ray Allen, *Land of Savagery, Land of Promise: European Images of the American Frontier in the Nineteenth Century*, New York: Norton, 1981.
Black Elk, *Black Elk Speaks: Being the Life Story of a Holy Man of the Oglala Sioux* (ed.), John G. Neihardt, intro. Vine Deloria, Jr, Lincoln: University of Nebraska Press, 1979 (1932).
Bold, Christine, *Selling the Wild West, 1860–1960*, Bloomington: Indiana University Press, 1987.
Boyer, Christine M., *Dreaming the Rational City: The Myth of American City Planning*, Cambridge, MA: MIT Press, 1983.
Boyer, Paul S., *By the Bomb's Early Light: American Thought and Culture at the Dawn of the Atomic Age*, New York: Pantheon, 1985.
Brand, Stewart (ed.), *Whole Earth Catalog*, Menlo Park, CA, 1968.
Brown, Julie K. (ed.), *Contesting Images: Photography and the World's Columbian Exposition*, Tucson: University of Arizona Press, 1994.
Bruegmann, Robert, *The Architects and the City: Holabird and Roche of Chicago, 1880–1918*, Chicago: University of Chicago Press, 1996.
Burnham, Daniel H., *The Final Official Report of the Director of Works of the World's Columbian Exposition*, vols 1–2, intro. by Joan E. Draper, New York: Garland Publishing, 1989.
Burroughs, John, *Camping and Tramping with President Roosevelt*, Boston: Houghton Mifflin, 1907.
Callenbach, Ernest, *Ecotopia*, Berkeley: Banyan Tree Books, 1975.
Carson, Rachel, *Silent Spring*, Cambridge, MA: Riverside Press, 1962.
Chase, Stuart, *Rich Land Poor Land: a Study of Waste in the Natural Resources of America*, New York: McGraw Hill, 1936.
Clark, Clifford Edward, *The American Family Home, 1800–1960*, Chapel Hill: University of North Carolina Press, 1986.
Coates, Gary J. (ed.), *Resettling America: Energy, Ecology and Community*, Andover, MA: Brick House Publishing Company, 1981.
Collins, Peter, *Changing Ideals in Modern Architecture, 1750–1950*, Montreal: McGill-Queen's University Press, 1965.
Colomina, Beatriz, "1949," in Robert E. Somol (ed.), *Autonomy and Ideology: Positioning an Avant Garde in America*, New York: Monacelli Press/Canadian Centre for Architecture, 1997.
Colomina, Beatriz, "Domesticity at War," *Assemblage* 16 (December 1991), pp. 14–41.
Colomina, Beatriz, "Reflections on the Eames House," in Diane Murphy (ed.), *The Work of Charles and Ray Eames: A Legacy of Invention*, Washington DC: Library of Congress/Vitra Design Museum, 1997: pp. 127–49.
Commoner, Barry, *The Closing Circle: Nature, Man & Technology*, New York: Alfred A. Knopf, 1971.
Craig, Lois, *The Federal Presence, Architecture, Politics and Symbols in United States Government Building*, Cambridge, MA: MIT Press, 1978.
Cranz, Galen, *The Politics of Park Design*, Cambridge, MA: MIT Press, 1982.

Crawford, Margaret, *Building the Workingman's Paradise: The Design of American Company Towns*, London: Verso, 1995.
Crawshaw, Carol and John Urry, "Tourism and the Photographic Eye," in Chris Rojek and John Urry (eds), *Touring Cultures*, London: Routledge, 1977.
Creese, Walter, *TVA's Public Planning: the Vision, the Reality*, Knoxville: University of Tennessee Press, 1990.
Cronon, William (ed.), *Uncommon Ground: Rethinking the Human Place in Nature*, New York: Norton, 1996.
Cronon, William, *Nature's Metropolis: Chicago and the Great West*, New York: W.W. Norton, 1991.
Cross, Whitney R., "Ideas in Politics: The Conservation Policies of the Two Roosevelts," *Journal of the History of Ideas* 14 (June 1953), pp. 421–38.
Cutler, Phoebe, *The Public Landscape of the New Deal*, New Haven: Yale University Press, 1985.
Cutright, Paul Russell, *Theodore Roosevelt, the Making of a Conservationist*, Urbana: University of Illinois Press, 1985.
Davis, Mike, *Ecology of Fear: Los Angeles and the Imagination of Disaster*, New York: Vintage, 1998.
Dimendberg, Edward, "Cinema, Highways, and Modernity," *October* 73 (Summer 1995).
Douthit, Peter (n.p. Peter Rabbit), *Drop City*, New York: Olympia Press, 1971.
Draper, Earle S. (ed.), *The Scenic Resources of the Tennessee Valley*, Knoxville, TN: Tennessee Valley Authority, Department of Regional Planning Studies, 1938.
Draper, Earle S., "Housing is More than Building Construction," in *Proceedings on the Conference on Low Cost Housing*, Atlanta: Georgia School of Technology, 1935, pp. 9–16.
Draper, Earle Sumner Jr., "The TVA's Forgotten Town: Norris, Tennessee," *Landscape Architecture* (March 1988), pp. 96–100.
Drexler, Arthur, *Built in the USA: Post War Architecture*, New York: Museum of Modern Art, 1953.
Duffus, R.L. and Charles Krutch, *The Valley and its People: A Portrait of TVA*, New York: Alfred Knopf, 1944.
Dyer, Thomas C., *Theodore Roosevelt and the Idea of Race*, Baton Rouge: Louisiana State University Press, 1980.
Easterling, Keller, *Organization of Space: Landscapes, Highways, and Houses in America*, Cambridge, MA: MIT Press, 1999.
Eaton, Allan H., *Handicrafts of the Southern Highlands*, New York: Russell Sage Foundation, 1937.
Eckbo, Garrett, "Outdoors and In: Gardens as Living Space," *Magazine of Art* 34, no. 8 (October 1941), pp. 422–7.
Eckbo, Garrett, "What is Landscape Architecture?" *Arts & Architecture* (October 1945), pp. 40–1, 52.
Eckbo, Garrett, *The Art of Home Landscaping*, New York: F.W. Dodge, 1956.
Eco, Umberto, *The Open Work*, trans. by Anna Cancogni, Cambridge, MA: Harvard University Press, 1989.
Eco, Umberto, *Travels in Hyperreality*, New York: Harcourt Brace Jovanovich, 1990.
Emerson, Ralph Waldo, *Nature: Addresses, and Lectures*, Boston: Houghton Mifflin, 1855.

Farrell, James J., *The Spirit of the Sixties: The Making of Postwar Radicalism*, New York: Routledge, 1977.
Fein, Albert, *Frederick Law Olmsted and the American Environmental Tradition*, New York: George Braziller, 1972.
Ferriss, Hugh, *Power in Buildings*, New York: Columbia University Press, 1953.
Fishman, Robert, *Bourgeois Utopias: the Rise and Fall of Suburbia*, New York: Basic Books, 1987.
Foglesong, Richard E., *Planning the Capitalist City: the Colonial Era to the 1920s*, Princeton, NJ: Princeton University Press, 1986.
Forty, Adrian, "Masculine, Feminine or Neuter?" in Duncan McCorquodale, Katerina Rüedi and Sarah Wigglesworth (eds), *Desiring Practices: Architecture, Gender and the Interdisciplinary*, London: Black Dog Publishing, 1996.
Frampton, Kenneth, "The Glass House Revisited," *IAUS Catalogue*, no. 9, New York: Institute for Architecture and Urban Studies, 1978, pp. 38–59.
Friedman, Alice T., *Women and the Making of the Modern House: a Social and Architectural History*, New York: Harry N. Abrams, 1998.
Fuller, R. Buckminster, *4D Timelock*, 1928, reprinted (ed. Steve Baer), Corrales, NM: Lama Foundation/Biotechnic Press, 1970.
Fuller, R. Buckminster, *Collected Works, 1932–*, n.p., n.d.
Fuller, R. Buckminster, *Fifty Years of the Design Science Revolution and the World Game*, Carbondale, IL: World Resources Inventory/Southern Illinois University Press, 1969.
Fuller, R. Buckminster, *Operating Manual for Spaceship Earth*, Carbondale, IL: Southern Illinois University Press/Simon and Schuster, 1969.
Fuller, R. Buckminster, *The Artifacts of R. Buckminster Fuller: a Comprehensive Collection of his Designs and Drawings*, 4 vols (ed. James Ward), New York: Garland, 1985.
Fuller, Buckminster R. and John McHale, *World Design Science Decade 1965–1975: Five Two-Year Phases of a World Retooling Design Proposed to the International Union of Architects for Adoption by World Architectural Schools*, 6 vols, Carbondale: World Resources Inventory/Southern Illinois University, 1967.
Gardner, Hugh, *The Children of Prosperity: Thirteen Modern American Communes*, New York: Saint Martin's Press, 1978.
Gaskin, Stephen and the Farm, *Hey Beatnik!*, Summertown, TN: Books Publishing Company, 1974.
Ghirardo, Diane, *Building New Communities*, Princeton: Princeton University Press, 1989.
Gilbert, James B., *Perfect Cities: Chicago's Utopias of 1893*, Chicago: University of Chicago Press, 1991.
Gilbert, James B., *Work without Salvation: American Intellectuals and Industrial Alienation, 1880–1910*, Baltimore: Johns Hopkins University Press, 1977.
Goetzmann, William H., *Exploration and Empire: the Explorer and the Scientist in the Winning of the American West*, New York: Norton, 1978.
Goldstein, Barbara (ed.), *Arts & Architecture: The Entenza Years*, Cambridge, MA: MIT Press, 1990.
Good, Albert H., *Park and Recreation Structures, 1938*, 2 vols, reprinted New York: Princeton Architectural Press, 1999.
Goodman, Paul and Percival Goodman, *Communitas: Means of Livelihood and Ways of Life*, New York: Vintage, 1960.

Grant, Nancy L., *TVA and Black Americans: Planning for the Status Quo*, Philadelphia: Temple University Press, 1990.
Grattan, Virginia L., *Mary Colter: Builder Upon the Red Earth*, Flagstaff, AZ: Northland Press, 1980.
Grinnell, George Bird (ed.), *American Big Game in its Haunts: the Book of the Boone and Crockett Club*, New York: Forest and Stream Publishing, 1904.
Grossman, James R. (ed.), *The Frontier in American Culture*, essays by Richard White and Patricia Nelson Limerick, Berkeley: University of California Press, 1994.
Gutheim, Frederick A., *TVA Architecture*, New York: Museum of Modern Art, 1940.
Gutheim, Frederick, "Greenbelt Revisited," *Magazine of Art* 4, no. 1 (January 1947), pp. 16–20.
Haddow, Robert H., *Pavilions of Plenty: Exhibiting American Culture Abroad in the 1950s*, Washington DC: Smithsonian Institution Press, 1997.
Hagedorn, Hermann, *The Bomb That Fell on America*, Santa Barbara: Pacific Coast Publishing, 1946.
Haines, Aubrey L., *The Yellowstone Story: a History of our First National Park*, 2 vols, Yellowstone National Park: Yellowstone Library and Museum Association, 1977.
Hales, Peter B., *Silver Cities: The Photography of American Urbanization, 1839–1915*, Philadelphia: Temple University Press, 1984.
Hall, Stuart, *The Hippies: An American "Movement"*, Birmingham, UK: University of Birmingham, 1968.
Haraway, Donna Jeanne, *Crystals, Fabrics, and Fields: Metaphors of Organicism in Twentieth-Century Developmental Biology*, New Haven: Yale University Press, 1976.
Haraway, Donna, *Primate Visions: Gender, Race and Nature in the World of Modern Science*, New York: Routledge, 1989.
Hargrove, Erwin C., *Prisoners of Myth: the Leadership of the TVA, 1933–1990*, Princeton: Princeton University Press, 1994.
Hargrove, Erwin C. and Paul K. Conklin, *TVA: Fifty Years of Grassroots Democracy*, Urbana: University of Illinois Press, 1983.
Harris, Neil, Wim de Wit, James Gilbert and Robert W. Rydell, *Grand Illusions: Chicago World's Fair of 1893*, Chicago: Chicago Historical Society, 1993.
Hatch, Alden, *Buckminster Fuller at Home in the Universe*, New York: Crown Publishers, 1974.
Hayden, Dolores, *Seven American Utopias: the Architecture of Communitarian Socialism, 1790–1975*, Cambridge, MA: MIT Press, 1976.
Hayden, Dolores, *Redesigning the American Dream: the Future of Housing, Work and Family Life*, New York: W.W. Norton, 1984.
Hays, Samuel P., *Conservation and the Gospel of Efficiency: the Progressive Conservation Movement, 1890–1920*, Cambridge, MA: Harvard University Press, 1959.
Heelas, Paul, *The New Age Movement: The Celebration of the Self and the Sacralization of Modernity*, Oxford: Blackwell, 1996.
Hession, Jane King, Rip Rapson and Bruce N. Wright, *Ralph Rapson: Sixty Years of Modern Design*, Afton, MN: Afton Historical Society Press, 1999.
Heynen, Hilde, *Architecture and Modernity, a Critique*, Cambridge, MA: MIT Press, 1999.

Hildebrand, Grant, *Designing for Industry: the Architecture of Albert Kahn*, Cambridge, MA: MIT Press, 1974.
Hines, Thomas S., *Burnham of Chicago: Architect and Planner*, New York: Oxford University Press, 1974.
Hines, Thomas, *Populuxe*, New York: Alfred A. Knopf, 1986.
Hise, Greg, *Magnetic LA: Planning the Twentieth Century Metropolis*, Baltimore: Johns Hopkins University Press, 1997.
Hobsbawm, Eric and Terence Ranger (eds), *The Invention of Tradition*, Cambridge: Cambridge University Press, 1983.
Hodge, Clarence Lewis, *The TVA: a National Experiment in Regionalism*, New York: Russell and Russell, 1938.
Hough, Emerson, *The Way to the West: and the Lives of Three Early Americans, Boone – Crockett – Carson*, illus. by Frederic Remington, Indianapolis: Bobbs-Merrill, 1903.
Howard, Ebenezer, *Garden Cities of Tomorrow* (2nd edn of *Tomorrow: the Peaceful Path to Real Reform*), London: S. Sonnenschein & Company, 1902.
Huxley, Julian S., *TVA – Adventure in Planning*, Cheam, Surrey, UK: Architectural Press, 1943.
Huxley, Julian S., *UNESCO, Its Purpose and Philosophy*, New York: United Nations, 1946.
Hyde, Anne Farrar, *An American Vision, Far Western Landscape and National Culture, 1820–1920*, New York: New York University Press, 1990.
Ian, Marcia, "When is a Body not a Body? When It's a Building," in Joel Sanders (ed.), *STUD: Architectures of Masculinity*, New York: Princeton Architectural Press, 1996.
Ickes, Harold, *Why I Favor a Program of Public Works*, Washington DC, 1936.
IL, *Diatoms, IL 28*, Stuttgart: Institute for Lightweight Structures, 1984.
Ingber, Donald, "The Architecture of Life," *Scientific American* 278, no. 1 (January 1988), pp. 30–9.
Ingraham, Catherine, "Missing Objects," in Diana Agrest, Patricia Conway and Leslie Kanes Weisman (eds), *The Sex of Architecture*, New York: Harry N. Abrams, 1996.
Isaacs, Ken, *How to Build Your Own Living Structures*, New York: Crown Publishers, 1974.
Jackson, John Brinckerhoff, "The Westward-Moving House," in Ervin H. Zube (ed.), *Landscapes*, Amherst: University of Massachusetts Press, 1970, pp. 10–42.
Jackson, Lesley, *"Contemporary": Architecture and Interiors of the 1950s*, London: Phaidon, 1994.
Jackson, Neil, "Metal Frame Houses of the Modern Movement in Los Angeles," *Architectural History* 32 (1989), pp. 153–72; and vol. 33 (1990), pp. 167–87.
Jackson, Neil, *The Modern Steel House*, London: E&FN Spon, 1996.
Jasen, Patricia, *Wild Things: Nature, Culture, and Tourism in Ontario, 1790–1914*, Toronto: University of Toronto Press, 1995.
Jones, A. Haworth, "The Search for a Usable American Past in the New Deal Era," *American Quarterly* 23, no. 5 (December 1971), pp. 710–24.
Jordy, William H., "'A Wholesome Environment Through Plain, Direct Means': The Planning of Norris by the Tennessee Valley Authority," *Arris: Journal of the Southeast Chapter of the Society of Architectural Historians* 5 (1994), pp. 6–30.

Kahn, Lloyd, *et al.* (eds), *Domebook One*, Bolinas, CA: Pacific Domes, 1970.
Kahn, Lloyd, *et al.* (eds), *Domebook Two*, Bolinas, CA: Pacific Domes/Random House, 1971.
Kahn, Lloyd, *et al.* (eds), *Shelter*, Bolinas, CA: Shelter Publications/Random House, 1973.
Karp, Walter, "When Bunkers Last in Backyards Bloom'd," *American Heritage* 31, no. 2 (February/March 1980), pp. 84–93.
Kaufman, Polly Welts, *National Parks and the Women's Voice, a History*, Albuquerque: University of New Mexico Press, 1996.
Keats, John, *The Crack in the Picture Window*, Boston: Houghton Mifflin, 1957.
Keller, Robert H. and Michael F. Turek, *American Indians and National Parks*, Tucson: University of Arizona Press, 1998.
Kepes, Gyorgy, *The New Landscape*, Chicago: Paul Theobald, 1956.
King, Judson, *The Conservation Fight: from Theodore Roosevelt to the TVA*, Washington, DC: Public Affairs Press, 1959.
Kirkham, Pat, *Charles and Ray Eames, Designers of the Twentieth Century*, Cambridge, MA: MIT Press, 1995.
Kirkham, Pat, *The Gendered Object*, New York: Manchester University Press, 1996.
Kolodny, Annette, *The Land Before Her: Fantasy and Experience of the American Frontier, 1630–1860*, Chapel Hill: University of North Carolina Press, 1984.
Kopp, Anatole, "Les Racines Européenes de la culture du New Deal," in Jean-Louis Cohen and Hubert Damisch (eds), *Américanisme et Modernité*, Paris: Flammarion, 1993.
Krausse, Joachim and Claude Lichtenstein (eds), *Your Private Sky: R. Buckminster Fuller, the Art of Design Science* (trans. Steven Lindberg and Julia Thorson), Baden, Switzerland: Lars Müller, 1999.
Kyle, John H., *The Building of the TVA: An Illustrated History*, Baton Rouge: Louisiana State University Press, 1958.
Lavin, Sylvia, "The Avant Garde is Not at Home," in Robert E. Somol (ed.), *Autonomy and Ideology: Positioning an Avant Garde in America*, New York: Monacelli Press/Canadian Centre for Architecture, 1997.
Lears, T.J. Jackson, *No Place of Grace: Antimodernism and the Transformation of American Culture, 1880–1920*, Chicago: University of Chicago Press, 1983.
Leavengood, David, "The Mountain Architecture of R.C. Reamer," *Mountain Gazette* 46 (1975).
Lejeune, Jean-François, "Democratic Pyramids: the Works of the Tennessee Valley Authority," *Themes in Architecture: Electricity, United States & USSR, France and Italy, Rassegna* 17, no. 63 (1995), pp. 46–57.
Leuchtenberg, William E, *Franklin D. Roosevelt and the New Deal, 1932–1940*, New York: Harper and Row, 1963.
Leuchtenburg, William E., *A Troubled Feast: American Society Since 1945*, Boston: Little, Brown and Company, 1973.
Lilienthal, David E., *Journal of David E. Lilienthal, vol. 1, the TVA Years, 1933–1945*, New York: Harper & Brothers, 1964.
Lilienthal, David E., *TVA: Democracy on the March*, New York: Harper & Brothers, 1953.
Lillard, Richard, *Eden in Jeopardy. Man's Prodigal Meddling with his Environment: The Southern California Experience*, New York: Alfred A. Knopf, 1966.

Limerick, Jeffrey, Nancy Ferguson and Richard Oliver, *America's Grand Resort Hotels*, New York: Pantheon, 1976.

Lippard, Lucy R, *Overlay: Contemporary Art and the Art of Prehistory*, New York: The New Press, 1983.

Lipstadt, Hélène, "Natural Overlap: Charles and Ray Eames and the Federal Government," in Diane Murphy (ed.), *The Work of Charles and Ray Eames: A Legacy of Invention*, Washington DC: Library of Congress and Vitra Design Museum, 1997, pp. 151–75.

Loos, Adolf, *Spoken Into the Void*, New York: Rizzoli, 1983.

Lorentz, Pare, *The River* (documentary film), Washington DC: US Farm Security Administration, 1938.

McCoy, Esther, *Case Study Houses, 1945–62*, 2nd edn, Los Angeles: Hennessey and Ingalls, 1977.

McCoy, Esther, Franz Schulze, Felix Candela and Craig Ellwood, "John Entenza," *Arts & Architecture* 3, no. 3 (1984), pp. 28–33.

McCoy, Esther, *The Second Generation*, Salt Lake City, UT: Gibbs M. Smith, 1984.

McDonald, Michael J. and John Muldowny, *TVA and the Dispossessed: the Resettlement of Population in the Norris Dam Area*, Knoxville: University of Tennessee Press, 1982.

McHale, John, *R. Buckminster Fuller*, New York: Braziller, 1962.

McHale, John, *Toward the Future/Design Quarterly*, no. 72 (1968).

MacKaye, Benton, "Appalachian Trail," *Scientific Monthly* 34 (April 1932), pp. 330–42.

MacKaye, Benton, "Tennessee, Seed of a National Plan," *Survey Graphic* 22 (May 1934), pp. 251–4.

McKay, Ian, *The Quest of the Folk: Antimodernism and Cultural Selection in Twentieth-Century Nova Scotia*, Montreal: McGill-Queen's University Press, 1994.

McWilliams, Carey, *Southern California Country: an Island on the Land*, New York: Duell, Sloan and Pierce, 1946.

Magoc, Chris J., *Yellowstone: the Creation and Selling of an American Landscape, 1870–1903*, Albuquerque, NM and Helena, MT: University of New Mexico Press/Montana Historical Society, 1999.

Mangan, J.A. and James Walvin (eds), *Manliness and Morality, Middle Class Masculinity in Britain and America*, Manchester: Manchester University Press, 1987.

Marcus, George H., *Design in the Fifties: When Everyone Went Modern*, Munich: Prestel Verlag, 1998.

Marks, Robert W., *The Dymaxion World of Buckminster Fuller*, New York: Reinhold, 1960.

Martin, Reinhold (ed.), *ANY 17: Forget Fuller?*, New York: Anyone Corporation, 1997.

Marx, Leo, *The Machine in the Garden: Technology and the Pastoral Ideal in America*, London: Oxford University Press, 1964.

May, Elaine Tyler, *Homeward Bound: American Families in the Cold War Era*, New York: Basic Books, 1988.

Mead, Margaret, "Are Shelters the Answer?" *New York Times Magazine* (26 November 1961).

Meadows, Donella H. and Dennis L., Jørgen Randers and William W. Behrens III, *The Limits to Growth: A Report for the Club of Rome's Project on the Predica-*

ment of Mankind, New York: New American Library/Potomac Associates, 1972.

Meikle, Jeffrey L., *The City of Tomorrow: Model 1937*, London: Pentagram Design, 1984.

Meikle, Jeffrey L., *Twentieth Century Limited: Industrial Design in America, 1925–1939*, Philadelphia: Temple University Press, 1975.

Miller, Timothy, *The 60s Communes: Hippies and Beyond*, Syracuse, NY: Syracuse University Press, 1999.

Mitchell, Lee Clark, *Reading the West: New Essays on Literature of the American West*, Cambridge: Cambridge University Press, 1996.

Mitchell, Timothy, *Colonising Egypt*, Cambridge: Cambridge University Press, 1988.

Mock, Elizabeth Bauer (ed.), *Built in the USA, 1932–1944*, New York: Museum of Modern Art, 1944.

Mock, Elizabeth Bauer, *If You Want to Build a House*, New York: Museum of Modern Art, 1946.

Moffett, Marian, "Looking to the Future: the Architecture of Roland Wank," *Arris: Journal of the Southeast Chapter of the Society of Architectural Historians* 1 (1989), pp. 5–17.

Moffett, Marian and Lawrence Wodehouse, *Built for the People of the United States: Fifty Years of TVA Architecture*, Knoxville: University of Tennessee, 1983.

Moffett, Marian and Lawrence Wodehouse, "Noble Structures Set in Handsome Parks: Public Architecture of the TVA," *Modulus: University of Virginia Architectural Review*, no. 17 (1984), pp. 74–83.

Montana Historical Society, *F.J. Haynes Photographer*, Helena: Montana Historical Society, 1981.

Moore, Arthur K., *The Frontier Mind: A Cultural Analysis of the Kentucky Frontiersman*, Lexington: University of Kentucky Press, 1957.

Moore, Charles, *Daniel H. Burnham – Architect, Planner of Cities*, 2 vols, Boston: Houghton Mifflin, 1921 (reprinted New York: Da Capo, 1968).

Morgan, Arthur E., "Benchmarks in the Tennessee Valley," *Survey Graphic* 23, 1934.

Morgan, Arthur E., "Tennessee Valley Authority Becomes Laboratory for the Nation," *New York Times* (25 March 1934), p. 1.

Morgan, Arthur E., "The Human Problem of the Tennessee Valley Authority," *Landscape Architecture* 24, no. 3 (April 1934), pp. 119–25.

Mumford, Lewis, "The Wilderness of Suburbia," *New Republic* 28, no. 353 (7 September 1921), pp. 44–5.

Mumford, Lewis, *Technics and Civilization*, New York: Harcourt, Brace and Company, 1934.

Nadel, Alan, *Containment Culture: American Narratives, Postmodernism, and the Atomic Age*, Durham: Duke University Press, 1995.

Nash, Roderick, *Wilderness and the American Mind*, New Haven: Yale University Press, 1967.

Nelson, George and Henry Wright, *Tomorrow's House: How to Plan Your Post-War House*, New York: Simon and Schuster, 1945.

Newton, Norman T., *Design on the Land: the Development of Landscape Architecture*, Cambridge, MA: The Belknap Press of Harvard University, 1971.

Novak, Barbara, *Nature and Culture: American Landscape, 1825–1865*, New York: Oxford University Press, 1980.

Nye, David E., *American Technological Sublime*, Cambridge, MA: MIT Press, 1994

Nye, David E., *Narratives and Spaces: Technology and the Construction of American Culture*, New York: Columbia University Press, 1997.
Oakes, Guy, *The Imaginary War: Civil Defense and American Cold War Culture*, New York: Oxford University Press, 1994.
Oliver, Paul (ed.), *Shelter and Society*, London: Barrie and Jenkins, 1969.
Olkowski, Helga, Bill Olkowski, Tom Javits and the Farallones Institute staff, *The Integral Urban House* (intro. by Sim Van der Ryn), San Francisco: Sierra Club Books, 1979.
Olmsted, Frederick Law, *Civilizing American Cities*, Cambridge, MA: MIT Press, 1971.
Olson, James C., *Red Cloud and the Sioux Problem*, Lincoln: University of Nebraska Press, 1965.
Owen, Marguerite, *The Tennessee Valley Authority*, Washington DC: Praeger Library of US Government Departments and Agencies, 1973.
Pawley, Martin, *Buckminster Fuller*, London: Trefoil Publications, 1990.
Pearce, Peter, *Structure in Nature is a Strategy in Design*, Cambridge, MA: MIT Press, 1978.
Phillips, Sandra S. et al., *Crossing the Frontier: Photographs of the Developing West, 1949 to the Present* (catalog), San Francisco: San Francisco Museum of Modern Art/Chronicle Books, 1996.
Pickens, Donald K., *Eugenics and the Progressives*, Nashville: Vanderbilt University Press, 1968.
Poling-Kempes, Lesley, *The Harvey Girls, Women Who Opened the West*, New York: Paragon Press, 1989.
Poulet, Georges, *Metamorphoses of the Circle* (trans. by Carley Dawson and Elliott Coleman), Baltimore, MD: Johns Hopkins, 1966.
Premis, John (ed.), *The Dome Builder's Handbook*, Philadelphia: Running Press, 1973.
Redfield, Robert, "The Folk Society," *American Journal of Sociology* 52, nos. 4–6, vol. 53 (1947), pp. 293–308.
Reiger, John F. (ed.), *The Passing of the Great West: Selected Papers by George Bird Grinnell*, New York: Winchester Press, 1972.
Reiger, John F., *American Sportsmen and the Origins of Conservation*, New York: Winchester Press, 1975.
Ritterbush, Philip C., *The Art of Organic Forms*, Washington DC: Smithsonian Institution Press, 1968.
Rojek, Chris (ed.), *Touring Cultures*, London: Routledge, 1997.
Rome, Adam, *The Bulldozer in the Countryside: Suburban Sprawl and the Rise of American Environmentalism*, Cambridge: Cambridge University Press, 2001.
Roosevelt, Franklin Delano, Message to Congress on Muscle Shoals Development, House Doc. 15, 73rd Congress, 1st Session, 10 April 1933.
Roosevelt, Theodore, *The Strenuous Life*, New York: Reviews Company, 1910.
Rosa, Joseph, *A Constructed View: the Architectural Photography of Julius Shulman*, New York: Rizzoli, 1994.
Rosen, Sidney, *Wizard of the Dome: R. Buckminster Fuller, Designer for the Future*, Boston: Little, Brown and Company, 1969.
Ross, Malcolm, *Machine Age in the Hills*, New York: Macmillan, 1933.
Roszak, Theodore, *The Making of a Counter Culture: Reflections on the Technocratic Society and Its Youthful Opposition*, Garden City, NY: Anchor/Doubleday, 1969.

Rothman, Hal K. (ed.), *Reopening the American West*, Tucson: University of Arizona Press, 1998.
Rotundo, Anthony, "Learning about Manhood: Gender Ideals and the Middle Class Family in Nineteenth-Century America," in J.A. Mangan and James Walvin (eds), *Manliness and Morality, Middle Class Masculinity in Britain and America*, Manchester: Manchester University Press, 1987.
Rousseau, Jean-Jacques, *The Social Contract*, New York: Hafner Publishing Company, 1947.
Rudofsky, Bernard, *Behind the Picture Window*, New York: Oxford University Press, 1955.
Runte, Alfred, *Public Lands, Public Heritage: The National Forest Idea*, Niwot, CO: Roberts Rinehart/Buffalo Bill Historical Center, 1991.
Rydell, Robert, *All the World's a Fair: Visions of Empire at American International Expositions, 1876–1916*, Chicago: University of Chicago Press, 1984.
Rykwert, Joseph, *On Adam's House in Paradise: the Idea of the Primitive Hut in Architectural History*, 2nd edn, Cambridge, MA: MIT Press, 1981.
Samson, Paul R. and David Pitt (eds), *The Biosphere and Noosphere Reader: Global Environment, Society and Change*, London: Routledge, 1999.
Schaffer, Daniel, "Benton MacKaye: the TVA Years," *Planning Perspectives* 5, no. 1 (January 1990), pp. 5–21.
Schama, Simon, *Landscape and Memory*, New York: Alfred A. Knopf, 1995.
Scully, Vincent Jr, *The Shingle Style and the Stick Style*, New Haven: Yale University Press, 1971.
Sears, John F., *Sacred Places: American Tourist Attractions in the Nineteenth Century*, New York: Oxford University Press, 1989.
Shi, David E., *The Simple Life: Plain Living and High Thinking in American Culture*, New York: Oxford University Press, 1985.
Sidlausskas, Susan, "Contesting Femininity: Vuillard's Family Pictures," *The Art Bulletin* 79, no. 1 (March 1997).
Sieden, Lloyd Steven, *Buckminster Fuller's Universe: an Appreciation*, New York: Plenum Press, 1989.
Simmons, Christina, "Modern Sexuality and the Myth of Victorian Repression," in Barbara Melosh (ed.), *Gender and American History*, London: Routledge, 1992.
Slotkin, Richard, *Gunfighter Nation: the Myth of the Frontier in Twentieth-Century America*, New York: Atheneum, 1992.
Slotkin, Richard, *The Fatal Environment, The Myth of the Frontier in the Age of Industrialization, 1800–1890*, New York: Harper Perennial, 1985.
Smith, Elizabeth A.T. (ed.), *Blueprints for Modern Living: the Case Study Houses*, Los Angeles: MoCA/MIT Press, 1989.
Smith, Henry Nash, *Virgin Land: the American West as Symbol and Myth*, Cambridge, MA: Harvard University Press, 1950.
Smith, Herby, *Strangers and Kin* (documentary film), Whitesburg, KY: Appalshop Films, 1984.
Smith, Neil, *Uneven Development: Nature, Capital and the Production of Space*, New York: Blackwell, 1984.
Smithson, Peter and Alison, "Phenomenon in Parallel: Eames House, *Patio* and *Pavilion*," *Places* 7, no. 3 (Spring 1991), pp. 19–23.

Snyder, Robert (ed.), *R. Buckminster Fuller – An Autobiographical Monologue/Scenario*, New York: St. Martin's Press, 1980.
Spanos, William V., *America's Shadow: An Anatomy of Empire*, Minneapolis and London: University of Minnesota Press, 2000.
Spears, Ross, *The Electric Valley* (documentary film), Johnson City, TX: James Agee Film Project.
Spigel, Lynn, "The Suburban Home Companion: Television and the Neighborhood Ideal in Postwar America," in Beatriz Colomina (ed.), *Sexuality and Space*, New York: Princeton Architectural Press, 1992.
Spigel, Lynn and Denise Mann (eds), *Private Screenings: Television and the Female Consumer*, Minneapolis: University of Minnesota Press, 1992.
St. John Wilson, Colin, *The Other Tradition of Modern Architecture: the Uncompleted Project*, London: Academy Editions, 1995.
Starobinsky, Jean, *Jean-Jacques Rousseau: Transparency and Obstruction*, Chicago: University of Chicago Press, 1988.
Steinberg, Salme H., *Reformer in the Marketplace: Edward Bok and the Ladies' Home Journal*, Baton Rouge: Louisiana State University Press, 1979.
Streatfield, David C., "The Evolution of the California Landscape," *Landscape Architecture* 66–7, "Part 1: Settling Into Arcadia" (January 1976) pp. 39–78; "Part 2: Arcadia Compromised" (March 1976), pp. 117–27; "Part 3: The Great Promotions" (May 1977), pp. 229–39; "Part 4: Suburbia at the Zenith" (September 1977), pp. 417–24.
Strong, Douglas Hillman, *Dreamers and Defenders: American Conservationists*, Lincoln: University of Nebraska Press, 1988.
Sussman, Carl (ed.), *Planning the Fourth Migration: the Neglected Vision of the Regional Planning Association of America*, Cambridge, MA: MIT Press, 1976.
Talbert, Roy Jr, "Arthur Morgan's Social Philosophy," *East Tennessee Historical Society Publications* 41 (1969), pp. 86–99.
Teilhard de Chardin, Pierre, *The Phenomenon of Man* (trans. by Bernard Wall, intro. by Julian Huxley), New York: Harper & Row, 1959.
Teyssot, Georges (ed.), *The American Lawn*, New York: Princeton Architectural Press/Canadian Centre for Architecture, 1999.
Theweleit, Klaus, *Male Fantasies*, 2 vols, Minneapolis: University of Minnesota Press, 1987.
Todd, John and Nancy Jack, *Tomorrow is Our Permanent Address: the Search for an Ecological Science of Design as Embodied in the Bioshelter*, New York: Harper and Row, 1980.
Todd, John and Nancy Jack, *Bioshelters, Ocean Arks and City Farming: Ecology as the Basis of Design*, San Francisco: Sierra Club Books, 1984 (reprinted as *From Eco-Cities to Living Machines: Principles of Ecological Design*, Berkeley: North Atlantic Books, 1994).
Trachtenberg, Alan, *The Incorporation of America: Culture and Society in the Gilded Age*, New York: Hill and Wang, 1982.
Treib, Marc and Dorothée Imbert, *Garrett Eckbo: Modern Landscapes for Living*, Berkeley: University of California Press, 1997.
Truettner, William H. (ed.), *The West as America: Reinterpreting Images of the Frontier, 1820–1920*, Washington DC: National Museum of American Art/Smithsonian Institution, 1991.

Tugwell, Rexford G., "Parts of a New Civilization," *The Saturday Review of Literature* 21 (13 April 1940).
Turner, Frederick Jackson, "Significance of the Frontier in American History," *Annual Report of the American Historical Association for the Year 1893*, Washington DC: Government Printing Office, 1894.
Tweed, William C., Laura Soulliere and Henry G. Law, *National Park Service, Rustic Architecture 1916–1942*, San Francisco: National Park Service, Western Regional Office, Division of Cultural Management, 1977.
US Dept. of Defense, *Personal and Family Survival*, Washington DC, 1966.
US Dept. of Defense, *The Family Fallout Shelter*, Washington DC, 1959.
US Dept. of War Information, *Valley of the Tennessee* (documentary film), 1944.
US Public Works Administration, *America Builds: the Record of the PWA*, Washington: US Government Printing Office, 1939.
Vale, Brenda and Robert Vale, *Green Architecture: Design for a Sustainable Future*, London: Thames and Hudson, 1991.
van Eck, Caroline, *Organicism in Nineteenth Century Architecture: an Inquiry into its Theoretical and Philosophical Background*, Amsterdam: Architectura et Natura, 1994.
van Leeuwen, Thomas A.P., *Skyward Trend of Thought: the Metaphysics of the American Skyscraper*, Cambridge, MA: MIT Press, 1988.
Vattimo, Gianni, *The Transparent Society* (trans. David Webb), Baltimore: John Hopkins University Press, 1992.
Ward, Barbara, *Spaceship Earth*, New York: Columbia University Press, 1966.
Warner, Sam Bass, *The Urban Wilderness: A History of the American City*, New York: Harper and Row, 1972.
Weigle, Marta, *The Lore of New Mexico*, Albuquerque: University of New Mexico Press, 1988.
Whisnant, David E., *All That is Native and Fine: the Politics of Culture in an American Region*, Chapel Hill: University of North Carolina Press, 1983.
Whisnant, David E., *Modernizing the Mountaineer: People, Power and Planning in Appalachia*, Boone, NC: Appalachian Consortium Press, 1980.
White, G. Edward, *The Eastern Establishment and the Western Experience: the West of Frederic Remington, Theodore Roosevelt and Owen Wister*, New Haven: Yale University Press, 1968.
White, Richard, *The Organic Machine: the Remaking of the Columbia River*, New York: Hill and Wang, 1995.
Whyte, William H. Jr, "Urban Sprawl," *Fortune* 57, no. 1 (January 1958), pp. 102–9, 194, 198, 200.
Wilson, Richard Guy, Dianne Pilgrim, and Dickran Tashjian, *The Machine Age in America, 1918–41*, New York: Brooklyn Museum/Harry Abrams, 1986.
Wrede, Stuart and William H. Adams (eds), *Denatured Visions: Landscape and Culture in the Twentieth Century*, New York: Museum of Modern Art, 1991.
Wright, Gwendolyn, *Moralism and the Modern Home*, Chicago: University of Chicago Press, 1980.
Zapatka, Christian, *The American Landscape*, New York: Princeton Architectural Press, 1995.
Zunz, Olivier, *Why the American Century?* Chicago: University of Chicago Press, 1998.

SIGNIFICANT PERIODICALS

American Architect (1932–6)
American Architect and Building News (1891–3)
American City (1933–8)
Architectural Design (1956–67)
Architectural Forum (1933–71)
Architectural Record (1940–9)
Artforum (1963–4)
Arts & Architecture (1944–61)
Co-Evolution Quarterly (1974–8)
Esquire (1965–70)
Forest and Stream (1892–1900)
Fortune (1933–6)
Futurist (1967–77)
House and Garden (1946–72)
House Beautiful (1946–55)
Interiors + Industrial Design (1948–60)
Ladies' Home Journal (1900–20)
Life (1950–71)
Literary Digest (1933–4)
Los Angeles Times Home Magazine (1946–62)
Magazine of Art (1938–41)
Modern Utopian (1970–2)
Nation (1933–67)
New Republic (1933–53)
New York Times (1934–67)
New York Times Magazine (1933–75)
New Yorker (1941–66)
Newsweek (1953–75)
Parks and Recreation (1934–40)
Pencil Points (1939–45)
Perspecta (1967–72)
Popular Mechanics (1939–58)
Reader's Digest (1955–61)
Saturday Review (1970–3)
Scribner's Magazine (1892–1934)
Sunset Magazine (1945–55)
Survey Graphic (1933–40)
The Century Magazine (1884–1903)
The Craftsman (1901–10)
Time (1941–67)
Whole Earth Catalog (1968–74)
Zodiac (1959–69)

ARCHIVES AND ORGANIZATIONS

Buckminster Fuller Institute, Sebastopol, CA.
California State Polytechnic University, Pomona, College of Environmental Design Archive, Architects Raphael Soriano and Craig Ellwood Collections.
Chicago Art Institute, Burnham & Ryerson Library. Daniel Burnham Papers.
Chicago Historical Society.
Chicago Public Library. C.D. Arnold Photograph Collection.
Cumberland Museum, Crossville, TN.
ESTO.
Los Angeles Public Library, History Department.
Minnesota Historical Society. Northern Pacific Railroad Collection.
Montana Historical Society, Helena. F. Jay Haynes Photographic Studio Collection
Montana State University, Bozeman. F. Jay Haynes Book and Manuscript Collection.
National Archives, East Point, GA. TVA Files.
National Archives, Washington DC.
New Alchemy Institute, Cape Cod, MA.
Newberry Library, Chicago.
Point Foundation, Sausalito, CA.
Julius Shulman.
Stanford University, Buckminster Fuller Archive.
Tennessee Valley Authority. Cultural Resources Section, Norris; Corporate Library, Knoxville; and Storage Facility, Chattanooga.
The Field Museum, Chicago.
University of California Berkeley, Bancroft Library.
University of California Berkeley, College of Environmental Design. Garret Eckbo and William Wurster Collections.
University of California, Santa Barbara, University Art Museum. Architectural Drawing Collection.
University of California, Los Angeles, Special Collections. Oral History Collection, Neutra Collection.
University of Montana, Missoula. K. Ross Toole Collection.
University of Southern California, Art and Architecture Library.
Yellowstone National Park Museum and Archives.

Index

Note: page numbers in italics refer to illustrations

Abell, Thornton 236–7, 257
Adams, Ansel 2, *121*
Adams, Charles Frances 82, 85
Adams, Henry 147
African Americans 63n23
Akeley, Carl 66n77
Albertson, Marjorie 104, 108
Albright, Horace 74–5, 110, 115
Althusser, Louis 339
American Association for the Advancement of Science 13
American Centennial Exhibition *12*, 13–14
American City 265
American Forestry Association 13
Ames monument 163, *164*
Appalachia 140, 175–8, 184, 197–8, 217n88; *see also* Tennessee Valley Authority
Arcadia 141–2, 200
Architectural Forum 272
architecture 6, 7, 215n56, 270; discourse 5–6; frontier 16, 42; gender 85–96, 130n43, 130n47, 167–8; hybrid 193, 195–6; landscape 2, 93; masculinity 165, 166; modernism 166–7, 228–9; national identity 41, 86; national parks 115–17, 134n116; Native Americans 119–22; nature 6, 303; rhetoric 7–9; space 241–2; technology 190–5
Army Corps of Engineers 149, 150, *151*
Arnold, C. D. 26, 47
Aron, Cindy 102, 113

Arts & Architecture 227, 234, 238, 243, 270, *271*
Arts and Crafts movement 82, 87, 90–2, 95, 97–101, 228–9
atomic bomb testing 264, *265*, 290n86
Atomic Energy Commission 210, 266
Augur, Tracy 190, 264–5
automobile camping 77, 112–15
automobile ownership 114–15, 200–1
automobile tourism 186, 197–208

Bach, Edmund 128n18, 128n21
back to nature movement 27
back-to-the-land movement 143, 326, 339
backyard 4
Baer, Steve 327–8, 332
Baker, Geoffrey 155
Banham, Reyner 152, 255, 295–6
Barber, Charles 192
Barthes, Roland 7–8, 10n13, 132n82
Bauer, Catherine 223
Bellamy, Edward 23, 182
Benjamin, Walter 123
Bernofsky, Gene and JoAnn 324
Bertoia, Harry 242
Bianculli, Mario 205
Bierstadt, Albert 2, 51, 98
big game 18, 29, 31, 47–9, 52, 53; *see also* wildlife
Big Ridge Park 201, 204
Bingham, George Caleb *40*
bioethics 338
Blackfeet 123
Blondel, Jean-François 85
Bond, J. Max 178

Boone, Daniel 65n57, 141
Boone and Crockett Club 36–40; class 57; hunting 55–6; Roosevelt, T. 47; scientific members 48–50; storytelling 47–8; *see also* Hunter's Cabin
Boulder Dam 148, 152, *153*, 173
Boyer, M. Christine 15, 27
Bradbury, Ray 273–4
Bradley, David 264
Brand, Stewart 317, 329, 331, 343–4n69
Bressani, Martin 344n71
Broadbent, Geoffrey 10–11n17
Brown, Jerry 338
Brown, Julie 14
Bruegmann, Robert 16
Brunelleschi 309
Buff, Straub and Hensman, architects 258
Burnham, Daniel 22, 24, 29, 35, 63n25, 68n102
Burnham and Root, architects 16, *17*
Burroughs, John 60
Butte 95–6
Button, Donald 238

California Look 228, 283
Calthorpe, Peter 332
Camillo, Giulio 314–15
camping 113–15, 133n111
Canyon Hotel 115
capitalism: class 57; conservation 73, 76, 96; gender 244; labor 96; nature/architecture 4, 6; overseas investment 60; White City 22–3
Cartwright, Lisa 288–9n69
Case Study House program 224–8; California Look 228, 283; class 236; Entenza 227–8, 247–50; furniture 234, 236, 242; gardens 234, 236, 259; gender 258; indoor–outdoor living 228–41; privacy 255–6, 260–2, 281–2; space 242–3; trellises 236–7, *240*; visibility 247–53
The Century Magazine 55–6
Chicago 16, *17*, 28

Child, Harry 76–7, 78–80, 113, 128n18, 128n21
Christian Century 272
Christianity 277–9, 291n95
Civilian Conservation Corps (CCC) 4, 140, 180, 201
civilization 14–21, 24, 31–5, 39, 57–8, 141
Clancy, Patrick and Flora 325
class: capitalism 57; Case Study House program 236; conservation 16; labor unrest 16, 57–8, 95–6; national parks 113–14; repression 339; tourism 104; Wooded Islands 28–9
Claude Lorrain 134n125
Clinch River Dam 147, *149*, 150, *151*
Colby, Charles 173
Cold War 277; *see also* Soviet Union
Cole, Thomas 2
Coleman, Charles Caryl 26
collectivism 171, 182
Collier's magazine 266
Colomina, Beatriz 8, 234
colonization 19, 21
Colter, Mary 119, 120–3
communism 179, 244, 277, 278–9
community 179–83
consciousness 293, 317–20
conservation: capitalism 96; civilization 58; class 16; frontier 62n19; hunting 31, 54–6; isolation 29; national parks 126; Roosevelt, T. 49–50; Tennessee Valley Authority 138, 141–2; wilderness 3, 19, 283
Cooper, James Fenimore 2, 57, 60
cooperatives 179, 181–3
Le Corbusier 152, 172, 241
counterculture 318–19, 323, 325–7, 333, 339
crafts 93–5, 97, 118–19, 123, 125, 183–8, 203
Crawshaw, Carol 98–9, 104
Creese, Walter 142, 183, 190, 212
Crockett, Davy 65n57, 99, 141
Cronon, William 31, 47, 62n19
Cuba 60, 61, 275

Cutler, Phoebe 201

Dale, Stephen 102
dam-building 172, 178, 188–9; *see also* Norris Dam; Tennessee Valley Authority
Darwin, Charles 57
Davidson, Julius Ralph 229, 236
daylighting, indirect 291n101
decentralization 196
democracy 253–4, 259
demonstration parks 201
Denevan, William 1–2
Department of Indian Affairs 21
Depression 3–4, 15–16, 137–8, 140, 143–4
Dimendberg, Edward 200
Dine, Jim 298
dioramas 32–3, 66n77, 68n110
discourse 5–6, 16, 97–100
Dobriner, William 256
Domebooks 318–19, 329
Domestic livestock 334, 336, 337–8
Drake, Gordon 228, *229*
Drake, O. S. T. 89–90
Draper, Earle S.: highways 198, 200; Norris town 173; recreation 201, 203; and Wank 150, 152, 195, 213n26
Drexler, Arthur 269, 287–8n51
Drop City 324–8, *327*, 339
Duffus, R. L. 171
Duncan, James 8
Dymaxion Earth map 296, 298, 313, *314*

Eames, Charles 228, 247, 283
Eames, Ray 243, 247–9, 283
Eames House 250–5
Earth: consciousness 317–19; development 317; Dymaxion map 296; natural resources 316–17, 325; photograph 292, 293, 340n1, 342n50; World Game 315–17
Easterling, Keller 112–13
Eckbo, Garrett 234, 236, 264
Eco, Umberto 300, 316
ecological architecture 333–8

ecology movement 5, 293, 338–40
economic expansion 16, 20, 39, 60–1
Eisenhower, Dwight 274, 291n95
Ellwood, Craig 259, *260*, 273, *274*, 275
Emmons, Frederick 281–2, *283*
English gardens 42, 132n82
Entenza, John 227–8, 247–50, 270
environment 264, 293
environmental activists 5, 325–6
erosion 137, 171
eugenics 58, *59*
Every Girl's Annual 89–90
expansionism 1, 60–1, 244, 276–7
Expo '67 292, 294, 295–300, *298*, 311–15

fabrique 42–6
fair chase 38, 55–6, 60–1
fallout shelters 275–81
family/nature 224, 234
family rooms 257–8
Faragher, John Mack 60
farmers 143–4, 196–7
Farnsworth, Edith 243, 256
Farrell, James 331
Federal Civil Defense Administration 266–7, 277
federal government, 6–7, 13–15, 71, 73–6, 137, 141, 207
fishing 108
folk 150, 172–8, 183–92, 202–3
Fontana Dam 205, *206*
food production 225; *see also* farmers
Ford, Henry 196–7
forests 13–14, 49
form/pattern 304–9
Forty, Adrian 85, 130n43, 130n47, 167
Foucault, Michel 3, 5–6, 9n6, 108
Frampton, Kenneth 270
freeways 198–200; *see also* highways
fresh air sleeping movement 229
Frisby, David 190–1, 219n122
frontier: architecture 16, 42; Boone and Crockett Club 39–40; conservation 62n19; end of 13–18; expansion 60–1; exploitation 141,

171; gender 61–2n10; metaphor 140, 200; Roosevelt, F. D. 140–1; Roosevelt, T. 15; Turner, F. J. 14–15, 43; wilderness 46–7
Fuller, R. Buckminster 8, 193; *Cloud Nines* project 311, *312*; Drop City 325; Dymaxion map 296, 298, 313, *314*; *Garden of Eden* project 301; geodesic domes 293–4, 300–3, 308–9, 310–11; geoscope 313–15, 321–2; intuition 320, 341n28; natural geometries 303–4; natural resources 325, 339; *Noah's Ark* 2 309–10; polarity principle 309; World Game 297, 315–17, 321–2
functionalism 153–6
furniture 234, 236, 242, 268–9

game reserves 31, 50–4
garden cities 172, 179, 224
gardens 42, 132n82, 234, 236, 259
gender: architecture 85–96, 130n43, 130n47, 167–8; capitalism 244; Case Study House program 258; domestic interiors 86; frontier 61–2n10; Norris town 183; Old Faithful Inn 87–96; Roosevelt, T. 68–9n120
General Grant National Park 31, 107–8
General Land Law Revision Act 13
geodesic domes 300–3, 308–9, 310–11; counterculture 318–19, 326–7; Drop City 324–8; how-to-build books 326–7; self/reality 328–9. *see also* Fuller, R. Buckminster
geoscope 313–15, 321–2
geysers 85, 99–100, 107
Ghirardo, Diane 7
Gibson, Hamilton 26–7
Giedeon, Siegfried 167, 241–2
Gill, Irving 134n116, 236
Glacier National Park Hotel 87–8
Glass House (Johnson) 267–70, 287–8n51
glass/transparency 230, 250, 274
government repression 338–9

Grand Canyon National Park 102, 107, 119, 120–3
Great Depression 138–40, 143, 172, 188
greenbelt 181
Greenbelt House (Rapson) 222, 224–8, 234, 236
Grinnell, George Bird 47, 48
Growth House (Simmonds) 325
Gutheim, Frederick 146–7, 162, 168–9, 171, 216n66

Hagedorn, Hermann 270
Haines, Aubrey 88
Hales, Peter 26
Hamlin, Talbot 168, 207–8
Haraway, Donna 56, 58, 66n77, 304, 309
Harris, Harwell Hamilton 228
Harris, Moses 77
Haskell, Douglas 171, 216n74
Hawthorne, Julian 55–6
Hayden, Dolores 7, 130n39
Hayden, Sophia 85–6
Haymarket riot 57
Haynes, Frank Jay 76–7, 78, 91, 92, 98, 99–100
Hays, Samuel 49–50, 96
heavenly valley 144, 173
Heidegger, Martin 41, 65n64, 315
Hersey, John 264, 289n74
highways: park to park 112–15; townless 197–8, 200
Hildegard von Bingen 318
Hill, Abby 132n70
Hill, Joe 96
Hill, Louis 123
Hillers, J. K. 71, 72, 126n1
Hine, Thomas 242, 243
Hines, Lewis 173, 192
Hiroshima 264, 276, 289n74
Hirst, Paul 6
Historic American Buildings Survey (HABS) 115
Hofer, Elwood 36, 37, 49
Holabird and Roche, architects 16, 37, 40, 41
Holidays, Gilbert 236

Hopi 118–22; see also Native Americans
Hough, Emerson 51, 53–4
House Beautiful 243
housing 4–5, 188–96, 219n124; see also Case Study House program
Howard, Ebenezer 218n96
Hudson River School 2
Hughes, Howard 281
Hunter's Cabin 18–19, 34–8, 40–8, 56
hunting: Boone and Crockett Club 55–6; class 57–8; conservation 31, 54–6; Kemeys 51–2; masculinity 56; sportsmanship 55–6; wilderness 60–1; Yellowstone National Park 108
Huxley, Aldous 290n83
Huxley, Julian 208, 219n124, 320–1
Hyde, Anne 83, 85, 93
hydroelectric power 138–40, 147, 156, 168–72, 197

Ian, Marcia 165
Indian wars 71, 77, 118; see also Native Americans
indoor–outdoor living 228–41
industrialism 20, 237–8, 239
information theory 316
Ingraham, Catherine 165
Integral Urban House 333–8, 339, 346n124
interdependency 293, 332, 339
interior design 90–1, 119–23
International Workers of the World 95–6
intertextuality 7–8, 10n13
intuition 320, 341n28
Inuit 21
irradiation 266
Ise, John 111
isolation 29–31, 64n45

Jackson, Helen Hunt 118
Jackson, William Henry 2, 78, 98
Jackson Park 19 (map), 25, 27
James Addams' Settlement House 28
Jencks, Charles 10–11n17
Jenkins, Leigh 123

Johns, Jasper 298
Johnson, Philip 267–70, 287–8n51, 289n70
Jones, A. Quincy 281–2, 283

Kahn, Lloyd 329, 330, 331, 332
Kant, Immanuel 215n56
Keats, John 259
Keller, Robert 123
Kemeys, Edward 16, 38, 50–4, 64n52, 67n84, 67n93
Kennedy, J. F. 275
Kepes, Gyorgy 303
Khrushchev, Nikita 244
Killingsworth, Brady and Smith, architects 259–60
Kirkham, Pat 87
Koenig, Pierre 228, 259, 260–2
Kolodny, Annette 61–2n10
Krausse, Joachim 309, 313
Krutch, Charles 141, 197

labor: capitalism 96; class war 16; dam-building 178, 188–9; women 218n101; working hours 200
Ladies' Home Journal 90–1, 102
landscape 1, 2; food production 225; painting 2, 98; photography 26, 71, 98–100, 102, 104–7; suburbs 224; Tennessee Valley Authority 4, 155–6, 209–12
landscape architecture 2, 16, 27, 93, 115, 234
Laugier, Abbé 42, 44, 47
Le Ricolais, Robert 309
Lears, T. Jackson 191
Leavengood, David 86, 93
Lefebvre, Henri 316
leisure 3, 71–3, 79, 85, 109, 119, 200–1
Ley, David 8
Lichtenstein, Roy 298
Life 264, 265, 277, 298
Lilienthal, David 141, 152, 192, 210
Living Machines™ 332
log cabins 35–37, 42–3, 45, 83–5, 88, 93, 116–17
Loos, Adolf 163, 215n56

Lorentz, Pare 171
Los Angeles 263–4, *265*, 271–2
Lowell, Robert 272–3

McCalls Magazine 257
McCarthyism 247, 264
McCoy, Esther 247–8
McDonald, Michael J. 190, 217–18n95
McHale, John 317, 323
McKay, Ian 176
MacKaye, Benton 197–8, 199
Mackintosh, Charles Rennie 87
MacMonnies, Frederic 23
Magazine of Art 146–7, 162, 168–9, 171
Mammoth Hot Springs Hotel 115
Marcuse, Herbert 325
Marx, Leo 13, 147, 195
masculinity 45–6, 56, 68n102, 162, 165–6
Mather, Steven 115
Matter, Herbert 228
May, Elaine Tyler 225–6, 244, 256
Maybeck, Bernard 134n116, 236
McKim, Mead and White, architects 23
Mead, Margaret 276
Mesa Verde *121*, 134n119
Mesoamericans 21
Mies van der Rohe, Ludwig 241, 243
military industry 271–2
millenarianism 277–9
Milyutin, Konstantin 182
miners *174*, 184
Mitchell, Timothy 31–2
Mock, Elizabeth 247
modernism: architecture 166–7, 228–9; Frisby 190–1; Heidegger 315; Mumford 160; Norris Dam 145, 150, 160, 161; sociology of 219n122; Tennessee Valley Authority 152, 153, 155; town planning 181–2; Wank 160
Montreal 295–6
Montreal Sun 298
monument 117, 162–6
Moran, Thomas 2, 98, 131–2n70

Morgan, Arthur E.: Clinch River 147, 149; Norris town 178, 182–3, 186; Tennessee Valley Authority 210, 212; tourism 201, 203; and Wank 150, 152, 181
Morgan, Lilian 192
Mount Rainier National Park 74
MOVE 338–9
Muldowny, John 190, 217–18n95
Mumford, Lewis 147; Clinch River 149–50; modernism 160; Museum of Modern Art review 152–3, 162; Norris town 182; visitors to Norris Dam 159–60; on Wank 168
Museum of Modern Art review 152–3, 161, 162, 168
mutually assured destruction 279
myth 7–8, 39–40, 140, 143

Nash, Roderick 1, 55
Nation 299, 303
national identity 1–2, 15, 41–2, 46, 86, 176
National Park Service 109–12, 114–17, 124–5, 200–1
national parks 33–4, 73, 107–8; architecture 115–17, 119–23, 134n116; class 113–14; conservation 126; highways 112–15; hotels 6, 78–9; leisure 85, 109; Native Americans 33, 108, 117, 118–19; railroad companies 70, 72–4, 75–6, 117–18; rangers 110–11; regional differences 109, 115–26; Roosevelt, F. D. 126; Roosevelt, T. 76; Sherman 63–4n40; tourism 3, 107–8, 114–15; US Army 71, 77; wilderness 3, 31, 71; women 113–14; *see also* Old Faithful Inn; Yellowstone National Park
national recovery 137–8, 140, 207–8
Native Americans: anthropological displays 20–1, 32–3, 68n110; architecture 119–22; craftwork 118–19; genocide 57–8; isolation 31; National Park Service 124–5; national parks 33, 108, 117, 118–19;

Native Americans *continued*
  reservations 31–4; sacred sites 126; tourism 120, 123, 124–5; World's Columbian Exposition 20–1, 63n23
natural resources 316–17, 325, 338, 339
natural selection 56–8
naturalists 47–50
nature 97, 99, 339; architecture 6, 303; capitalism 4, 6; family 224, 234; individual homes 224; leisure 3; national identity 1–2; pattern integrity 304–9; as resource 3–4, 14; as social good 27–9; structures of 303–4; suburbs 339–40; technology 272, 301; transparency 253–5
nature tourism 73–4, 108–9, 111
naturization 173–6, 210
Nelson, George 242, 257
neotechnic 147, 159
Neutra, Richard 228, 229–30, *231*, 250, 272
New Deal 4, 140, 171, 172, 207
New England Kitchen 45
New York Times 155, 176, 303
New York Times Magazine 276
New Yorker 264
Newsweek 298, 326
Nietzsche, Friedrich 8
Nixon, Richard 244
Noble, John 13
noosphere 319–20, 322
Norris, George 138, 140
Norris Dam 146–52; labor 188–9; modernism 145, 150, 160, 161; Museum of Modern Art review 162, 168; pyramid comparison 162, 166; setting *136*, 155–6, 161; sublime 145, 147; visitors 156, 159–60, 187–8, 197–8, 201, 204–5; Wank 156, 159–60, 214n30; *see also* Tennessee Valley Authority
Norris town: community life 182–3; craftwork 183–8; Draper 173; electrification 192; farming 196–7; folk culture 184, 189–90, 191–2, 203; gender 183; houses 188–96, 219n124; Morgan 178, 182–3, 186; race 178; Tennessee Valley Authority 8–9, 144–5, 179; town planning 173, 178–81; Wank 179–80, 192, 195
Northern Pacific Railroad *70*, 73–4, 75, 78
nuclear fallout shelters 275–81
nuclear testing 274
nuclear war threat 267, 272–3
Nye, David 147

Oakes, Guy 277
Old Faithful Inn 10n15, 76, 82–3, 129n27; bedroom 91, *93*; gender coding 87–96; lobby 87–9, *90*; log cabin model 83–5; morality 97; national identity 86; Reamer 80–3, 93–6, 115; roof 89; setting 93–4
Olkowski, Mike and Helga 333, 338
Olmsted, Frederick Law 16, 24–9, 42–3
open plan living 241
organic machine 138, 144–5, 197–8, 203, 210
ornamentation 147, 149, 160, 167–8

Pacific Islands 240
Paris Match 298
Parkman, Frances 38, 39, 47
patterns in nature 304–9
Pedestrian Pockets™ 332
personalism 331
Peter Rabbit 324
Phelan, James 281
photography: Eames House 250–5; Earth *292*, *293*, 340n1, 342n50; Evans 173; Haynes 78, 98; Hillers 126n1; Hines 173; human fetus 342n50; kodaking 99, 102, 104–7; landscapes 71; Northern Pacific Railroad 78; wilderness 2; Wooded Islands 26; Yellowstone National Park 98–9
pilgrimage 98
Pinchot, Gifford 49, 138, 142
pioneer 45, 52, 140–1, 176, 200
Pitcher, John 76–7
Plath, Sylvia 259

Plexiglas 244–7
poaching 54–110
pollution 264
Post, Emily 113–14
Post, George B. 23
postcards 99–100, 104–5
Poulet, Georges 317
Premis, John 329
primitive hut 40–7
primitivism 39, 56, 83–5, 176
privacy 247–53, 255–6, 260–3, 281–2
public transport 338
purification 33–4, 64n45
pyramids 162, 166

Quakers 183, 184

race 58, 178, 217n88, 339
radiography 288–9n69
radiolaria 305–7
railroad companies 70, 72–4, 75–6, 117–18
rangers 110–11
Rapson, Ralph 228; *Arts & Architecture* 238; Greenbelt House 224–8, 234; trellis 236
Reamer, Robert 8; Canyon Hotel 115; Child 78–9; hotel at Grand Canyon 112; Hunter's Cabin 85; Mammoth Hot Springs Hotel 115; Old Faithful Inn 80–3, 93–6, 115
recreation 201, 203; *see also* leisure
recycling 236, 325, 332, 334, 336, 337
Red Cloud 32, 33
redwood tree 12, 13–14, 18; *see also* sequoia
reflectoscopes 123, *134n125*
regional plan 138–45, 45, 173–4, 197–9, 208
regionalism 2, 80, 93–6, 109, 115–19, 191–5
Remington, Frederic 16
Renwick, Edward 37
resettlement 4; Tennessee Valley Authority 137, 142, 173–8, 188–9, 210; urban dispersal 264–5
resource management 49, 141
responsibility, personal 331

Richardson, Henry Hobson 16, 86, 163, *164*
Richert, Clark 324–5
Ritterbush, Philip 304
road building 112–15, 197–200
Rohm and Haas company 244–7
Romney, George 298
Roosevelt, Franklin Delano: Depression 138; farmers 143, 196–7; frontier 140–1; home ideals 192; Morgan 147; national parks 126; New Deal 140; Tennessee Valley Authority 137, 138, 140
Roosevelt, Theodore: Boone and Crockett Club 47; civilization 57–8; conservation 49–50; frontier 15; gender roles 68–9n120; Hunter's Camp 35–6, 37–8; hunting 60; national parks 76; sportsmanship 67–8n98; trust-busting 128n21; wilderness 56
Rosenquist, James 298
Roszak, Theodore 323
Rotundo, Anthony 56, 68n104
Rousseau, Jean-Jacques 65n68, 253–4, 259
Ruderman, David 314
Rural Electrification Administration 4
Ruskin, John 41
Russell Sage Foundation 184
rusticity 81–5, 89, 92–5, 116–17
Rykwert, Joseph 41

Saarinen, Eero 227–8, 242, 247
Sadao, Shoji 295
Saint-Gaudens, Augustus 27
Santa Fe Railway 117–18
Saturday Evening Post 258
scenic resource 199
Schindler, Rudolf 228
Schulz, Franz 289n70
Schweikart, Russell 293
Scribner's Magazine 26–7
Sears, John 98, 126
self/reality 328–9, 344n71
self-reliance 333, 334
Semper, Gottfried 43
Sequoia National Park 31, 74, 107–8

sequoia trees 107–8; *see also* redwood tree
Sherman, Mary Belle 63–4n40
Shi, David 91
Shingle style 82
Shulman, Julius 228
Simmonds, Charles 325
simple life 3, 36, 39, 83–5, 184; *see also* primitivism
skylights 236
skyscrapers 10n12, 16, *17*
sliding track walls 229–30
Slotkin, Richard 57, 61–2n10
Smith, Whitney R. 230, *232*, 237
Smithson, Alison and Peter 252–3
smog 263–4
social commentary 270
social contract 253–4
social engineering 181
social values 283
socialism 96, 144, 182
solar energy 9n5, 324–5, 332
soldiers, returning 223
Sondist, Alan 325
Sontag, Susan 107
Soriano, Raphael 259–60
Soviet Union 264, 275
space 241–3, 259–60
Spalding, A. W. 79, *80*
Spaulding, Sumner 230
sphericality 304–5, 309–11, 332
Spigel, Lynn 241
spirituality 322–3
sportsmanship 55–6, 67–8n98
Stickley, Gustave 91, 95
storytelling 47–8
Strangers and Kin film 176
strenuous life 56
structuralism 342n28
subjectification 3, 9n6
sublime 71, 145, 147, 203; *see* technological sublime
Subsistence Homestead 181, 189, 195
suburbs 4–5, 6, 223–4; display/space 258; fallout shelters 275–6; landscape 224; nature 339–40; Norris 178, 190; pioneer homesteads 277; privacy 256; visibility 258; wilderness 190
Sullivan, Louis 21, 86
sunglasses 290n83
Sunset Magazine 228, 236, 238, 241
Superman 279, 281, 291n97

Tange, Kenzo 289n74
technological sublime 145–7, 195
technology 147, 203, 272, 301
Teilhard de Chardin, Pierre 319–20, 322–3, 344n73
television 258
Tennessee Valley Authority 6, *139*, 161, 208; biological re-adjustment 203–4; conservation 138, 141–2; craftwork 203; Depression 137; farmers 143–4; folk culture 191–2, 203; freeways 198–200; landscape 4, 155–6, 209–12; masculine metaphors 162; modernism 152, 153, 155; Morgan 210, 212; New Deal 207; Norris town 8–9, 144–5, 179; powerhouses *170*, 171; recreation 201; regional regeneration 171–2, 212; resettlement 137, 142, 173–8, 188–9, 210; Roosevelt, F. D. 137, 138, 140; visitors 207; Wank 150; *see also* Norris Dam
Thompson, D'Arcy 306–7, 342n40
Thoreau, Henry David 58
Tieche, Aline 106
Time 277, 323
Todd, John 332
tourism: automobile 112–14, 200–1; behavioral norms 99, 108–9; cameras 104–8; class 104; depression era 186; leisure 119, 200–1; Morgan 201, 203; national parks 3, 71–4, 107–8, 114–15, 122, 126; Native Americans 120, 123, 124–5; stagecoach 101–4; TVA 153, 156; *see also* nature tourism; visitors
town planning 172–3, 178–83, 188–97

Toynbee, Arnold 175
Trachtenberg, Alan 16
trade unions 200
transparency 230, 250, 253–5, 259, 274
trellises 236–7, *240*
Truman, Harry 266, 277, 289–90n79
Turek, Michael 123
Turner, Frederick Jackson 14–15, 46, 61–2n10, 141
Turner, Victor and Edith 98

unemployment 15–16, 172
UNESCO 320–1, 344n81
Unwin, Raymond 161
urban dispersal 264–5
urban parks 27–9; see also national parks
urban sprawl 4–5, 223–4
Urry, John 98–9, 104
US Army 22, 33, 71, 77, 108, 110
US Information Agency 297, 298
US Pavilion, Expo '67 292, 294, 295–300, 311–15

van Brunt, Henry 86, 129–30n39
van der Ryn, Sim 2, 9n5, 333, 338
Van Gogh, Vincent 41, 65n64
Vattimo, Gianni 315, 339
Veblen, Thorstein 97
vernacular architecture 41–2
Viollet Le Duc, Eugene 41
visibility: Case Study House program 247–53; daylight 291n101; fallout shelters 281; privacy 247–53, 262–3; space 259–60; suburbs 258
visitors: Norris Dam 156, 159–60, 187–8, 197–8, 201, 204–5; Tennessee Valley Authority 207; Wank 205–6; see also tourism
Vitruvius 85
Voyd, Bill 324, 327–8

wage levels 196–7
Walker, Rodney 237
Wallace, Henry 140–1
Wank, Roland 8; Draper 150, 152, 195, 213n26; materials used 159, 168; modernism 160; and Morgan 150, 152, 181; Mumford on 168; Norris Dam 156, 159–60, 214n30; Norris town 179–80, 192, 195; Tennessee Valley Authority 150; visitors 205–6
Warshall, Peter 331
waste recycling 334, *336*, 337
wastewater treatment 332
Watts Bar Dam 205, *206*
Weigle, Martha 117–18
Western Architect 89
western films 2, 164
Wheeler, Olin 101
Whisnant, David 184
White, Peter 117–18
White, Richard 34, 47, 83, 172
White City 21–3
Whole Earth Catalog 317, 329, 331, 340n1, 343–4n69
Whyte, William 223–4
Wiener, Norbert 265
Wigley, Mark 166–7, 256
wildlife: beans 99, 106, 107; see also big game
wilderness 14, 23–7; conservation 3, 19, 283; discourse 16; European settlers 1–2; frontier 46–7; Hunter s Cabin 18–19; hunting 60–1; isolation 29; national identity 15; national parks 3, 31, 71, 82–3; photography 2; Roosevelt, T. 56; skyscrapers 16; storytelling 47–8; suburbs 190
Williams, Raymond 61
Wilson Dam 196
Wister, Owen 16, 38, 47
Wolfe, Tom 329–31
Wölfflin, Heinrich 130n47
women 113–14, 133n111, 218n101; see also gender
Wonderland 100
Wooded Islands 26–31, 34–5; class 28–9; isolation 29–31; Olmsted 24–9; photography 26; see also Hunter's Cabin
World Game 297, 315–17, 321–2
World War II 4

World's Columbian Exposition 14, 16–17, 18–23, *24 (map)*; Hayden 86; industrialism 20; landscape architecture 27; western landscapes exhibition 71; White City 21–3; Wooded Islands 26–31, 34–5
Works Progress Administration (WPA) 115, 140
Wright, Frank Lloyd 2, 134n116, 241, 243
Wright, Henry 257
Wright, Russel 236
Wurster and Bernardi, architects 236–7, 257
Yeats, W. B. 87
Yellowstone National Park 31, 74–6; fishing 108; front stage/back stage 107–8, 112; Haynes 98; hunting 108; Jackson 98; Native Americans 33, 108; Northern Pacific Railroad 70, 73–4; paintings 98; photography 98–9; postcards 99–100, 104–5; stagecoach tours 101–4; tourists 71, 107–8; wildlife 36, 49, 99, 106, 107; *see also* Old Faithful Inn
Yellowstone Park Hotel Company 128n18
Yellowstone Park Transportation Company 128n18
Yosemite National Park 31, 33, 74, 98

Zeisel, Eva 236
Zimmer and Reamer, architects 80
zoological societies 49